BRITANNIA'S SHIELD

LIEUTENANT-GENERAL SIR EDWARD HUTTON AND LATE-VICTORIAN IMPERIAL DEFENCE

From British colonial conflicts in Africa and Egypt to the turn-of-the-century war on the South African veldt and its complicated aftermath, *Britannia's Shield: Lieutenant-General Sir Edward Hutton and Late-Victorian Imperial Defence* presents an in-depth, international study of imperial land defence prior to 1914. The book makes sense of the failures, false starts and successes that eventually led to more than 850 000 men being despatched from the Dominions to buttress Britain's Great War effort – an enormous achievement for intra-empire military cooperation.

Craig Stockings presents a vivid portrayal of this complex process as it unfolded throughout the late-Victorian Empire through a biographical study of Lieutenant-General Sir Edward Hutton. As a true soldier of the Empire, the difficulties and dramas that followed Hutton's career at every step – from Cairo to Sydney, Aldershot to Ottawa, and Pretoria to Melbourne – provide key insights into imperial defence and security planning between 1880 and 1914.

Richly illustrated, *Britannia's Shield* is an engaging and entertaining work of rigorous scholarship that will appeal to both general readers and academic researchers.

Craig Stockings is an Associate Professor of History at the University of New South Wales, Canberra. His areas of academic interest concern general and Australian military history and operational analysis, and he has published a number of titles on these subjects.

OTHER TITLES IN THE AUSTRALIAN ARMY HISTORY SERIES

Series editor
Peter Stanley

Phillip Bradley *The Battle for Wau: New Guinea's Frontline 1942–1943*

Mark Johnston *The Proud 6th: An Illustrated History of the 6th Australian Division 1939–1946*

Garth Pratten *Australian Battalion Commanders in the Second World War*

Jean Bou *Light Horse: A History of Australia's Mounted Arm*

Phillip Bradley *To Salamaua*

Peter Dean *The Architect of Victory: The Military Career of Lieutenant-General Sir Frank Horton Berryman*

Allan Converse *Armies of Empire: The 9th Australian and 50th British Divisions in Battle 1939–1945*

John Connor *Anzac and Empire: George Foster Pearce and the Foundations of Australian Defence*

Peter Williams *The Kokoda Campaign 1942: Myth and Reality*

Karl James *The Hard Slog: Australians in the Bougainville Campaign, 1944–45*

Robert Stevenson *To Win the Battle: The 1st Australian Division in the Great War, 1914–1918*

Jeffrey Grey *A Soldier's Soldier: A Biography of Lieutenant-General Sir Thomas Daly*

Mark Johnston *Anzacs in the Middle East: Australian Soldiers, Their Allies and the Local People in World War II*

Mark Johnston *Stretcher-bearers: Saving Australians from Gallipoli to Kokoda*

Christopher Wray *Poziéres: Echoes of a Distant Battle*

BRITANNIA'S SHIELD

LIEUTENANT-GENERAL SIR EDWARD HUTTON AND LATE-VICTORIAN IMPERIAL DEFENCE

CRAIG STOCKINGS

CAMBRIDGE
UNIVERSITY PRESS

CAMBRIDGE
UNIVERSITY PRESS

Shaftesbury Road, Cambridge CB2 8EA, United Kingdom

One Liberty Plaza, 20th Floor, New York, NY 10006, USA

477 Williamstown Road, Port Melbourne, VIC 3207, Australia

314–321, 3rd Floor, Plot 3, Splendor Forum, Jasola District Centre, New Delhi – 110025, India

103 Penang Road, #05–06/07, Visioncrest Commercial, Singapore 238467

Cambridge University Press is part of Cambridge University Press & Assessment, a department of the University of Cambridge.

We share the University's mission to contribute to society through the pursuit of education, learning and research at the highest international levels of excellence.

www.cambridge.org
Information on this title: www.cambridge.org/9781107094826

First published 2015

A catalogue record for this publication is available from the British Library

A Cataloguing-in-Publication entry is available from the catalogue of the National Library of Australia at www.nla.gov.au

ISBN 978-1-107-09482-6 Hardback

Please be aware that this publication may contain several variations of Aboriginal and Torres Strait Islander terms and spellings; no disrespect is intended. Please note that the terms 'Indigenous Australians' and 'Aboriginal and Torres Strait Islander peoples' may be used interchangeably in this publication.

For Emma, Georgia, Charlotte and Thomas Stockings

Contents

Photographs

Acknowledgements

One pleasant aspect of completing any book is that it brings with it the opportunity to give proper thanks to all of the individuals and institutions that helped to make it possible. I would first to acknowledge the generous support provided to this endeavour by the Australian Army History Unit. Dr Roger Lee and his team remain a key institution in promoting the study and understanding of Australian – and in this case imperial – military history. My particular thanks also to Professor Peter Stanley, a fount of valuable advice and the editor of the series to which this book belongs. I would further like acknowledge the University of New South Wales, my faculty, UNSW Canberra, and the School of Humanities and Social Sciences, for their generous support.

At a personal level I would like to thank a number of my colleagues for their wise counsel and patient discussions, including Professor David Lovell, Professor Jeffrey Grey, Associate Professor Eleanor Hancock, Dr John Connor and Dr Rob Stevenson. I am particularly indebted to Emeritus Professor Peter Dennis and Cathryn Game for their patient and invaluable editorial assistance. Professor Dennis gave of his time and counsel with a generosity I cannot repay. Thanks, too, to Laura Dennis for her mastery of microfilm. I also wish to express my gratitude to Isabella Mead and Vilija Stephens at Cambridge University Press.

Throughout the process of research and writing the helpfulness of archivists from various state offices of the National Archives and the Australian War Memorial was greatly appreciated, as was the cheerful support offered from staff at various Australian state records offices and libraries, the National Archives, Kew, UK, and of the British Library. For their invaluable research assistance across a wide range of Canadian libraries and archival repositories I give my heartfelt thanks to Sarah Cozzi and Samantha Bourgoin. Thanks too for advice on Canadian sources and aspects of this project to Dr James Wood and Dr Mike Bechthold.

For me, as always, the most important factor in the completion of this book has been the unremitting support of my family. My wife Emma is a true partner. Let me also thank my children, Georgia, Charlotte and Thomas, who never cease to lighten my heart.

Last, my gratitude to Balzare – you know what for.

Introduction

On 6 August 1914, two days after Britain entered the Great War, the British Prime Minister, Herbert Asquith, concluded an address to parliament with a call to arms. 'Let us now make sure that all the resources, not only of this United Kingdom', Asquith urged, 'but of the vast Empire of which it is the centre shall be thrown into the scale.'[1] The Prime Minister was sure that the Empire would rally around Britain in the war that followed, and subsequent events proved his confidence well founded. The dominions of Canada, Australia and New Zealand alone contributed expeditionary forces of more than 840 000 men to the conflict. The origins of such imperial military cooperation, however, pre-dated the war by decades. The physical manifestations of intra-Empire military cooperation might have unfolded on the shores of Gallipoli, the fields of France and the deserts of Palestine, but conceptions of how, or even whether, this situation was ever to come to pass had been the subject of tentative, halting thought and discussion since the late-Victorian era.

This book is a study of the military career of Lieutenant-General Sir Edward 'Curley' Hutton. Yet it is not a traditional biography. Rather, Hutton is a means by which to shed light on late-Victorian thinking on the 'land' defence of the British Empire and the embryonic structures of imperial (military) defence during this period. Developed in an era when traditional military mechanisms and assumptions in London were increasingly seen as inadequate to cope with rapidly changing global circumstances, these were issues concerned fundamentally with whether and how the white self-governing colonies could contribute to the collective security of the

Empire at large. They were complex questions, which spoke to a wide range of issues beyond a narrow – and at times shallow – contemporary defence debate in Britain and at the edges of the Empire. This work aims to shed light upon them; to investigate on the form, failings and accomplishments of the theory and practice of this notion of 'imperial defence'. A close study of Hutton's career is particularly well suited to untangle the many threads of the imperial defence paradigm of the era. A British regular officer, his various appointments across the Empire, and the controversies they engendered, provide a unique window through which to view and interpret a range of key issues at the heart of the imperial defence conundrum. His career illuminates key aspects of a wider issue. First, however, that larger question, the very concept of imperial defence, needs to be placed in context.

The second half of the nineteenth century marked not only a material high point for Britain and the Empire but also key transitions in the very conception of imperialism in Britain and the self-governing colonies. For much of the period relative stability and prosperity coincided with continuing British commercial and maritime dominance overseas. At the same time, however, the British world was being transformed – and fast. One of the most obvious conceptual manifestations of such change concerned thinking about the Empire itself. In the first half of the century many had concluded that the British Empire 'as both an idea and a physical edifice' was crumbling.[2] Natural processes of evolution and maturity in the Anglo-Saxon colonies would see them move, inexorably, towards independence, especially considering the mid-century grant of responsible self-government to the Australasian colonies and Canadian Confederation in 1867. This in itself was no disaster. After all, what was really to be gained by underwriting an empire, a large proportion of which Britain effectively no longer controlled – and one that represented a drain on the Exchequer? Such sentiments reflected not only pragmatic politics and economic concerns but also a large measure of the popular mood.

Yet change was in the air. After some decades of intellectual and sentimental 'neglect', from the 1870s the Empire was again a subject of discussion. What was, or should be, its character? What was its value to Britain, and what, if anything, should be done to shape it? Indeed, by the late 1870s differences of philosophy and its practical application with respect to the imperial project came to be split along party lines. The division was brought to a head over the aggressive foreign policies of Benjamin Disraeli, which British Liberals characterised and criticised as 'imperialism' – a label still at this stage considered a taunt in its implications of military recklessness, undue expenditure, foreign entanglements and land-grabbing. For British Liberals such policies were simply incompatible with 'values that should be fostered at home and abroad'.[3] Conservatives countered by charges that the Liberals wished (and had been trying) to dismember the Empire from the inside out. It was an exchange won from the 1880s onwards decidedly, in the public sphere if not always in Parliament, by an ever-growing chorus of advocates of Empire.

Key to the conversion of British public and political opinion from the indifference (and sometimes antipathy) of 'Little Englandism' in mid-century to overt imperial enthusiasm at its end were two important issues: sentiment and fear.[4] These two were not separate, but rather worked to buttress each other. With regard to the first, appeals by intellectuals and authors such as John Robert Seeley to embrace the noble sentiment of Empire, not simply to reduce the imperial ledger to an account-balancing or entirely practical exercise, found fertile ground. This was so much so that by the 1880s the very concept of imperialism had become respectable, in the political and public sphere. In fact, this 'respectability' and notions of a 'greater good' at home and abroad resulting from the imperial paradigm soon reconciled many British Liberals towards their own brand of imperial enthusiasm. It was a transition assisted, no doubt, by a concurrent crisis of Liberal Gladstonian thought that appeared to have no answer to emergent international challenges. Nor were more traditional antagonistic British Liberal attitudes to Empire easy to maintain in the face of the issue of Irish Home Rule in the 1880s. Liberals accused of trying to weaken the Empire in Ireland by their Conservative critics were tempted to prove their imperial credentials by advocating greater connections between Britain and the white Empire overseas, and so imperial momentum gathered steam.[5]

Transforming political attitudes were, of course, only part of the story. The growth of popular support for the sentimental and physical importance of the Empire in the late-Victorian era was central. In 1870 a petition of 104 000 working men was presented to the Queen in favour of retaining the colonies and the consolidation of the Empire. The emergence of Victoria from mourning in 1876 to be crowned Empress of India and the Jubilee celebrations in 1887 at which colonial representatives gathered for the first Colonial Conference were important public symbols. Popular romanticism in the British world in literature and art, and increasing literacy, further spread imperial ideas. Aside from Seeley, authors from Dilke to Froude and from Tennyson to Kipling waxed lyrical on the value of the colonies and the future of imperial relations.[6] All of this was set against the backdrop of significant social uncertainty and upheaval. Continuing urbanisation and the breakdown of traditional communities in Britain, and an economic depression from 1868 to 1876 that shook the faith of many free-traders, for example, merged with an extended franchise from 1867, which encouraged a rise in general political consciousness. An outlet, an explanation, perhaps even a distraction was required; a 'sense of where it all fit'.[7] The answer was the Empire. Such sentiments were further encouraged in the self-governing colonies by self-government, which allowed a vision of partnership (rather than dependency) within the Empire. Meanwhile, free of the burden of direct control of such colonies, Britain could now strengthen imperial connections within the white Empire more easily than in the past thanks to steamships, telegraphs and cables laid to Canada in 1866 and to Australia in 1872.

Importantly, these powerful emergent imperial ideas were embraced not only by political elites in Britain but also by those in leadership positions in the colonies. At the periphery the Empire was led and managed by members of the ruling classes: governors, senior military and naval officers, and administrators who came to share a set of common, if unspoken assumptions about the role and future of the Empire. Often sharing similar social positioning, education and a reasonably common ethos, in the main this ruling elite believed their duty extended to the Empire, its growth and preservation. This was a powerful manifestation of Robinson and Gallagher's 'official mind'.[8] Moreover, the notion of inter-imperial defence cooperation often became a part of the vision shared by those who worked for a closer and more consolidated Empire. As international competition with Britain grew more serious, the self-governing colonies grew more powerful and, instead of favouring independence, seemed to want to move closer to Empire. All of this meant that various schemes and plans for defence cooperation began to be raised and discussed.[9] Such historians as John Darwin may be correct in suggesting that British imperial policy in the late-Victorian era was *ad hoc* and therefore lacked clarity, coherence and consistency.[10] The common interests of a 'gentlemanly capitalist' class (a merger of the emergent financial and 'service' sector and the older ruling class) might also have set the imperial policy agenda.[11] Regardless of the causes, however, most influential agents of Empire at home and abroad were agreed that 'the Empire must be maintained and threats must be countered', even if few had definitive plans on how.[12]

A growing and pervasive fear that the Empire was under increasing external threat was another key ingredient in the rise of imperial identification and sentiment as the century drew to a close. For a generation

Britain had been on top, but by the late 1860s and 1870s there were signs that serious challenges were mounting. There was a sense in intellectual circles that a crisis loomed, which preceded the material challenges that manifested in the next decade. Just as such nations as the newly unified Germany and a post–Civil War United States emerged as serious competitors, Britain's influence on international affairs was at a low point (well represented by the Danish Crisis of 1862–64). Money was short, and one considerable and undeniable burden was the colonies. Many Liberals in the 1860s favoured cutting ties, yet this movement was countered, ironically, by Liberal prime ministers such as Palmerston, Russell and Gladstone who did not share this view. By the end of the decade, encouraged in part by rising international competition, a Conservative reaction against Liberal rank-and-file attitudes to the Empire was underway.[13]

For a growing number of politicians, military figures and British intellectuals, one key answer to the problem of international competition to Britain from the 1870s was to look to the white Anglo-Saxon Empire – Canada, the Australasian colonies and those in South Africa – for physical, moral and economic support. Perhaps a 'Greater Britain' might be mobilised and the growing strength of the self-governing colonies used to reinforce the centre.[14] Such ideas were, after all, firmly in the context of global pan-racial movements, which encouraged thinking of the white Empire as an Anglo-Saxon family. By the 1890s the pressures helping to move attitudes in this direction grew more powerful still. Increasing international industrial capacity demanded larger fields of commercial exploitation. Empires consequently grew larger, rapidly and, in some places such as Africa, pressed each other at their edges. Military threats followed. Britain, with the largest Empire of them all, seemed increasingly exposed, and British statesmen responded by looking even more closely to a stronger and more consolidated Anglo-Saxon Empire. By now the white settlements were looked on quite differently from India and the direct-rule colonies.[15] In this transition of conception, from a ruling centre with subordinate outposts to some sort of collaboration between Anglo-Saxon nations, the self-governing colonies were generally more than willing participants.[16]

Of course there is no question that such late-Victorian conversions of thinking about the white Empire were not universal. Segments of society, in Britain and the self-governing colonies, naturally did not subscribe to it, especially elements of the working classes and labour movement. But to suggest, as some have done, that the late-century explosion of imperial sentiment was predominantly a middle- and upper-class phenomenon goes too far. The imperial movement was mass and popular. Meaningful broad-based conclusions about it do not require universality in order to be valid. As Lehane notes, the presence of small groups that were not caught up in the tide of imperial enthusiasm 'does not negate the value of searching for positions of consent' – or working with them.[17] In any case, it is safe to conclude that by the new millennium early nineteenth-century attitudes throughout the Empire to the idea of Empire had reversed. Imperialism as a social and political force had grown more symbolic, more strident than ever before. The crisis of the Second South African War of 1899–1902, and Empire-wide reactions to it, coincided with it and to some extent represented a climax of imperial sentiment.[18]

At this point it is important to consider what 'imperialism' meant to people throughout the Anglo-Saxon Empire in the late-Victorian era.[19] For the purposes of this study, the key aspect in this regard is the *idea* of Empire, rather than the physical act of empire-building in the period. In this respect, the term was itself politicised and malleable. The imperial idea was not only a rhetorical device but also a weapon in the political battles waged between Conservatives and Liberals. It was also an inherently ill-defined and adaptive notion in that it attempted to represent a wide variety of colonies with unique governments, physical and economic circumstances. The Empire was never a single or homogenous whole, despite the ceaseless imperial mantras of common ethnic past and destiny.[20] Moreover, what the word represented to self-governing colonies was not the same as that which applied to India or the direct-rule colonies. Throughout this book therefore 'imperialism' refers to a type of Empire-wide nationalism, or even patriotism, shared between Britain and the self-governing colonies. It is the drive to celebrate and strengthen what was considered to be a shared ethnic, cultural and even religious heritage in a way that saw the whole as more than the sum of the constituent parts.

Importantly, late-Victorian imperialism was fundamentally rooted in conceptions of race – a shared Anglo-Saxon identity as a distinct cultural and ethnic group, itself a notion well aligned with emerging ideas of social Darwinism. Shared beliefs in unique racial characteristics were a means of self-identification and 'ethnicity' a shared value that needed to be protected. Such ideas, more than any other single factor, created the 'strategic mental mind maps' of the era.[21]

So too late-Victorian British imperialism developed within the context of the broader rise of nationalism across the globe from 1880 but at the same time remained separate from it. It never meant, for example, ignoring or making subservient the imperatives or interests of the self-governing colonies. The interests of Britain and these colonies ran side by side. As it concerned the white Empire, this was not 'an imperialism of the despotic, grasping, oppressive mould; but, rather, a type of nationalism, a sense of belonging to a common nation', the Empire.[22] The dominant vision of that Empire was one of British English–speaking communities living British lives in strange and far-away places. National identities were accepted, but were asserted within a wider imperial framework. As Thompson points out, however, it was not the differences between these parts but the similarities that were emphasised. By the 1890s even the language of imperialism – voiced by men like Joseph Chamberlain – was a key currency of political debate in Britain and right across the Empire.[23]

The rise of the imperial idea in the late-Victorian Empire included, and was to some degree stimulated by, a rise in military consciousness. This was, again, a consequence of feelings of increased external threat mixed with popular and romantic sentiment. From the 1870s the Victorian army was constantly involved in colonial conflicts and, with some notable exceptions such as Isandlwana in Zululand (1879) and Majuba Hill in Natal (1881), it was most often victorious. Popular heroes like Wolseley, Roberts and even Gordon found fame as protectors of the Empire and the imperial ideal. Extensive press and popular coverage of military affairs and adventures reflected the influence of rising imperialism and its associated cultural drivers.[24] Yet the Victorian army was a small organisation by European standards and was constantly stretched, sometimes close to breaking, by various commitments throughout the globe. Its famous regiments of cavalry and foot were, in many ways, a 'bluff that masked considerable weakness and vulnerability'.[25] Although sufficient troops might be scraped together to put down an indigenous rebellion or two, this was not the same as maintaining a force capable of prevailing in a general war with a European power. Moreover, this uncomfortable truth was well recognised by a small but growing military reform movement.

A key response to changing late-Victorian attitudes to the Empire, and its preservation, was the birth and development of the idea of 'imperial defence'. This was an important evolution of thinking over earlier assumptions that British soldiers and sailors would protect any and all parts of the Empire when needed – although Britain never retreated from responsibility for underwriting colonial security. Rather, as noted, the idea slowly developed that some type of mutual defence arrangement might be possible as the self-governing colonies grew in power and confidence. Perhaps the colonies, contributing not only to their local defence but also to the military strength of the Empire as a whole, might even help to offset obvious British military weakness and the danger posed by other emergent and existing powers with increasing imperial ambitions of their own. This was a two-way street. The colonies looked to Britain for security, and Britain gradually came to view the colonies as sources of potential military strength, and to realise how much her imperial position relied upon the self-governing colonies. Gradually, from the 1870s, the issue of imperial defence and organising to defend the Empire became a key aspect of the evolving relationships within the Empire.[26]

Clearly the most important instrument for defending the Empire during the late-Victorian period remained the Royal Navy.[27] Before 1914 the navy was 'intellectually, physically, symbolically and intuitively regarded as the embodiment of the martial nature of imperial defence'.[28] The army was in many ways a poor cousin. The army's regular force, especially early in the period, was often posted to garrison duties to support bases important for the navy, while the defence of India remained a central consideration. Yet military forces, even outside the army in India, were important and grew increasingly so as military challenges to the Empire mounted. Moreover, it was military officers, thinkers and politicians, much more than their naval counterparts, who encouraged truly cooperative aspects of imperial defence thinking. This book is therefore concerned, in the main, with the 'land' defence of the Empire – not to question the central importance of the navy, but to shine a light on less well known but equally important areas.

It is important to understand that the idea of imperial military defence was in flux in this period, certainly much more so than it would become by the eve of the Great War. There were continual shifts in how the notion was conceived by political and military elites in London, and by their contemporaries at the edges of the Empire. Such shifts were, of course, themselves representative and part of the wider evolution of how the Empire itself was conceived. So too a range of factors of a non-defence nature always intruded upon and shaped imperial defence attitudes and practices in London, including domestic politics, economics, technology and the European balance of power. At all times British policy-makers were severely constrained as to how imperial defence initiatives might be implemented. They could not cost too much money or consume too many other industrial or human resources. They also had to be sure that 'the act of producing imperial defence [in no way] altered the very fabric of what was being protected'.[29] That is, decision-makers were restrained by theories of free trade and what it ought to mean in terms of international relations, ideas of democracy, standing armies, liberal notions on the use of military force, religious ideas about role of the Empire, volunteer traditions and a range of other factors. Equally, it was never a question of simple military strategy in the colonies. Ideas of imperial defence mingled with notions of colonial self-respect and the perceived prerogatives of new self-governments, local pressures and politics. It is also true that, largely as a consequence of such issues, imperial defence for much of the period was more an intellectual and theoretical exercise than a physical reality in terms of firm structures, definite plans or consistent thoughts, but it was no less important because of this.[30]

Within this context the earliest ideas about imperial military defence emerged and developed. It is upon this scaffold that key questions must be asked and answered. To what extent, for example, did the idea of imperial defence represent a set of clearly defined plans and concerted effort from London in this era? To what extent they were *ad hoc*, the result of local initiatives or the personal plans of various imperial officers abroad? Was there any measure of duplicity or coercion from the War Office to entice the colonies to offer up manpower to be sacrificed on command from Whitehall in war? Or were intra-Empire military initiatives better described as natural responses to shared concerns, with a significant two-way interplay? Answers to questions of this type shed light on more issues than those directly associated with defence – they illuminate important aspects of the Empire as a whole and the attitudes that held it together and drove it apart. This is a study therefore of more than military concerns, plans and strategic scheming. At the political level, for example, the issues involved include the jealously guarded prerogatives of relatively new nations – protective of their sovereign rights and constitutional responsibilities, interacting with agents, particularly in the War Office, which often failed to understand such sensitivities.

The military career of Edward Hutton has been chosen as a vehicle by which to investigate the imperial defence in the late-Victorian era for a number of reasons. First, his unique experiences and appointments in the self-governing colonies help to overcome the danger of a narrow national (and nationalist) approach. Not only was Hutton, in his capacity of General Officer Commanding, the 'creator' of the post-Federation Australian Army in 1901 but also he had by that time led the New South Wales colonial forces (1893–96) and the Canadian militia (1898–1900), as well as fought in four of Britain's expeditionary wars. This included, crucially, command of troops from Britain, the Australian colonies, New Zealand and Canada within the 1st Mounted Infantry Brigade in South Africa in 1900. Most of these commands unfolded during the key Colonial Secretaryship of Joseph

Chamberlain, from June 1895 to September 1903. A good speaker with a flair for publicity, as a junior member of the 'Wolseley Ring' of outspoken army reformers, Hutton became a leading advocate of the use of mounted infantry and colonial troops. At the same time his marriage into the aristocracy in 1889 and appointment as aide-de-camp to Queen Victoria in 1892 afforded him a degree of influence unusual for an officer of his rank and station. Hutton's various commands put him at the centre of key imperial defence issues. Indeed the frustrations and successes of his colonial career, and its associated professional crusades, are a microcosm of the difficulties and debates over late-Victorian intra-Empire military cooperation in a general sense. Operating at the practical end of philosophical and practical debates surrounding the issue, Hutton is an ideal individual case study by which imperial defence can be better understood.

Despite Hutton's centrality to such important questions of Empire, the man who had been 'undoubtedly the most influential British army officer serving in the self-governing colonies before 1910' has no published biography.[31] Perhaps more than anything else this reflects the narrow focus of many past studies. For authors writing on Canadian military affairs, for example, a few years spent in charge of the militia (even if Hutton is recognised as the most important and controversial of any British officer to hold this appointment) seems insufficiently significant. For British historians, on the other hand, interested in the difficulties of the late-Victorian army and various initiatives for harnessing the military potential of the self-governing colonies, the temptation is to focus on the centre, while men like Hutton worked at the periphery. Yet the scope of Hutton's career throughout the Empire as a whole – from London to Sydney, to Ottawa, to Pretoria and to Melbourne – placed him at the centre of the issues fundamental to imperial defence in the era. The man is intimately connected to, and his career in many ways representative of, this much larger issue.

Two other issues make Hutton a worthy case study through which to examine imperial defence issues in this period, as well as an interesting biographical candidate in his own right. The first is that Hutton himself pursued a personal vision of building a comprehensive system of what he called 'Cooperative Empire Defence'. This was his grand project, his overarching professional goal. Partly as a consequence of his colonial experiences, and partly the result of an agenda that he took with him to the edges of the Empire, as time progressed Hutton's dream of an imperial military partnership between the self-governing colonies and Britain, each fielding relatively cheap, self-contained volunteer militia armies capable of local defence and defence of the Empire, took form. It was a scheme that embraced key elements of the reform-minded military professionalism Hutton himself grew to hold dear. It was a plan that also incorporated his convictions regarding the value of mounted infantry and the natural martial advantages of the British race generally, and colonial stock in particular. This was not a system of coercion or compulsion. Indeed the whole basis of his assumption was that in a time of catastrophe, in context of the peak of imperial sentiment that grew throughout the white Empire in the late nineteenth century, volunteers would come. Empire-wide sensibilities regarding citizen-soldiery and compulsory military service would not need to be offended. Taken in total, this vision was Hutton's solution to match or even surpass the military potential (and danger) represented by the mass conscript forces of Europe. Britain, through the Empire, might then be equipped to deal with the European war that would decide its fate and which Hutton and many of his fellow officers thought was not only inevitable but also looming.

A second factor that makes Hutton a valuable choice was his personality, which tended to draw out, polarise and set up confrontations between the actors, agendas and inherent contradictions of imperial defence in the era. He was all at once, and in no small measure, brilliant, determined, vigorous, ambitious, arrogant, stubborn and ruthless. For Morton, Hutton was 'cast in the pro-consular mould, aggressive, imaginative, energetic, with a nearly limitless self-confidence'.[32] To Buchan he was 'a propagandist, a missionary fired with apostolic zeal, and apostles do not think greatly of tact'.[33] Hutton was also an intellectual trailblazer. His vision for imperial defence cooperation was based on a scholarly approach to Empire-wide strategic questions uncharacteristic of the officer corps in general, particularly at his rank.[34] Educated at Eton but caught socially half-way between the middle class and the aristocracy, he found personal legitimacy through professional competence and attainment, not an inherited title. In the context of a rise in the professional classes more generally Hutton saw himself as a new-style professional officer in the reformer mould. 'To be a successful soldier you must work and work thoroughly and conscientiously,' he told an audience at Eton in 1880. 'Knowledge is power ... Men will not believe in those whom they know to be ignorant.'[35] He was as a result possessed of a considerable internal drive and work ethic. Although he came to possess independent means, 'able to move between court, military and political circles with ease', Hutton at once despised his aristocratic dilettante brother officers and worshipped them, as only one on the outside looking in could.[36] A streak of insecurity therefore ran side by side with an indomitable self-confidence. It motivated him to self-aggrandise, to crave the approval of his mentors and never to stop seeking official recognition.

Hutton was well aware of his powers of the mind, organisational ability and of a level of professional competence rarely matched by his peers. He was, consequently, absolutely convinced of the correctness of any position he took while being intolerant of, and condescending to, dissenting views. His high opinion of his military rank, ability and accomplishments, and the gravitas that in his eyes ought to be attached to them, gave him what he thought ought to be an unassailable position of authority in colonial contexts. The colonials, however, did not always agree. Nothing was as important in Hutton's eyes as his own projects. That others might be slow or reluctant to agree with him was understood by Hutton to be a consequence of their lack of intelligence, experience or a hidden agenda. He was too self-confident to be wrong. He was therefore both tactless, easily offended and slow to forgive.[37] Yet no one was more conscious of his faults than the man himself. Hutton wrote in June 1902 to a former subordinate and friend from the Second South African War:

> My very strong points constitute my weakness – for example my nature as you know is quick in perception and enthusiasm, amounting to strong impulse. These very qualities lead me to being impatient with others whose thoughts work slower than my own. I am strong in my views and the very strength which constitutes the value of most I try to do, betrays me sometimes into impressing my will too strongly upon those around me. I am my dear fellow very very conscious of my failings, and try as all the best of us try, to overcome them.[38]

The key point here is that Hutton's personality, his strengths and his weaknesses, elicited strong reactions in all his appointments. Caught on the outer spirals of the Empire, Hutton juggled a wide range of competing agendas, some of his own devising, others thrust upon him. He won friends and made bitter enemies. Once again the controversy that resulted illuminates many important issues associated with the idea and practicality of imperial defence.

The research informing this study has by necessity, and like its subject, been a multinational endeavour. Along with a host of contextual and specific secondary material published in Britain, the former colonies and elsewhere, archival and primary material has been examined from repositories in Australia, Canada and Britain. Hutton's own papers, held in the British Library and available in Australia on microfilm, are a key source. Overall this collection provides a unique insight through official, private and personal correspondence into many of the institutional and personal attitudes central to the issue of imperial defence. Yet it is a large but problematic collection. There is no question, for example, that Hutton ordered his own personal papers with due consideration for how they might be used by future historians. He wrote to George Reid, former Premier of New South Wales, and at the time Australian High Commissioner in London, in February 1916, noting: 'I have also been engaged for some time past in putting together my own papers, not for publication, but because hereafter and long hence they may prove of some historical value when contemporaneous history comes to be written.'[39] Most difficult of all are a series of draft memoir chapters within Hutton's papers drafted during and immediately after the Great War. These are key documents but need to be read carefully, sensitive to Hutton's self-serving purpose. Even beyond these drafts, many of Hutton's footnotes are self-aggrandising and seek to show his actions and their reactions in a positive light. Inserts and additions are used to exaggerate his role, and align with his belief in own achievements. It was Hutton, after all, who selected the order of his papers and what appeared within them. Although he wrote: 'I leave to history and to the future generation the real estate of work done, and of the result achieved',[40] he was not averse to shaping its path.

It is important to note that for all the utility of Hutton's military career as a lens through which to investigate imperial defence, before his appointment to New South Wales in 1893 the two ran on essentially separate tracks. Up to this date, as a low- and middle-ranking officer, Hutton certainly felt the practical consequences of the evolution of ideas as to how the Empire could or should be defended, but he was too junior to shape the course of such developments. At the same time, when thrust into his first colonial appointment, at the 'coalface' of imperial defence concerns, Hutton's actions and reactions were contingent upon wider thinking about such issues in Britain and the colonies that had been unfolding throughout the latter half of the nineteenth century. So too they were the product his own personality, attitudes and convictions, which were, as for all of us, developed over time. The first chapter of this book therefore will trace key themes and developments in the imperial defence idea up to the early 1890s. This foundation, or scaffold, is followed in the next chapter by a focus on the parallel progress of Hutton's early military career. From 1893 (and chapter 3) onwards, these two separate threads become intimately interwoven, each shaping and helping to illuminate the other.

CHAPTER 1

'THE COMMON DUTIES OF THE EMPIRE'

DEVELOPMENTS IN THE IMPERIAL DEFENCE IDEA, 1848–92

The British regular army of the mid-nineteenth century essentially remained the small and elite force it had been a hundred years earlier whereas its European counterparts were being transformed by mass conscription. At the same time British military prestige had been declining since Waterloo as the effectiveness of such an army in a significant European war was questioned at home and abroad, inside and outside military circles. The difficulties exposed by the Crimean War were a clear sign that reform was overdue, not only of the British regular force but also of the auxiliaries: the traditional county-based militia, the mounted yeomanry and the rapidly growing and predominantly city-based volunteer movement. In 1859 a royal commission on the fortifications of British harbours found that the Royal Navy, the regular army and the auxiliaries combined could not ensure Britain's safety from invasion.[1] Meanwhile, Liberal government policies favoured financial and fiscal conservatism, caution in international affairs and reduced defence expenditure. The Gladstone government of 1868, in an environment of general retrenchment, subsequently gave the Secretary of State for War, Edward Cardwell, an impossible mandate to modernise the British Army and to cut costs while increasing efficiency.

Cardwell's subsequent reforms, although significant, were more evolutionary than revolutionary. He was prepared to push for reform against prevailing military conservatism, and did so with a greater level of parliamentary support than his predecessors. Like Earl Grey, Cardwell saw the recall of imperial garrisons abroad as a key step. If the need to maintain these military outposts was removed, then reorganisation of the home army became a real possibility.[2] In any case the scattered garrisons had never added anything to the defence of the British Isles. Moreover, colonial service had always been costly in money and men, given the higher rates of disease, death and desertion on such postings, factors that aggravated the consistent problem of military recruitment. Expenditure on the army in India came out of the Indian budget, yet the other colonial garrisons accounted for a full third of the military vote, and the burden was growing, an acute concern to free-trade liberals.[3]

At the same time there was more than economics at work. During the 1859 war scare a select House of Commons committee had been established to look into 'any, and what, alterations may be advantageously adopted in regard to the defence of the British Dependencies'. The resultant Mills Report, tabled in 1861, concluded that the garrisons should be brought home and that the self-governing colonies 'ought to assist in their own defence'.[4] For a growing number of British elites, colonial self-government implied a responsibility for self-defence. Yet the presence of British regulars abroad had perhaps hindered the development of such attitudes in the colonies.[5] In this context the Commons passed a resolution on 4 March 1862 favouring the recall of imperial troops.[6] Cardwell's recommendations thus mirrored a long-standing policy preference in Britain. On 7 March 1873, the Undersecretary of State for the Colonies, Edward Knatchbull-Hugessen, announced that although Britain still guaranteed colonial security, imperial troops had returned and the self-governing colonies had assumed responsibility for their local defence.[7]

In the self-governing colonies, defence issues, up to the 1870s, had never assumed centre stage. To take the Australian example, although the population was familiar with guns, they were used primarily for hunting and for sport and to a lesser degree for self-defence. Meanwhile, small British regular detachments, whose primary purpose up to 1852 was guarding transported convicts, had watched over government treasuries, hunted bushrangers and harried the Aborigines. There was no real or even perceived need for much else. Few European powers, certainly no non-European power, could challenge the Empire. The peace of 1815 and the Royal Navy made serious defence considerations unnecessary; rather, the focus was on building wealth and material prosperity.[8] Certainly, from time to time local interest in defence spiked in accordance with various European military crises.[9] At such times, when colonies felt vulnerable, the scattered redcoats and few British ships in Australian waters looked a thin shield, particularly with the French presence in New Caledonia and the departure of British regulars to the New Zealand Wars.[10]

Spasmodic crisis-related bursts of military interest and the *ad hoc* establishment of volunteer units from the 1850s (which followed similar patterns in Britain and throughout the Empire) suited the Australian colonial governments as they represented a relatively cheap defence alternative and one that satisfied an old, imported British antipathy to regulars.[11] Volunteerism also provided its predominantly middle-class adherents some of the same social capital as their British volunteer counterparts. It was 'a hobby', General Sir John Monash once called it, 'with great social opportunities'.[12] As in Britain, part-time volunteer units assembled as 'clubs', largely free of overt regulation. From time to time efforts were made to funnel this spirit into part-paid militias, subjected to discipline in between that expected of regulars and purely volunteer units. Success in this regard, however, was only ever mixed, primarily due to the cost involved. The idea took root that there was little need for European-style military systems or structures as armed colonial citizens would make for a fine 'reserve' of soldiers if required. Yet, behind the scenes, in narrow military circles questions regarding the effectiveness of local citizen-soldiers were never far from the surface. From the 1860s onwards a degree of fear lingered as Europe conscripted its armies, which mixed with budding feelings in the colonies linking responsible government and the duties of citizenship with some form of serious military service.[13]

Nonetheless, the Australian colonies, with the Royal Navy supreme on the high seas, were generally unperturbed about Cardwell's withdrawal of the garrisons. New South Wales, Victoria and South Australia were to some extent relieved to be released from the need to subsidise British troops over which they had no real control.[14] Years of neglect and ad hoc volunteerism had, however, left them without effective local defence structures, models, plans or even people. Military advice sometimes came from resident Royal Navy officers or governors, but the colonies were largely left to their own devices to do (or not) what they would. Some limited attempts at greater professionalisation were attempted. In the larger colonies former regulars were occasionally appointed as instructors or as technical staff, or to man fortifications at key harbours. Efficiency targets for volunteer attendance and rifle practice were also occasionally set with 'capitation grants' to offset costs. From the early 1860s 'training camps', although still predominantly social occasions, were sometimes attempted. The efficiency dividend of such enterprises was, however, always questionable.

The attitudes and approaches of the other Anglo-Saxon colonies had much in common with the Australian example, yet diverged in some key ways in response to local conditions, pressures and experiences. Canadian defence and military structures had developed, for example, in response to a significant perceived threat from the United States. Canada also had to deal with the Fenian incursions from 1866 to 1871 and the Riel Rebellion of 1869–70.[15] At the same time Canadian attitudes towards citizen-soldiers, influenced by interpretations of the War of Independence, the War of 1812 and the American Civil War, and contrary to the actual performance of such troops in these conflicts, asserted that volunteers fighting for their homes would always be the most effective type of army. The result was a concern to ensure firm political control over any military activity, an infatuation with volunteerism and prevailing defence parsimony.[16]

The same spasmodic interest in military affairs, tied to various international crises, that encouraged spurts of volunteerism in the Australian colonies also shaped Canadian citizen soldiery. Raised in 1808 on a British model, the Canadian militia languished after 1812, but was temporarily reinvigorated thanks to the Crimean War. A decade later the American Civil War sparked not only Canadian Confederation but also a renewed interest in defence. A new Militia Act in 1868 established the 'modern' Canadian militia. Although this Act contained a latent universal obligation and the power to conscript all males between 18 and 60 years in an emergency, it was in reality another statement of preference for volunteerism. It set the 'active militia' – those who wished to serve in peacetime – at 40 000 volunteers, the vast majority of whom served part-time and were paid during short periods of annual training. The active militia also contained a small, full-time paid cadre of 'permanent' soldiers.[17]

In Canada (like New Zealand) the withdrawal of British troops was not well received. Thanks to a set of much more realistic threats than faced in Australia, and despite Britain's continuing guarantee of the Canadian frontier, the 'air was full of accusations and recrimination'.[18] Soon thereafter, however, with an improvement in Anglo-US relations, interest in the active militia fell rapidly. Some even questioned the purpose of the militia in that any war between Canada and the United States was surely a forgone conclusion. Yet a minority continued to involve themselves in the volunteer active militia.[19] The appointment in 1874 of a British general to command the organisation – the first such appointment by a self-governing colony – and the establishment of a military college in 1876 to train local officers for the militia or for British commissions did little, however, to reverse the tide of public and political (particularly Liberal) apathy.[20]

Back in London Cardwell's reforms continued with the command structures of the British military being completely overhauled. The old army headquarters organisation, the Horse Guards, was moved to Pall Mall, co-located with the War Office and soon found itself 'swamped in a vast sea of civilian clerks'.[21] This ended the system of 'dual control' of the army with, in theory, the Commander-in-Chief now clearly subordinate to the Secretary of War. The Secretary's real influence, however, was determined by his inclination to wrestle the military establishment into subservience. Indeed, the problem of how to integrate civilian power with professional expertise was at the core of many subsequent War Office reorganisations. Other key Cardwell initiatives with a significant influence on army culture and practice included short service enlistment for twelve years (six years each to be served at home and abroad) rather than for life, the abolition of commission by purchase from 1871 and the beginnings of a reorganisation of army regimental structures the following year.[22]

Unsurprisingly, conservative elements in the army came to oppose the Cardwell initiatives, whereas small groups of self-styled reformers, even young and not yet influential officers like Hutton, embraced them – except on the issue of civilian interference, where their opposition was generally shared.[23] At the head of the conservatives was the army's Commander-in-Chief, the Duke of Cambridge, the Queen's cousin, who had held the position since 1856. Cambridge and his followers were guided by experience, tradition and army successes of the past. They developed somewhat of a citadel mentality and feared that radical change might undermine the prestige, status and traditions of the army, reflecting uncertainties linked to wider social changes unfolding around them. Opposing the conservatives were officers seeking to continue the post-Crimea reform program. It was a split, however, over more than military reform and was in many ways rooted in personalities and in the very social, class and traditional structures of the army.[24] After his triumphant return to England after leading the victorious Ashanti campaign in 1874, Major-General Garnet Wolseley, for example, drew the attention of many reform-minded officers, who began to gravitate towards him as their highest profile campaigner. Wolseley himself developed a coterie of like-minded and trustworthy acolytes, which included a number who had served with him in West Africa. This 'Wolseley Ring' was the most prominent reform group opposing Cambridge's traditionalists who still rejected such innovations as the replacement of parade-ground drills with field manoeuvres and the development of professional and technical branches (as in Europe). The reformers, however, were always a small minority, who were divided in their approaches and who risked their careers in advocating change. Wolseley himself was removed from his position as Inspector-General of Auxiliary Forces in 1875 after drawing government attention to the Horse Guards' deliberate stonewalling of Cardwell's recommendations.[25]

Photo 1 Major-General Sir Garnet Wolseley, GCMG, KCB (1833–1913). (Royal Collection Trust/© Her Majesty Queen Elizabeth II 2014, RCIN 2500946)

Despite support by such reformers as Wolseley, the Cardwell initiatives did not fundamentally alter the attitudes, traditions and structures of the army overnight. Nor did they solve immediate problems such as recruiting, planning and overall efficiency. The final end of the purchase system, for example, was hardly definitive. It neither altered the social homogeneity of the force nor removed the requirement in many cases for officers to have some form of independent means.[26] The point was that British officers of the late-Victorian army were linked more by civilian interests, lifestyle and the accepted norms of the ruling classes than by a shared self-identification as members of a separate profession. The army was not led entirely or even predominantly by aristocrats; around half of all officers were of the middle class and only 12 per cent from the peerage or baronetage. Nonetheless, traditional aristocratic values dominated. Even those whose social roots were elsewhere indulged in such traditionally upper-class pursuits as hunting and preserved old ideals and traditions in regiments and messes. Social relationships were therefore often more important than professional ones. Indeed, the very notion of professionalism, for some, insofar as it meant a dedication to the military, was seen as an unsavoury militaristic spirit.[27]

Such attitudes within the officer corps at large were increasingly out of place in context of an ever more competitive, expanding and aspirant professional class in the wider community. At the same time they were understandable in the context of the importance placed on recruiting officers of good character over those with intellectual or administrative potential. Intellectual expertise 'was frequently linked with undesirable attributes', for example, 'which implied that the intellectual was the boor [*sic*] and the prig who knew books better than men and who preferred work at the desk to delights in the saddle'.[28] This outlook was itself tied to the schooling shared by the majority of the officer corps as the products of philosophies that defined education as a training ground for leadership over scholarship. The 'character over intellect' argument was clear, for example, in the training programs at the Royal Military Academy, Woolwich (which prepared officers for the Royal Artillery and Royal Engineers) and the Royal Military College (which trained cavalry and infantry officers). It was also apparent in the selection of officers to fill staff and command appointments throughout the Victorian period. In any case, promotion by seniority acted against professional endeavour as under normal circumstances it took an officer of intellect and accomplishment just as long as any other to reach high rank.[29]

The net result was a stifling of the spirit of professionalism within the army, and Hutton and other reform-minded officers struggled against this tendency. It was certainly true that an aristocratic title and a professional outlook were not mutually exclusive – Prussian officers were proof of that – yet the values that attended them in Britain discouraged reform at an institutional level. Although forces for change certainly existed and the paternalistic role of commanding officers within the regimental system allowed for experimentation at that level, the overall system discouraged professionalism. Wolseley understood the problem and a young Hutton seemed to intuitively understand the issues at stake, but they were exceptions to the rule.[30]

Meanwhile, Benjamin Disraeli's Conservative Party was returned to government in February 1874 with its first clear majority in the House of Commons since the 1840s. Political attitudes to the Empire shifted with Disraeli, who soon made conservatism equate to 'patriotism, royalism and imperialism' and who took a much more aggressive imperial policy stance than his predecessor.[31] One of the consequences of Disraeli's imperial position was a new war scare during the Russo-Turkish conflict of 1877–78, when fear of a Russian seizure of the Suez Canal prompted the Prime Minister to despatch the fleet. Britain and Russia approached the brink of open conflict before a settlement was negotiated. This was followed in 1879 by the Anglo-Zulu War, thanks to the plans of Sir Henry Bartle Frere, High Commissioner in Southern Africa, to build a British-dominated confederation in the region. The subsequent destruction of Zulu power then presented the Transvaal Boers with an opportunity of reasserting their independence after the British annexation of 1877. An ensuing revolt became another war in late 1880, which ended only after a significant Boer victory at Majuba Hill. This moment was, above all, another disaster for British military prestige, and it inspired, as had been the case after the British defeat at Isandlwana in Zululand, a significant public over-reaction.[32]

A year and a half after Majuba Hill, British troops once more found themselves fighting a new colonial war, this time in Egypt. Threats to British and French investments and a subsequent crisis led to an intervention that forced the Khedive to accept Anglo-French usurpation of Egypt's sovereignty in the form of control over the treasury, customs and other national institutions. Such a move provoked a backlash from unpaid Egyptian army officers led by Ahmad Urabi Pasha. The successful suppression of Urabi's revolt during the Anglo-Egyptian War of 1882 did not, however, mean the end of British problems in the region. The need for a

British contingency plan for the Sudan, under Egyptian administration since 1819, soon arose owing to a continuing insurrection led by a Muslim religious leader, Muhammad Ahmad, the self-styled 'Mahdi'. Under British instructions, the Egyptian government ordered all Egyptian troops in the region to be withdrawn. Major-General Charles George Gordon was chosen to coordinate the extraction, which did not go as planned, owing in part to Gordon's stubborn determination to conduct the operation as he saw fit, rather than to follow the clear intent passed to him from London. Subsequently, in March 1884 the Mahdist army laid siege to Khartoum. Under pressure from the public, in August 1884 the British Government decided to reverse its hands-off policy and send a relief force to Gordon's aid. Although the relief of Khartoum failed, the Mahdist revolt was repressed.

While such colonial military outbreaks held public attention, behind the scenes important developments in the nascent philosophy of imperial defence were unfolding. A lack of coherence was no surprise at this stage. After all, from the middle of the century when reference to the army's role of maintaining the balance of power in Europe was dropped from the Mutiny Act, the British Government had, officially, no formal military policy at all.[33] Nonetheless, the idea that the colonies might one day contribute to the defence of the Empire endured and emerged from time to time. In his evidence to Mill's Committee in 1859, Gladstone, for example, noted: 'I have not the smallest doubt ... that they [the self-governing colonies] will be disposed to go beyond the bare idea of self-defence and to tender loyal and effective assistance in the struggles of the Empire.'[34] This was, as yet, the echo of an idea and represented neither a statement of policy nor an enduring strategic sentiment.

The idea of imperial defence resurfaced in Disraeli's famous Crystal Palace speech of June 1872. During this speech, along with rhetoric of preserving the Empire from competitors, the Prime Minister argued that formalised responsibilities for defence ought to have been implicit when self-government was granted to the Anglo-Saxon colonies. Such an arrangement, Disraeli continued, should have defined the means by which 'this country should call for aid from the Colonies'.[35] No such bargains, however, had ever been struck, and the new 'states' were inaugurated without any formal reference to defence responsibilities. From this point, with concerns about money always to the fore, low-level debates on the issue continued in London. On 7 March 1873, for example, Lord Eustace Cecil proposed in the House of Commons that colonies be invited to contribute to the costs of defending the Empire in proportion to their size and wealth.[36]

Meanwhile, John Colomb, a former Royal Marines artillery officer, had published *The Protection of Commerce and Distribution of Naval Forces*, which advocated to the few who might listen the use of colonial troops in a coordinated imperial defence system.[37]

Contrary to pre-election rhetoric, on gaining office, Disraeli's government made no effort to encourage the colonies towards an intra-imperial defence system, or even effective local defence. The concept was, however, subsequently championed by Lord Carnarvon, Disraeli's Secretary of State for the Colonies. In 1876, in the context of Australasian agitation for a greater British strategic presence in the Pacific to offset the French, Carnarvon attempted to secure the acceptance in principle that the colonies ought to share the burden of defence and to 'accept their membership in the common duties of the Empire'.[38] He found little support from the colonies, which again pointed to the anomaly of paying for an instrument they did not control. Nor was the military establishment in Britain interested. Cambridge was far too busy running a continuous battle to thwart the Cardwell reforms, while the best and brightest of Wolseley's reformers were consistently absent fighting colonial wars that acted against their consideration of larger issues.[39]

The war scare with Russia, however, and consequent realisation of Britain's unpreparedness for a large-scale conflict, eventually encouraged the Conservative government to action, particularly given its decision to reinforce Malta with troops from India during the crisis, a distinctly imperial solution. In the first instance the idea of a Colonial Defence Committee (CDC) was conceived by Carnarvon to 'weave loosely together some imperial defence response', but this committee lasted only as long as the war scare.[40] Importantly, however, a series of studies into intra-Empire defence problems were subsequently initiated that marked a move towards meaningful conversations about imperial defence cooperation.[41] The most important of these was the Royal Commission on the Defence of British Possessions and Commerce Abroad, established under the chair of Lord Carnavon in 1879, after he had resigned as Colonial Secretary in protest against Disraeli's brinkmanship the previous year.[42] The Carnarvon Commission was primarily directed to consider whether an 'organised system of imperial defence was required' to examine associated costs and what portion might be hived off to the colonies.[43] Its work was interrupted by a change of government in 1880, but the commission eventually produced three reports. The first discussed the importance of commerce to the Empire, the second the defence of trade routes and ways by which Britain and colonies might contribute, and the third the specific problem of defending the Australasian colonies.

A number of key colonial politicians testified before the Carnarvon Commission, including such prominent men as Sir John A. McDonald of Canada and Sir Henry Parkes of New South Wales. The former argued that 'no common system of defence, embracing all the states of the Empire, could be established' as local conditions varied too much.[44] It was better to trust to individual loyalty and volunteering at time of crisis. McDonald's argument was echoed by Parkes, who added that any defence agreements in peacetime would have to come with a hand in shaping Empire policy and that public opinion in Australia was not ready for such an initiative. Other Australian witnesses, such as Frederick Sargood, future Minister for Defence in Victoria, were less hostile to the notion of cooperation. Overall, the commission stopped short of recommending any formal system of imperial military defence; rather it trusted, in time of war, that the colonies 'would readily come forward' of their own accord.[45] The commission thought it not unreasonable, however, that the richer colonies might increase the effectiveness of their local defence arrangements and be called on to defray the cost of the wider British defence budget. There was no reason, for example, that the Australian colonies could not help to pay for the cost of the naval squadron stationed there (especially after receiving a proposal from them in 1881 to increase its size). After all, defence expenditure per head showed a wide discrepancy, from 2s 4d in New South Wales, the highest in Australia, to 15s 7d per head in Britain.[46] Thus began an early pattern of thinking of the defence of the Empire in terms of a connected whole, with a centralised authority and colonial contributions.[47] At the same time there was much to be done. The commission had to depend for data collection on officers of itinerant naval vessels, for example, illustrating the lack of Empire-wide defence machinery of any kind. Although at this stage the immediate practical outcome was further emphasis on fortifying Britain and the colonial ports to protect imperial trade and a reinvigoration of the Royal Navy, it was, at least, a start.[48]

Important embryonic imperial defence developments were concurrently unfolding in the self-governing colonies. The withdrawal of garrisons, combined with a laissez-faire liberal outlook and distaste for 'European militarism', began a period of limited interest in defence in the colonies, punctuated by the momentary excitement of various war scares. Although the advice of various touring imperial officers, such as the comprehensive reports prepared by Major-General Sir W.F.D. Jervois and Colonel P.N. Scratchley on the state of defences in Australia, was regularly proffered, it was less regularly implemented in its entirety.[49] This neglect was occasionally raised as a concern in London, but little was done to address it from Whitehall. More to the point, there was not much that could be done. British politicians and military figures interested in imperial defence during this era tended to ignore, or remain ignorant of, the limitations on colonial policy-makers in this regard. Like their British counterparts, colonial politicians were influenced by the requirements of their political system and by what was practical within their parliamentary context. Added to the mix was often a strong drive to guard the rights of local self-government, which tended to clash with a degree of ignorance of colonial constitutional rights and sensibilities on the part of many in London. So too no matter how individuals might have felt about reform and imperial defence, little could be done in the colonies and less could afford to be spent, unless supported by public opinion, which was largely uninterested except in moments of crisis.[50]

Yet the strength of imperial sentiments within the colonies was amply shown during periods of military emergency. Sir Edmund Head, Governor-General of the Province of Canada, had seen the Crimean War as a reason why Canada should take on imperial defence responsibilities. Similarly, Sir William Denison, Governor in New South Wales, considered it his colony's duty to assist Britain in the defence of the Empire as a whole as well as take care of its own internal order.[51] The Indian Mutiny of 1857 saw militia units and individuals in Canada volunteer in large numbers, although their offers were rebuffed by London. At the same time in New Zealand, Colonel Robert Henry Wynyard, commanding British troops in the colony, called for his government to offer military support to Britain during the mutiny.[52] In March 1858 the Canadians were approached for recruits to the British Army, and as a result the 100th Royal Canadians was raised, the first colonial unit to be formed to serve wherever Britain wished. Later, in the debates surrounding Canadian Confederation, Macdonald announced that in a real crisis Britain might rely on the colonies to 'assist in enabling her again to meet the whole world in arms as she has done before'.[53] Back in New Zealand, in 1869 William Fitzherbert, the colony's Treasurer, developed a plan whereby the cost of the British fleet in Australasian waters might be shared with Britain. Sir Julius Vogel, New Zealand's Prime Minister, also expressed support for some form of cooperation for defence.[54]

As in Britain, the war scare with Russia stimulated thinking about imperial defence in the self-governing colonies. In New Zealand and Australia, money for local defences (temporarily) flowed. This crisis saw more offers of service from Canadians and a suggestion by the British commander at Halifax, General Patrick McDougall, that a Canadian unit be specifically organised for imperial service. Cambridge at the War Office approved the idea, as did the Canadian Government, although with the end of the crisis it lost momentum. Yet the idea was nurtured by the incoming Governor-General, the Marquis of Lorne, who called on his government to create an imperial reserve in Canada, to be armed and paid for by Britain. McDonald thought it worth a try, but the scheme foundered on the inevitable issue of control. Such a force must be at Britain's call for service anywhere at any time, but how might that be enforced?[55] Continuing the tradition of crisis and response, the Majuba Hill disaster saw the South Australian Government offer 300 volunteer troops for service in Natal in March 1881, the first such offer by an Australian Government, although it was declined.[56] Such displays of imperial loyalty in the self-governing colonies were hardly surprising given the nature of colonial identity in the period leading up to the early 1880s. Even the short-lived separation movement that sprouted in Canada from around 1870, for example, never seriously challenged ideas expressed by one of the fathers of Canadian Confederation, Thomas D'Arcy McGee, five years earlier: 'Canada is itself the Empire in North America.'[57] In all of these cases and throughout this period, one key principle emerged: that the self-governing colonies seemed more than willing to offer troops to meet an imperial crisis, *during* times of crisis. This sentiment did not, however, extend to formal or standing cooperative arrangements in times of peace.

Hence, despite all the talk, little was actually done by British or colonial governments to ensure intra-Empire defence cooperation up to the mid-1880s. Yet important groundwork, even if only in terms of shared perceptions, was laid. All the while the transition of public and political consensus towards the notion that Britain might be best served by *strengthening* colonial connections grew ever stronger. Preserving the Empire became a popular catch-cry. The notion that the colonies should be seen as an asset rather than an encumbrance was reinforced by European grabs for more of their own, including the French in Pacific and the Germans in New Guinea. Meanwhile, Social Darwinist notions added to the mix as a type of scientific rationale for an aggressive defence of Empire as a test of racial characteristics and national power, and religious approaches began to encourage a vision of a white self-governing Empire united by faith.[58] At the periphery the self-governing colonies continued to grow in power and wealth; the military potential of four million white citizens in Canada, two million in Australia and 300 000 in New Zealand was becoming harder to ignore.

Meanwhile, British governments from the mid-1880s were not only pressured to respond to the rising tide of imperialism in the electorate; they were also pressed by vocal interest groups such as the Primrose League, the

Imperial Federation League and its offshoots, the British Empire League and Imperial Federation Defence Committee. British Liberals, in particular, with their traditional political philosophies challenged on all fronts, were to some degree forced to advocate imperial unity as a consequence of debates surrounding the Irish Home Rule Bills of 1886 and 1893, which opened them up to criticism that they cared little for the Empire. Lord Salisbury credited this particular issue with awakening a deep imperial sentiment in Britain.[59] Some Liberals deserted Gladstone over policies in Ireland that they thought would contribute to Empire disintegration. It was no surprise that when the Conservatives were in power in the period, government policy sought to draw the bonds of Empire closer in every way. Lord Ripon was appointed Secretary of State for the Colonies in 1892 for the express purpose of countering Conservative criticisms in this regard, pledging to 'confirm and to strengthen the union which ought to bind together every part of the British Empire'.[60] By this time even the language of 'patriotism' had shifted to merge with 'imperialism' – sentiment towards state could no longer easily be separated from the imperial vision. A family metaphor of a mother country, sister/daughter relationship was often used. Britain would lead the imperial household in terms of defence and foreign policy, but it would be conscious of children's individual needs and wishes.[61]

As the 1880s and early 1890s progressed, the Empire nationalism of the self-governing colonies (the self-identified connection and celebration of membership in the imperial community) grew even stronger than at the centre. Alongside, in parallel, local patriotism and the protection of self-interests continued to develop.[62] Most white colonists, save the French Canadians and other minority groups with alternative cultural heritages, still thought of themselves as British settlers with first and natural loyalty to the Empire, of which their colony was, in any case, an extension.[63] One obvious manifestation of such sentiment was the growth of Imperial Federation League branches in Canada, Australia, New Zealand, Barbados and British Guiana after the organisation was established in Britain in 1884. Although the British branch was dissolved in 1894, the league lived on in the colonies, especially in such places as Victoria and Ontario, thanks largely to the efforts of key local adherents.[64] Defence was often a key issue of consideration for many of the league's notable members, such as George Denison in Canada, who argued in 1890 that 'an empire of 320 000 000 banded together as a solid phalanx would be able to say to the world, just leave us alone and we will not interfere with you'.[65]

Importantly, the view from London suggested that such a 'phalanx' was becoming a real possibility. In the early stages of the crisis in Sudan, with news of the fall of Khartoum and with Gordon's fate still uncertain, the Acting Premier of New South Wales, William Bede Dalley, made an important choice. On tenuous constitutional grounds given the lack of legislative provision for troops from his colony to serve overseas, he offered to furnish two batteries of permanent field artillery and an infantry battalion, at his colony's expense, for service in the Sudan.[66] A chain reaction followed. The next day a cable was sent from Premier James Service of Victoria to British authorities declaring that 'if England values assistance of Colonies in Egyptian campaign, assure Imperial Government that Victoria is ready to do her part as an integral portion of the Empire'.[67] On 14 February, after being pressed by the Colonial Office on the grounds of its symbolic value and under the mistaken impression that it was a pre-formed force, the War Office agreed to accept Dalley's offer. Three days later more Victorian telegrams were sent with specific offers of a contingent of 600–700 men. Queensland then followed suit, as did South Australia with its own offer of 250 infantrymen and a scheme for a federal Australian contingent. The federal idea was sunk, predictably, by inter-colonial jealousy in that New South Wales opposed the initiative given that its, and only its, contingent had thus far been accepted. In two weeks Dalley's force of 770 men was recruited, and on 3 March 1885 it sailed.[68]

Photo 2 The departure of the Australian contingent for the Sudan, by Arthur Collingridge (1853–1907). (AWM, ART16593)

Similar forces were at work in Canada. In August 1884 the Canadian Governor-General, Lord Lansdowne, received a ciphered message from the Colonial Office asking for '300 good voyageurs' to be sent to join Wolseley's expedition up the Nile.[69] Macdonald gave his consent, but as an imperial, not a Canadian enterprise. Nonetheless, Lansdowne continued to agitate for official Canadian involvement. Meanwhile, a host of Canadian militia officers, including Major-General John Wimburn Laurie (a British-born officer living in Canada) and Colonel Arthur Williams, volunteered to raise and lead contingents and offered their own regiments or their individual services to the War Office. The Canadian Government had no objection to them going – so long as Britain paid the bill. None, however, were accepted.[70]

The importance of the colonial contingents offered for service in the Sudan was what they symbolised. Major-General Alexander Tulloch, in command of Victorian military forces, described them as from 'a political point of view ... magnificent', even if the rather inglorious campaign actually 'fought' by the New South Wales detachment fell somewhat short of public expectations.[71] The immediate result of Gordon's death was another upsurge of imperial sentiment, which had provoked a clear display of colonial loyalty.[72] Pressure had come from the colonies to Britain to accept their troops, not the other way around. Moreover, such offers were made in spite of local interests regarding the economic danger of sending men of fighting age abroad, a militia/volunteer ethos stressing home defence, and a general lack of parliamentary sanction. The crowd of around 200 000 Sydneysiders that farewelled the only contingent accepted by Britain spoke for itself.[73] Importantly, the message received by a range of British politicians and statesmen from such offers was that perhaps the colonies were at last ready to share the burden of imperial defence, doubly significant given Britain's increasingly isolated international diplomatic position.[74] Cambridge called it 'the first step towards vigorous co-operation with the Mother Country should the necessity for it arise again'.[75] In years that followed, imperial defence advocates in Britain repeatedly referred to Sudan and the 'new era' it heralded.

The apparent willingness to assume imperial responsibility aroused in the colonies over Sudan was further stimulated by the Penjdeh Crisis with Russia from March 1885. Dalley, for example, actually agreed to the New South Wales contingent being diverted to India if needed.[76] Further, in May 1885 Robert Stout, the New Zealand Premier, sought parliamentary approval to despatch a thousand men to Afghanistan, for use there, 'or any other part of the globe where Her Majesty's Government might require them'. Sir George Grey, politician and previous Governor of New Zealand and the Cape Colony, told the New Zealand parliament in June 1885 that any enemy of Britain would 'have to encounter the effect that will be produced by the resources of a very large proportion of the world'.[77]

Such conclusions in London, however, were much too premature. Colonial troop offers were spontaneous. They were neither automatic nor representative of any desire to codify a standing military commitment. In Canada, where all offers had been unofficial, Macdonald's position was clear. 'The time has not yet arrived', he wrote, 'nor the occasion, for our volunteering [official] aid to the Mother Country.'[78] This position was reaffirmed in the wake of the North-West Rebellion of 1885, which kept the focus of Canadian defence attention local. The prevailing political opinion was that the Canadian Government would assist Britain in an official capacity in a time of real crisis, not over an imperial trifle. In the meantime, unofficial volunteers were always free to offer themselves.[79] This was the balance between sentimental and material ties to the Empire and the principle of no military taxation without representation. For his part, Henry Parkes in New South Wales feared that his colony's deployment risked the birth of a 'spurious spirit of military ardour'.[80] The truth was that the colonies had not yet formulated a clear concept of the relationship between themselves and the British Government on military questions – nor was there any imperative to formulate one.

Yet it is possible to trace the first tentative steps towards organised cooperation commitments in this direction during this crucial period. The Russian scare of 1885 prompted pressing questions from colonies about their defence that required joint decisions from the Colonial Office, War Office and Admiralty, which 'could not be dealt with by existing machinery with the rapidity required by the importance of the subject at a time of political tension'.[81] On the suggestion of Robert Henry Meade, Assistant Undersecretary of State of the Colonies, the CDC was re-formed. Before its first meeting in April 1885 its President, Sir Andrew Clarke, was informed that his committee was to carry on past the current crisis and to 'consider representations as to their defence from the Colonies'.[82] The basic idea was to work out local colonial defence arrangements with contributions from all three departments in peacetime, not cobble them together in war. The CDC was therefore not really focused on imperial cooperation so much as on the oversight and organisation of local measures. It was by no means even the embryo of an imperial general staff (there was no colonial representation), and for the next decade none of the highest-ranking or most influential military or naval figures were among its members. Nor was it a decision-making body. Rather its reports, based the comments of its members on the schemes and papers laid before it, were to be considered 'advice'. Nevertheless, the committee represented pioneering work in inter-departmental defence liaison, and over time it became an important, if often accidental, contributor to imperial defence debates.[83]

Another important practical development was that from 1885 London began pressing British officers on to the colonies to command local troops, whereas previous requests had come from the colonies themselves. The War Office also began despatching more highly performing and more senior active officers. Whereas in 1883 relatively obscure and junior officers like Majors Thomas Robert Disney and George Arthur French took charge of the Victoria and Queensland forces respectively, after Sudan such officers were much more carefully selected, a policy soon to affect Hutton directly. As a consequence of British murmurings of disquiet over the quality of colonial officers sent to the Sudan, such imperial appointees would in future also be expected, as suggested by the Carnarvon Commission, to improve local colonial forces.[84] Meanwhile, the War Office drew up a dormant Order in Council to extend the British Army Act to the colonies if required in the future.[85]

Any idea, however, that British commandants might act as prime movers for local colonial defence improvement in the 1880s, let alone imperial defence unity, was a grave mistake. George Sydenham Clarke, the first Secretary of the CDC, who knew nothing of local circumstances, prerogatives, sensibilities and pressures, might have expected the commandants to voice the opinions of his committee, but they did not. By 1892 only Victoria and Queensland had even complied with the CDC request to submit their defence plans. There was nothing at all from other Australian colonies or New Zealand. With respect to the defence plans that were sent to London, the CDC could not get the commandants to agree on the threats they faced, let alone a common policy. Clarke complained in 1890 that 'they have neither the knowledge nor the experience necessary to qualify them to deal with the larger questions of Imperial defence'. In the same year one official at the Colonial Office argued that any attempt to dictate to the colonial commandants from London 'would no doubt be resented by the officers and would leak out and involve us in some considerable trouble'.[86] In reality the commandants and the CDC acted as a check on each other – not at all as a mechanism to impose London's will. Even had they a mind to execute what they might have thought to have been the War Office's bidding, the commandants themselves were subject to the local financial constraints and local political imperatives. These were the real puppet strings, and over them London had precious little control.[87]

Moreover, British military policy-makers remained overwhelmingly preoccupied with domestic concerns, without wrestling with the problems of the Empire. Plans in 1882 for an expeditionary corps of 25 000 men to Egypt had broken down under the strain of the campaign and led to a new scheme of mobilisation developed by Wolseley for two army corps and a cavalry division that he (and Cambridge) thought necessary to deal with the emerging European threat. Yet these too were 'paper' plans, given continued recruiting problems and that supplementation from the auxiliary was uncertain as no militia unit could serve abroad without the consent of members and, until 1888, the Yeomanry could not be required to serve outside their own county (and thereafter anywhere in Britain but not Ireland).[88] In any case, as the influential parliamentarian Sir Charles Dilke had pointed out, the auxiliary forces were incomplete in all arms and services and therefore incapable of mobilisation as formations. Meanwhile, friction over the division of power between the Commander-in-Chief and Secretary of State for War also remained, and the rift between senior army officers and politicians grew wider than ever. Wolseley wrote to the Queen: 'When professional soldiers and sailors warn the people on these serious subjects, professional politicians jump up and pooh pooh all their warnings. The foolish public prefer to believe the tradesman who has become politician to the gentleman who wears your Majesty's uniform.'[89] To complicate matters further, a growing antagonism between Cambridge and Wolseley was also evident. Another War Office reorganisation of 1888 did little to solve its problems, but rather increased Cambridge's personal authority and conservative influence.

A subsequent parliamentary investigation of military affairs resulted in establishment of the Hartington Commission in 1891 to conduct a full-scale examination of the army and navy and their relationship with the Treasury. This commission recommended further radical reform, including abolition of the position of Commander-in-Chief and its replacement by a War Office Council, the establishment of a General Staff for planning purposes and wholesale decentralisation of control. Only the War Office Council proposal was implemented immediately, however, and the position of Commander-in-Chief remained, thanks largely to the Queen's determination not to see her cousin removed.[90] While such reformers as Dilke and Colomb might have applauded the Hartington recommendations, little of substance really changed. Outside Aldershot the professional and reformist approach advocated by the more senior members of Wolseley's coterie remained a minority position. Even at Aldershot, Major-General Evelyn Wood, a Wolseley man, was publicly rebuked by Cambridge in front of his troops for experimenting with night training.[91] In mid-1892 Edward Stanhope, the Secretary of State for War, wrote to Wolseley: 'I have my doubts [about successful reform]' and that 'until old age removes one of the difficulties, it is impossible to advance as one would wish'.[92] The irony, of course, was that Wolseley's own policy of constantly appointing his own small circle of acolytes as staff officers and to operational command kept their minds away from internal army reform, limited the wider pool of experience, hindered professional development and retarded rise through merit outside his ring.[93]

Encouraged by the peak of imperial sentiment sparked by Gordon's death at Khartoum, the small military and political movement in London interested in imperial defence issues got their chance with the Queen's 1887 Jubilee. The associated celebrations included a Colonial Conference, the first of its kind, organised at the behest and agitation of the Imperial Federation League, planned to run from 4 April to 9 May.[94] Stanhope, in his invitation to the colonies to attend and again with Sudan as the example, stressed his 'desire to arrive at ... a common basis of action' and to 'attain a better understanding as to the system of defence which may be established throughout the Empire'.[95] It was in his mind a 'question which is at once urgent and capable of useful consideration'.[96] The implications were clear for the colonies in that such language seemed to imply the future use of colonial troops for imperial defence, and the message was well received by the few at the periphery already thinking in such directions. Brigadier-General John Owen, commandant in South Australia, for example, pressed his premier to support the prospect of using local troops outside his colony, particularly in the Pacific in case of a war with France.[97]

In his opening address to the conference, the British Prime Minister, Salisbury, emphasised the changing strategic circumstances of the Empire as a whole. He urged the colonies to look to a future where 'those who are born in the Colonies will take personal part in the defence of the Empire in all its portions'.[98] Two plans for military cooperation were actually tabled during the discussions that followed. The first was made by the Colonial Secretary, Sir Henry Holland, who had taken on the appointment in January. Based on a memorandum from Lord Knutsford of the Carnavon Commission, this was an attempt to secure an agreement whereby colonial forces, paid by the colonies, would '[w]ith the assent of the

Colonial Government and in the event of the Government providing the means . . . aid Her Majesty in any wars in which she might be engaged'.[99] Such a brash request did not get far. The Canadians objected in that they already spent more on defence than required under their 1865 defence agreement with Britain. The other colonial delegates were equally uninterested. The second proposal came from Jan Hofmeyr of the Cape Colony, who called for an imperial customs tariff to be used to raise funds for improvement of imperial defences. Again, the idea drew no significant attention. Faced with such responses, Holland did not press the issue.[100]

More was achieved at the 1887 conference concerning Empire-wide cooperation in naval defence, thanks to Australian and New Zealand fears of European designs in the Pacific. The 1881 inter-colonial conference in Sydney had earlier called on Britain to increase the size of the Australian Squadron, but nothing had happened. In 1885, leveraging off such fears, Rear-Admiral George Tyron took command of Australia Station and began to negotiate a scheme with the colonies whereby his squadron would be expanded, but with costs of its maintenance defrayed by them. Colonial support for the idea was hesitant, however, on the basis that they would have no control over the positioning of any subsidised British vessels and the voting public would like to see the ships it paid for. The Victorian Governor, Lord Loch, warned the Colonial Secretary, Lord Derby, that if 'Victoria was going to pay the imperial piper', then it would also want to 'call the imperial tune'. Premier Robert Stout of New Zealand was of much the same mind in that he was happy to pay but expected a pay-back in the form of a Royal Navy port. Importantly, this was an issue about local interests, local political prerogatives and cost (especially in the context of financial problems in New South Wales); it was not at all a rejection of imperialism or imperial cooperation, nor an expression of local nationalism above and beyond the Empire. Indeed, the Australasian colonies were wary of even meeting with each other to discuss Tyron's ideas for fear of sacrificing individual political prerogatives to collective action. At the time the Colonial Office understood and accepted this reluctance.[101]

From a British perspective, however, subsidies seemed the only answer. The Admiralty wished to discourage local Australian naval ambitions, especially in Victoria, lest the actions of colonial ships on the high seas risk setting imperial policy. At the same time, the Australia Station could not simply be expanded – its costs needed to be minimised. A version of Tyron's scheme was therefore tabled at the Colonial Conference as something of a compromise, whereby the Admiralty would undertake to pay for the construction of five cruisers and two torpedo boats as an 'Auxiliary Squadron' to the Australia Station. Further, against prevailing naval strategic wisdom, British authorities agreed that the Auxiliary Squadron was not to leave local waters without colonial consent. For their part, the colonies signalled a significant concession, contrary to a long-established preference, in that they agreed to pay a small percentage of the original cost of the ships plus £126 000 per annum towards the cost of maintenance and manning. The subsequent Australasian Naval Defence Act of 1887 was an important step. A compromise had been reached and some level of colonial control ceded.[102]

At the conclusion of the colonial conference the rhetoric of British policy-makers demonstrated an enthusiasm beyond its actual results. Salisbury claimed that its decisions 'may not be of this moment of vital importance' but rather 'the beginning of a state of things to come which is to have great results in the future'.[103] Holland noted that while the colonial naval contribution was trifling, it was nonetheless 'the first step towards a federation for defence which would not only add strength to the Empire, but would tend to bind its members in closer union'.[104] Clarke of the CDC was equally enthusiastic.[105]

Such conclusions were, however, again based on a fundamental misreading of the colonial position. In the absence of a war scare, local interests were foremost. During the discussion surrounding the naval agreement, Alfred Deakin of Victoria complained that the colonies were being asked to fund a fleet over which they still had fundamentally little control. Samuel Griffiths of Queensland echoed the sentiment. There were fears also that any plans to use colonial funds without colonial input might undermine local political autonomy, an issue of particular (and perpetual) sensitivity. Conversely, in New Zealand, where public and political security fears were more acute, Premier Harry Atkinson was much more positive and reminded his parliament that 'we are not a sovereign country ourselves' and while New Zealand had the chance 'of laying the first stone of the edifice ... we should seize that opportunity'.[106]

Fear led to the naval agreement, and the degree of fear set the tone of discussions surrounding it. Deakin, Griffiths and Atkinson were all in basic agreement. In fact Deakin went on to note (along with Adye Douglas of Tasmania and John Forrest of Western Australia) that the whole issue should not be perceived from a narrow colonial aspect but a larger imperial one. All answered to local constituents and pursued local political agendas – the provisions of the agreement reflected this – and all did so under the shared umbrella of Empire nationalism. The relative balance of these two considerations depended on circumstances. The 1887 Naval Agreement was therefore never 'a calculated method of locking the colonies into imperial policy'.[107] There was no imperial policy in this regard. It was rather a compromise of shared interests. It is equally mistaken to conclude that 'a heightened sense of colonial nationalism on the matter of defence prevailed at the 1887 conference' or that the Australians were 'not enamoured' with any scheme 'that hinted at imperial responsibilities'.[108] Rather, a heightened state of local interest was evident, and any lack of enthusiasm concerned control and cost. The friction between these factors framed the imperial defence debate for the next twenty years.

After the colonial conference, interest in imperial defence cooperation in London waned. The clear shortcomings of British military structures at home continued to absorb most of the available time and energy of those interested in defence issues. Meanwhile, the absence of an overarching military policy continued in the late 1880s and early 1890s. The service departments still lived in their own worlds. While the Admiralty discounted the possibility of invasion, for example, the War Office worried about home defence and sending the regular army abroad on *ad hoc* expeditions as the need arose. Meanwhile, Cabinet received no consistent advice on imperial defence issues.[109] Wolseley's late 1886 mobilisation plan was approved by Stanhope in the 1887–88 estimates, yet there was still no real guidance as to the army's purpose. With the poor state of British defence a topic of considerable press concern in mid-1888 Colomb and Cambridge renewed the call for real strategic guidance. Finally, Stanhope provided a list of 'priorities' for the army, in order of precedence, to aid to civil power, garrison India and the colonies, and provide home defence and potentially a reduced two-corps expeditionary force to Europe. There was no mention of any collective effort at imperial defence.[110]

Meanwhile, the British army had to improvise, as always, without detailed advance planning. Defence policy was firmly subservient to foreign policy; there was little connection between them. Political ultimatums were therefore often made with no reference to military capacity. This haphazard approach was actually advocated by some outspoken politicians, including the Liberal Secretary for War in 1886, Henry Campbell-Bannerman, who equated the preparation of war plans in advance of a crisis with a type of militarism.[111] It was an attitude reaffirmed with the return of the Liberal government in 1892. In the same year Redvers Buller, as Adjutant General, admitted to the Wantage Commission that army establishments were not fixed according to prescribed duties but rather 'incidentally', while Ralph Knox, a long-term civil member of the War Office inner circle, claimed that no plan had ever been worked out by any committee of the War Office for an overseas deployment in a crisis.[112] If this was not enough, the War Office and the Admiralty still failed to cooperate effectively. The 'two-power standard' for the navy was introduced, for example, at the same time as Stanhope was advocating for a string of forts to be built around London. Within such a context it was entirely unsurprising, perhaps even inevitable, that any real attempt at implementing an imperial defence policy remained the elusive dream of a few.

Nevertheless, incremental and divergent progress on imperial defence had been made. One important, if not immediate, outcome of the Colonial Conference from an Australian perspective, for example, was the idea that a British 'Inspecting Officer' might be sent to report on colonial defence arrangements – an initiative in line with the Carnavon Commission's earlier suggestions.[113] Major-General James Bevan Edwards, Commander of British Troops in China and Hong Kong, was appointed. He arrived at Brisbane in July 1889, inspected fortifications and troops in each colony and reported to the colonial governments in October. Edwards argued that the Australian colonial forces lacked effective training, organisation, equipment and the ability to operate together in defence of the continent. His most significant recommendation was, in effect, the military federation of the forces of the different colonies.[114] There was more, however, to Edwards' agenda. In recommending Edwards for this task, the occasional imperial military adviser to Victoria and New South Wales, Major-General Edward Harding Steward, suggested that in time of war the Australian colonies might 'initiate such operations as may make the Enemies of the Empire in the Pacific and China Seas and Indian Ocean look after their own possessions'.[115] So too before going to Australia Edwards told Cambridge that his inspection might 'pave the way to their being able to give the Mother Country most material assistance in time of war'.[116] Although such direct language was unsurprisingly absent in his official report, in 1891 Edwards went on to lecture in London that Australian troops would be best placed to attack enemy possessions in the Pacific and Indian Oceans in the event of a large-scale war involving Britain. The CDC agreed with this principle, even if it thought Edwards had exaggerated the threat.[117]

It is important to note, however, that the Australian colonies had invited Edwards to make his report; he had not been imposed upon them. Local fears of non-British imperial incursions in the Pacific were at play and had been since 1883 when Sir Thomas McIlwraith, Queensland Premier, took possession of New Guinea in the name of the Queen as a direct consequence of German and French interests in the region, an action approved in the colonies but repudiated in London. The Australians were very much alive to a perceived security threat in their neighbourhood and what might be done to defray it. Along with the naval agreement, improved local military defence was part of their solution.[118] In truth, Edwards' report was representative of the wider paradigm of imperial defence of the era. It was a spontaneous response to an ill-defined feeling of the military potential of the colonies held by a small number of senior officers and policy-makers in Britain. It was made possible, momentarily and coincidentally, by a local colonial imperative. It was entirely disconnected from any standing imperial policy or structure. Some officials at the War Office could not help but look to a future where colonials might be able and willing 'to assist the mother country ... should she be engaged in any considerable war', but this was still a world away from a practical proposal, let alone a reality.[119]

The idea, nonetheless, kept resurfacing. General Sir Frederick Roberts, Commander-in-Chief of the Indian Army, for example, suggested in 1889 that the colonies should be prepared to aid imperial defence including a formal affiliation between India, the Australasian colonies and those in South Africa.[120] Sir Henry Loch, Governor in Victoria and then Cape Town from 1889, argued to Alexander Stuart, former New South Wales Premier, for 'some understanding which would give the colonial forces a direct interest in the Imperial Army' and requested a meeting with Stanhope to discuss his plan for an Australian force formed for service in India.[121] Two years later, the War Office established the Joint Naval and Military Committee as an interdepartmental body under the Undersecretary of War to make technical recommendations concerning coaling stations and military outposts across the Empire. Further, by 1892, thanks to support from the leader of Opposition, Arthur Balfour (himself influenced by men like Dilke and Colomb), the idea of a Cabinet Defence Committee grew closer to a reality. All the while George Sydenham Clarke at the CDC developed his own aspirations for an imperial system of defence. This was all the more important as Clarke, through his relationship with Meade, was fast becoming 'the unofficial defence adviser to the Colonial Office'.[122] These were small steps, but steps nevertheless. Despite the setbacks and institutional barriers, a 'continuity of discussion' of imperial defence questions was maintained.[123]

At the same time, at the height of the new imperialism, remarkably little had been accomplished in practical terms, especially from 1883 to 1892, to secure constructive cooperation in the defence of that Empire. Some conceptual groundwork had been laid, but much less of a structural or policy framework had been put in place. An imperial defence agenda and its small band of adherents had thus far had little of practical substance to offer. In any case, such was the state of the imperial defence conundrum to 1892, as Edward Hutton prepared to make his first significant impact upon it. Meanwhile, up to this point Hutton's own experiences, attitudes and agenda were being set, and it is to these that attention now turns.

CHAPTER 2

'An intelligent and most active officer'

Hutton's formative years, 1848–92

Edward Hutton was born on 6 December 1848 into a respectable middle-class family, with traditions of military service. Although he later mixed in the highest social circles, Hutton was not born to the aristocracy and was always sensitive about his social positioning. His ancestors, the Huttons of Lincolnshire, had their roots in the 'yeomanry of Nottinghamshire' of the early seventeenth century. His great-grandfather, Henry, was a barrister and elected Recorder of the city of Lincoln in 1784, establishing the family's respectability by taking possession, through his wife's inheritance, of Sherwood Hall near Mansfield in 1804. Henry's eldest son and Hutton's grandfather, Edward William, joined the 4th Royal Irish Dragoons in 1805 and retired as a lieutenant-colonel in 1838, after considerable operational service. His grandfather, Hutton later reflected, 'much impressed my childish imagination as a Peninsular War veteran'. Three of Hutton's paternal uncles were also military officers. One, Thomas, joined the 4th Light Dragoons and commanded a squadron in the Crimean War at the Battle of Alma, the Siege of Sebastopol and at the ill-fated charge of the Light Brigade at Balaclava. Hutton's own father, Edward Thomas, however, did not choose a military career but rather, after school at Rugby, became a junior partner in the West Riding Bank.[1]

In 1845 Hutton's father married Jacintha Charlotte (always known as Charlotte), daughter of the Reverend James Phipps Eyre. The Eyres of Hampshire were strongly liberal in political outlook and had a lineage that could be traced to members of Oliver Cromwell's Council. The joining of such a strongly Whig family to the Huttons was not viewed with satisfaction by Edward Thomas's parents. Consequently, when Hutton's father died on 15 February 1849, two months after his son's birth, Charlotte and her in-laws grew steadily estranged. Alone and isolated, Charlotte doted on her son and received his deep affection in return.[2]

In January 1854, with Hutton now six years old, Charlotte married Lieutenant-Colonel Arthur Johnstone Lawrence, of Fox Hills, Chertsey, at that time commanding the 2nd Battalion, Rifle Brigade. From this point Lawrence, who went on to become General Sir Arthur Lawrence, became a powerful influence on Hutton. Not only did he stimulate an early interest in a military career but also Lawrence ensured that it would mirror his own *professional* approach to soldiering, not the gentlemanly distraction it represented for many of his peers.[3] The bond between them was always strong. 'From the first my step-father regarded me as a son', Hutton later wrote, 'treating me in all respects as if I was his own.'[4] Hutton's two younger half-brothers, George D'Aguilar Lawrence and Frederick Eyre Lawrence, were born in 1860 and 1862 respectively.

In April 1862 Lawrence sent his stepson, at 13 years of age, to board at Eton – a mark of significant social distinction within the expanding middle classes. Unsurprisingly, Hutton remained attached throughout his life to Eton as a symbol of the social status he craved. At school he formed friendships with some notable future officers with whom he always maintained an association, such men as Reginald Pole-Carew, Henry Gordon-Lennox, Charles Byng and Charles Prideaux-Brune – the last joining the army the same day as Hutton and becoming a life-long friend. Like many at Eton, three of these boys, Hutton's friends yet social superiors, held or later inherited titles.[5]

Not long into his school career Hutton fell under the influence of one of his masters, Dr Edmond Warre, whom he remembered as 'By instinct a soldier and by circumstances a schoolmaster'. Hutton never forgot Warre's maxim that the 'safety and success of an army depends more than ever upon the intelligence and professional knowledge of the officers', and the two years Hutton spent with Warre were crucial in extending Lawrence's ideas of professionalism in Hutton's mind.[6] Warre was also instrumental in shaping Hutton's ideas on masculinity and the importance of athletic and physical strength, sporting success and outdoors skill – all of which were considered vital military traits in this era.[7] Moreover, for the young Hutton a 'manly, physical bearing [began to be] substituted for aristocratic blood as the basis for the right to leadership'.[8] For Hutton the physically powerful and professionally accomplished gentleman became a masculine ideal.

Warre also instilled ideas of 'moral' gentlemanly values into Hutton, which extended beyond physical prowess into loyalty and service to the nation. This 'high sense of honour', championed by Warre, provided an early sense of self-identity for a young man caught in many ways between his current social circles and his real social status.[9] The internalisation of such ideas might have been typical in this era, but Hutton grasped and held onto them strongly and lastingly. Reflecting on his school days in 1886 and echoing these dominant contemporary attitudes, he contended that 'so long as the present manly tone is fostered and encouraged at all our great public schools, so surely will a race of men be produced, who are ready and able not only to maintain the legacy of this great Empire left us by our forefathers, but also still further to extend it'.[10]

In mid-1865 Lawrence decided that Hutton should spend a year in Switzerland to learn French and continue his classical education in Latin and Greek, required subjects for army entrance examinations. The following year Hutton also studied for a short time with the Swiss painter Charles Louis Guigon in Geneva and later in London with Collingwood Smith, then the President of the Old Water Colour Society. These experiences he later credited with providing 'the power of observation invaluable to a soldier' – and a military career was always Hutton's path. Lawrence had initially intended that Hutton should join his own regiment, the Rifle Brigade but, to his stepfather's intense disappointment, there were no vacancies when Hutton returned from Switzerland. Rather than lose seniority by waiting, Lawrence purchased him a commission (at a cost around £450) in the 60th Rifles (the nickname of the King's Royal Rifle Corps). This was a respectable middle-class infantry regiment of no particularly high prestige or fashion, but with a reputation for innovation. Hutton joined the regiment at Winchester in October 1867 as a 19-year-old ensign and was appointed to the 4th Battalion under Colonel R.B. Hawley, who had served under Lawrence at Aldershot in 1859. Hutton's new unit was stationed at Saint John, New Brunswick, Canada.[11]

Hutton's experience in Canada was a happy one. Hawley was himself a well-known innovator, and the 4th Battalion was a well-trained and administered unit. Hawley warmly welcomed Hutton on account of Lawrence. 'Anything I can do for your boy', Hawley wrote, 'you may depend upon it.' Hutton was further encouraged that many of his fellow officers were fellow Etonians. 'I found', he later reflected, 'that the spirit of Eton was in a large measure the spirit of the Regiment.'[12] Always class conscious, he was further pleased to find little 'cavalry swagger' about them.[13] It was at this point that another Etonian and Hawley's adjutant, Redvers Buller, came into contact with Hutton for the first time. It was an important connection for the future, solidified by a shared admiration for Warre.[14]

Above all else Hawley's command crystallised many of Hutton's developing attitudes to professionalism and military reform. He later credited his commanding officer's tactical and training reforms as paving the way for the principles gradually adopted by the army at large over the next twenty years. Hawley also took 'assiduous care in organisation' and instilled 'discipline in all the ranks' – qualities Hutton vigorously demanded of his own future commands. His approach was characterised by care for troops, a preference for individual initiative over automatic responses, a much-relaxed relationship between officers and men (by the standards of the era) and comprehensive training of all ranks. Unusually within the context of the times, 'Every captain and every subaltern personally taught his own men.' Hawley also prided himself on battlefield innovation. His battalion practised widely extended or skirmishing movements of a type rarely attempted by others. Hutton called it an 'advanced school of military theory and practice' and wrote enthusiastically to his mother in October 1868 that 'in the time that any ordinary Line regiment would be thinking about it we would have deployed into line and commenced firing'.[15] In his personal manner Hawley allowed an appearance of severity to overlay any instincts of sympathy and affection – a mask also copied by Hutton in years to come.

Hawley's methods also shaped Hutton's views on military service and the Empire. Hutton believed that Hawley's preference for individual initiative was possible only as a consequence of the character and self-reliance of Anglo-Saxons as contrasted to the 'machine-like methods of collectivism, as practised in the conscript armies of Europe'.[16] Importantly, the professionalism Hawley encouraged in his officers reinforced the ideas that Lawrence, Eton and Warre had already planted. The notion of technical mastery hence came more and more to represent to Hutton a method by which to transcend his middle-class origins and to move as an equal within the aristocratic circles he could never join. Such a professionally oriented outlook also focused Hutton's sharp mind. The conviction that problems could be overcome by hard thinking and hard work later drove Hutton to try to solve the military problems of the Empire in a rational way.[17]

Hutton's emerging military attitudes were, of course, tied to a much wider social phenomenon connected to the rise of professionalism in the middle classes. The natural extension was for Hutton to regard himself as a reformer and to gravitate towards like minds, such as Hawley. This type of self-identification, however, inevitably set him against what he saw as conservative forces within the army best represented by dilettante aristocrats (or middle-class officers projecting similar attitudes). Such officers became obstacles in Hutton's mind to necessary military reform. The key to command success, and indeed the right to authority, for such men was their social standing. For one without such blood lines, like Hutton, it was increasingly to be found in technical competence. Hutton was charting a difficult path in this regard. Despite the emergence and growing influence of wider middle-class professionalism, political and military elites in the late-Victorian era always valued and even favoured the role and contribution of aristocratic dabblers.[18]

With the end of the American Civil War and the Fenian Raids and as part of the general phasing out of British garrisons in the self-governing colonies, British troop numbers in Canada were reduced and Hutton's battalion returned to England in July 1869. Hutton was soon caught up in the wider military reform debate (although yet too junior to shape it), centred at Aldershot and fuelled by the Cardwell transformations. He witnessed the effect of Hawley's low-level reforms, which began to attract positive attention from some of the army's leading generals, as well as the press. Such interest was itself encouraged by the outbreak of the Franco-Prussian War in 1870. In particular, for Hutton, by this point a firm supporter of the idea of recognition by merit not birth, there seemed hope 'that the professional education of officers would be dealt with and placed on a compulsory basis'.[19] While at Aldershot Hutton also met Major Henry Evelyn Wood, one of Wolseley's Ashanti protégés and a key future friend, as Wood set up a system of instructors to enable officers to study the subjects they were now required to pass.

From this point Hutton was drawn more and more towards Wolseley and the reform movement he represented. Yet even here there were complex forces at play. First, Wolseley was the son of a relatively junior officer, not born an aristocrat. He was raised by a penniless widow and received a free commission in the army as thanks for his father's service. His background was even more humble than Hutton's, yet Wolseley was a national hero and an emerging force within the upper echelons of the army. Importantly for Hutton, he had achieved this as a consequence of professional and battlefield competence. Second, membership of the type of late-Victorian clique like that beginning to grow around Wolseley represented an important opportunity for Hutton in that it offered a mechanism for advancement beyond the slow regimental system and the role of social hierarchy within it.[20]

In early October 1870 Hutton's battalion moved to Winchester and his mother, after a painful illness, died, leaving Lawrence to care for his two young half-brothers. By now driven by a desire for professional improvement and perhaps in an attempt to move his mind on from this personal tragedy, Hutton determined to go to France, as 'the death-knell of the French Regular Army had sounded', to witness the final stages of the Franco-Prussian War for himself. Hutton knew Henry Bonham-Carter, the organiser of the National Aid Society helping the sick and wounded of the campaign, and called on him to offer his services. He was subsequently asked to take a consignment of fragile medical stores to hospitals behind the German lines and left London on 28 October, in this semi-official capacity. During his trip Hutton visited various battlefields, including Sedan, and was 'deeply impressed by the organisation and discipline of the German Army'.[21] This quick tour further encouraged a military career and professional outlook. 'My ambitions had been stirred by visiting the seat of war', he later wrote. 'Knowledge is power and I applied myself to the close study of my profession.'[22]

Back in Winchester, Hutton settled into regimental life while following his professional impulses. When a hunting fall laid him up a few weeks, for example, and remembering his visit to France, he set out to learn German, and he took leave for two months to stay with a family in Dresden to improve his grasp of the language. Hutton was promoted lieutenant in 1871, and in March 1873 his mentor Hawley retired his command to become Assistant Military Secretary at the War Office. Hawley was replaced by Lieutenant-Colonel Charles Williamson, and Hutton's battalion moved to Verne Citadel, Portland. In June Hutton was appointed its adjutant. By this time, encouraged by Lawrence, Hutton had made up his mind to secure a posting to Staff College, where 'it was possible to have leisure to think and to study the great problems which the Army and the study of war presented'.[23]

In late July 1874, Hutton's unit left for Dublin. There, he found it difficult in the new surroundings to maintain the high level of discipline and training he prized. This was especially so given that Lieutenant-Colonel Rowley Willee Hinxman, who had replaced Williamson following his untimely death, was new to the battalion. Hinxman had no taste for the relaxed relations between officers and men in Hutton's unit, or for Hawley's improved training and tactics. As Adjutant, Hutton found it difficult to maintain Hawley's principles, but the battalion was destined for Indian service so he tried 'by tact and patience' to make it work.[24] The new environment was especially hard for Hutton to reconcile given that he was at the time writing his first book on 'Light Drill', which affirmed his commitment to a professional approach and tactical innovation, lauded the value of individual soldiers and implicitly opposed Hinxman's old-fashioned contempt for the other ranks.[25]

In June 1876 Hutton's battalion moved to Fermoy in advance of a deployment to India. Soon quartered at Agra, Hutton enjoyed 'happy days' spent at 'polo, pigsticking, race meetings, gymkhanas, hunting, shooting, fishing'. Conscious of his reliance on an allowance from his stepfather, all such pursuits in India, he noted, were 'accessible to a subaltern even with slender means'.[26] Hutton eventually (and inevitably) clashed with Hinxman over a minor disciplinary incident in the Officers' Mess, explaining that 'the perfect understanding usually supposed between a Commanding Officer and his adjutant no longer exists'.[27] Showing an early glimpse of what became a characteristic stubbornness, he resigned the adjutancy of his unit over the issue on 29 March 1877 and was granted two months leave of absence in India (including a month of tiger-shooting in the Terai jungle), pending transfer back to England.[28]

Hutton returned to Southampton in mid-June 1877 and happily rejoined Lawrence at Fox Hills. He was careful to seek out the right people after his difficulties in India and dropped in to see both Hawley and Buller, the latter now a staff officer at the Horse Guards following service as Wolseley's intelligence officer in the Ashanti campaign. Both received him cordially. These two officers arranged a new appointment, and on 26 July Hutton joined the 3rd Battalion, 60th Rifles, back at Aldershot. 'I found myself among many old friends ... and a very happy family we were!' Hutton later mused. He saw much of Lawrence and his two half-brothers, now at Eton, and had sufficient time for 'close and determined study for the Staff College examination', which he had resolved to take the following year.[29] Interestingly, in line with Hawley's lessons and his own ideas on reform at the lowest level, Hutton also busied himself addressing what he saw as excessive drunkenness in his unit by organising a regimental restaurant where troops could get cheap suppers 'without making use of the canteen and exposing themselves to the ill-effects of excessive drinking'.[30] Such facilities soon became general throughout the army.

The 1878 war scare with Russia unfolded as Hutton studied for his Staff College entrance exams. On the mobilisation of the British 1st Division, its commander, Major-General David Anderson, invited Hutton to act as his aide-de-camp. Although no deployment followed, Hutton knew he was being noticed by more senior officers and that his career prospects were brightening. He therefore spent the winter studying harder than ever.

'To my great satisfaction', Hutton later reflected, 'and rather to my surprise, I passed high and my name appeared on the Lists on the 24th September.'[31] At this point Hutton's battalion moved to Colchester, and he was offered and accepted a position as aide-de-camp to Major-General William Pollexfen Radcliffe, commanding Eastern District, until required to join the Staff College.

On 1 February 1879 Lieutenant Hutton began his period at Staff College and was thrilled to be elected 'whip of the Drag Hounds' and subsequently captain of the college cricket team – pointing out once more the dominant aristocratic and public school attitudes of the army and Hutton's own love/hate relationship with what they implied. On a pragmatic level, Hutton knew that these were important social distinctions 'much in demand and considered to be the antecedents to coveted Staff appointments later'.[32]

Meanwhile, in southern Africa, following the Zulu rejection of Sir Henry Frere's deliberately provocative and unacceptable ultimatum of December 1878, Lord Chelmsford invaded Zululand with around 15 000 British troops. The initial movement of all three of Chelmsford's columns was unopposed. On 22 January, however, the British centre column was devastated at the Battle of Isandlwana. This defeat made it obvious that a considerable expeditionary force would be despatched from Britain to retrieve the situation, and Hutton was subsequently recalled from Staff College to command a company of the 3rd Battalion, 60th Rifles, which was then embarking for service. He reached Cape Town in mid-March 1879, as Chelmsford prepared a force to relieve Eshowe. This advance began at the end of the month, and after a tedious, three-day advance Chelmsford's column, which included Hutton's company, reached the Inyzane River and set up a large defensive square on a low ridge in an area known as Gingindlovu – 'Elephant Tusk'.[33]

After sunset on the night of 1 April, Zulu fires were reported on the opposite side of Inyzane, and an hour before dawn the following morning the British square was called to 'stand to'. Soon afterwards a Zulu Impi of close to 12 000 troops attacked the laager. In spite of heavy British fire, the Zulu advance pressed close and, on Hutton's face of the square, got within 10 metres at some points. After a while, however, unable to make headway, the attackers began to withdraw. Demonstrating a distinctly aggressive streak on the battlefield, Hutton made urgent requests to send skirmishers to harry the Zulu retreat but was forbidden to do so. For his steadiness during the battle Hutton was mentioned in despatches.[34]

After the successful relief of Eshowe, Chelmsford learned that Wolseley was being sent to replace him so he worked furiously to launch a second general invasion before he was removed from command. As part of Chelmsford's new plan to converge his forces on the Zulu capitol of Ulundi, Major-General Henry Hope Crealock was detailed to command British troops on the coast, formed into the 1st Division, while Chelmsford's main force and Evelyn Wood's 'flying column' operated further inland. At this point Hutton was surprised to receive a letter inviting him to act as one of the general's two aides-de-camp. This was a key opportunity for Hutton, offered by Crealock because of what he had heard 'of the manner in which you did your duty in the march to Eshowe'. Crealock congratulated Hutton 'on an appointment which I hope may afford the opening that every man who is fond of his profession should lose no opportunity of gaining'.[35] As his first chance of a career outside his regiment the appointment meant new pathways of promotion for Hutton. He felt it was 'a new and fresh start to my career' and an 'unexpected change of fortune'.[36] Nevertheless such an opportunity represented a high-stakes career gamble for an officer like Hutton. Being noticed by Crealock gave him the all-important patron he required, but it also forced him into the world of informal intra-army alliances. The day after accepting his new post Hutton was told that Redvers Buller had also asked for him to be released to act as second-in-command of his regiment, the Frontier Light Horse, attached to Evelyn Wood's column on the Upper Tugela. Buller and Wood were Wolseley men, Crealock was not. Yet Crealock was a senior officer, and Hutton was unaware that Wolseley was on his way. Hutton was happy, for now, with the outcome. 'I am better off where I am', he wrote to Lawrence, 'a certainty of promotion under a dashing and young general.'[37]

The performance of Crealock's division in the second invasion of Zululand was less than spectacular, despite the fact that the Zulu king, Cetshwayo, still hoping for an end to hostilities, refrained from attacking its vulnerable supply lines. 'After various vicissitudes and constant delays', Hutton lamented, his column finally reached Port Durnford.[38] Meanwhile, Chelmsford's main force clashed and routed the Zulus at the Battle of Ulundi. The Zulu army dispersed, and Cetshwayo became a fugitive. It was a hollow victory for the 1st Division, which played no part in the final battle. Moreover, every officer under Crealock knew that in Wolseley's opinion their division had been entirely irrelevant.[39] Even Hutton conceded that his commander's 'methods may have lacked the energy Evelyn Wood was so well known to possess'.[40] Worse, 'we on his staff', Hutton wrote to his stepfather, 'come in for our share of ill-favour'. His patron was disgraced. Hutton had thought he was likely to be promoted, but 'as it is I can hope for nothing'. Soon afterwards Hutton was ordered back to Staff College. On the way home he lamented that two of Wolseley's rising protégés, Wood and Buller, had offered an entry into their coterie but, hitched to Crealock's falling star, he had for the moment missed his chance.[41]

Photo 3 King Cetshwayo, who became a fugitive after the Battle of Ulundi (4 July 1879). He was taken prisoner in August by a British detachment under Major Richard Marter, King's Dragoon Guards, and guarded for a short period by Hutton's company. Deprived of his kingdom, he was sent into exile at Cape Town. (Council of the National Army Museum, London, NAM 1965–06-46–1)

Nevertheless, Hutton had learned important professional lessons in Zululand. He realised full well, for example, that the keys to Crealock's difficulties were logistic and administrative. On 26 May his division had still required 600 oxen before it could move at all. '[A] stronger General might have been able to overcome the apparent indisposition of those in authority at the base to comply with his requisitions', Hutton reflected, but Crealock could not.[42] A second difficulty was sickness. Within the division, a force of less than 6000 men lost 2566 to hospital admissions. Such appalling logistic and medical situations made a deep impression on Hutton, who saw it all from his position on Crealock's staff.[43] A third enduring lesson Hutton learned in Zululand was the importance of the press. Wolseley's, Wood's and Buller's reputations and career prospects rose considerably thanks to public awareness of their exploits. In the first few months of the war Hutton had in fact been paid as correspondent for *The Times*, only to have relinquished the job when appointed to Crealock's staff.[44]

Back in England, on 1 February 1880 Hutton reported to Staff College hoping to devote himself 'exclusively to theoretical study'.[45] He worked diligently and was praised by his instructors, including Colonel Lonsdale Hale, whose influence extended far beyond the college. Hutton was a successful and happy student. At this point he also began to think and write about the embryonic concept of 'mounted infantry' within the British Army at this time. After delivering a lecture on the subject in early May, Hutton's former general, Crealock, wrote to congratulate him on the 'intelligence which you have been able to show in giving a lecture on the subject'.[46]

Hutton's studies were again interrupted in early 1881 when British reinforcements were sent to Natal as a consequence of the outbreak of hostilities with Transvaal. Among them was a small force of mounted infantrymen raised and led by Major Percy Barrow, 19th Hussars, who had commanded a squadron of mounted infantry in the Anglo-Zulu War. Hutton's earlier lecture on the subject had caught Barrow's eye, and he invited Hutton to command one of his two squadrons. Hutton received permission to accept and again took leave from Staff College.[47] On arrival in South Africa, he marched for Ladysmith and was met by the now Major-General Evelyn Wood (who had succeeded to the command of British forces) who told Hutton of the disastrous defeat of British forces at Majuba Hill. Determined to reach the scene of action, Hutton arrived at Newcastle on 10 March and joined a growing British force gathered there. Under pressure from a British government eager to disengage itself from hostilities, Wood had, however, already signed a peace treaty with the Transvaal President, Paul Kruger, which brought the war to an end a little over two weeks later. Hutton and his mounted infantrymen remained for the next six months, camped not far from the slopes of Majuba.[48]

Hutton used his time near the Transvaal border to reflect on the series of British failures during the conflict. He came both to admire Boer mobility and effectiveness as citizen-soldiers and to attribute British reversals at Laing's Nek and Ingogo to a lack of mounted troops. Hutton blamed British over-confidence and poor defensive procedure (as at Isandlwana) for the defeat at Majuba. His predispositions towards mounted infantry, volunteer citizen-soldiers – he thought the Boers resembled the 'best class of yeoman farmers at home' – and the importance of professional competence were further strengthened.[49] Another important conclusion Hutton and many fellow officers drew from South Africa was that British military prestige, upon which much of the stability of the Empire relied, had been shattered thanks to the inappropriate and weak-willed interference of politicians. Hutton called the peace settlement 'preposterous'.[50] Gladstone and his fellow politicians, Hutton and other officers fumed, had betrayed the Empire and could not be trusted to act in the 'right' way. Such attitudes festered and had significant consequences for Hutton in the years to come.[51]

In early June 1881 Sir Hercules Robinson, the new Governor of the Cape and High Commissioner in South Africa, made his way to Pretoria to negotiate the final peace settlement with Transvaal. Hutton, with a half-squadron of men, was ordered to accompany him and remain as Robinson's official escort. It was a fortunate chance for Hutton to rub shoulders with another influential potential patron. Even more opportunely, Hutton was again noticed by Wood and Buller, themselves increasingly interested in the value of mounted infantrymen. They asked him whether he would be prepared to command a force of permanent mounted infantry troops to be raised in South Africa.[52] 'I hesitated', recalled Hutton, 'and Sir Evelyn and Redvers Buller asked me to give my own views on the suggestion quite frankly.'[53] Hutton replied that a system of mounted infantry instruction would be better than a permanent unit, with a school at Pietermaritzburg to train mounted detachments from the various British battalions serving in South Africa. Buller liked the idea and asked Hutton to draw up a scheme for such a school, which subsequently opened under the command of Captain Hallam Parr. Robinson then asked Hutton to remain as his military secretary. It was another tempting offer, but Hutton balanced his options and chose to complete the Staff College course. He set sail back to England on 1 September, beginning 'a strenuous three months of hard study', to make up for lost time.[54] His late arrival in South Africa had meant no promotion for Hutton, yet again the powerful and rising stars Wood and Buller, not to mention Robinson, had him in their sights.

Back in England Hutton passed the final Staff College exam with distinction and special mentions in three subjects, an achievement that further lifted his profile. Upon leaving the college Hutton returned to Fox Hills and received unofficial word that there might soon be a vacancy in the War Office Intelligence Department, exactly the staff job he had hoped for and one 'which at that time was much sought-after'. Until this position was open Hutton accepted an appointment to the 1st Battalion, 60th Rifles and was sent to Ireland to take command of a detachment of two infantry companies and a cavalry squadron quartered at Castlebar. Here, in the middle of the Irish Land War (1879–82), he 'had some experience of the usual concomitants of garrisoning outlying towns in that distressful country'. During this period Lord Spencer, the new Viceroy, offered Hutton a position on his staff. 'Attractive as this was to me', Hutton wrote, 'I preferred to wait until the vacancy in the Intelligence Department at the War Office, which I coveted.'[55]

Such an opportunity at last presented itself when, in early 1882, Major-General Sir Archibald Alison, Deputy Quartermaster-General, Intelligence, appointed Hutton as his private secretary. This was a critical posting for Hutton, not only in Alison's potential patronage but also by his service as secretary on a range of War Office committees. Alison was firmly part of Wolseley's circle after having been selected by Wolseley as his second-in-command during the Ashanti campaign. Importantly, in early June 1881, as secretary to a committee concerned with the training of the British Army 'Reserve', as part of Cardwell's short service system, Hutton came into direct contact with Wolseley, at the time chairman of a Mobilisation Committee for a contemplated expedition to Egypt. Wolseley invited Hutton to be the assistant secretary to this committee, and he soon became involved, in the strictest secrecy, with the already well-advanced preparations for a campaign in Egypt.[56] Here was Hutton's opportunity to impress Wolseley, whom he admired above all others and who influenced him directly and indirectly for the remainder of his career. For Hutton, Wolseley combined the elements he defined himself by – qualities of bravery and strength, with the expertise of a professional man rather than the affectations of a dilettante. Many of Wolseley's personal attitudes, such as a distrust of politicians (and party politics) and fear for the security of Empire in the event of a great European war, complemented and extended Hutton's developing views on such subjects.[57]

By the end of July Captain Hutton had accepted Alison's invitation to travel with him to Egypt as his aide-de-camp and military secretary in the event of his being appointed to command an advance British ground force, which was at the time being assembled in response to Urabi's nationalist insurrection. Reaching Port Said on the morning of 16 July, Alison met and conferred with British and French naval officers and decided to proceed forthwith to Alexandria. On their arrival Alison's men immediately set about relieving the naval force garrisoning the city. Following the Royal Navy's earlier bombardment, Urabi had withdrawn, but the whereabouts of his large force was unknown. Hutton suggested that a small corps of mounted infantry might be raised from British troops in Alexandria, some of whom had served as such in South Africa. Alison agreed, and by nightfall Hutton's small mounted party had established that no Egyptian troops were in immediate striking distance.[58]

On 15 August British reinforcements arrived under Wolseley, who took command of the overall campaign. The small force of mounted infantry Hutton had organised in Alexandria had been among the first to land. Wolseley praised them heartily, and Hutton basked in the reflected glory. Alison's Highland Brigade, to which Hutton was attached, subsequently joined the main British force on 9 September at Kassassin. An audacious night march against the Egyptian fortified position at Tel-el-Kebir was planned by Wolseley, with an assault scheduled for dawn. After a nervous few hours marching in the intense blackness of moonless night Alison's men found themselves just short of the Egyptian defences as dawn broke. The order was given to fix bayonets without halting. Early in the assault Hutton was separated from Alison, but found a 'rough sally port' used by Egyptian pickets, and pressed himself through the defensive works.[59] After gathering a small group of men, he assaulted a redoubt containing three Egyptian guns, then personally manned one of them with considerable effect against the flank of the Egyptian line. When Hutton finally arrived at Tel-el-Kebir Bridge he found Alison with Wolseley, discussing the situation. Hutton had already been reported as badly wounded and looked a fearsome sight, covered in blood from his wounded horse. He was heartily received, and his reputation soared.[60]

Photo 4 'The Guards at Tel-el-Kebir, 13 September 1882', by Richard Caton Woodville (1856–1927). (Royal Collection Trust/© Her Majesty Queen Elizabeth II 2014, RCIN 407434)

After Tel-el-Kebir, Urabi's army was broken. The whole deployment was another reminder to Hutton of importance of preserving British military prestige. So too it affirmed his growing contempt for politicians. Hutton, and many other officers in Egypt, considered Urabi as basically a patriot, encouraged by the example of British political weakness regarding the Boers.[61]

When Wolseley and the bulk of British troops departed Egypt, Alison was given command of the army of occupation, and Hutton was appointed as his military secretary. Hutton had a new patron and was not shy of informing Alison of his desire for 'employment on the General Staff'; that is, at the War Office. Alison told him that following the occupation 'he [Archibald] would return to England and be in a position to put my claims for staff employment in a way that could not be overlooked unless his own [Archibald's] were passed over'. 'I am very fond of Sir Archie', Hutton continued, 'so I have made the right choice.'[62] Nor did the opportunities stop there. Major-General William Pollexfen Radcliffe in England, for example, wrote to Hutton praising his work in setting up the mounted infantry school in South Africa.[63] Further, on 7 November Lord Dufferin arrived from Constantinople as an inspecting

British commissioner, to investigate the reorganisation of Egypt and invited Hutton to assist him in military matters. 'I was fortunate in being thrown for a time both officially and socially in close contact with the High Commissioner and his family', Hutton wrote. 'Looking back, I recall many of his views and opinions which have helped me in later life.'[64] Meanwhile, the connection with Evelyn Wood continued as Wood raised the new Egyptian army. At one point Wood offered Hutton the command of a battalion with the local rank of lieutenant-colonel and £750 per annum in this new Egyptian force. Hutton declined on Alison's suggestion that his career prospects were better where he was. All the while Hutton's connections to Wolseley's Ring grew closer, in the shadow of Wolseley's own growing fame and influence. Hutton wrote to Lawrence, excited that 'Sir Garnet might have mentioned my name in connection with the Mounted Infantry Corps, since the first idea was mine'.[65]

In March 1883 Alison's health began to fail, and he was forced to return home. Hutton had himself earlier contracted a tropical disease at Tanta and had fallen ill. Once again he was reminded of the substandard state of British Army medical services, which he considered were 'only a slight improvement upon those of the Zulu War two years before'.[66] On 12 May Alison departed, and Hutton followed him at the end of the month. The deployment was a defining moment in Hutton's career. He had lived up to his own high expectations in terms of competence, valour and physical prowess. Aside from the important personal connections he made or strengthened in Egypt, Hutton was praised in Alison's official despatches to the War Office not only as 'an intelligent and most active officer' and for his exploits in Alexandria and at Tel-el-Kebir, but also for the value of the mounted infantry unit he had raised, particularly its reconnaissance work in Alexandria.[67] Hutton, predictably, began to identify even more with this branch of service as his pathway to prominence and as a representation of the technical innovation and reform to which he remained committed.

Back in England, Hutton was appointed brigade major of the 1st Infantry Brigade at Aldershot, under the command of Major-General Mark Walker. Here he developed and publicised his ideas on mounted infantry. This was both an outlet for his intellectual energy and a reform agenda that ensured he would come to the notice of the right type of senior officer. In March 1883 he had sent Cambridge his ideas for a scheme of how a brigade of mounted infantry volunteers might be raised in England, as he had recommended in Egypt. The Commander-in-Chief called it 'very well worked out' and gave his 'compliments on the zeal and intelligence' displayed in drawing up this plan.[68] Further enthused, Hutton published an article on mounted infantry in early 1884 in the *Illustrated Naval and Military Magazine*, discussing a scheme for creating a corps of mounted troops through the establishment of a school at Aldershot based on the principles he had drawn up for Evelyn Wood in Pretoria (1881) and for Alison in Cairo (1882). The article attracted considerable military and public attention.

Meanwhile, with a deteriorating situation in the Sudan, it seemed that another Egyptian deployment might be possible, and Hutton began to make use of his strengthening Wolseley Ring contacts. In early 1884 he wrote to Buller, attempting to secure service in any future expedition, and was told: 'I would be very glad to have you with me – ask Wolseley.'[69] Alison wrote to the Military Secretary at the War Office, Lieutenant-General Sir Edmund Whitmore, on Hutton's behalf, that he knew of 'no officer better suited' for such employment.[70] As a result Wolseley instructed Hutton to consider developing an expanded mounted infantry force for use in Egypt. Hutton drew up a scheme to this effect and, shortly afterwards, the officer in command of the small mounted infantry corps already in Cairo was accidentally killed in a steeplechase competition. Hutton was asked whether he would go to Egypt to fill the vacancy and put into effect the plan he had devised. He readily accepted.[71]

On 13 June Hutton left Aldershot for Egypt, arriving a week later, 'just as if I had never been away'.[72] In early July his small force was raised from one to two companies, and it appeared that Hutton's more ambitious plans for an expanded mounted infantry corps in Egypt were on the verge of realisation. By this stage British planners were preparing for the relief of Khartoum, and Hutton realised, thanks to weather and terrain, that horses would be of little use. He therefore began to think of using camels as war mounts, an idea hitherto untried by white troops. Despite the 'cries of derision' by officers with Indian and Egyptian experience, his experiments succeeded and, as Hutton recalled, 'the British soldier and the Hedin camel made friends with one another in an astonishing manner'.[73] After watching one of Hutton's demonstrations, General Sir Frederick Stephenson, Commander-in-Chief of the British Army of Occupation in Cairo, backed the initiative.[74]

For the planned relief of Khartoum a large force of Hutton's camels would be needed, and he was soon overworked in arranging, training, equipping and working out a system of drill for his camel-riders. Such labour was not just for his own mounted infantry corps, as Hutton also developed a scheme of organisation and equipment for three additional battalions of camel troops and sent it to Wolseley at the War Office.[75] 'All this strenuous work fell on my shoulders and I had but little staff assistance', Hutton later wrote. 'I began to feel the effects of the heat in combination with the arduous and constant work.'[76] In early August Hutton had two attacks of sun stroke, and a medical board ordered two months leave and a return to England, forcing him to abandon, in his words, the 'finest command a young officer has ever had'.[77] Mortified not only at abandoning his work, Hutton also had to face the emasculating and horrific reality of 'physical' failure. Such medical problems were very common in late-Victorian colonial campaigning, and Hutton's exaggerated response to his situation shows how deeply he had invested in concepts of manly fortitude and strength.

After recuperating in England for a month, Hutton re-embarked for Egypt, reaching Alexandria on 6 October and proceeding thence to Cairo. A few days later he set out for Philae where boats were gathered to support the British advance to Khartoum, under the command of Wolseley himself, who had decided that the fastest way of reaching Gordon would be to ascend the Nile. Hutton dined with Buller and Wood and was thrilled that both generals seemed genuinely pleased at his arrival. He felt 'intense responsibility ... not only for the Mounted Infantry Camel Corps, but for the success of the three other camel corps of whose equipment and organisation I was in a large measure the author'. On 28 October Hutton moved with the force towards Dongola, but his previous symptoms returned. On arrival he dismounted from his camel almost delirious and was sent back to Wadi Halfa hardly conscious. For two days Hutton was comatose and near death. Buller came to visit murmuring 'words of sympathy and sorrow which I could never forget'.[78] The shame at feeling to have failed professionally and in terms of his expectation of himself as a man once more hit hard.[79]

Hutton soon began to recover physically, but 'was overcome with heavy depression of mind'.[80] Once recuperated, he was allocated desk duties as staff officer on the British Lines of Communication headquarters under Evelyn Wood. He received letters of sympathy and support from his friends in Egypt, his stepfather and from Wolseley, who wrote: 'I am extremely sorry that I am not to have the benefit of your help in the Mounted Infantry during this advance of Khartoum.'[81] Yet none could lift his spirits. Importantly, however, Hutton spent much time with Wood, and their relationship grew strong. During this period Hutton managed to impress Wood with arguments concerning the potential of the mounted infantry arm of service. Slowly Hutton began to write of a determination to 'get over my disappointment' and look to the future.[82]

The relief of Khartoum had meanwhile struck problems. Early in the New Year news of Gordon's increasingly critical situation encouraged Wolseley to split his force into two parts. A combined force of four battalions of camel-mounted troops were despatched from Korti across the desert to reach Khartoum as soon as possible, while the remainder of Wolseley's force continued up the river. This 'desert column', under Colonel Stewart's command, was attacked by 10 000 Mahdists at Abu Clea wells on 17 January and again at Abu Kru two days later, before news of Gordon's death and the fall of Khartoum removed its purpose. Nevertheless Hutton's camels and his mounted infantry corps had distinguished themselves.[83] Hutton was proud and was soon referring to his own role in their success, encouraged by Wolseley, who praised the performance of the mounted infantrymen. Official recognition was published in orders of 10 March 1885 for the 'excellent service they have rendered'.[84]

In the wake of fall of Khartoum, the British decided to move another force from Suakin towards Berber as a diversion, and a second mounted infantry battalion was to be raised as part of the expedition. Hutton was directed to create and lead it, as far as his health allowed, until relieved by a permanent commander. A rush of volunteers highlighted the growing popularity of the mounted infantry idea. In late February 1885, Hutton handed the new battalion to Colonel R.F. Grant (later a lieutenant-general). Dispirited, Hutton wrote sorrowfully to Lawrence, wondering whether he might 'ever be permitted to command a battalion of my own training'.[85]

Such continuing disappointments encouraged Hutton to throw even more of his intellectual energies into developing his ideas on mounted infantry. Thanks to another war scare with Russia in early 1885, Hutton was encouraged to rethink the mounted infantry concept as a way to deploy troops rapidly in an emergency. In March 1885 he drafted a scheme for a full brigade of 2000 mounted infantry volunteers 'for immediate service in war'. The system very much reflected his developing ideas concerning part-time citizen-soldiers in that it would exploit 'the latent military power and soldierly qualities of the Volunteer Force'.[86] The proposed brigade, based at Aldershot, would complement the cavalry in that certain routine cavalry duties could be devolved to the mounted infantry. Moreover, the recent campaign in Egypt had proved that this concept could work. Hutton sent the scheme to the War Office and was pleased that it was 'most handsomely complimented by Sir Archibald [Alison] and HRH [Cambridge]'.[87]

By the middle of May 1885 orders from London were to concentrate all British troops in Egypt and abandon operations in the Sudan. Hutton was still ill and was ordered in front of a medical board and given four more months of sick leave in England. He continued to reproach himself. '[O]n the journey home I realized I had disappointed my friends', he wrote. 'Through my break-down in health, I had not come up to their expectations. I had failed in the active work in the field which after all is the one and only test of an officer's value.'[88]

Once he had recovered, Hutton returned to duty with 3rd Battalion, 60th Rifles, at Devonport in late November 1885. Here he concentrated on developing a paper on the mounted infantry, building on the scheme he had developed and sent to the War Office while in Egypt, which would capture and publicise his views, energise debate on the issue and continue to keep his name in front of influential senior officers.[89] This was, in part, an intellectual endeavour, stimulated by perceptions of failure in Egypt and in part a natural extension of his professional ideas about the unique military potential of Anglo-Saxon mounted troops. Hutton also knew, given the success of the mounted infantry battalions in Egypt, that public and professional interest was assured. At the centre of the picture that emerged was the establishment of a mounted infantry school to train a small cadre capable of expansion in war. Hutton discussed his ideas with Wolseley, whom he knew would be sympathetic and who offered to chair the reading of his paper at the Royal United Services Institution.[90]

Hutton's paper, 'Mounted Infantry', was presented on 2 June 1886 and printed in the Institution's journal. In it he argued that the presence of more such troops would have prevented past disasters, such as those at Isandlwana and Majuba Hill. Further, he contended, mounted infantrymen should be seen as an economical alternative for the limited numbers of British cavalry for small-scale colonial service, to relieve the cavalry of 'many of their most tiresome and irksome duties', such as outposts and escorts in larger campaigns, and to act in conjunction with cavalry troops if and when required. Hutton outlined a plan to detach individual troops from various infantry battalions, to be trained at a mounted infantry school at Aldershot, before being rotated back to their regiments. The system would thus produce twelve mounted infantry qualified officers and 300 men annually. In line with his emerging ideas of harnessing the latent but very much unrealised military potential of part-time citizen soldiers, he further challenged his audience with the radical suggestion that British yeomanry cavalry might be more effectively trained as mounted infantry, perhaps even opening up the possibility of their serving overseas.[91]

With his paper Hutton was deliberately putting himself in the centre of an institutional debate, positing himself as a progressive and a reformer. On the one hand his scheme underscored his ideas on professionalism (and even class) in that it challenged the aristocratic conservatism of the cavalrymen, who would invariably view with contempt with any perceived attempt by the infantry to encroach upon their traditional roles. On the other hand, infantry officers would doubtless be wary of a system that would take detachments of quality troops from the regiments.[92] Hutton was at pains to invite the attendance of as many of the leading soldiers of the day as possible to the reading of his paper and more especially those generals 'under whom the Mounted Infantry had served'.[93] The result was a crowded, enthusiastic and impassioned audience.

Unsurprisingly, Hutton's proposals were bitterly opposed by such senior officers as General Edward Hamley, an infantryman who objected to detachments from battalions that could ill afford to spare them to create a temporary corps. Cavalry officers such as Lieutenant-General Sir James Hills-Johnes and Colonel Frank Russell argued that cavalry, better trained for foot duties, would be superior to mounted infantry.[94] Wolseley's men came to the rescue. Alison supported the idea in all its details. Redvers Buller also endorsed Hutton's plan, adding that 'in the next Great War will the value of Mounted Infantry be the most notable feature'.[95] A range of other luminaries participated in the debate, adding to Hutton's stocks, and Wolseley concluded: 'I think there is one point on which everyone in the English Army – certainly everyone who has had much experience in recent wars – will agree and that is that Mounted Infantry as a Force in the field is of incalculable value.' 'In the future', he continued, 'the army that will have with it in the field a large mounted infantry force ... will have an enormous advantage.'[96] Wolseley clearly supported Hutton's proposals. For his part Hutton was 'more than satisfied with the general expression of approval by those whose opinions and influence counted'.[97]

During winter 1886–87 Hutton continued work on his mounted infantry school scheme, and it was not long before his efforts paid further dividends. Early in 1887 he asked by Major-General George Byng Harman, Military Secretary at the War Office, if he was interested in temporary duty as a staff officer at Aldershot, with the promise that it would facilitate a future appointment as the Deputy Assistant Adjutant General the following summer. Hutton eagerly agreed to what he saw as the 'Blue Ribbon [appointment] of the Army for officers of my standing'.[98] Hutton was now more than ever part of the Wolseley reform group entrenched at Aldershot and had the opportunity to help put their innovative agendas into practice. He also worked hard on the Queen's Jubilee celebrations at Aldershot in 1887, which saw concentration of almost 60 000 troops in two separate corps, under the charge of his patrons Alison and Wood. Much of the staff arrangements for the review fell upon him. This work brought Hutton into close contact with volunteer troops and he warmed further to them and what they represented, despite their organisational faults. '[T]here could be no mistake about the soldierly bearing', he wrote 'and the excellence of the material of which the ranks were compose.'[99]

Hutton's rise continued during the summer of 1887 when he was directed by the War Office to accompany Major-General Sir John Dunne to observe a series of Swiss military manoeuvres. Hutton was surprised to find that, in contrast to low estimations at the War Office, part-time Swiss citizen soldiers were 'well organized and reasonably well equipped'. He was amazed they 'could attain such general excellence in so short a period of training' and thought the Swiss system so 'eminently sound' that it shaped his thinking on the mass employment of part-time troops from this point.[100] On his return to England Hutton found Dilke publicly criticising the recent Jubilee review as a sham in that the auxiliary units that had paraded were bereft of support services and thus unable to mobilise if required. '[O]ur army in a modern sense', Dilke argued, 'may be said to be non-existent.'[101] Dilke advocated a Swiss militia model for British auxiliary forces, which sat very well with Hutton.[102]

Meanwhile, in September 1887 Hutton's mounted infantry school moved a step closer to a reality when, on Wolseley's request, he had sent another memorandum to the War Office, this time calling for a mounted infantry regiment to be raised at Aldershot of eight companies (forty officers and 1052 other ranks), to be trained in four separate 'courses', each for two companies at a time.[103] In November and December Alison wrote to both Wolseley and the War Office advocating that Hutton's school be established on a two-year trial (stressing its low cost at only around £840 per annum). At last, on 21 January 1888 the War Office directed that a mounted infantry regiment was to be raised at Aldershot as part of the Cavalry Division of the 1st Army Corps. Regulars from various infantry units would cycle through a two-month course of training each year. Hutton, with a small staff, was appointed to command and instruct these companies.[104]

In truth, a number of key factors that had little to do with Hutton had helped to ensure that his school was established. Wolseley's mind, for one, had long been made up.[105] The Commander-in-Chief had, in fact, written the Wellington Prize Essay in 1871 on the topic of how to deal with a continental enemy, noting that 'the General of the future' will 'take care to have him well supplied with mounted infantry'.[106] So too Wolseley faced the problem of finding enough mounted troops to fill the expeditionary force plan for two army corps and a cavalry division that he had helped develop. The cavalry units theoretically available were deliberately kept under strength to save money. There were also no cavalry reserves. Part of the answer for Wolseley was the mounted infantry, an 'ingenious expedient', especially in the face of the government's financial parsimony towards the army.[107] Wolseley's plan was that Hutton's graduates would, on mobilisation, come together in two battalions of around a thousand men, one each for the two planned army corps. The snub such troops represented to the cavalry, a branch of service increasingly viewed by Wolseley as overly conservative, resistant to reform and tactically anachronistic, was an additional bonus for both him and Hutton.[108]

The mounted infantry school in itself, however, was still insufficient to satisfy Hutton's ambition. He sought additional outlets for his desire for reform (and to been seen as a reformer). To this end he felt that there should be a means to encourage the military intellectual spirit at Aldershot, beyond the Royal United Services Institution, which he thought had 'drifted into the hands of senior officers and lacked the enthusiasm requisite to attract the rising generation'.[109] In his staff appointment Hutton was responsible for the Prince Consort's Library at Aldershot and its building, at that time lying moribund. He thought to use both as the nucleus of a new military society. With Alison's support, Hutton therefore sought to build a forum to discuss technical military questions, still considered in many regiments as taboo, or at least 'poor form', and 'to assist in promoting a study as well as an interest in all professional matters among officers'.[110] While Alison gained the sympathies of the generals, Hutton began a campaign to elicit support from younger officers 'in the hunting field, in the racquet courts, playing cricket and on the race-course'.[111] During summer of 1887 considerable interest was aroused, and the first general meeting of the Aldershot Military Society was held on 23 December 1887, with Alison in the chair. Hutton immediately began planning a series of lectures from Colonel Sir Henry Halford on the magazine rifle, to Edward Warre on the history of tactics, to John Robert Seeley on the Empire itself. The series was well attended and, importantly for Hutton, extensively reported in the press. At the same time the society represented a sincere desire on Hutton's part to spread his own spirit of professionalism within the wider army.[112] Hutton was praised by Wood and Wolseley for his work with the society and remained honorary secretary for the next five years.[113]

Meanwhile, as the mounted infantry school developed under his supervision, Hutton's military reputation continued to rise. He was emerging as *the* recognised expert on this branch of service and influenced it more than any other officer over the next twenty years. Hutton's good fortune continued when Alison was replaced at Aldershot at the end of 1888 by another one of Hutton's patrons, Evelyn Wood. An enthusiastic supporter of the mounted infantry branch since Egypt in 1885, Wood was soon echoing Hutton's philosophies in this regard and reporting on Hutton and his school in glowing terms. At a small cost and 'with no permanent staff and with only a clerk', reported Wood to the War Office, 'this Officer has succeeded in welding together a single and thoroughly practical corps'.[114] The experiment was also watched from on high with a visit by Cambridge and Buller in March 1888 to inspect its progress. As light infantry movements were demonstrated on horseback and dismounted, Hutton claimed the Commander-in-Chief was 'shocked' at the efficiency reached after only a month's training.[115] Wolseley, too, showered praise, and Hutton took the opportunity to further ingratiate himself. 'Your Lordship will, I think, believe that I am in no way a member of the Old School', he wrote, 'but rather a Progressivist of your own School.'[116] In early 1889 Hutton delivered a second mounted infantry lecture, a sequel to that of June 1886, this time presided over by Buller. It was standing room only, and the mood was overwhelmingly supportive. Hutton was jubilant.

Yet the more Hutton's mounted infantry experiment succeeded, the more opposition and controversy it engendered, which did no harm to Hutton's reputation. The Inspector-General of Cavalry (also commander of the Cavalry Brigade at Aldershot), Major-General Sir Drury Curzon Drury-Lowe, complained to Wolseley that the idea was flawed in that it relied on using the horses of cavalrymen on leave.[117] Drury-Lowe's opposition was 'shared by the cavalry generally'.[118] So too, Colonel Lonsdale Hale, the *Times*' military critic, wrote of his fear that if 'Hutton's hands were free, the Mounted Infantry would ... literally override the cavalry'.[119] Twenty years Hutton still recalled the 'bitter criticism, not unmingled with scornful invective, which was experienced from our comrades of the Cavalry'.[120] Yet the context of such opposition was always much wider than Hutton or his school. It was in many ways a debate about the role and future of cavalry in Britain, with resources at its heart. Once Wolseley made the mounted infantry an 'official' branch of service in 1887, the spectre of 'conversion' for many cavalrymen felt real. This was especially so after the publication of 'The Field Exercise of 1889', which allotted the new branch the traditional cavalry roles of scouting and patrol duties. There were serious institutional and social stakes involved here, complicated by the patronage and personal loyalties of the late-Victorian army.[121]

Meanwhile, Hutton pursued his own reform program at Aldershot. He busied himself, particularly under Evelyn Wood, implementing new systems of fire discipline, subunit training, field operations and tactics, and agitated for instruction for higher officers through field exercises with umpires (a practice never before attempted). The work had its challenges as, even at Aldershot, the habits of devolving training and supervision of troops to non-commissioned officers died hard. Another important movement of the moment, and one embraced by Hutton and his fellow reformers, was the improvement of soldiers' conditions of living, leave and messing, a movement in line with wider changing upper- and middle-class social attitudes towards a type of paternalism for the lower classes.[122] Hutton took over the School of Cookery, established in the 1860s by Sir Arthur Herbert, for example, and reinvigorated it. He made contact with the chefs of 'the principal London hotels', explained the problem and enlisted their help.[123] A new syllabus of training and new standards emerged. Always keen for publicity, Hutton ensured that the press was involved, culminating in a four-page article in *Truth*. The resulting principles of messing and administration were still in use in 1914.

Throughout this period Hutton's attitudes to class and social status grew more complex. On one hand his advocacy of the mounted infantry implied a stiff rebuff to the conservative and aristocratic elements of the cavalry. Yet, on the other, his personal life provided a limited avenue of participation (not entry) into these same social circles. In his late thirties and having established his career, towards the end of 1888 he met, at Adderbury Manor, Warwickshire, Eleanor Paulet, daughter of the late Sir Charles Paulet and niece of the Marquess of Winchester and of Field Marshal Lord William Paulet.[124] The acquaintance continued through winter, and the two were engaged in February 1889. Lady Paulet, 'after a little hesitation' owing to Hutton's middle-class background, gave her consent. Hutton's recent professional successes helped. Lord William wrote to Lawrence that he had heard 'from all sides that Major Hutton is a first-rate soldier, popular and likely to prosper in his profession'.[125] In June the two were married in London, followed by a honeymoon at Amport House, Hampshire, on loan from Eleanor's first cousin and the current Marquis. By the middle of the month the pair were settled in Hutton's modest cottage at Aldershot.

To what extent Eleanor represented for Hutton a path into the social circles inhabited by many former Eton classmates may only be guessed at. There is no question, however, that in addition to providing him with far more secure financial circumstances, his improved social connections also led to his being appointed an aide-de-camp to the Queen in December 1892. Yet it is equally certain that there was more for Hutton in the marriage than Eleanor's connections. He had found a partner to share his ambitions and to subordinate herself to them. The couple worked as a team.[126] According to Hutton, from the beginning Eleanor understood that 'professional duty is the first consideration in all circumstances of a soldier'.[127] Evelyn Wood called her a partner who realised that 'duty came first and a wife dances on her husband's time'.[128] The union was thus not only of considerable career benefit; it was also both a long and, insofar as may be judged, a happy one.

Hutton's appointment at Aldershot ended in September 1892. He was rewarded by a promotion to the rank of brevet colonel, which, after a decade of strenuous work, at last 'made up for my ill-fortune as regards promotion in Egypt in 1882 and on the Nile in 1884/85'.[129] After a six-week vacation with Eleanor on the French Riviera, Hutton returned to England at a loose end, on half-pay and without a military position. His ambition and convictions regarding military professionalism and reform, however, were as strong as ever. He compared the 'earnestness and the persistency with which foreign [European] officers devote themselves to the training of their men', with what was still needed to improve the British Army.[130] Hutton's various writings and lectures on this topic and other technical military questions in early 1893 proved an unsatisfactory outlet for his intellectual energy. Friends suggested he might consider a political career, but Hutton was dissuaded by Sir Howard Vincent, Conservative member for Sheffield, advocate for closer imperial unity and prominent member of the military faction in parliament. Vincent argued to Hutton he would have less chance of effecting the military reforms he advocated within the political system than from outside it.[131] In fact, the small but influential band of military reformers at the War Office and in parliament, with which Hutton had associated himself as a junior member of the Wolseley Ring, had other plans for him, plans that would send him about as far from Aldershot as was conceivable.

Hutton's time at Aldershot also proved crucial in developing his nascent ideas on imperial defence. Like many officers of the period, he was convinced that a decisive European war was coming – a 'great struggle which must inevitably fall to our lot as a nation within the next few years' – and one that the British Army was manifestly unprepared to fight.[132] He therefore spent more and more of his intellectual energy trying to frame a solution to this problem, and his answer was increasingly the 'Empire'. He was influenced in this regard by men such as Seeley, who urged far greater ties with the white colonies as extensions of Britain itself, the consolidation of a 'Greater Britain', a 'new state, English in race and character'. It was a type of inspirational, uplifting and even moral message whereby Britain might harness its full imperial potential to remain a dominant and civilising power. For Seeley the choice was clear: imperial consolidation or disintegration. This type of imperial nationalism resonated with Hutton (and many others given that Seeley's *Expansion of England* sold 80 000 copies in its first two years) and fired him with a sense of urgency. In many ways Seeley's imperial concepts brought together many of the different strands of Hutton's own developing worldview. This included his public school values, the importance of education and professional competence, the idea of an empire to be protected by soldiers (but not necessarily politicians) and a role for self-governing colonies (which meant citizen soldiers) in some form of mutual defence arrangement.[133]

Seeley was of course not the only influence. George Parkin (future secretary of the Imperial Federation League and long-time friend), for example, lectured at Hutton's Aldershot Military Society on the need to consolidate the Empire. Parkin's message encouraged Hutton in this 'new field for military enterprise and thought'.[134] Hutton was further influenced by Dilke who, in addition to his criticisms of British auxiliary forces, with Spencer Wilkinson published *Imperial Defence* in 1892, which argued that the existing military system in Britain was inadequate to meet the looming catastrophe.[135] As a consequence, by 1893 Hutton was thinking about the Empire in new ways, later describing himself as 'imbued with the ideas of imperial expansion and solidification'.[136] So too in Cairo Hutton would have been aware of the colonial contributions to the 1884–85 campaign, which perhaps further signalled an imperial potential. Equally, his advocacy of the mounted infantry was a least partly framed by such considerations inasmuch as it exploited ethnically based notions of unique British adaptability, individuality and resourcefulness unavailable to the conscripts of Europe, while fitting Wolseley's wider agenda of a deployable professional force to be used on the continent in a general war. Aldershot was both a high point of Hutton's professional achievements thus far and an environment well suited to stimulate such ideas. To develop, however, they required a wider stage.

By the early 1890s the dual streams of Hutton's professional career and personal outlook and wider developments in imperial defence were converging. Soon they could no longer be discussed in parallel; rather they would merge and mingle, each influencing the other. With the day of crisis apparently looming for the Empire, Hutton's answer was increasingly a volunteer, yet professional citizen army of which the mounted infantry were a key component. All that was left for him was to add an 'imperial' ingredient. In addition, at this point Hutton was more determined to establish his military reputation than at any time thus far in his career. The deployment to Sudan was a high point and the task of creating a mounted infantry force for the campaign a pinnacle of professional recognition, by Wolseley of all men. It had been the culmination of his intellectual endeavours and efforts at military reform since first working for Hawley. Failure here was an assault on all the pillars of his self-identity; such failure could not be countenanced in the future. To this end Hutton soon found opportunity to match his ambition.

CHAPTER 3

'I SUPPOSE HE SENT ME A BLISTER'

A COLONIAL COMMANDANT, 1893–96

Events moved at a rapid pace for Hutton in early 1893. At further meetings in January with Colomb and Vincent it was suggested that he might consider taking up an appointment to command the military forces of New South Wales. The particular hook was that, in such an appointment, he might have a hand in 'strengthening the tie between Australia and the Mother Country' and even to 'assist so far as possible, in bringing about the long-discussed political union of the six States of Australia'.[1] While key figures in the Colonial and War Office worried that Federation might edge the Australian colonies away from Britain, for many ardent imperialists in it represented an opportunity for fresh and even stronger ties. A newly federated nation, united in the context of prevailing imperial sentiment in both Britain and the Australian colonies, might offer more to the Empire than the sum of its colonial constituent parts. This was particularly so for defence. A sound military system for New South Wales might subsequently be developed into a federal scheme, which in turn might help solve the strategic dilemmas of the Empire along the lines advocated by such men as Seeley. The notion fired Hutton's imagination. Here was an opportunity to exert an influence on the imperial questions that had increasingly been occupying his thoughts. From three threads – an effective force for the colony, the hope that it might be the basis of a federal military arrangement for Australia and the potential this force offered the Empire – was woven the fabric of the next phase of his career.

There is little question that well-connected and influential men like Vincent and Colomb made use of their personal relationships at the War

Office and elsewhere in order to ensure the appointment of an officer like Hutton to New South Wales, as part of their own imperial agendas. Here was a young, energetic, outspoken, intelligent, ambitious, imperial-minded and reform-minded Etonian, eager to make his mark and seemingly happy to take 'advice' from his mentors. After all, his efforts with the mounted infantry had, not coincidentally, been shaped by and corresponded with Wolseley's wider program. Their discussions with Hutton were also no doubt a way to feel him out on behalf of the War Office. It was therefore of little surprise when on 23 February Hutton met with his Wolseley Ring senior, Redvers Buller, now Adjutant General of the Army, and General Sir Reginald Gipps, Military Secretary, to be told he would probably be appointed as Commandant in New South Wales if he desired the position. Later the same day Hutton visited Lord Carrington, a former Governor of the colony, who gave him a glowing account of both the place and its people and who impressed on him that the job was 'pregnant with great results to anyone who could do it justice'. 'It seemed like Providence had thrown it my way', wrote Hutton, 'the very opportunity for which I was looking.'[2]

On 2 March Hutton's nomination from the War Office was accepted by the New South Wales Government, and his appointment was confirmed.[3] A round of interviews followed. On 9 March he twice met with Robert Meade, Undersecretary of State for the Colonies, who drew attention to the same triple purpose of his appointment as had Vincent. Meade first focused on the need for improved organisation and administration for the 'material defence of Sydney'. Second, he told Hutton that while general Australian Federation was at present outside 'the sphere of practical politics',[4] as a preliminary it might be possible to bring about a federal defence initiative. 'It appeared to me', Hutton later reflected, 'that the time was ripe for ... [s]uch a Scheme, [which] if successfully affected, should prove to be a sure stepping stone towards the larger federation.'[5] The two men then discussed the potential for a federal force, as had been noted by Bevan Edwards, to act in the Pacific, or elsewhere, in defence of imperial interests if required. Meade further urged Hutton to foster existing sentiment towards the defence of the Empire in the colony, as he thought it entirely possible that, in a serious military crisis, 'the Colonies may be invited to assist by a contingent of troops or otherwise'.[6]

Hutton's expectations were further shaped by a meeting on 18 April with Captain Cyprian Bridge, director of the newly established Naval Intelligence Department at the Admiralty and soon to be appointed Commander-in-Chief of the Australian Squadron. Bridge argued that

Sydney 'was over-fortified' with static defences but that a 'mobile Field Force' was missing.[7] Moreover, and echoing Meade, Bridge 'did not think that England realized at the time and even now, the vast importance of the principle of mutual combination for defence between the mother country and her colonies' represented by offer of troops for the campaign in the Sudan in 1885. Bridge thus 'laid great stress on the importance of the NSW forces being organized not only for the defence of the Colony itself, but for use also as a movable force in case of hostilities with a great foreign power in which the Empire might be involved'.[8] Such arguments made an impression.

Before he departed for Sydney Hutton also met Captain W. Peacocke, an old friend from Staff College and the newly appointed secretary of the CDC. Peacocke gave Hutton a set of papers on imperial defence that had been prepared by his predecessor, George Sydenham Clarke. Hutton later reflected that close study of these papers on the voyage to New South Wales – essentially Clarke's thoughts on the issue – gave him the ambition to consider how the principle of imperial defence cooperation might be given practical form; that is, although guided by the vague and general framework of expectations given by Meade and Bridges, from the very first Hutton was thinking in his own terms about how the forthcoming opportunity in New South Wales might lead to concrete outcomes for the colony, the continent and even how it might feed into his ideas about the future of the Empire's defence. True to his personal drive and professional thoroughness, on his own initiative Hutton followed his call on Peacocke with a visit to Shoeburyness and the Isle of Wight to get a better feel for coastal defence and Hythe to observe latest methods of rifle-shooting instruction in order to take the latest in military theory and practice with him to his new appointment. Hutton also arranged to dine with Major-General Edwards at the Savoy to gain his insights into Australian defence more generally.[9]

Hutton's friends and professional associates wished him well on the eve of his departure for Australia as the youngest (local rank) major-general in the British army. Evelyn Wood congratulated him on the appointment but in the same breath, conscious of the single-minded determination Hutton had shown during his operational service and during his period of struggle in support of the mounted infantry at Aldershot, warned Hutton to tread lightly with the locals.[10] With similar motivations Buller suggested the way to deal with them 'was by deference and flattery'. 'You cannot drive them', Buller continued, 'but you can lead by the nose with a soft ring.'[11]

After disembarking in Melbourne, Hutton finally arrived in Sydney and took up residence at Green Oakes on Darling Point on Sunday afternoon

28 May 1893, having by coincidence travelled northwards in same train as his new Premier, Sir George Dibbs, who concurrently held the portfolio of Chief Secretary, the minister responsible for the colony's military forces. Like most of his fellow colonial commandants across the Empire, nothing in his previous experience could adequately prepare Hutton for his new role. Certainly much was familiar. Around 20 per cent of the population had been born in the United Kingdom, although the proportion was declining. Popular imperial sentiment was still very strong, if a little less vocal than in 1885. 'Britishness' remained the dominant white colonial social and cultural point of self-identification. Symbols of the Empire were everywhere, from flag-waving public ceremonies to school curricula. The colonists were generally literate, thanks to free or cheap schooling, and well read. They knew their British military heroes. Meanwhile, more material ties endured. Three-quarters of all imports and exports and virtually all colonial debt was connected to Britain. Limited constitutional ties also remained, especially in the form of the Governor.[12]

Other important forces were also at play of which Hutton was less aware, but which would nonetheless shape his tenure as commandant. By the time he arrived in the colony a severe, decade-long depression was already underway, and from 1891 immigration all but ceased. British loans had begun to dry up. Unemployment rose and wages fell. In an era of growing labour organisation (and employer resistance to it) confrontations resulted, and a wave of strikes began that seemed to threaten the easy social order. The consequent mobilisation of citizen troops, particularly during the 1890 maritime dispute, had appalled segments of the community, especially the labour movement, which became acutely sensitive to the role and use of colonial armed forces from that moment onwards. In the wake of such developments a wave of limited colonial radicalism emerged, although one that generally ran in parallel with, not opposition to, prevailing imperial sentiment. In fact, if anything, the banking failures of 1892–93 curbed nationalist tendencies in the colony as the reliance on British capital was underscored.[13]

Despite his cursory discussions with Meade on the issue, the fact was that Hutton also knew little of the complex, long-running debate on Federation, which had been unfolding within and between the Australian colonies. In 1867 Henry Parkes, as Chief Secretary in New South Wales, had first proposed the idea of a Federal Council. Although rejected by the Colonial Secretary in London at that time, Parkes raised the issue once more at the Intercolonial Conference of 1880, and a Bill was drafted in support of such an organisation at the next Intercolonial Conference in 1883. Delegates successfully petitioned the British Government to pass the Federal Council of Australasia Act two years later. The Federal Council was thus formed to represent collective colonial interests, although it was hamstrung by a lack of executive power and a refusal by New South Wales to participate. Parkes, now New South Wales Premier, had come to fear that the body might help to solve some of the problems driving the colonies towards political union and that it therefore represented a stumbling block to Federation. Meanwhile, the smaller colonies remained guarded in their support for the federal idea, concerned about what form a federal government might take and worrying about domination by New South Wales and Victoria, the potential abolition of local tariffs (especially given New South Wales' anti-protectionist policies) and a range of other parochial concerns.[14]

Nonetheless, slow progress was made, and intercolonial discussions on the federal issue were continuous. In his historic Tenterfield address in October 1889, Parkes seized the opportunity of Edwards' military report to emphasise that federal defence was necessary for colonial security, making the time ripe for Federation. He called for a convention to begin the process. The subsequent February 1890 Federation Conference, a meeting of representatives of the colonies (and New Zealand) in Melbourne, concluded that the time for federal political union had indeed arrived and paved the way for the National Australian Convention of March 1891. Meanwhile, in London, Sir Andrew Clarke, who maintained a deep interest in the Australasian colonies, began to draft a federal Constitution, which returned with him to Australia in late 1890. With Parkes as president, the 1891 convention outlined the form of government a federal system might take and prepared a Commonwealth Bill for the establishment of a federal Constitution based on Clarke's draft. When it was to be submitted to the New South Wales assembly, however, George Reid moved a hostile amendment. George Dibbs then moved a vote of no confidence, which was only narrowly defeated, and Parkes resigned on 22 October 1891. With Parkes' removal, the difficulties of prolonged negotiations and the impact of economic depression, the federal movement lost momentum.

Importantly, the discourse surrounding Federation in Australia always had a defence aspect. This connection was certainly not a link of Meade's making in his discussions with Hutton in 1893. Rather, the Colonial Undersecretary was responding to an existing framework. The Carnarvon Commission of 1879 had found that there would be considerable efficiency in defence cooperation and even 'defence federation' in Australia. Colonel P.N. Scratchley, a resident British officer and adviser on defence issues to the Australian colonies, gave various lectures in the same year in which he showed himself to be a keen advocate of a federal scheme. So too a royal commission into the state of the New South Wales military forces of 1881 recommended a federal military college and arsenal and federal manoeuvres. During the 1887 Colonial Conference in London an acknowledgement was made of need for federal defence by the Australian premiers in their decision to cooperate in order to fortify Albany and Thursday Island. The following year Sir Henry Loch, who supported military federation throughout the Empire, passed an invitation through the colonial office for Wolseley to visit Australia to give his views on combining the colonial forces into a federal service.[15] Wolseley refused, but Edwards took the task a year later, and he too recommended (publicly) the union of colonial military forces. The CDC's remarks on Edwards' report, sent to colonial governments, also supported the notion of a federal military system. Fredrick Sargood, the Victorian Minister for Defence, subsequently called for and presided over a Commandants' Conference in 1890 to determine what each colony could pledge to federal defence in peace and war.

Meanwhile, following Henry Parkes' Tenterfield speech, Alfred Deakin of Victoria proposed that before a federal Constitution could be adopted something immediate should be done regarding defence and argued that the Federal Council should be used to this end.[16] After the National Australian Convention met in Sydney in 1891, Parkes noted: 'I then come to one [issue] to which I expect an almost unanimous agreement: that the military and naval defences of Australia shall be entrusted to federal forces, under one command ... that should be strictly defined by the Convention before we can proceed to construct a Bill to confer a constitution.'[17]

This connection again emerged in early 1892 when Dibbs invited Major-General Tulloch, Victorian commandant, to lead a royal commission into his colony's defence force. The commission took three months, from June to September 1892, before tabling its report to parliament in October. It found that while New South Wales was paying more on defence than other Australian colonies, it was not getting value for the money, an important consideration in the depressed economic climate.[18] Extensive reforms were recommended, largely endorsed by the CDC, including the 'military federation of the Australian Colonies'.[19] Moreover, when Tulloch's report was read by Clarke at the CDC, he argued to Meade that the time was right to turn all the discussion of Australian federal defence issue into fact. All that was needed was for Britain to be 'represented by a soldier and sailor who <u>know</u>'.[20] Meanwhile, the health of the current New South Wales commandant, Major-General John Soame Richardson, was failing, and Tulloch advised Dibbs to seek a new British commandant during a forthcoming visit to London. Dibbs followed Tulloch's suggestion. A colonial request for an active imperial officer therefore pressed the War Office from one direction just as Vincent and Colomb pressed it from another. Hutton's appointment was a much more complex confluence of circumstances than simple manipulation from any one party – Vincent, Meade or anyone else.

For his part, the new commandant was bursting with energy, self-confidence and ambition, which acted against his approaching his new role with the prudent caution that would perhaps have eased the transition. Hutton's first duty was to assess the state of the New South Wales forces, an organisation of around 6000 men (exclusive of a nominal reserve), based on a nucleus of permanent troops (a scattering of headquarters staff, three companies of garrison artillery, a field battery and a small number of submarine miners), with the balance split between unpaid volunteer units and part-paid volunteer militiamen. Even accepting that it was in Hutton's interests to portray a force he was supposed to improve in negative terms – in order to be seen as the solution there needed to be a problem – his conclusions were damning and with good reason. He told Dibbs, less than a week after arriving, that the condition of the force 'was even worse than had been represented to the Country in the Proceedings of the recent Royal Commission of 1892'.[21] Specifically, with Dilke's complaints against Britain's part-time soldiers no doubt in mind, Hutton lamented to Lord Hampton, future Governor of the colony, that 'every department and every organisation here was either obsolete or incomplete'.[22] To Parkes he argued that 'the organisation and administration (everything in fact which makes an army an effective machine) [was] chaotic'.[23] Conditioned to equate organisation with professionalism and efficiency, Hutton railed against 'a general want of ... proper system'.[24] There was no mobilisation plan for the colony, for example, and an absence of rigour and continuity in training. In addition, Hutton contended that in the wake of Tulloch's damning commission, the force was held in a type of 'quiet contempt', which dissuaded 'educated men to come forward to serve as officers or the best of the working and middle classes to join the ranks'.[25] Confidence in those responsible for command of the forces had all but disappeared.[26]

Hutton saved his most severe criticisms for the colonial artillery and its two most senior officers, Colonel Warner Wright Spalding in overall command of the artillery (and Hutton's second-in-command) and Brevet Colonel George John Airey, in charge of colonial field artillery. Both were former Royal Marines officers who had arrived in the colony aboard HMS *Challenger* in 1866. Both were criticised by Tulloch in his 1892 report, and both, in a grave affront to Hutton's professional sensibilities, were non-experts and technically incompetent, while enjoying the local social privileges of their rank and appointments. Hutton found Spalding 'without any professional knowledge of artillery attainments' and described Airey 'with like incapacity'. Neither had 'any military education', he complained to Peacocke at the CDC, 'beyond what they learnt during a few years as officers in the marines'.[27] Hutton warned Parkes that both were ignorant of the technicalities of their profession and that modern guns and good troops were 'of little avail in war without officers of high attainment'.[28] For Hutton the two colonels represented a type of officer who treated their duties 'as a species for past-time', with little concern for efficiency or their subordinates – the same typecast he had riled against at Aldershot.[29] These two incompetent officers, he wrote to Buller, were incapable of improving the broken organisation over which they presided.[30] For his part, it should be noted, Spalding had been looking forward to replacing Richardson as commandant and lost no time undermining the cuckoo in the nest. Before Hutton had even arrived, for example, Spalding warned the colonial parliament: 'Allegiance to Imperial authority could not fail to be the first consideration of Imperial officers; obedience to officers of this country, their second.'[31]

Hutton was, predictably, absolutely determined that Spalding and Airey be removed from their positions. Rottenness at the top, he argued to Cambridge, had left the colonial artillery in a 'demoralised and chaotic condition'. '[N]o system existed', he continued, 'for utilising it upon any intelligent, much less modern lines.'[32] As a result, Hutton claimed rather dramatically, 'Sydney was practically defenceless and at the mercy of an Enemy's cruiser which would be prepared to run the gauntlet of a few ill-controlled stray shots.'[33] If Hutton was exaggerating, it was not by much. The artillery forts were deficient in equipment of all kinds and their magazines practically empty, without any regular record of ammunition. The training of officers and men had been neglected for at least three years. The New South Wales field artillery regiment 'existed only in name'; the harness for one of its batteries was not even assembled.[34] Until Spalding and Airey were retired, Hutton reported to Peacocke, 'it is useless to talk of the Artillery here being efficient, or the port of Sydney being safe as a Naval Base'.[35] Yet neither colonel would be removed without a fight. The ensuing struggle revealed much about Hutton's personality, the inherent difficulties and contradictions of colonial commandant appointments and

Photo 5 Bombardier Knox, Hutton's 'cycle orderly' at his headquarters and a member of the New South Wales artillery – the branch of service so harshly criticised by Hutton upon his arrival in the colony. (Council of the National Army Museum, London, NAM1985–07-29–4)

even something of the inherently problematic nature of ideas of imperial defence when run up against the realities of local interests.

Leaving aside the issue of Spalding and Airey, Hutton threw his efforts into restructuring and reforming the New South Wales forces. Here was a level of authority and licence to implement the ideas he had fostered at Aldershot that would never have been available in Britain. By late August 1893 Hutton had completed a scheme of defence for the colony, based on the assumption that the most likely threats to be countered were raids by enemy ships on ports to obtain coal, create diversions, threaten bombardment and thereby levy an 'indemnity', or induce panic in the population.[36] Hutton's defence against such attacks was to be based on the static protection of key ports such as Sydney, Newcastle and 'Wollongong-Bulli', primarily by volunteer units and by the creation of a 'movable column' consisting of well-equipped, well-organised, all-arms militia troops 'capable of being moved into any part of the Colony at the shortest notice'.[37] This was a miniature army, more or less, under Hutton's direct command and ready to act in defence of any portion of the colony. These were not entirely original ideas. Indeed, the notion of a mobile 'Field Force' of part-paid militia, with volunteers to man the forts, was part of the 1890 Commandants' Conference recommendations. Hutton's scheme also incorporated Tulloch's suggestions (which he read *en route* to Australia) and the CDC's response to it.[38] Yet if the essentials of the new defensive scheme for the colony were borrowed by Hutton, the forcefulness and energy with which he implemented the reforms demanded by it was a novel military experience for New South Wales – a world away from Richardson's relaxed indolence.

Hutton's privileging of the militia over the volunteers in his defensive plan for New South Wales was entirely in line with his pre-existing experiences and attitudes. 'The general defence of the colony must undoubtedly be placed in the hands of the partially paid troops,' he told the *Sydney Morning Herald* within a month of his arrival.[39] As they were paid, militiamen were subject to a much greater level of enforceable military discipline and regulations, and therefore training and professional competence, than their volunteer counterparts. The militia, also on account of being paid, were more open to a wider segment of the community and served a far lesser social purpose than the volunteers. Again, dilettante/professional divides were prominent in Hutton's mind. Fortunately for him, the trend in the colony (since the burst of volunteerism in 1885) was already towards converting many volunteer units to militia status. Hutton therefore largely avoided the powerful backlash that often accompanied such transformations across the Empire at other times and places. His advocacy of the militia in New South Wales was also in line with aspects of his nascent plan on how the Empire as a whole might by defended in a time of crisis. Throughout his time in New South Wales and beyond, Hutton's faith in white, part-paid, militiamen never wavered, nor did his distaste for less professional unpaid volunteers.[40]

Along with the formulation of a defensive scheme for the colony, another significant early reform was Hutton's successful agitation to restructure the defence branch of the Chief Secretary's portfolio. Previously, the offices of Commandant (a military representative) and Military Secretary (a civil representative) ran a parallel chain of military advice and authority to the Chief Secretary. The situation in 1893 was further complicated in that the Military Secretary was Colonel C.F. Roberts, a former British regular officer who had retained his rank and title when seconded to the job. Not only was the idea of sharing authority with a 'civilian' abhorrent to Hutton – ever jealous of his personal and command prerogatives – but also it was out of line with a series of War Office reviews, from the Stanhope reforms of 1888 onwards, which clearly charged the British Commander-in-Chief with acting as a single point of contact with the Secretary for War. Roberts was henceforth made subordinate to Hutton, who was now the sole adviser to the minister and head of the military branch of the Chief Secretary's office. Yet Hutton went further, soon requesting that the Military Secretary be cut out of direct ministerial correspondence and moved to Victoria Barracks to work directly under his own watchful eye. He subsequently, and unsuccessfully, tried to do away with the civil branch completely by subsuming control for the Ordnance Department and sending the balance of Roberts' financial staff to work for the Colonial Treasurer.[41] Despite this setback, by late 1893 there was no question of who was in control of the forces. Although he had given his consent to the reorganisation, Dibbs began to notice disturbing signs of his commandant's penchant for independence.

Unsurprisingly, another item on Hutton's reform agenda was the New South Wales mounted force. Here he continued both his advocacy for and development of the mounted infantry concept. In July 1893 Hutton told his colonial mounted troops: 'I intend to devote myself for the next three years to the work of making you ... one of the best forces in the world.'[42] In August he remodelled the colony's existing cavalry regiment (the New South Wales Lancers) and mounted infantry regiment (the New South Wales Mounted Rifles) into the Mounted Brigade, the centrepiece of his 'movable column', which, when mounted support services were added, became 'perhaps the first combat-capable and organised multi-unit formation in the colony'.[43] Behind his back the commandant's devotion to this brigade earned them the name 'Hutton's pets'.[44] At the same time, with his Aldershot experience very much in mind, Hutton was cautious not to offend the colonial cavalrymen with any direct suggestion that they be transformed into mounted infantry. Nevertheless there was no question that his focus was in that direction, and soon the Lancers were practising the carriage and tactical use of rifles and honing their dismounted skills. Further underscoring the importance he placed on this formation, Hutton also managed to persuade Dibbs in July 1893 to secure the services of a British officer to act as its second-in-command.[45]

Nor did Hutton's intellectual investment in the mounted infantry concept slow down in the colony. In August 1894 he gave a well-received paper, 'The Tactical and Strategical Power of Mounted Troops in War', to the United Services Institute of New South Wales.[46] Within it he confirmed his belief that this branch was essential to the modern battlefield and recommended a range of practical and tactical reforms appropriate for part-time mounted forces from the colonies. It was clear at this stage that such troops were figuring more and more prominently in Hutton's wider conceptions of imperial defence. He later reminisced that the part-time volunteer soldiers he found in New South Wales were 'the beau ideal of Mounted riflemen' and that '[a] contingent of such men would be worth their weight in Australian gold in any campaign in which British troops may be engaged'.[47] All the while, in another obvious rebuke to the cavalrymen of Britain, he urged his audience, with respect to mounted service, to be 'unfettered by the traditions of the past'.[48]

An essential component of all of Hutton's various reforms in New South Wales was a sustained effort to increase the standard of training of the force, just as it had been at Aldershot under Evelyn Wood. For Hutton, as always, only through thorough training – not the vacillating interest and social posturing of the amateur – came legitimacy, professional mastery and competence. To this end, by August 1894 he had established schools of instruction for mounted troops, field and garrison artillery, infantry, engineers, medical staff and 'military equitation'. Hutton also began a system of company-level annual training for militia troops on the Aldershot model, a novelty in the colony, and later concluded that the experiment had 'proved successful beyond my most sanguine hopes'.[49] Part-time troops from the colony strove to obtain badges of proficiency Hutton instituted to those who qualified. 'I see no difficulty in achieving really satisfactory results', he told Cambridge in August 1894, 'from this Militia system of Annual Field Training.'[50] For the higher education of officers (and interested civilians) Hutton worked with Sir William Charles Windeyer, one of the University of Sydney's earliest graduates and its Vice Chancellor in 1894 (and Chancellor, 1895–96) to establish a 'Military Chair' within the university, which was eventually filled in 1906 by Colonel Hubert Foster.[51] Meanwhile, competitive examinations were instituted for officer entry into the colony's permanent artillery regiment. Hutton also successfully agitated for a system of detaching permanent colonial officers to Britain for training, or to British and Indian units, to widen their military experiences.[52] '[T]he effect of this is most wholesome', he noted in 1894, 'and is showing already most excellent results, as it not only raises the standard of military efficiency but it brings Australian troops in thorough touch with the British troops elsewhere.'[53]

Overshadowing all of Hutton's reform successes and accounting for much of his frustration was an ever-present shortage of funds. In 1890 in New South Wales £264 000 was spent on defence, which fell to around £225 000 in 1892 and only £175 000 by 1894.[54] Government reluctance to spend on its military forces, in a period of relative strategic calm, a severe and continuing depression and an acute banking crisis in early 1893, was entirely understandable. Hutton, however, with a tunnel-visioned fixation on his own objectives, too readily equated this position with deliberate obstructionism, despite his knowledge of similar pressures on military expenditure in Britain. His frustration at this situation and the conflict it engendered with his civil masters soon grew in intensity and importance.

In September 1893 Hutton carped to Cambridge that the 'difficulties here of reorganisation have been very considerable due to the necessity for general retrenchment. The task of squeezing the pocket and insisting on harder work is no easy one.'[55] A month later he complained bitterly to Buller: 'The Government have seen fit to cut down our military Estimates.'[56] Hutton's reaction to this particular decision inevitably set him on a collision course with Dibbs. In 1893 the commandant was initially instructed to make savings of £40 000 in the following year's estimates. Hutton chose to comply by instituting pay cuts for the troops but as compensation promised them an Easter training camp, the first in three years. Yet the camp would itself cost £30 000 and hence, as Hutton was only too aware, little real saving would follow. Dibbs predictably cut the camp from the prepared estimates. Hutton protested and used the press to warn of a severe degrading of the efficiency of the force without his proposed camp. Dibbs resented it, accusing Hutton of being 'dictatorial' in his tone.[57] The conflict was made public when reported in detail in the *Evening News*. Dibbs took the press report as an attempt by Hutton to criticise his decisions publicly and as a direct challenge to his constitutional authority. The Premier struck back through the *Daily Telegraph*, claiming: 'If he [Hutton] had his own way, I should merely become his recording clerk.'[58] In parliament, during debates on the military estimates, Dibbs practically accused his commandant of a breach of confidence for voicing his contrary opinion. Hutton was saved by George Reid, Leader of the Opposition, who supported him for political rather than philosophical reasons.[59] With no real alternative, however, Hutton capitulated and conducted a series of less ambitious local camps in the following year without exceeding the budget for paid drills.

Serious damage was done to the relationship between Dibbs and Hutton as a consequence of the friction surrounding the 1993 defence estimates. It is worthwhile to spend some time investigating this controversy and other points of disagreement between the two men because they serve to illuminate much wider issues than a personality clash between two public figures in colonial New South Wales. Indeed, the conflict was in many ways representative of the inherent contradictions of the military–political interface throughout the Empire in this era. This was particularly so when the issues at stake involved authority and control. An agreed division of duties, responsibilities and authority was equally missing in New South Wales as it was in Canada, Wellington and, to some extent, in London.

Meanwhile, Hutton, always convinced of the correctness of any position he took and unable to countenance circumstances that did not align with his wishes, continued to wilfully ignore financial realities of the colony and constantly pressed for more money. Some Sydney papers accused him of 'making party capital' out of Dibbs' attempts to curtail military spending and of having 'heckled our irascible and impetuous Premier'. Hutton understood neither the reason for Dibbs' anger nor its intensity – 'a storm in a tea cup', he explained to Buller.[60] The commandant's methods in this regard were also questionable. Emboldened by CDC concerns over falling defence expenditure in the colony, for example, Hutton exploited colonial fears of credit ratings in London by using his official annual report in 1894 to imply that all-important British capital would be guaranteed for New South Wales only if its security was similarly ensured. 'Any feeling of distrust in the defensive power of the Colony', he warned, 'would invariably be followed by a want of confidence on the part of those capitalists who have so largely promoted the commercial interest of the Colony.'[61] Such an approach did nothing to smooth the breach with Dibbs.

Concurrently, Hutton's deliberate and calculated use of the press won him few friends in the colonial legislature. In this approach Hutton was following lessons he had learned when campaigning and Wolseley's maxim that 'the press has become a power which a man should try and manage for himself ... it is an influence which one cannot deny and therefore should try to make one's own.'[62] Hutton was quite deliberately outspoken and made himself openly accessible to the press in order to get 'upon good terms with the public'.[63] Indeed, he attributed much of his reform achievements to the power of 'the Press placing them before the public on fair and just lines'.[64] Hutton's speeches were many and widely reported, as were his opinions on government policy.

To be fair, part of Hutton's motivation in this regard was an honest and energetic attempt to 'educate' public opinion, to 'awaken intelligent interest in the community at large', to raise the public profile and prestige of forces and to put 'military service upon the highest level as a duty to God as well as a duty to the State'. From the beginning he was convinced that to achieve his aims, he 'must win ... the confidence of the Press and the sympathy of the public'.[65] This was the same impulse behind his insistence on a grand and expensive 'Naval and Military Review' in Centennial Park for the new Governor, Sir Robert Duff, in July 1893. Such a parade had never before been conducted and certainly succeeded in garnering significant media approbation. His subsequent support for public military events was consistent with a drive to ensure that 'the Force would be presented in its most attractive light to the public and become popularised accordingly'.[66] It is also clear that such an approach was a wider mission, in which Hutton perceived himself to be part, of educating the Empire on the importance of defence and role of the military within it, before the looming international calamity took hold. The immediacy of this threat, a persistent theme at the War Office, was never far from his mind.[67] 'To cultivate the military instinct', he wrote in 1894, was imperative.[68] Nevertheless, the more immediate outcome of Hutton's outspoken approach was to further poison his relationship with Dibbs.

One important result of the worsening relationship between Dibbs and Hutton was an outright refusal by the Premier to have meetings with his commandant. In June 1893 Hutton had made an arrangement with Dibbs whereby, in order to avoiding unnecessary correspondence and misunderstandings, the two would meet at 3.00pm each Monday and Friday to discuss papers and issues of importance. For four months from August 1893, however, Hutton was denied any audience with Dibbs, in spite of repeated attempts. The situation, in Hutton's words, 'became so embarrassing that I put on paper the impossible position to which I had been officially reduced'.[69] More to the point, no personal interviews made Dibbs' Principal Undersecretary, Critchett Walker, the sole medium of correspondence, and therefore military advice, to the Premier. For a jealous Hutton this was a grave and unacceptable usurpation. His opinions were not to be represented by 'an irresponsible and non-military third party'.[70] Hutton sent his memo to Dibbs on 27 September 1893, outlining his concerns, especially in that 'the vital point of personal interviews so as to avoid unnecessary correspondence and misunderstandings has been allowed to lapse entirely'. Hutton further claimed that inappropriate notes and minutes placed on his correspondence by Dibbs proved such misunderstandings had arisen and that he was not deserving of the censure implied by them. 'It is quite beyond my power to act up to the spirit of your wishes', he argued, 'unless I have personal access to you as the Minister to whom I am responsible.'[71]

The issue was finally forced to a head in early November. True to form, while visiting Melbourne Hutton gave a press interview alluding to his frustrations, particularly over funding cuts, which had hamstrung his plans for annual training camps. Dibbs fired back the next day with his own press interview: 'I cannot believe that his statements have been reported correctly', claimed Dibbs. 'General Hutton knows his position too well to attempt to censure his Minister.' Dibbs went on to complain, incorrectly, that the 'War Office in England would not allow any discourtesy to a Minister'. '[H]e is a good soldier', the Premier continued, 'but he writes and talks too much. He means well . . . but he has much to learn in regard to his official duties.'[72] Hutton complained to Buller about the Premier's 'offensive and indeed insulting' remarks.[73] On his return to Sydney Hutton insisted on a personal interview, this time granted (in Hutton's opinion after pressure on Dibbs from his Cabinet).

The fateful meeting with Dibbs (with Walker present) began at 9.00am, 13 November. Walker began by producing a copy of Hutton's earlier memo, which Hutton read a paragraph at a time to Dibbs, outlining his dissatisfaction with the treatment he had received. He further accused the Premier of resisting his reforms for personal reasons, in particular his refusal to allow the removal of Spalding and Airey. When he had held his line on this issue, Hutton continued, Dibbs 'endeavoured by every means in his power to make my position untenable and to this end subjected me to numerous acts of official discourtesy and incivility'.[74] Hutton further claimed, 'very firmly and in measured language', that he had been treated in 'a highly discourteous and inconsiderate manner, that I had been denied access to him since August, in spite of repeated attempts' and that such a condition rendered the success of his command impossible.[75] He then challenged Dibbs to have the offensive memos written in the Premier's own hand and placed on his papers, printed and made public. Dibbs declined.

For his part Dibbs denied that the condition of the forces was as bad as Hutton represented and also argued that the commandant seemed to think himself more as serving the Governor than himself as Chief Secretary. Dibbs reminded Hutton that when he arrived in Sydney he did not officially call on him. This was a significant snub, and Hutton knew it. The fact that the two had shared a carriage from Sydney to Melbourne, conversing for hours, was no excuse. Dibbs also complained that 'many things have appeared in the Press connected with Military matters, hinting at questions that had not been submitted to me or decided on'. Yet the meeting seemed, at least from Hutton's perspective, to end well. Hutton reported that the result of his determination to make his point was that Dibbs, 'who with all his bluff and rudeness was at heart an admirer of determination and pluck', changed his manner completely and 'yielded to my representations in a manner which was as satisfactory as it was sudden'.[76]

The meeting ended with Dibbs asking Hutton if he knew Redvers Buller well. 'Yes, I have known him for the last 25 years,' said Hutton. 'Ah! A strong man, I should say', replied Dibbs. 'He didn't like my refusing to take the old gentleman with a large family which he wanted to send us.' 'Probably not,' Hutton replied. 'In revenge', Dibbs quipped, 'I suppose he sent me a blister.'[77] Incredibly, Hutton later claimed that 'so apprehensive was I of what might occur from Sir George Dibbs' well-known hasty temper that, being in uniform at the time, I arrived on the scene with my revolver concealed in my greatcoat pocket'.[78] If this was more than an embellishment, a creative effort both to discredit Dibbs and to maintain 'personal honour' by Hutton, twenty years after the event, it was certainly not evidence (as some have argued) that such 'sinister preparations' were indicative of an intention to do physical violence or mount some sort of meeting-room coup.[79]

Although the November meeting allowed an airing of differences and led to a temporary restoration of the relationship between Hutton and Dibbs, the commandant gravely underestimated the strength of the Premier's lingering hostility. Hutton wrote Buller that it was all a 'storm in a teacup, & will all blow over'. Buller replied five days later reminding Hutton of the stiff financial position of the colony and that its government could not be expected to spend much on defence under the circumstances. 'I think, therefore, you will be well advised if you should try for a year or so to be as low as possible.'[80] As sage as Buller's advice was, such a way forward was simply not in Hutton's nature. Nor, it seemed, was burying the hatchet a priority for the Premier.

From January 1894 Dibbs' policy of avoiding contact with Hutton resumed, again in spite of Hutton's repeated and constant applications, official and unofficial, to meet him. Frustrated, Hutton used his first official report, tabled in March 1894, to place all he saw deficient in the New South Wales military before parliament, including the shortage of available funds and the still unresolved issue of Spalding and Airey – again threatening that the defence of Port Jackson could not be assured without a new artillery commander and that as such Sydney's future as a naval base was uncertain.[81] For Hutton this was a further attempt to 'bring matters to a head', of forcing Dibbs' hand and to 'bring forth an expression of public approval of my reforms'.[82] The gamble failed. Dibbs was livid. He considered the report an insult, 'intended as a slap in the face', and refused to table it.[83] Worse, Dibbs was grilled on the issue and embarrassed in parliament, and the whole controversy was made public.

Hutton was subsequently instructed, through Walker, that the Premier 'cannot permit you, or any officer of your department, to embody recommendations of which he does not approve in a report to be placed before Parliament'. '[S]uch a course', Dibbs continued, 'would be fatal to the proper subordination, which he will insist on so long as he administers this office.' Specifically, Dibbs once more opposed official references that the two ageing artillery colonels were incompetent and told Hutton he would not 'allow vague charges of this character'.[84] Hutton countered with accusations to friends at the War Office and the CDC that his report was shelved 'for personal and private reasons' in that Spalding's wife was 'the 'protégé or protégée of Sir G. Dibbs' and Airey's wife 'a friend of another influential Minister'.[85] In private he went further, describing Dibbs' stubbornness on this issue as caused by 'an infatuation for an intriguing Delilah', which 'could deaden the natural acumen and generous minded instincts of our Samson and reduce him to political failure in his high office'.[86] Hutton's pre-existing distaste for politicians, which had been brought into focus in the shadow of Majuba Hill in South Africa and encouraged by similar signals and attitudes from Wolseley and his ilk, flared white hot. 'As happens in such cases of Colonial Politicians', he complained to Peacocke, 'every sort of petty obstacle and annoyance' was placed in his way 'as a result of giving my opinions and insisting upon a remedy'.[87]

From this point the relationship between Dibbs and Hutton degenerated into little more than public and private mud-slinging. Hutton grumbled to Cambridge that his 'real difficulties' lay with 'political wire-pulling'. He had 'frequently cause to exercise great forbearance in my dealings with Sir George Dibbs and the politicians of the Colony', Hutton admitted and 'I find it difficult occasionally, while being firm, to exercise the requisite tact'.[88] Hutton's continual press interviews and speeches soon led Dibbs to direct him formally to 'refrain from any public utterance on matters connected with the administration of military or other public affairs in New South Wales' and to pass his views on military issues to the Chief Secretary's office, not the papers.[89]

The degenerating situation was saved only by the July 1894 elections in New South Wales, which returned a liberal free trade government under George Reid. From the first Hutton built a better relationship with Reid, in part because the new Premier shared many of Hutton's views on the place of the colony in the Empire. Reid was no imperial federationist and rather, like Hutton, thought that the Empire ought to be united by the bonds of shared sentiment and race. The new Chief Secretary, James Nixon

Brunker, knew little and seemed to care little of military affairs and tended not to intervene. Hutton lost no time in trying to shape his new environment, writing to Reid on 27 July requesting an early meeting to discuss the artillery question and further cuts in pay appearing in the latest military estimates. There was a predictable lack of tact in Hutton's approach, telling Reid: 'I am unable to any longer accept the responsibility of the Command here unless I have the assistance of a properly qualified Commanding Officer of artillery' and that he felt 'sure that you cannot be aware of how severe have been the reductions of pay made in the case of our Staff Officers'.[90] Reid doused Hutton's fires, agreeing to personal access to Brunker and assuring him he 'might rely on all his recommendations being carried out which were not inconsistent with the policy of the government'.[91] In a subsequent interview with Brunker, Hutton persuaded his new civil master that their two appointments ought to mirror the relationship between the Commander-in-Chief and the Secretary for War in London; that is, the Principal Undersecretary, Walker, was sidelined from this point onwards as nothing but a medium of routine correspondence. Another win, it seemed, for the commandant.[92]

Yet, although both Reid and Brunker were far more careful to shepherd Hutton's considerable ego and more inclined to avoid ruffling his prickly sensibilities than their predecessors, both men were politicians and still faced the same set of practical and political constraints that had influenced Dibbs with regard to the military defence of the colony. For his part, Hutton remained blind to any consideration or set of circumstances that did not promote his personal objectives. Reid, for example, while assuring Hutton he personally agreed that Spalding and Airey had to go, knew better than to risk parliament's indignation, particularly that of its Labor members, if he recommended pensions for the two colonels, if they were retired, during a period of general retrenchment and stringency.

Nonetheless, single-mindedly, Hutton refused to let the issue go. In his 1894 report he again placed on the official record that he was unable to guarantee 'the security of Sydney as a naval base in time of war' unless he had 'the assistance of a Commanding Officer of Artillery upon whose expert knowledge I can rely'.[93] He increasingly used his imperial connections to try to coerce and manipulate his civil superiors in the colony. He privately requested Bridge, Cambridge, Wolseley, Hampden, Peacocke and his successor, Captain William Nathan at the CDC, for example, all to try to pressure government into acceding to his demands.[94] Bridge and the CDC responded with memoranda hinting at removal of the Royal Navy's base from Sydney if Hutton's recommendations (principally concerning Spalding and Airey) were not acted on.[95] In August 1895 Hutton informed Cambridge that if the government continued to refuse to act on the issue, he would be forced to resign. Cambridge warned him that such a move 'would be open to grave misinterpretation', and Hutton recalculated his options.[96] Reid, however, was not a man easily moved. The two colonels stayed. Only the fact that Brunker at least was aware of and perhaps tacitly supported Hutton's exaggeration of the threat to get his way explains the lack of friction between himself, Reid and Hutton from mid-1894 over this issue. Meanwhile, Hutton continued to simmer. He told Evelyn Wood in November 1895: 'We have few if any Statesmen, only politicians ... Our public men here follow – they do not lead ... Like John the Baptist I feel as if I was the voice of one crying in the wilderness.'[97]

For all it was intensified by Hutton's temperament and attitudes, it is important to note that the type of political friction he experienced in New South Wales was entirely consistent with a broader pattern of difficulties experienced by commandants in similar positions throughout the Empire, each largely the result of ill-defined roles, powers and prerogatives of the commandants relative to their civil authorities. There was little in British army traditions or experiences to prepare such officers for colonial service, or the types of colonial political environments and values to be found there. The technical and constitutional facts of self-government and the local sentiments they encouraged remained a mystery to most. For almost two years in the 1880s, for example, a running battle between Colonel Thomas Robert Disney (commandant) and Frederick Sargood (Minister for Defence) in Victoria over their respective duties and responsibilities had raged. Like Hutton, Disney expected a free hand to reform and complete control over all aspects of military. His attitude meshed poorly with colonial political constitutional viewpoints concerning the subordination of his position to parliament, as well as their responsiveness to financial circumstances and public opinion. Disney lost the argument.[98]

Such problems were mirrored in Queensland when Major-General John Fletcher Owen ran into difficulty with the press and parliament trying to disband a volunteer unit commanded by a parliamentarian and lawyer, Andrew Joseph Thynne. In the process Owen tried unsuccessfully to assert that the government ought not to interfere with military discipline. Owen also faced a lack of funds and equipment of all kinds, and a minister with little interest in defence aside from reducing the budget, and complications encouraged by his abrasive personality. Only the end of his tenure in 1894 saved the situation.[99] Across the Tasman the situation was worse. By 1894 the disagreements between Captain Francis John Fox, commandant in New

Zealand, and his minister, Richard Seddon, had in Buller's words 'reduced the military question in New Zealand to an impasse'.[100] Again the issue was about relative power. Like Hutton, Fox thought his position was to some degree 'independent', showed no consideration of local political pressures and was not averse to trying to force ministers' hands. The whole debacle became public, strained imperial relations and did nothing for military effectiveness in the colony. Meade was scathing: '[H]e [Fox] begins by putting a pistol at the Minister's head and dictating to him in an absurd manner.'[101] Hutton's complaint to London of 'a system of log-rolling and political wire-pulling which most effectually prevents any real military efficiency' was part of a much wider chorus.[102]

It was a tune, too, that never stopped sounding from England. In many ways political friction and the resentment of political interference in military affairs in the colonies was a reflection of the attitudes held by senior British officers at home. Such a stance was itself innately political and represented a growing involvement by British officers in politics.[103] Throughout his entire tenure as Commander-in-Chief Cambridge, for example, was openly uncooperative with politicians and actively sought to block or circumvent ministerial directions when he did not agree with them. So too, contrary to notions that increasing professionalism decreased the likelihood of political involvement by soldiers, late-Victorian reformers such as Wolseley, Roberts and later Kitchener very much accepted and embraced a political and policy-shaping role. After replacing Cambridge as Commander-in-Chief on 1 November 1885 Wolseley privately and later publicly railed against ceding any level of control to civilians in the War Office. On the political front, by the 1890s Wolseley had reversed his overt support for the Liberals in the wake of the Home Rule Bill, fearing it would break up the Empire. He vigorously supported some government policies and denounced others, and grew increasingly critical of any politician's ability to implement necessary military reform. Wolseley deplored to his inner circle the 'baleful effects of party considerations upon contemporary politics' and was convinced that politicians needed to be forced into action by public opinion and the threat of election defeat.[104] None of this was lost on Hutton. The growing sense of professionalism of such men at once made them resent political encroachment on what they considered their domain while at the same time providing the self-appointed justification to strain the boundaries of civil–military relationships.[105]

The issue was not limited to the most senior military echelons in Britain. The British Army's officer corps as a whole in this period was in many ways 'morally committed to preserving the army from political influence'.[106]

Throughout the 1880s and 1890s, the Horse Guards demanded that civilians be excluded from many of their internal meetings. This agenda was behind Cambridge's efforts to preserve the role of the monarchy in military affairs. He lectured to British officers in the colonies to get rid of such interference – one of the few issues on which he and Wolseley agreed. In fact it is not too much to suggest that a general dislike for democratic processes and party politics was widespread in late-Victorian elites more generally. Certainly many imperial governors, for example, often resented parliamentary 'interference' in the belief that real weighty issues ought to be above the petty compromises of party politics. Civilian military reform advocates like Dilke ran similar arguments. In February 1894, for example, Dilke helped to write a letter to Gladstone, Balfour, Salisbury and Chamberlain emphasising the view that imperial defence ought to transcend party politics.[107] It was of little surprise that such attitudes were reflected at the periphery. Although Dibbs and Hutton could not see it, their problems were but one echo among many.

In line with the wider patterns of imperial relations of the era, as much as the frictions between Hutton and Dibbs in New South Wales were set within a common, Empire-wide context, they were also stimulated by local and even personal issues. Hutton's frustrations were derived from an expectation that the role of Commander-in-Chief and its relationship with politicians that Wolseley and other officers strove for in Britain was, or ought to be, replicated in the colonies. In his mind parliament should vote adequate funds and then leave military matters to military officers. The efficiency of the force (camps) and appointments (the colonels) were his responsibility. This frustration encouraged, again on Wolseley's model, use of the press to manipulate opinion in order to force political action. But in colonies the government's view was invariably that the commandant was a public servant and therefore subordinate. Colonial politicians were especially sensitive to public rebuke that affected their chances of political survival. This outlook itself offended Hutton's sense of professionalism and ideas about his rightful status as a British officer.

Added to such a mix was the clash of the professional with the amateur volunteer (as Dibbs was also an officer in Newcastle Artillery Corps) and, further, the fact Hutton operated in an environment where many parliamentarian citizen soldiers had themselves inherited, like the movement they represented, the British militia tradition of viewing itself as protectors of parliament over regal authority. In as much as Hutton symbolised the Crown, it was their duty to check him.[108] Career and class issues were no doubt present as well. In the first instance Hutton well knew that his career depended on success in the colony and pleasing his patrons at home. He had every incentive to care little for his constitutional position, ill-defined as it was by legislation. In the second, Dibbs was a merchant sailor and in Hutton's eyes – with all the insecurity of one on the edge of his own social circles – his social inferior.[109] Last, the simple issue of personality was never too far from the surface. In Reid's words, 'the trouble with Major-General Hutton arose between a highly irascible gentleman in the person of the ex-Premier and a highly independent gentleman at the head of the forces'.[110]

Photo 6 Sir George Dibbs in carpenter's attire, c. 1900. The relationship between Dibbs and Hutton was not helped by issues of class and Hutton's feeling that the Premier was his social inferior. (State Library of New South Wales, P1 2071)

One key outcome of his disagreements with Dibbs was that Hutton believed, for rest of his life, that the public controversy surrounding them was the cause of Dibbs' election defeat. This was a gross and wild exaggeration of his personal role in a political loss that owed much more to financial difficulties in the colony than to any issue connected with defence. It also 'inflated Hutton's estimation of his own political skills' and reinforced in him the dangerous notion that by manipulating public opinion via the press and by skating on the edges of his constitutional position he could get his way.[111] Although similar tactics by Fox in New Zealand ended his career, for Hutton they encouraged more of the same in future postings.

Yet, despite his difficulties with his political masters, Hutton managed to accomplish much for the good of the colonial military force from 1893 to 1896 – the first objective given to him by Meade. His energetic inspections, public addresses, military lectures, reviews and advocacy of rifle clubs revived the flagging spirit of the forces and raised their public profile considerably. His reform of the colony's headquarters staff was a welcome improvement. So too the creation of administrative support units for its fighting corps – a lesson learned in Zululand and never forgotten. By January 1896 Hutton's Mounted Brigade, with a peacetime footing of close to a thousand troops, for example, boasted Maxim guns in 'galloping carriages', a mounted section of engineers for field telegraphs and a mounted Bearer Company.[112] By August 1895 Hutton was satisfied that, aside from the artillery dilemma, the force was 'fairly complete as a Military factor', with a fair proportion of all arms and a 'due proportion of the Departments necessary for an Army however small'.[113] He also instituted a number of long-overdue technical improvements. Electric lights were placed in forts, for example, and telephone lines laid between them in Port Jackson.

Moreover, there is no question that under Hutton's command the overall military knowledge and proficiency of the New South Wales force rose considerably. He made military training realistic and useful at a time when, in Britain, officers even at Aldershot still hunted for five to six days a week in winter, artillerymen still deployed in lines with no consideration of cover and where as late as 1899 some battalions were still practising close-order battlefield manoeuvre 'with a final assault launched with "the battalion formed up in a line, dressed by the right within 200 yards of the enemy and then walked forward cheering"'.[114] All this was achieved in a period of acute economic depression, which removed any real political interest in military affairs other than reducing the defence budget. From the dark depths of Tulloch's 1892 report, by 1896 New South Wales was in many ways 'a model of military organisation to be emulated'.[115] An officer who had served under him in New South Wales in the 1890s, Major-General James Macarthur-Onslow, later argued that Hutton brought to the colony

> not only sound and proved professional qualifications, but also enthusiasm, untiring industry and an inspiring personality. Often misunderstood (and therefore opposed and resented) he not only reorganised, but revivified, even electrified, the NSW Military Service ... Never sparing himself the performance of duty, he expected the same of his subordinates. To incompetence and negligence he was most stern. Good service he never forgot and those who gave him that found him the most loyal of commanders. Of his soldierly qualities and power of command none could doubt.[116]

Yet Hutton's eyes had always looked beyond New South Wales. In a speech to Sydney Church of England Grammar School December 1894, drawing on his own worldview, he told the students that the Empire was their inheritance but that they would 'need to maintain that birthright', as 'Australian natives and British citizens'. He urged them to take 'to themselves the line that duty dictated and then, cost what it might, carry out that line'.[117] This Hutton did with characteristically single-minded determination, especially with regard to Meade's other two objectives in New South Wales: his proposed federal and imperial enterprises.

CHAPTER 4

A 'TROJAN HORSE' IN THE COLONY?

FEDERAL AND IMPERIAL DEFENCE IN AUSTRALIA, 1893–96

From his earliest meetings with Howard Vincent in January 1893 to his discussions with Robert Meade in March and his close study of George Sydenham Clarke's papers on the voyage to Melbourne, Hutton busied himself considering exactly how he might initiate a federal defence scheme or system for Australia. Success in this regard would make a mark and his reputation. He was therefore, in his own words, 'determined to risk all in my efforts ... to bring about [such] a scheme'.[1] It was an ambitious objective. Much stood in Hutton's way. The issue of a federal defence plan for the Australian colonies had been under discussion from the time of the Carnarvon Commission, but little had eventuated. By 1893, in addition to political inertia, colonial parochialism and lack of funds that had long acted to stifle such an initiative, the apparent closeness of political union encouraged opposition to interim defence measures. So too the fundamental question of who or what would control a federal military force in the absence of political union had never been adequately addressed. The idea of a British federal military commander, as suggested by Bevan Edwards, was out of the question. Nor, without executive authority (or even representation from New South Wales), could it be the Federal Council. Indeed, Sir Henry Parkes, for one, believed that the establishment of a federal defence system would take more effort to effect than political Federation itself.[2] Once set on a course, however, as he had already and amply demonstrated, Hutton possessed an ability to ignore any and all realities that suggested otherwise. His efforts to use his time in New South Wales to achieve this federal purpose, and perhaps even leverage success in this regard towards imperial ends, was no different.

Hutton's immediate reform agenda for the New South Wales forces and his mounting friction with Dibbs did not allow him to press the federal issue in the initial period of his command, although developing an effective military system in the colony that could serve as a federal model was an important early step. From very beginning, however, Hutton hinted at a federal defence system in his interviews with the press. By September 1893 he was actively describing his efforts in New South Wales as a 'means to bring about a General Federation for Defence among the Australian colonies'.[3] That is, his plan for the colony was to be effected 'in such a manner as to prove a model to the other remaining States . . . to facilitate its further development later into complete federation'.[4] In the period of August and September, while Dibbs refused to meet him, Hutton worked out a formal federal military system involving a version of his New South Wales scheme writ large. This plan again involved a 'Field Force' for active defence and 'Garrison Troops' for the passive defence of key areas.[5] In fact, Hutton later boasted that his 'movable column' in New South Wales had been created in the first place with a federal objective in mind.[6] Under his federal plan the field forces of the six states would be considered available 'for the co-operative defence of the whole'.[7] Little could be done without Dibbs' support, however, and Hutton was forced to wait until the temporary thaw in relations between the two in late 1893 to make his pitch. Dibbs, surprisingly, seemed interested and in early January 1894 instructed Hutton to draw up his federal defence plan by way of a memorandum to be sent to the other colonial premiers.[8] It was all the encouragement Hutton needed. He wrote excitedly to Buller of his intention to use his reforms in New South Wales 'to form the basis of a Federation for Defence' for the 'whole of the Australian Colonies'.[9] Buller replied that 'your ideas for military federation for defence seem perfectly sound' and again, in vain, advised Hutton to watch the tone of his language with the Australian politicians.[10]

Hutton began by seeking the views of his fellow commandants. An early rebuff from Fox ruled out any thought of including New Zealand troops in his scheme, but the Australians appeared enthusiastic. Major-General Owen in Queensland suggested a conference to discuss the issue. Next, true to form, Hutton began to sound out public opinion and on 24 January 1894 took the opportunity during a military inspection at Bathurst to give a speech outlining his proposed federal system, including a single defence policy for the six colonies, common defence legislation, a common organisation of their forces while preserving their identity, a federal regiment of artillery and a 'Council of Australian Federal Defence'. The speech received significant press attention in all the colonies. Dibbs was not the only one to be unimpressed with Hutton's public approach. Parkes wrote to Hutton with 'some concern', reminding him that 'the ground taken up is very old ground with us, which has been examined time and time and virtually abandoned'.[11] Parkes again argued that there could be no federal defence plan without a federal government as no other authority could control it and that he would oppose Hutton's plans. Hutton disingenuously replied that he had hoped only 'from a soldier's standpoint' to describe the 'lines upon which I make bold to hope an ultimate Federation for Defence may be evolved', when 'statesmen like yourself considered the moment had arrived'. Yet he went on to suggest that a federal defence system might persuade Australians of the practicality and possibility of political union and that 'the greater question of Federation generally might be brought forward' under the leadership of New South Wales.[12]

Hutton's flattery, however, was clumsy, and Parkes was no fool. 'It is curious how you insist upon misapprehending me', wrote Parkes, who was all in favour of a federal military force but, he reiterated, 'as I have pointed out a hundred times ... this can only be done by the Australian colonies uniting under one federal government'. In the end Hutton withdrew from the confrontation. 'I hope that you will regard my humble attempts to aid the good cause as those of the soldier and not of the statesman', he again pandered with false humility. 'I have some knowledge of the former, but little if any of those with the latter.'[13] In private, unable to understand why Parkes might stand against a system that, if successful, would rob the Federation movement of one of its key platforms, Hutton mocked Parkes' position as 'characteristic of his old age' and that any delay to the implementation of his scheme must be 'the height of imbecility'.[14]

At the end of January 1894, Hutton submitted his controversial 1893 Annual Report and left for a holiday in Tasmania, during which time he completed the details of his federal scheme and continued his press campaign, telling the Hobart *Mercury* he was 'strongly impressed with the importance of federation for defence as being the most effective and by far the cheapest arrangement to ensure adequate military protection for Australia', as well as a 'preliminary step to the greater federation for general purposes'.[15] By this stage, even before he learned of Dibbs' reaction to his 1893 report, Hutton was worried about colonial political opposition to his plans. He wrote to Cambridge: 'Politics in these Colonies is too fickle and uncertain a factor to be sure of any given end.' 'Sir Henry Parkes is now too old and lost much of the public confidence', he continued, while 'Dibbs is at once too big and too small. His larger, broader views being warped by want of grasp and by his local prejudices.'[16] Hutton returned Sydney on 18 February to find his concerns were well warranted. Dibbs had changed his mind and abandoned the federal defence idea.

Hutton had no idea of the complex political manoeuvrings that had first inclined Dibbs to support his scheme, then to abandon it. Characteristically placing himself at the centre of the issue, he simplistically believed his constant insistence on the immediate retirement of the two artillery colonels was the beginning and end of Dibbs' reversal. Hutton had no idea that Edmund Barton had joined Dibbs' ministry in October 1891 as Attorney-General on the condition that Dibbs further the federal cause, which had ground to a halt after the 1891 Federal Convention. A federal defence initiative was an easy opportunity for Dibbs to satisfy Barton. Barton, however, resigned in December 1893, leaving Dibbs to follow a slower evolutionary approach towards federal union. He no longer needed Hutton's federal defence scheme.[17] A lack of real interest in the idea from the other premiers also swayed Dibbs' hand. Despite his feigned enthusiasm to Hutton, Owen advised the Queensland government that the problem of federal control suggested against the possibility of a federal military scheme, and the Queensland Premier sent the message back to Dibbs.[18] The Victorian and South Australian governments were also lukewarm about the idea due to perceived practical difficulties. The federal scheme, like Hutton's annual report, was pigeon-holed.

By March 1894 Hutton was despondent. He told Buller that his federal scheme was completed but, given Dibbs' attitude, he was 'not sanguine' of 'achieving anything at present'. The Premier had 'never moved the point with me since he asked me to draft the scheme in January'.[19] Hutton would not, however, be deterred. He soon set himself to move 'full steam ahead', 'with or without the Government at my back'. As a guest at a Victorian military camp, Hutton made speeches about a federal military system, which were well received by Sargood and the Victorian Premier, Sir James Patterson. He preached the same message to Queensland officers during a visit to Brisbane in June, and again he felt the message was well received.[20]

Hutton returned to Sydney in early July with an election imminent. George Reid's subsequent victory at the polls was a turning point for Hutton's federal plans. 'So far, so good!' he told Cambridge in late

August. 'Sir George Dibbs has passed into the cold shades of opposition' and his federal scheme 'may now see the light'.[21] Subsequently, on 12 October, Reid asked Hutton for the details of his scheme. Hutton complied three days later, with the addition of a proposal for a conference of commandants as soon as could be arranged. He was quite surprised when Reid 'suddenly' agreed not only to support the idea of federal defence but also to hold such a conference as soon as could be arranged. Invitations to other colonies were soon accepted. In addition to Hutton, the delegates included Tulloch from Victoria as President, Colonel Joseph Maria Gordon from South Australia, Colonel Edward Robert Drury from Queensland and Captain Arthur Parker from Tasmania. An agenda was prepared by Hutton and submitted to the New South Wales Government, along with the scheme he had prepared for Dibbs.[22]

Yet Hutton was just as mistaken in his assumptions about Reid as about Dibbs. Reid was elected on a federal platform, despite his questionable personal commitment to federal union. He was therefore expected to take

Photo 7 George Houstoun Reid, Premier of New South Wales, 3 August 1894 – 13 September 1899. (National Archives of Australia, A1200, L11178 B)

a lead on the Federation question, which, through the influence of Barton and others, was once again growing into a pressing political issue. A federal defence system was a convenient way to help Reid present himself as the leader of a restarted federal movement, but it was only a minor and relatively unimportant part of a wider agenda. Hutton never understood the true context of Reid's apparent support for his federal scheme. What was for Hutton of central importance was for Reid a means to an end.[23]

The subsequent intercolonial military conference convened in Sydney on 24–26 October 1894. Hutton presented his scheme, based on the New South Wales model, and overall, with some minor changes, his basic plan was carried unanimously. The specific allotment of troops from each state was agreed, as was the need for some form of federal legislation. The Queensland Militia Act, which included compulsion in war, was chosen as a model in this regard, and it was decided that Hutton should draft it. The only real sticking point at the conference was, predictably, over the issue of control. Hutton proposed a 'Council', composed of delegates from all the colonies, to be set up at short notice in an emergency. It would appoint a Military Head, who, in conjunction with the British naval commander-in-chief of the Australia Station, would be responsible for the defence of Australia. Tulloch argued that it should exist in peacetime as well. Hutton, however, prevailed. The commandants knew the limitations of their decisions, in view of the lack of their executive power, and therefore called for an inter-colonial ministerial conference to settle the issue of what form the council would take and to consider the need for a common Defence Act. It was a substantial achievement for Hutton. His federal scheme, mirroring his system in New South Wales, was now an official intercolonial endeavour.[24] He was pleased at the result, praised the 'energy and political vigour of the Reid Ministry' and reported his 'success' back to the War Office and CDC.[25]

Hutton continued to tie the 'greater good' of his federal scheme tightly to his own career prospects. His need to control the process spoke both to his personality and to his determination to reap the credit for it. By November 1894, for example, he worried about the appointment of Major-General Sir Charles Holled Smith to command in Victoria, replacing Tulloch. Hutton feared that Smith's appointment, given he was senior to Hutton, would place Victoria (and another officer) at the head of the federal defence initiative. He sought to discredit Smith, writing to Buller: 'He never impressed with the idea of being an administrator, or of being able to head a measure such as the present.'[26] Lieutenant-General Sir Reginald Ramsay Gipps, Principal Secretary to Cambridge, wrote back telling Hutton to calm down and that Smith's seniority as a colonel did not place him above Hutton.[27] Hutton later attempted a similar hatchet job on Tulloch who, back in England, began to criticise his federal scheme, which had been sent to the War Office by Reid, on the grounds that Hutton had excluded the minutes of the 1894 conference that showed Tulloch's objections to a number of the 'agreements' made. Tulloch made the mistake of listing his grievances with Hutton before he sailed in November 1894. 'I am afraid I shall enter an official protest wi.[th] re.[gard] the last lot of papers you sent', complained Tulloch, 'It looks as if I agreed to them. The contrary is the case ... I will stick my pen into you as greatly as if you were being vaccinated.'[28] Concerned that back in England Tulloch might personally represent at the War Office 'the objections which he had reviewed in his letter to me' and thereby take the shine of his perceived 'success', Hutton pre-empted him and wrote directly to Buller, the Adjutant-General, enclosing Tulloch's letter.[29] When he arrived in England Tulloch realised that the proceedings of the conference had beaten him by a fortnight. He was interviewed by Buller, but Hutton's letter had also arrived first. Tulloch received no personal acknowledgement of his involvement in the federal defence conference.

Meanwhile, back in the colony, Hutton was encouraged on 12 November 1894 when Reid called for a Premiers' Conference in Hobart to discuss 'questions of federal union, intercolonial free trade, federal defence and other subjects'.[30] The real motivation for Reid was not Hutton's federal defence plan at all but, again, mounting pressure on him to take a leadership role on the issue of federal union from the Federation League and his fellow premiers (and to deflect Parkes' criticisms in this regard). Yet federal defence was on the agenda, and that was enough for Hutton to conclude that it was central to the forthcoming discussions and that Reid was somehow acting to satisfy his agitation in this direction.[31] The Premier did ask Hutton to prepare the defence discussion points for the meeting, and Hutton set about preparing a submission, including a draft 'federal defence agreement', which would provide a legislative framework and details for the federal defence council. He used this as a substitute for a draft 'Bill' the commandants had agreed he should prepare. Hutton also, rather deviously, bound the draft 'agreement' with the report of the 1894 Conference 'effectively blurring the distinction between what had been accepted by the commandants and what was purely his own work'.[32] These papers were printed and considered by Reid's Cabinet before being sent on to the other colonial premiers.

Smug in his misunderstanding of the real nature of the Premiers' Conference, Hutton expressed his hopes to the War Office that 'some result may follow, even if the whole scheme is not accepted'.[33] On the way to the conference the premiers gathered in Melbourne on 25 January where Hutton, on leave, chose to join them in order to provide advice on his federal scheme when required. Unsurprisingly, he was not needed. Informal discussion on the steamer to Hobart between the premiers settled this comparatively insignificant item of business by accepting the scheme in principle, but refraining from any suggestion of its official adoption. Reid and the other delegates had much bigger fish to fry. Hutton consoled himself with the comfortable but doubtful contention that his federal defence plan was helping bring about Federation and that the scheme itself, its associated draft Federal Defence Agreement and even a draft agreement on the powers of a future Council of Australian Federal Defence, remained available in case of an emergency.[34] He was happy, for the moment, with Cambridge's 'warm commendations'.[35]

Hutton's single-minded obsession once more led to underhanded methods that instigated a significant challenge from an unexpected quarter. In May 1895 Rear Admiral Cyprian Bridge, now in command of the Australia Station, wrote to the Governor, Lord Hampden, noting he agreed 'heartily' with general principles laid down in Hutton's federal scheme but, in the draft agreements outlining the duties and responsibilities of the proposed Federal Council of Defence, he saw an attempt to 'define the responsibilities of the Admiral in command of the Squadron on the Station'. To this he gave 'strongest opposition'. Worse, Bridge resented the fact that it 'has been retained in the present reprint despite my known inability to accept it' and that it had been sent to London without his knowledge, 'an unusual and serious departure from the well-understood and universally accepted Conventions of official procedure'.[36] Hutton was caught out by a man he had earlier described as his 'stout and outspoken co-adjuter'.[37] Bridge had attended the 1895 Premiers' Conference and pointed out to Hutton his concerns, but Hutton had chosen not to amend the offending clauses. He had in fact included a minute in the papers sent to London in April with an assurance that Bridge had agreed with the scheme and accepted the principles therein. Bridge forwarded further complaints to the New South Wales Government and the Colonial Office.[38]

Exposed, Hutton sought to flatter his way out of trouble. He wrote to Bridge in early May 1895 apologising profusely that his plans had been 'construed into a disregard of your wishes'. 'I do hasten to assure you', he added, 'I cannot hope to have the knowledge or experience of the necessities of Imperial Defence policy which you are bringing to bear on Australian Defence and I trust that you will excuse me, if in my zealous endeavours to compass what is of such vital consequences to the Military Forces of Australia, I make occasional mistakes.'[39] He followed it with a very different letter to Reid outlining a mere 'misapprehension on the Admiral's part'.[40] The net result of the incident was that the Admiralty became resistant to the scheme, and the CDC certainly withheld its approval. By April, whether Hutton admitted it or not, his federal initiative had stalled.

Yet Hutton continued to try to keep the federal defence idea alive, while working on the fine detail of his scheme. In his words, 'no opportunity was lost by public speeches and by military displays, of keeping the matter before the public'.[41] Nor was Hutton averse to exploiting colonial security fears to this end. He had written to Buller in October 1894: 'These Colonies are curiously subject to panic and if we should have even a symptom of war scare we soldiers will boon.'[42] In late March 1895 the Sino-Japanese War gave Hutton the chance to urge Reid to send to other colonies a formal proposal for 'the immediate adoption of the Federal Military Scheme by Co-operation without delay', pointing to 'the rise of Japan as a Military and Naval power ... and an imminent danger to Australia'.[43] Reid did not do so but instead forwarded another circular letter to the premiers with Hutton's minute enclosed. Reid added that he thought it 'expedient if possible to mature plans for federal action in case of any National Emergency arising' and suggested another Premiers' Conference.[44] Hutton admitted to Cambridge three weeks later that the war had 'given me the pretext for again urging upon the Government of New South Wales the necessity of taking some immediate measures to bring about Australian Federal Defence', greatly exaggerating the actual effect of his lobbying. Reid's latest call, however, was not supported by the other colonial governments or Hutton's fellow commandants, who were increasingly convinced that the federal scheme needed to wait for Federation. The subsequent impasse encouraged Hutton in mid-1895 to decline an offer from Reid to extend his three-year term. The CDC urged him to reconsider, but Hutton was thinking of the future. He told Cambridge he saw no chance of advancing the federal defence initiative further and that most of the difficult military reorganisations in New South Wales had been completed.[45] He explained more candidly to Meade in May the following year, however, that had he accepted the extension it would have precluded him returning to Australia as head of its federal forces when Federation eventually took place.[46] The loss of his younger half-brother, Captain Frederick Lawrence, killed on active service in East Africa in October, cemented Hutton's desire to return to England as soon as he could. 'It has been a great blow to me', he told Evelyn Wood, 'and I am now doubly anxious to reach home and settle his affairs.'[47]

If the federal defence question was kept alive – barely – by Hutton's manoeuvrings in the first half of 1895, it was given new life by the key appointment of Joseph Chamberlain as Colonial Secretary on 1 July 1895. An ardent imperialist, Chamberlain declined the Exchequer, unwilling to be constrained by conservative spending plans, and also refused the office of Home Secretary. Instead, he secured the lesser political post of Colonial Secretary with a self-appointed project of increasing imperial unity, a unity he considered essential if Britain was to remain a great power. Before Chamberlain's appointment an imperial political federation, preferential tariffs laws and functional system of imperial defence had all been proposed, but little had been done. Chamberlain, however, brought enormous energy and personal drive to the task of turning such discussions into reality. As they shared many common imperial outlooks, non-aristocratic origins and professional attitudes, it was not long before Hutton was drawn towards Chamberlain's vision for the Empire.

Meanwhile, Hutton had been formally informed by the CDC of its decision not to endorse the federal scheme until all the colonies had approved it. In reply, Hutton complained that it would take the CDC to endorse the plan to shake the colonies out of their apathy.[48] It is likely that such discussions caught Chamberlain's eye. At his suggestion the CDC considered the scheme again November 1895 and gave its general approval, excepting the clause that placed the Admiral of the Australia Squadron on its governing council. In an illustrative twist, the CDC recommended that a Military Head replace Hutton's proposed council to avoid the potential conduct of war by committee.[49] The military wisdom of this suggestion was clear. Yet it revealed the depths of CDC ignorance with regards colonial realities. Hutton was appalled. He knew full well that such a position would need to be filled by an imperial officer and that 'the public feeling in Australia would never allow such an Officer control of its Defence Policy'. 'Such a course', he continued, 'has never, so far [as] my knowledge goes, been sanctioned by any Self-Governing Community.'[50] To try to impose this he knew would destroy what remained of his scheme.[51] Yet CDC could not grasp the problem. It was a pattern set to continue.

Under Chamberlain's watchful eye, the generally positive CDC remarks on Hutton's federal scheme were provisionally approved by the War

Office and Admiralty before being returned to the colonies in late November 1895.[52] As part of its report, the CDC suggested that a second commandants' conference be held to negotiate a number of points of finer detail. Reid responded in early January 1896 with an offer of such a conference later in the month, to be followed by another Premiers' Conference in February. In order to encourage his fellow premiers, by now even more unenthusiastic about federal defence initiatives outside the wider ambit of political Federation, Reid gave the commandants the prosaic purpose of 'reporting on the best pattern of modern Magazine Rifle to be adopted as the universal small arm for the Australian Troops'.[53] Federal defence was to be on the agenda, including the difficult issues of the Draft Federal Agreement, powers of Council for Defence and the CDC's suggestions, but Hutton was not optimistic. He told Captain Matthew Nathan, Secretary of the CDC, that if nothing else the conference would keep the issue from being forgotten.[54]

Never one to doubt himself for long, however, and on the basis of no obvious evidence, within weeks Hutton had convinced himself that real progress on the federal defence initiative was once again possible and that Reid had promised to 'launch the Federal Ship before my departure!!'[55] He threw his energies into the latest conference, which sat in Sydney on 29–20 January. Here, representatives from Victoria, Queensland and South Australia joined Hutton and formally reaffirmed the 1894 proposals for the employment of the forces of every colony in the joint defence of Australia under the control of a Council of Defence, with only minor amendments. With this endorsement, Hutton looked forward to both his scheme and the Federal Military Agreement being adopted at the forthcoming conference of premiers foreshadowed by Reid, with perhaps his council formed to launch it afterwards. He reported as much to Buller in mid-February and thanked Major-General Robert Grant, President of the CDC, for the views of his committee, which had 'shown to all concerned that the expert opinion at home endorsed the proposals framed here'. He exclaimed to Nathan it was all more than he had hoped 'even in my most sanguine moments'.[56]

In contrast to the messages he sent back to Britain, however, real progress was an illusion of Hutton's own making. Any lingering potential for a federal defence scheme was being overwhelmed by the larger issue of Federation. It was difficult, for example, for Reid even to convene a Premiers' Conference for February 1896 with federal defence as a central issue. A number of colonial politicians, by now wary of Reid's real commitment to Federation, asked why he wished to discuss defence when the focus might have been on electing delegates to the constituent conference, a key step towards Federation. Nonetheless, the conference convened on 2 March, without the Queensland or Victorian premiers, and Hutton's scheme shared the agenda with a range of other items. Hutton delayed his departure from Australia in order, once more, to be on hand if his advice was required. Again, he was not needed. Reid proposed that Hutton's federal plan be accepted, but the delegates complained of its cost and agreed instead to simply adjust their various Defence Acts to allow forces to serve in any colony and to standardise equipment and conditions of service where possible. Even then, these were mere expressions of opinion, not executive decisions. The overwhelming feeling was that Federation was necessary before a federal force could be seriously considered.[57] The conference concluded, and Hutton's scheme was sidelined. He prepared to leave not only the conference but also the colony.

Thousands lined up at Redfern railway station platform at 5.15pm, 5 March 1896, to farewell Hutton and his wife. Those who wished him well included a 200-man guard of honour, Sir Frederick Darley (the Chief Justice and Lieutenant-Governor of the colony), Brunker, Critchett Walker, a range of civil figures and most of the senior officers of the New South Wales forces. As the train pulled away a thirteen-gun salute sounded and the crowd sang 'Auld Land Syne'. It was a touching conclusion to a problematic final few months for Hutton. The scheme proposed for a federal defence system in Australia was in abeyance with no prospects for further development without some type of emergency to drive it forward. Moreover, Hutton had never satisfactorily addressed the problem of control. In truth, the scheme was never close enough to reality to bring to a head the colonial rivalries that would likely have ruled out any agreement about his proposed council. Rather, after Hutton departed the colonies acted pragmatically, reorganising their forces along common lines and obliging them to cooperate in times of war to defend Australia, all without a truly federal system.[58]

Hutton had never grasped the true place of the issue of defence within the federal movement. He misunderstood and exaggerated its importance, which distorted and inflated his opinion of the significance and influence of his scheme. He was puzzled, for example, that in Reid's autobiography, published in 1917, that only twenty-seven out of 381 pages were devoted to the period of Hutton's command, with no references at all to his defence policy.[59] Hutton failed to grasp that what was the centre of the universe for him was not for those around him. The whole question of a federal scheme, always overshadowed by political Federation, was in the end smothered by it. This was especially true for the smaller colonies in that they feared paying for a force of more benefit to Victoria and New South Wales than to themselves; better to wait for a federal political union.[60] Nor did Hutton have any insight into the politics of Federation as they affected his plans. Reid's encouragement, for example, was for political mileage, not for the purposes of federal defence or, necessarily, Federation. In his ignorance Hutton took all at face value. This is why he mused, years later: 'For some reason – with which I am not acquainted – Sir George Reid did not press the Federal Movement after the Second Military Conference in February 1896.'[61]

The natural conclusion for Hutton, with an ingrained tendency for self-aggrandisement, was that his scheme, even if it failed to result in a federal system, nonetheless helped bring about political union in Australia. He was convinced, after his departure, that 'it was due to the Defence system and the manner in which the defence of Australia was presented to the Australian public, that the first practical commencement of a Federal of Commonwealth system had been brought upon the arena or practical politics'.[62] In 1911, speaking at the Royal Society of Arts, he congratulated himself 'in playing some small part in the establishment of the Commonwealth' in that 'preliminary arrangements, based on the Federal Defence of Australia, were carried through with that object in view'.[63] Twenty years later Barton was still trying to persuade him otherwise. 'That indissoluble union was not attained', wrote Barton, 'by any scheme of Defence, however perfect, but by voice of the people, who most of them knew little or nothing of any such scheme.' Barton agreed that many were perfectly happy to be defended upon a scheme hatched in New South Wales, but 'it did not follow as to any one of them that he was a Federalist; some of them were and some hated the thought and the name'. Of Reid's role Barton counselled: 'Believe me, who know; there never was a greater mistake than to suppose that support given by Sir George Reid to any measure, military or other, was given out of a desire for Federation.'[64]

Yet Hutton remained convinced of the role he ascribed for his federal military scheme in relation to Federation for the rest of his life. Fortunately for him his military masters in London were equally ignorant of what had actually been achieved. The War Office thus praised his scheme as 'a solid basis for future use', especially in that 'its importance has been accentuated a hundred-fold by the rise of Japan into a first rate Power by land and sea'.[65] After Hutton had departed the colony the CDC referred to the 'happy results of the Federal Military Conferences of 1894 and 1896'.[66] Hutton therefore returned a hero to himself and his patrons, quite independent of the material results obtained. His inflated opinions of his successes and his negative opinion of colonial politicians were subsequently reinforced by letters from his former colonial subordinates. Captain (and future major-general) James Gordon Legge, for example, assured him: 'There are so many of us here who wish the "old general", as they call you, were back again.'[67] Colonel Henry Beauchamp Lassetter was another who assured Hutton that after he left that '[p]olitical intrigue was rampant and [Major-General] [George Arthur] French [Hutton's successor] became a tool in the hands of Parliament'.[68] The messages stayed with him.

The federal issue to one side, the wider question of defending the Empire was always at play throughout Hutton's tenure in the colony. To one set of authors, the relationship between Hutton's tenure in New South Wales and imperial defence is straightforward. The commandant was a single-minded imperial agent, a 'Trojan horse' planted by Britain in the colony.[69] The issue of local defence was never his true purpose. Rather, the real interest was 'in establishing an Australian force for an expeditionary role', either to enable Australian forces to seize New Caledonia, New Hebrides or New Guinea in a war with European power, or for more general imperial purposes.[70] Hutton's overriding aim then was to create a situation whereby the colonies would 'provide troops for service abroad under British command', somehow independent of Australian interests.[71] Hutton's reforms of the colonial forces, along British patterns, were therefore solely for the purpose of '"Imperialising" the troops for service abroad'.[72] Hutton's interest in Australian political Federation, like Meade's, was promoted by the wish 'to implicate the Australian colonies in imperial defence strategies' as a national force 'could be more easily deployed on overseas operations than six separate forces'.[73] The British desire 'to secure intra-Imperial defence co-operation' was therefore the driving force behind attempts to federalise Australian defence during the 1890s.[74] The promotion of this idea *before* political union was achieved was simply a consequence of impatience. Hutton's presence in the colony was, from first to last, part of a plan 'to achieve their imperial objective'.[75] The colonial government, such arguments go, 'would have been aghast had they known the full facts of his appointment'.[76]

A necessary assumption behind this imperial conspiracy theory is a familiar, yet flawed conception of a nationalism/imperialism divide. Under this model those wary of Hutton's federal scheme were worried about British command of it, or its use outside the colony, as affront to the 'raw nerve of Australian nationalism' and it was this supposed nationalism that meant Britain's (and Hutton's) true intentions could not be publicised.[77] British manipulation and manoeuvring were by necessity covert. Following this formula one step further, Hutton's political problems were derived from the fact that his imperial scheming, directed from London, gave him an 'arrogant disregard for the practice of self-government' and ran counter to the objectives of colonial politicians with true colonial interests at heart.[78] It was local nationalism, apparently, that conspired to frustrate British plans.[79]

Of course, such explanations of Hutton's activities in New South Wales fall well short of the mark. They ignore the role of domestic colonial politics and political prerogatives. They also generally fail to engage with the essential duality of colonial identity. Even a man like Sir Henry Parkes, a vocal critic of Hutton's federal scheme, was a devoted imperialist who, like Hutton, feared a general European war and assumed that Australia would have a role in it. Parkes called himself in parliament 'a loyal Englishman, which means loyal Australian' and the populace of his colony 'faithful members of a common country'.[80] Hutton's constant speeches expressing the notion of the Empire as a family joined by race, religion and kinship and the important role of the military in nation-building transcended Meade's loose directions; they were heartfelt truths. The commandant as imperial agent argument also makes light, as it must, of the real military improvements he implemented, reforms equally crucial for defending the colony as they might potentially be for contributing to the Empire. Most of all for Hutton and the majority of those in the colony, the Empire's interests *were* colonial interests. These were two sides of same coin. The 'Trojan horse' analogy requires opposing sides, opposing 'nationalisms', that simply did not exist in the Australian colonies in this era.

Like all good conspiracy theories, however, there is a kernel of truth here, even if subsequent conclusions fly astray. There was, for example, some press uneasiness in the second half of 1893 regarding Hutton's imperial loyalties and intentions. Leaving aside the predictable line of the *Bulletin*, which worried that Hutton 'seemed under the ghastly delusion that he was here to train men for imperial service', the *Daily Telegraph*, *Newcastle Herald*, *Truth* and the *Illustrated Sydney News* all ran articles questioning the future use of local forces outside the colony and also Hutton's potential loyalty to Whitehall rather than the colonial government.[81] Yet there were many more articles in same and other colonial newspapers praising the 'commandant's discrimination and acuteness' and his efforts at reform and suggesting that 'Hutton deserves sympathy' for his efforts at economy and reform and the resistance he encountered.[82] In fact, it was Hutton himself who initially fuelled such stories with indiscriminate public remarks early in his command concerning the need to stand by Britain in an emergency. The frequency of such press reporting dropped off significantly in 1894 and 1895, just as his advocacy of the federal defence scheme spiked. Similarly, balance is required in reading Dibbs' early confrontations with Hutton over this issue. On the one hand it appeared that the Premier suspected London's influence before Hutton even arrived. He wrote to Hutton 3 May 1893 advising him to 'Close your ears & eyes to all representatives of cliques and subtracters in reference to military affairs here, until you have had an opportunity of forming your own conclusions ... Often times an officer coming here has been primed afar & opinions formed for him.'[83] Yet such remarks are perhaps more reflective of Dibbs' uneasiness about his colony's reputation for poor military efficiency than anything else.

In line with his discussions with Meade in 1893 it is clear, however, that Hutton always foresaw a limited expeditionary role for Australian troops within his federal defence scheme. Discussions at the 1894 commandants' conference in Tasmania raised the issue of such a role for the proposed federal force. It was not Hutton but Colonel Drury, however, who proposed extending its range of operation from 'Australia and Tasmania' to 'Australia and elsewhere'.[84] Hutton, conscious of what was actually possible and what would draw an inevitable political backlash, had the proposal struck out. At the same time he knew that a later clause in his scheme remained, which allowed for troops to be transported 'to any Colony of strategical position which it may be in Australian interests to protect or seize'. He had already told Meade, beforehand, 'you will note the "Federal Force" proposed by me would be available for service wherever the policy of the Australian Colonies might indicate'.[85] In context, however, this was not such a bold stroke. It was entirely in line with similar provisions in Britain for citizen troops to be used in the Channel Islands and in Canada, where militiamen could be despatched anywhere the Canadian Government saw fit.[86]

Hutton went on to use the opportunity of drafting the Defence Agreement for 1895 Premiers' Conference to reintroduce an expeditionary possibility. Here he defined 'Australia and Tasmania' as a geographic area that included New Caledonia, British New Guinea and the New Hebrides. This had not been approved at the conference and was not in its report. Yet such was the lack of imperial coordination and understanding of colonial limitations in London that such efforts received censure, not support, from the CDC. Nathan complained to Hutton of the absence of a plan for offensive action which 'seems the chief *raison d'être* of the whole scheme'. Hutton wrote back in January 1896 that this expeditionary possibility had been 'steadily in view throughout all the Schemes, both for New South Wales and for Australia, which I have drawn up, but I have never dared hint publicly at the possible necessity of moving Australian Troops out of Australia Waters'.[87] He promised, however, to discuss this and the other CDC recommendations at the forthcoming commandants' conference.

Photo 8 Edward Hutton in civilian attire in New South Wales, c.1894. (Council of the National Army Museum, London, NAM 1985–07-29–1)

Hutton's federal plan was extended and developed further at the 1896 commandants' meeting. Again, however, it was not Hutton but another, in this case Major-General Howel Gunter from Queensland, who suggested that the definition of Australia and Tasmania be extended to include all Pacific islands south of the equator and west of Tonga, including portions of Java, Borneo and German New Guinea. Hutton thought this amendment might pass without political or public reproach and shepherded it in this direction, while fighting successfully *against* Gordon's support of a CDC recommendation for a provision for general overseas service. It was not that Hutton did not agree with a wider imperial role for a federal force, but he knew such a possibility would be ruled out if his proposals went too far in this direction. He told Cambridge that the conference proposed 'just so much as the existing conditions of public opinion are likely to concede us'.[88] Crucially, however, Hutton feared not a rejection on the basis of colonial reluctance to defend the Empire in an emergency (a powerful expression of imperial nationalism), but rather he understood colonial reservations of ceding *control* of troops, which meant ceding parliamentary prerogative, to anybody, even an Australian council, especially in times of peace. The powerful local political sensitivities of reasonably new parliaments were grasped by Hutton to a much greater extent than by Gordon, the CDC and others in London.

For all Hutton's subsequent self-delusions and inflated claims, the federal defence scheme never represented a British attempt to secure an Australian partnership in imperial defence. It was, rather, a long-standing Australian issue, fanned briefly into renewed life by Hutton, which lived and died by Australian colonial decision-making. It was, after all, Reid who kept the flame alive for his own purposes from 1894. London had few levers to pull and, in truth, no plan by which to pull them. Tenuous links to a commandant with tenuous links to his government were not a mechanism for effective influence. Throughout his tenure in the colony Hutton never ventured to suggest, until the occasion of a final speech in the Union Club in Sydney on the eve of his departure, that the day would come when Australia would be expected to assume her share in the defence of the Empire and that such a defence must include operations elsewhere than Australian soil.[89] This parting broadside, however, caused barely a ripple.

Yet there is no question Hutton considered himself as an instrument of imperial policy in New South Wales, and his posting as commandant was a perfect platform from which to champion his emerging ideas on imperial defence. Meade's briefing fitted well with his own pre-existing beliefs, and his mountains of correspondence to the War Office and the CDC show Hutton to have been careful to please his patrons. This was a neat alignment of career opportunity and earnest desire to shape imperial and colonial policy for what he considered to be the better. Hutton was always careful to keep imperial authorities well informed of his plans and activities. He sent 'private' copies of the defence scheme of the colony and the establishment of its forces back to London. He also wrote privately to Buller and Cambridge before and after the 1894 commandants' conferences, with enclosed copies of the report itself and its minutes and proceedings. So too he sent Buller the circular letter from Reid to other premiers containing Hutton's complete scheme for federal defence. Similar information was sent to Gipps, Evelyn Wood, Wolseley and the CDC in early 1896.[90] None of this correspondence was sent with the blessing or knowledge of the colonial government. Yet even this seemingly underhanded activity was, in fact, common practice for British commandants abroad, who made such private communications often on their own initiative rather than at London's bidding. Such correspondence was an important means for ambitious officers like Hutton to keep themselves connected to the War Office and their patrons. This requirement, combined with Hutton's energy for self-promotion and drive for recognition, properly contextualised the volume of his correspondence home. Now, more than ever, Hutton needed his connections. His next promotion was to the substantive rank of major-general, and there were only around seventy such officers in the British Army. Hutton needed to maintain his profile and the only way to do was through his pen.[91]

As part of his line of communication back to London, and quite conscious that such messages would resonate with the right people at home, while in New South Wales Hutton made continual private reference to his efforts to prepare colonial troops for a possible imperial role. In May 1894 he assured Buller that he understood 'the importance of maintaining my position here on Imperial grounds'.[92] In July he confided in Hampden his dual aims of improving 'the efficiency of the Military Forces of Australia' and to 'enable those forces hereafter to be rendered available for joint operations with Imperial troops'.[93] As late as 1896 Hutton was imploring the War Office: 'Don't forget that if you want men to lick the Boers (or indeed any troops) you have a magnificent description of Mounted Troops here in Australia.'[94] Importantly, however, the message was often tempered with recognition of the importance of local defence. Hutton told Cambridge in late August 1894, for example, that his whole military system in the colony was based on the principle 'of providing adequately for the local defence of harbours, rivers and coast line and of further supplying a movable column which shall be available for Federal Defence, or indeed for any service wherever the National Policy may direct'.[95] For Hutton, who saw the future of the Empire as a racially, culturally and militarily homogenous whole, there was no contradiction here. Adequate local defence was important, as were federal defence and naturally the defence of the Empire. One led seamlessly into another. For Hutton and those of like mind there was no subjugation of colonial interests to those of London. Rather, those interests were shared. Further, as he explained to the Governor of Queensland, Sir Henry Norman, his plans for federal defence would 'enable these forces hereafter to be rendered available for joint operations with the Imperial troops *should the Colonial policy allow of it*'.[96] The last caveat was an important one and repeated often in his correspondence with the War Office. Hutton not once, in any official or private communication, intimated that any Australian military expedition could or would ever be made without local government consent. Imperial defence for him was based on cooperation, not coercion.

There was, of course, a wider backdrop to Hutton's thoughts and actions with respect to federal and imperial defence in New South Wales from 1893 to 1896 that helps to contextualise his efforts. Britain's difficult international diplomatic and strategic situation continued. Tension in early 1893 with France over its influence in Siam underscored the point. In March (the month Meade briefed Hutton), French gunboats pushed up the Mekong to take possession of various Siamese islands. The situation was tense and French intentions uncertain, a key background, perhaps, for Meade's suggestion to Hutton that Australian forces might be used against New Caledonia. It was in this context that the Imperial Federation League presented Gladstone with a draft scheme for the political federation of the Empire, which included plans for a defence council and representation on an imperial Cabinet to Canadian, Australian and South African members. Gladstone did not act, but spoke warmly of union for defence. The League was not impressed but, nonetheless, the more pragmatic of its members in Britain and the colonies who believed full imperial federation to be unlikely began to focus more heavily on the notion of cooperative Empire defence.[97] The idea was supported by Gladstone and Salisbury, so long as it meant British control. Lord Ripon's support for greater union with the colonies, which included aspects of imperial defence, similarly excluded imperial federation but included British control. The idea of mutual defence was a good fit for those who wanted closer imperial union without federation in a manner acceptable to free traders; that is, most British politicians.[98] Sir Francis Edwards, a British Liberal parliamentarian, wrote to Hutton in May 1894 reminding him of such developments and that: 'While you are working in Sydney for general Australian defence, some of us are much interested in "Imperial" defence, in which all parts of the Empire will take part'.[99] Such talk, however, as in the past, yielded more rhetoric than real progress.

The Conservative/Liberal-Unionist election victory of 1895, which brought Wolseley to the post of Commander-in-Chief and Chamberlain to that of Colonial Secretary, was a key development not only in keeping Hutton's federal defence scheme alive but also for the wider issue of imperial defence. The 'united Empire', advocated by Seeley and romanticised by Rhodes, was embraced by Chamberlain as a matter of policy. Echoing Disraeli's 1872 speech, Chamberlain's view of colonial self-government implied imperial consolidation based on intra-Empire economic connections and tariffs, political representation in some form of imperial council and by a system of imperial defence. The Colonial Secretary's mind was focused in this regard by the Venezuelan Crisis, which had threatened to involve the United States and Britain in a confrontation in the winter months of 1895–96. So too the ongoing crisis in the Transvaal at once confirmed to Chamberlain (and others) the limits of British military power and the potential means to remedy the shortfall.[100]

Colonial reaction to Venezuelan and Transvaal affairs was also important in shaping Chamberlain's and wider attitudes with regard to imperial military cooperation. Here, again, without any real sense of local considerations and circumstances, the message received in London seemed clear. On 13 January 1896 the Australian colonies cabled Lord Salisbury that they viewed 'with satisfaction the prompt and fearless policy adopted by Her Majesty's Government in the defence of the integrity of the British Empire'. 'We desire to convey to you our united assurances', the message continued, 'of loyal support.'[101] George Reid, for one, promised military support if war broke out in South Africa.[102] The New Zealand Government noted that the 'patriotic conduct of Imperial Government with reference to the Venezuela and Transvaal Republic has been such as to intensify loyal sentiments'. The Canadians too assured Britain of their 'unalterable loyalty and devotion to the British Throne and the Constitution' and their resolution to send troops to any point 'where the honour and interest of the Empire were threatened'.[103] It was to the Empire then that Chamberlain looked to strengthen Britain's hand. 'What is the greatest of our common obligations?' he asked the Canadian Club in 1896. 'It is Imperial Defence.'[104]

Tangible developments, however, still lagged the rhetoric of imperial defence consolidation. Long, drawn-out economic downturns in the leading self-governing colonies undermined defence initiatives of any sort, including cooperation. While in Australia the wider issue of Federation also obscured the issue, the New Zealanders were preoccupied during their depression years with social reform programs, which kept attention from defence matters. The Committee of National Defence (Defence Committee of Cabinet) was established in 1895 in London, as a result of the Hartington Commission, yet no plans for imperial defence were developed by it, much less enacted. This was largely a result of its members already being overworked in their own departments.[105] Meanwhile, the CDC worked on, with Nathan as its secretary from May 1895. While Nathan was certainly an imperialist and shared the views of his friend, George Sydenham Clarke, his committee remained a toothless, subordinate and marginalised organisation, bereft of members with high military or politic rank, challenged regularly by War Office and Admiralty interests and without any official remit to consider the coordinated defence of the Empire as a whole.

Moreover, the CDC could still only provide *guidance* and could (and did) do nothing when colonial governments decided not to accept the advice given. Despite consistent CDC pressure, for example, a South Australian defence scheme was not complete until 1896 and the Victorian plan of 1898 was criticised as ignoring previous CDC recommendations. New Zealand submitted its first defence scheme only in 1889, Canada in 1898 and Tasmania not at all. So too the CDC's emphasis continued to encourage the improvement of local defences, rather than pressing for any imperial defence collaboration. Its memoranda reaffirmed the maintenance of Royal Navy maritime supremacy as the basis of imperial defence, not colonial military offerings. The furthest the committee went in this regard, aside from an attempt to encourage a potential role in the Pacific for a non-existent federal defence system in Australia, was to suggest that colonial authorities standardise their forces on British patterns to facilitate 'their working with Imperial forces if called upon to do so'.[106] There was never any hint here of British control of colonial troops abroad. Such vague advice was completely in line with an absence of official British interest in the practical mechanics of imperial military cooperation.

Any government action in London or the colonies on these issues was further hampered by the absence of a clearly enunciated military defence policy in Britain that spelled out the strategic role of the services, or the method by which they were to defend the Empire. This 'elementary condition of success', to borrow Hutton's phrase, which had been an obstacle for the military reforms attempted under Cardwell as Secretary of State for War in 1868–74, was still lacking after the Salisbury government took power in 1895.[107] Wolseley's thinking with regard to imperial defence was a function of his military expeditions, all of which were mounted from home. Unlike Lord Roberts, who advocated an army concentrated in India to counter Russia, Wolseley's approach was 'global and amphibious',[108] and 'accepted as a military principle ... the best defence was a vigorous offence'.[109] This school of thought influenced Hutton, as it did Wolseley's wider coterie. Yet Wolseley's expeditionary mindset was focused on the British regular army and to a lesser extent on the British auxiliaries, not on the colonies. The key issue for Wolseley was whether the army could man, equip and mobilise the three corps that had been called for by the Liberal Secretary for War, Henry Campbell-Bannerman. There was little real or official consideration of a role for colonial troops beyond contribution to the defence of their own colonies and limited external operations such as the CDC's suggested role for Australian troops in the South Pacific. Hutton's larger ruminations for an imperial cooperative system were therefore his own and not based on any blueprint from the War Office. No such plans existed. Hutton might well have reflected of his time in New South Wales that '"defence by co-operation" promised to provide the answer to the long discussed question', but it was not an answer framed in any official manner.[110]

There was therefore no larger conspiracy behind Hutton's activities in New South Wales in 1893–96. He was rather an ambitious and energetic – even zealous – commandant, determined to make his mark and equally determined to further his career. There is no question that Hutton did his best to please what he thought to be the objectives of his patrons and his contacts at the War and Colonial offices. Yet the vigour with which he pursued his agenda also reflected his earnest belief in the 'mission' given to him by Meade and his view that his efforts regarding federal and imperial defence in New South Wales would further the interests of all, including those of the colony. Hutton's expectation that in a time of real crisis the Australian colonies would prove ready and willing to participate in an imperial war was correct. Under such circumstances they would not need to be compelled, duped or coerced. Hutton knew this, just as his juggling of CDC and local expectations concerning his federal scheme showed that he knew far better than many in London how counter-productive any attempt would be to codify such a commitment in peacetime. Yet with imperial sentiment still on the rise, in Britain as in the colonies, it was natural that in some quarters the strong independent colonies might be thought of as moving towards the assumption of a larger role in the defence of the wider Empire. As Gordon notes, 'This was part of the imperial rhetoric of the age of imperial federation.'[111] But a line of thought, perhaps more coherent and forceful than in the past, was all it was. Hutton and his patrons were part of this intellectual movement, but there was no coherent plan behind the scenes to towards which they were working.

There was no consensus in the Colonial Office, for example, as to whether Australian Federation would assist the imperial federation movement or separate Australia from the Empire. Meade's position in this regard was his own. The New South Wales Governor, Sir Robert Duff, sent to the colony *at the same time* as Hutton, was a staunch Liberal and disagreed with the commandant about the benefits of drawing the Empire together in any way; Duff's was not an appointment consistent with British plotting. So too British commandant appointments were all voluntary and the officer selected – even the need to have one – was in the end a colonial decision. Hutton was not the first choice for New South Wales as Dibbs had rejected the War Office's initial nomination as being too old. Hutton's replacement, Major-General French, was also hand-picked by the colonial government. The individual nature, skill, attitudes and conduct of commandants as a group throughout the Empire in the 1890s was therefore largely uneven and uncoordinated. Some, like Tulloch in Victoria, sent much more overt messages to the press regarding colonial participation in imperial wars than Hutton. 'The colonies in such an event', Tulloch told the *Evening News* in July 1893, 'would be expected if necessary to offer their last dollar and their last man.'[112] Others expressed no opinion in this regard at all. It is also worth remembering that British commandants were not the only example of supplementing local knowledge with imperial expertise. Similar appointments were made in the public service, medicine and other professions.[113]

Although little of substance was achieved towards an imperial defence system in London or the colonies during Hutton's time in New South Wales, his own concepts of the future direction of such a program were clarified. His earlier ideas on the Empire and military reform were now tempered with experience of the realities of colonial attitudes, limitations and prerogatives. The result was a reasonably complete conception of a plan for imperial defence, progressively refined from this point onwards. Hutton later reflected that it was during the voyage to Melbourne that it 'seemed clear, even at this early period, while studying the methods for effecting a co-operation for defence among the six States, that this system, if successfully launched in Australia, might easily become the prototype of a similar system which could be adopted by Canada, by New Zealand, by South Africa and ultimately by the Mother Country'.[114] His experiences in New South Wales confirmed for Hutton the principle of 'the defence of the Empire as a whole by a co-operation between all of its parts'.[115] Moreover, all that stood in the way of implementing such a scheme in Hutton's mind were public attitudes, which could be corrected through engagement with the press and the elimination of undue political interference. Hutton mistakenly believed that he achieved both in New South Wales and that his federal scheme, which he again erroneously saw as a 'success', was the result. All that was required then was to follow the pattern on a wider stage.

Nothing on Hutton's return to England disabused him of such ideas. He was heartily congratulated by Vincent, Colomb and 'My many friends in the House of Commons'. Hutton was also invited to address a number of like-minded parliamentarians 'in Committee at the House to explain the NSW system in detail' and 'its bearing upon a general system of Co-operative Defence throughout the Empire'. With all the convenience of retrospect, the self-confidence of self-delusion and an unerring knack of perceiving events as he wished them to be, rather than as they really were, Hutton later reflected that 'a great and most important movement forward towards the solidification and unity of the Empire had been made and that it only remained to preach the same doctrine in the other great self-governing Dominions in order to unify the whole upon a system which was well calculated to satisfy their views of constitutional government, as well as to gain one of the most important objects on union, namely that of defence upon a co-operative basis'.[116]

The opportunity to 'preach the same doctrine' was, in fact, not too far distant. Hutton had already written to Gipps, a fellow Etonian, in mid-1895 that 'I believe that the command of the Militia in Canada to be vacant in the course of a few months' and indicating his interest in the appointment.[117] For the moment, however, Hutton was back in London basking in the apparent success of his time in New South Wales.

CHAPTER 5

'One general policy – elastic as it may be'

Back in Britain, 1896–98

When Edward Hutton returned from New South Wales to London on 16 April 1896 he was riding on the crest of a wave of *perceived* success in the colony and wasted no time calling on key figures at the War Office and various Colonial Office officials, including Joseph Chamberlain. Hutton was thrilled to be received privately by the Duke of Cambridge a week after his return. 'Nothing could have exceeded the cordiality and kindness which I everywhere received', he later reminisced, 'and the congratulations which were conveyed to me, by all officials concerned with military and imperial interest, were gratifying in the extreme.' Hutton later claimed that it was suggested to him that he might be promoted major-general for his services, but he declined as it would have passed him over the heads of his seniors and he did not relish the jealousy and 'professional unpleasantness' which would result.[1] Be that as it may, such official recognition fired Hutton's imagination, reaffirmed his self-belief and stoked his ambition to greater heights than ever before. With more time on his hands than had been available in New South Wales, Hutton was also free to devote his considerable intellectual energy to his emerging ideas concerning imperial defence.

Hutton spent much of his time immediately after his return to Britain seeking the company and counsel of the members of the CDC. He was aware that the committee was at that point on the cusp of moving beyond its restrictive traditional focus on local colonial defence issues towards the consideration of the wider issue of defending the Empire. How best to do so was a subject that at once held Hutton's attention and one he hoped to influence. He helped Captain Nathan, for example, prepare in May 1896 the first CDC memorandum ever drafted that gave a solid set of principles behind its conception of imperial defence. The memo was itself a consequence of a Colonial Office request to prepare a paper that could be used to 'educate colonial public opinion in the right principles of defence'.[2] In it the CDC (and Hutton) confirmed 'the maintenance of sea supremacy . . . as the basis of the system of imperial defence', while at the same time staking a claim, if only a moral one, to the defence resources of the colonies. Should the situation arise in which Britain was at war, it suggested in a follow-up memorandum in December that 'the increasing strength and resources of the self-governing Colonies will enable them to materially assist the Mother Country, by placing at her disposal for operations in any quarter of the globe bodies of troops formed from the excellent material of strong, self-resilient colonists'.[3] Hutton was at the centre of imperial defence considerations by the CDC at this time and prized the fact.

Hutton's newfound closeness to the CDC, and with other officials at the War and Colonial offices, also gave him the chance to continue to press his Australian federal defence scheme, well after it had lost all relevance in the colonies. He sat with the CDC when it discussed his report of the 1896 commandants' meeting and was not shy in describing what had been 'accomplished'. Meade praised him fulsomely. Even if no agreement for troops to be used outside Australia had been reached, Hutton argued, they could always volunteer for such service. Although the War Office published part of the scheme, Hutton was disappointed in a Colonial Office decision not to do so on the basis of continuing Admiralty unease concerning his proposed council of control. Illustrative of just how successful his self-delusion really was with respect to the federal scheme, at this point Hutton argued that if it had been published then colonial public opinion and the Australian press would have seen it adopted. Meade was happy enough that a scheme existed that *might* be adopted, if required, in an emergency.[4]

By July 1896 Hutton was drawn away from the seats of imperial policy-making in London and appointed for a three-month stint to command a militia brigade at Aldershot, under the command of Prince Arthur, the Duke of Connaught, to whom Hutton referred to as 'a friend of long standing'.[5] The posting was in advance of a future appointment as the Assistant Adjutant General, Dublin Military District, a reasonably high-profile staff position. Hutton, however, immediately riled at the old-fashioned and 'unprofessional' training practices within the brigade. He complained to Headquarters, 5th Division, that training for militia battalions was carried out by their unit's adjutant and permanent staff rather than their own part-time officers. 'Officers cannot handle their men', he carped, through a 'lack knowledge and "moral influence"'.[6] He urged British militia officers to take responsibility. 'I would add that while in command of the Military Forces of New South Wales a similar system of company training was instituted in the Militia Regiments of the Colony which was followed by an almost marvellous improvement in discipline as well as military knowledge.'[7]

Beyond a reaffirmation of his professional attitudes the real importance of the second half of 1896, in the context of a job that taxed neither Hutton's time nor mental energy, was that he began to formalise his ideas on imperial defence and to write them down. Hutton was influenced in this regard not only by his experience in New South Wales but also by the ongoing difficulties of the British Army, with which he was all too familiar. Wolseley's advocacy of an expeditionary role for the regular force was at this point finding influential supporters. Vice Admiral Phillip Colomb, for example, told the Royal United Services Institution that a much larger expeditionary force was required than that available and that more funds should be spent on a larger and more mobile army. The problem, however, was always money and men. In 1896 defence ate up 38 per cent of the national budget in Britain (up by almost 11 per cent from mid-century largely owing to the two-power naval standard).[8] There was a shortage of funds to pay for new recruits – a problem partially alleviated by the continued difficulty of finding them. The answer for Hutton was the Empire.

Hutton chose the professional think-tank he had created, the Aldershot military Society, 'the van of Military Progress and Military Efficiency' as he called it, as the forum through which to publicise his scheme of cooperative imperial defence. His paper, 'Our comrades of Greater Britain', was read on 24 November 1896. The principles outlined therein captured all of the essential elements of Hutton's thinking about the issue. First was the immediacy of the problem in that the Empire was under threat and that it fell to the soldiers to protect it. 'During the long rest of 80 years from any great life struggle other nations have been pressing in our wake', he wrote, 'the day may at any moment break when we must keep up with the sword what we have gained by the sword.' Next was his lament that British policy-makers had successively failed to develop a joint naval and military strategic plan. The issue had 'never yet been adequately or authoritatively considered', noted Hutton, and it was equally 'certain that no practical solution of this problem has ever yet been enunciated as a basis upon which the preservation of the Empire may safely rest'.[9]

Hutton's solution, implied in his paper, was based in his own experiences. There was a strong recognition, for example, of Seeley's vision of a white partnership of Britain and the self-governing colonies into the union of a greater empire. In this regard Hutton hoped to convey 'something of the vastness and something of the similarity of national feeling and of national instinct which permeates the whole Empire alike'.[10] On the practical side he noted that the enormous growth in wealth and power of self-governing colonies in the last twenty-five years had significant military implications, especially as Australians paid on average 2s 9d per capita on defence, the Canadian 1s 3d, but the British 9s 1d for the army and 17s 4d per capita for the combined military vote. For Hutton, if the colonies came to be educated as to the benefits they derived from the British security umbrella then they would surely be content to contribute more. Such an 'education' was further necessary to popularise military service in the colonies (and in Britain). This service would of itself be for the good of the nation and the Empire in that this 'sacred and solemn duty' and 'national privilege' built self-discipline and civil responsibility. In line with the Etonian lessons that never left him, such service would further provide even more in terms of 'manly qualities' than 'even cricket, hunting or racing'; all qualities that had 'given us our freedom and free institutions'.[11]

Hutton's conceptions of ethnicity, born of his own military expeditions in Africa and Egypt and congruent with the times, also figured in his principles of imperial defence. So too his professional outlook and even his preference for part-time and mounted troops. In a 'safe' parallel message, equally applicable to British auxiliary troops and one not lost on his audience, Hutton extolled the virtues of white part-time Australian citizen-soldiers, while warning of the lingering unease in the colonies with regards to regulars. He praised the 'quick intelligence and strong individuality' of the Anglo-Saxon colonial citizen-soldier, whom if properly led could achieve the heights of martial success but, if commanded by professionally ignorant or incompetent officers, would lead the army to disaster.[12] At a time when a cavalry backlash against the mounted infantry movement in Britain had gained momentum, Hutton was careful to point out the value of colonial mounted infantrymen as 'self-reliant and excellent marksmen ... never seen to a greater advantage than when mounted and riding across bush or difficult country'.[13]

Echoing Wolseley's speeches and writings, 'Comrades of Greater Britain' also discussed the historical importance not only of defence of the Empire but also of the maintenance of offensive capability. This 'great principle of offensive-defensive policy' and an expeditionary capability, under the principle of fighting an enemy on their soil, was another of Hutton's key tenets. Hutton foresaw the passive defence of strategic areas by local garrisons and the maintenance of another mobile force, contributed to by all parts of the Empire, to be despatched 'wherever necessitated by political events'. Yet it would by necessity be a force of troops whose service was given by their colony to the wider Empire on a voluntary basis. He therefore argued against notions of applying a formal and binding peacetime framework for defence throughout the Empire. 'Attractive as this may seem', he warned, 'a sojourn in our Colonies, even of a short duration, will soon demonstrate the impossibility of such a system being accepted by the majority of our fellow subjects of Greater Britain.'[14]

All the essential elements of Hutton's imperial defence thinking were thus on the table for pubic critique: a vision of an Empire-wide force of volunteer white part-time militiamen, preferably with a high proportion of mounted troops, properly trained and led by professional officers, charged with defending their colonies and cooperatively contributing to the defence of the Empire at any point that might be required, with the consent of local governments. He urged his audience to overcome the institutional conservatism that stood in the way of embracing such ideas. In the main those who attended the reading seemed to do just that, and the paper went on to attract significant press and military attention.

Towards the end of 1896 Hutton's staff appointment to Ireland commenced. Away from London, his web of contacts widened somewhat from the Wolseley Ring. He saw 'much of Dublin society under the cheery auspices of the then Lord Lieutenant and his wife, Lord and Lady Cadogan' and was thrown into contact with Field Marshal Lord Roberts, Commander-in-Chief of British forces in Ireland, for the first, but by no means the last, time. In early May 1897 Hutton was transferred to act as the chief staff officer at Curragh Camp, on the eve of drill season, as troops began to concentrate for battalion, brigade and divisional manoeuvres. At Curragh his immediate commander, Major-General Boyce Albert Combe, fell ill, making Hutton 'practically in command of this important training centre', providing him with experience with not only British regulars but also with the auxiliary army at home.[15] Still advocating more professional and realistic training, he induced Roberts to permit him to organise a three-day Staff Ride for more than 200 officers in early summer, the first of its kind held in Ireland. Roberts was impressed.

Importantly, in September 1897 Hutton and three fellow officers at Curragh arranged official permission to attend German and French manoeuvres to take place at Homburg and around St Quentin and Bapaume respectively. They wore plain clothes, but were free to ride wherever they wished. At one stage, observing the Germans and with the Kaiser himself present, Hutton watched '80 000 men engaged in mimic warfare, making up a scene not easily forgotten'.[16] On 10 September he proceeded to St Quentin and was given all help and hospitality by the French general staff. On his return Hutton again gave his thoughts to the Aldershot Military Society. Aside from making a number of accurate observations on the strengths and weaknesses of French and German tactical and operational methods that would be borne out in 1914 and less reliable deductions concerning the difference between Teutonic and Celtic racial characteristics, the key point for Hutton resulting from the experience were the huge numbers involved. Such 'mass' drove home to him that a small regular army like Britain's would be all but irrelevant if war broke out on a large scale in Europe. The true comparison was therefore between the continental systems and an imperial army of volunteers. Britain's Empire would live or die in the next general war by the efforts of troops raised from the civilian population at home and abroad. This raised in Hutton 'a deep and abiding feeling of anxiety and concern' as, in their current state, British auxiliaries 'would be incapable of making solid resistance'.[17]

With a British military still practically the same as it had been at the time of the Napoleonic Wars, Hutton argued, after watching the French and Germans, that the time had arrived for serious change. Along with comprehensive field training, a sense of wider professionalism and a 'single hearted feeling of patriotism' among the officer corps, this must involve a 'generally accepted military policy' for the defence for the 'whole Empire'.[18] Hutton noted recent remarks by Lord Lansdowne, Secretary of State for War, that 'the possession of a large fleet does not relieve us of the need for an efficient army' and that no country can have a powerful defence 'unless it is powerful for offence also'. He concluded that the Empire needed both a small regular force 'for the maintenance of order' and a much larger army 'for offensive-defensive and defensive purposes'. The key for providing the latter was once again an Empire-wide 'Militia System', complete in all arms and administrative functions. Hutton henceforth began to think seriously about the detail of such a 'cooperative system' as it might apply to Australia, Canada, New Zealand and South

Africa, with each portion of the Empire taking its share of responsibility. In fact, he rather disingenuously claimed that such a system was already practically accepted by the Australian colonies. Further, he was 'convinced the time [was] at hand when our colonies with responsible government will be prepared to consider upon a broad and adequate basis the defence policy of the future'.[19] The principles sketched in 'Comrades of Greater Britain' were crystallising into a plan.

Meanwhile, as Hutton had been working in Ireland, the Queen's Diamond Jubilee celebrations were in full swing. Importantly, invitations to the premiers of the white colonies included a request for a colonial conference that would 'afford a most valuable opportunity for the discussion of many subjects of the greatest interest to the Empire, such as Commercial Union, Colonial Defence, Representation of the Colonies'.[20] Here was a chance for Chamberlain to make some progress towards his own Empire project, and imperial defence seemed to be the perfect building block towards his vision of wider union. In London, at least, important ground had been prepared in this regard. On 3 December 1896, the Duke of Devonshire, chairman of Cabinet Defence Committee, had given his famous Guildhall speech, quoting extensively from the CDC's May memorandum on the principles of imperial defence. Devonshire's basic message was that while Britain underwrote the security of the Empire, the colonies were responsible for contributing to defending themselves as a 'step towards a practical measure of federation for the purposes of defence'. The theory was to make 'available for Imperial defence the whole resources, both of the British Empire and of her Colonies'.[21] Through Devonshire it appeared that the Imperial Government wanted a system that might defend the Empire as a whole through the cooperation of its parts. With international competition and tension mounting and war scares a result, far from the burden of the 1860s and the irrelevancies of the 1870s and early 1880s, the colonies now seemed to represent a natural and important resource to be harnessed. The sum of military forces already in the self-governing colonies, for example, amounted to almost 70 000 men, roughly size of the British Army in India. Meanwhile, the Imperial Federation (Defence) Committee stressed again the disparity between colonial and British defence expenditure, a theme that resonated in the House of Commons, which was all too conscious of an increasing defence burden.[22]

On 24 June, two days after the Jubilee celebrations, the colonial premiers gathered at the Colonial Office, and Chamberlain made his pitch. He outlined his vision for a united Empire, which included a common commitment to share the weight of imperial defence. He began by flagging the idea of great 'federal council', containing colonial 'representative plenipotentiaries' for the Empire as a whole as a step towards imperial federation. Aside from some limited attention from Sir Edward Braddon of Tasmania, the Australians were not interested in any form of imperial union if it implied taxation, especially one that would not give representation independent of population. Besides, their focus was on Australian political union. Richard John Seddon, Premier of New Zealand, was in favour, reflecting his colony's tradition of earnest imperial commitment. Wilfrid Laurier of Canada, essentially happy with conditions as they were, vacillated somewhere between these positions.[23]

The second item on Chamberlain's card concerned imperial defence. He contended that it was 'of first importance that we, all having a common interest, should have before-hand a scheme of common defence against any possible or at all events any probably enemy'.[24] In the first instance this meant colonial contributions to the upkeep of imperial forces – notably the navy – to help meet rising costs. Chamberlain also suggested the exchange of military units as a 'practical step in the direction of Imperial unity' and went so far as to argue: 'I see no reason why these colonial troops should not, from time to time, fight side by side with their British colleagues.'[25] Few positive responses resulted. The Australians rejected Admiralty suggestions to remove the restrictions on the Australia Station's auxiliary squadron from operating only in Australian waters. They were prepared to consider a minor increase to its upkeep, but only if the Station was strengthened. Laurier urged delegates to look at imperial defence more broadly, but admitted no Canadian contribution was likely, given local political circumstances. To the idea of exchanges the premiers murmured approval but gave no firm undertakings, and the issue was soon bogged down under problems of military law, the availability of local forces and cost: 'They all with one accord began to make excuses.'[26] Only the South Africans, fearful of Transvaal, responded as Chamberlain had hoped. The Cape Premier, John Gordon Sprigg, offered a cruiser to the Royal Navy while Natal agreed to provide £12 000 per year towards imperial naval defence. Chamberlain was assured by George Reid of New South Wales that in a time of real crisis Britain could be sure of support from the colonies, but in peacetime he and his fellow premiers would be reluctant to make firm offers or agreements.[27] Again, there was no distaste for the idea of fighting for the Empire in a serious crisis, but in parallel with powerful imperial sentiments was a pragmatic recognition of local priorities, parochialism and prerogatives.

Overall, the results of the gathering were extremely disappointing for Chamberlain. In place of his imperial council, he received only a mechanism for future imperial conferences. Rather than substantial colonial defence commitments he got mere promises of increasing uniformity in equipment, training and organisation, closer contact between colonies on defence matters and the minor pledges of the South Africans. Not even Reid's eleventh-hour attempt to revive the Australian federal defence scheme, supported by Chamberlain on CDC advice, amounted to anything; not that Reid necessarily expected it to. Yet here was another example of the division between firm imperial sentiment and earnest intention in a military crisis, so consistently offered by the colonies, and a rejection of formal arrangements to this end in peacetime, also consistently flagged by them and Hutton while he had been in New South Wales. Laurier subsequently spoke at a banquet of colonial representatives on 18 July 1897, declaring: 'If the day were ever to come when England was in danger, let the bugles sound, let the fires be lit on the hills and in all parts of the colonies; though we may not be able to do much, whatever we can do shall be done by the colonies to help her.'[28] Such sentiments were more in line with Hutton's voluntary conceptions of imperial defence than Chamberlain's desire for formalised arrangements. It was a point of difference set to continue between the two men, who otherwise found little to disagree upon.

Despite the colonial rebuff at the 1897 conference, various initiatives in the direction of formal imperial defence ties continued to appear in its wake. The Victorian Governor, Lord Brassey, for example, thought to lever such a scheme off the popularity of the colonial military contingents sent to the 1897 Jubilee, telling the CDC in August 1897, 'I would urge that the Imperial Government take advantage of our exceptional resources for raising a force of 5000 mounted rifles in Australia under engagement for general service in time of war.'[29] Brassey followed this up with similar letters on 31 August and 14 December and met with the CDC when in London to further his cause. The committee endorsed the broad sentiments behind Brassey's argument but pointed to problems of cost, efficiency and political considerations, in that to remove so many men from the colonies in case of war could not be effected without colonial agreement. Moreover, the committee pointed out, 'Imperial federation for defence is undoubtedly desirable but it might be checked if an Australian corps . . . were wanted for Imperial purposes in circumstances with regard to which popular feeling in Australia was not fully in accord with the decision of the Home Government.'[30] In other words, no such force was worth the potential damage to imperial relationships. In this case the CDC recognised that '[p]olitical conditions have to be considered' with regard to ceding the control of colonial forces to imperial authorities. Many policy-makers beforehand, and many to come, assiduously failed to grasp this key point.

Nonetheless, the local initiatives kept coming, while conceptions of what form any imperial defence cooperation might take remained inconsistent in London. In July 1898, the CDC floated idea of raising a permanent Australian regiment for imperial service to foster imperial unity and to allow a material Australian contribution to imperial defence. Major-General Sir John Ardagh (head of the Intelligence Department at the War Office and a friend of Hutton who had served with him on headquarters staffs in Egypt in 1882–83 and again in 1884–85) and Wolseley supported the idea. Lansdowne, however, was less enthusiastic, and Evelyn Wood, now Adjutant-General, worried that no recruits would volunteer. The Colonial Office was also lukewarm, yet in December Chamberlain sent the proposal to Australia. No response was forthcoming.[31]

Meanwhile, as Hutton penned his report on the German and French manoeuvres in the autumn of 1897, his mind began to fixate on where or how he might get an opportunity to convert his cooperative imperial defence plan into reality. In early 1896 Hutton's friend, fellow Etonian, fellow mounted infantry officer in Egypt in 1882 and fellow advocate of Britain's auxiliary forces, Lord Minto, who had been military secretary to Lansdowne during his governor-generalship of Canada in 1883–85, had written to Hutton about his possible appointment as General Officer Commanding the Canadian militia at some future date.[32] The kernel began to germinate. It was encouraged in Spring 1897 when it was suggested to Hutton that he might be nominated by the War Office for this appointment should it become vacant. 'I immediately drew up a plan of action', Hutton later wrote, 'so as to ensure something at least of the success which had attended my efforts in New South Wales.'[33] By late 1897 he was in contact with Ardagh and Wolseley, claiming that both were anxious he go to Canada, to 'undertake the reorganisation of the whole Defence System and the placing of the Canadian Militia in a reasonable state of efficiency'. In early 1898 Redvers Buller suggested to Hutton that with the approaching retirement of Major-General William Julius Gascoigne, the current incumbent in Canada, the probability of his being selected was 'assured'.[34] Hutton was subsequently informed that his name had been submitted to the Canadian Government. Even the Toronto *Globe* was, by July 1898, reporting rumours that Hutton was likely to be chosen.[35] Yet no official announcement was made. Hutton later claimed to have been told by Lord Tennyson that the reason for the delay was that Gascoigne had objected on the grounds Hutton was a 'martinet' and 'impossible to work with'.[36] Familiar with the conditions, difficulties and limitations faced by a British general in Canada, Gascoigne proved something of a prophet.

As Hutton waited to see whether his hopes for a Canadian appointment would be realised, he set his mind once more to perfecting his scheme of intra-imperial defence cooperation. During late 1897 and early 1898 Hutton spoke regularly to Ardagh who, like himself, was convinced of the need for some type of cooperative, Empire-wide military system. Both thought a policy needed to be developed that was acceptable to both Britain and colonies, and an extension of the New South Wales scheme, refined in line with principles laid down in Hutton's recent public speeches, seemed to be the key. 'I had taken him [Ardagh] into my confidence', Hutton later recalled, 'and described the methods of co-operative defence which I had in mind with a view to the unification and solidarity of the Empire through its defence system. In all points my old friend more than endorsed my views.'[37] Hutton received further inspiration and affirmation of his developing scheme from reading George Sydenham Clarke's *Imperial Defence*, published in 1897, which called for 'Imperial co-operation in a general scheme of defence framed in accordance with national requirements'. Clarke, it appeared, endorsed many of the fundamental tenets of Hutton's own scheme and wider outlook. 'The Anglo-Saxon people, doubtless from hereditary causes', wrote Clarke, 'is specially prone to believe in the efficacy of imperfectly trained men ... to trust overmuch its natural fighting capacity and to under-rate the vital need for organisation and of careful preparation for war.' 'Unprofessional armies promiscuously brought together when danger appeared imminent', he warned, 'no longer sufficed.' Such sentiments well matched Hutton's own professional outlooks and aspirations for imperial citizen soldiery. Militiamen, Clarke continued, 'if properly nurtured' would be 'fully capable of furnishing a large and mobile force' – something akin to the 'cheap and excellent system of Switzerland', which Hutton had seen and praised himself in 1887. Clarke went further, paralleling Hutton's New South Wales scheme in that an imperial militia force might be organised and made available for field operations, with volunteers manning forts. The greatest need of Empire in coming war, he concluded, would be 'forces available for field service', not local or port defence. The idea then was to assign each to their place in an imperial scheme.[38] Yet Clarke was less ambitious than Hutton in that he argued for local colonial forces operating primarily (but not exclusively) within the geographic divisions of the colonial naval commands; that is, Australasian troops, for example, free to act anywhere covered by Australia Station. Hutton, however, envisaged an imperial militia that might be sent wherever it was required.

On 10 May 1898, Chamberlain gave a speech to the Commons foreshadowing that a great and general war as looming and declaring: 'The sons of Britain throughout the world shall stand shoulder to shoulder to defend our mutual interests and our common right.'[39] This level of imprimatur, such a declaration, in Hutton's words, so 'forcibly laid down . . . in a great public speech', was enough not only for Hutton to finalise much of the detail of his own 'cooperative scheme' but also to make it public.[40] Ardagh gave 'full concurrence', although he remained careful to avoid committing himself to any official approval. On 19 April 1898 Hutton therefore delivered a paper entitled 'A Co-operative System of Defence of the Empire' to the Royal Colonial Institute, chaired by Lieutenant-General Sir James Bevan Edwards, who had inspected the Australian colonies in 1889 and who was now a member of parliament. Hutton began by speaking of a 'generally expressed hope that a military policy may be evolved from the existing conditions of uncertainty and upon it may be erected some solid and satisfactory military scheme of defence'. Surely the 'time has arrived', he continued, 'when all potions of Her Majesty's Dominions . . . should be prepared to co-operate for mutual defence and should decide to accept one general policy – elastic as it may be'. This was an issue 'pregnant with the whole future existence of the Empire'.[41]

The problem with current defence arrangements, in Hutton's mind, was that Lansdowne's speech in December 1897, which set out a plan for a garrison for home defence in Britain and two regular army corps (60 000 men) for offensive purposes outside the British Isles, was flawed. Two corps was hardly enough in a real crisis, especially in a general war in Europe. Moreover, it in no way capitalised on the military potential of the Empire. Hutton again argued that the regulars 'should be more properly regarded as an Imperial constabulary and cannot be reckoned upon as the true factor in the defence of the Empire'; there was just not enough of them to mount offensive operations of any real significance, and the deployment of Lansdowne's corps would leave the current British auxiliary forces bereft of cavalry, artillery and administrative departments.[42] Hutton's grand solution, building further on (and from) his developing scheme of imperial military cooperation, was for the volunteers and militia of Britain and the self-governing colonies to be organised along the lines he had pursued in New South Wales; that is, such forces arranged as complete military organisations and formations with all constituent administrative parts. The volunteers and yeomanry in Britain and part-time volunteer troops elsewhere were to be utilised for passive local defence, while the more thoroughly trained militia throughout the Empire could be used for either local defence or in accordance with Wolseley's principle of defence by strong offence. Only this type of arrangement and troops of this type, Hutton argued, could provide the numbers needed, some 173 000 troops, or six corps, from Britain alone. Such legislation as the British Militia Act of 1882 and similar Acts in the colonies already had most of the framework in place to raise and maintain militia numbers if required (enforced by ballot or compulsory service if needed). This would, as Hutton argued had been the case in New South Wales, 'utilize what was already in existence . . . into one generally accepted plan'. 'Mutual defence' therefore would be 'guaranteed by one and all parts alike of the Empire'.[43] More detail was thus slowly added to Hutton's grand scheme of imperial defence.

Like his federal plan for Australia, however, Hutton's imperial vision still failed to address the politics of a controlling body, which would invariably need to deal with the sovereign, financial, philosophical and parochial concerns of the self-governing colonies. Such a plan was simply untenable without a robust system of control, which would inevitably at this stage be run from London and would therefore be likely to be unacceptable at the periphery, not because of issues of subimperial nationalism but again rather thanks to the same raft of local prerogatives, issues, agendas and self-interest that had hampered Hutton in 1895–96 and frustrated Chamberlain at the Jubilee conference in 1897. All Hutton could suggest in this regard was some sort of 'representative system . . . some system of offensive defensive alliance, or Federal Agreement'.[44] Yet Hutton's views were once more well received by the small but influential circle of imperial defence advocates and military experts in and out of parliament and the army. In addition to Edwards, within Hutton's audience at the Royal Colonial Institute sat Sir Charles Dilke, Liberal and reformist politician and co-author of *Imperial Defence* (1892). Sir John Colomb, a member of parliament, and his brother Admiral Phillip Colomb, were also present. So too were General Sir Henry Norman (former Governor of Queensland), Major-General Ardagh and Hugh Oakeley Arnold-Forster (MP and future Secretary of State for War). All supported Hutton's general principles. In the discussion that followed, Dilke argued that the time 'for smooth words' was past and that it was now 'necessary to speak plain words and call upon the Colonies as patriots, to take their part with the Mother Country in the common defence of the Empire'. Again, Hutton's paper was reported widely in the press and generally praised in Britain and the colonies. The *Canadian United Service Magazine*, for example, called it the 'foundation stone of an imperial system of defence' that would act as 'a strong element for the preservation of peace'.[45]

Hutton's paper also marked a watershed in his own mind. His imperial scheme was now finalised and ready for implementation. Only a personality like Hutton's, stimulated by the public pronouncements of such men as Devonshire and Chamberlain and such private voices as that of Ardagh, had the ambition, single-mindedness and arrogance to make the attempt. Moreover, his cooperative scheme from this moment onwards became more than a practical solution to an imperial problem. Rather it grew into a personal crusade, almost an obsession. Its attainment would at once seal his reputation, epitomise his professional accomplishment and save the Empire from fickle politicians unable 'to grasp the problem of the defence of the Empire', let alone frame a solution.[46]

In early August 1898 Hutton's public speeches and private representations bore fruit. Major-General Gascoigne, General Officer Commanding the Canadian Militia, and Lord Aberdeen, Governor-General in Canada, were both due to return to Britain. In this changing of the guard policy-makers in London saw a chance for real military reform in the largest self-governing colony. The former would be replaced by Hutton and the latter, in all likelihood, by Lord Minto.[47] Both now publicly expressed similar views with regard to the Empire and imperial defence with each other and with Chamberlain. As had been the case before his departure for New South Wales in early 1893, a round of interviews preceded the announcement. The first of these was with Wolseley, who had previously served in Canada and who urged Hutton at a meeting on 29 July to 'minimise and if possible eradicate politics and political interference' – a dangerous mission for a man already sharing with his Commander-in-Chief a general distaste for politicians and a mistaken belief of his triumph over Dibbs in New South Wales.[48] Hutton had in fact reaffirmed his negative view of colonial politicians in his 'Comrades of Greater Britain' paper in that 'the most dangerous and sinister effects of constitutional Government in our Colonies is the ever recurring tendency on the part of individual members of the Legislature to interfere for various reasons with the workings of and with the personnel of the military machine'.[49] On 3 August he had an interview with Lansdowne, who similarly lamented the influence of political interference in Canadian militia affairs. Hutton also noted Lansdowne's specific wish that the Canadian militia should be made into a complete militia 'army', in line with his own cooperative imperial defence scheme and his philosophy for auxiliary forces more generally.[50]

Photo 9 The Earl of Minto, Governor-General of Canada (1898–1904). Minto was an old friend and comrade of Hutton and a key figure during his time in Canada. (William James Topley, Library and Archives Canada/C-001009)

The most important of Hutton's preappointment interviews was with Chamberlain on 9 August. The Colonial Secretary began by telling Hutton that his government was 'most anxious' not only that Canadian defence arrangements 'should be placed on a satisfactory condition' but also that reforming the Canadian militia organisation was a task 'requiring great tact'. Indeed, a lack of diplomacy and discretion had proved fatal for Hutton's predecessors in Canada, none of whom had stayed for their full term. The problem was, Chamberlain reiterated, with sections of the Canadian Government in that, with respect to military affairs, 'politics were allowed to be the determining factor'.[51] Hutton again agreed that political interference was the ruination of discipline. Chamberlain suggested: 'Much might be done by quietly urging measures of reform' and that 'above all "festina lente" should be the motto'.[52] Although the classical adage was certainly in Hutton's Latin vocabulary, Chamberlain did not yet realise that the idea of 'more haste, less speed' was simply not within his nature. Chamberlain also reminded Hutton of the importance he attached to the idea of exchanging military units. By this stage, however, although Hutton respected Chamberlain and welcomed suggestions on reform and the removal of political influence, where they aligned with his wider cooperative scheme, he had no intention of furthering initiatives that ran counter to it. Hutton never subsequently advocated the idea of exchanges with any force. Of the wider imperial project Hutton told Chamberlain he well understood and shared his desire see the colonies 'prepared in a spirit of Empire patriotism, to participate in the defence of the Empire as a whole'.[53]

The messages Hutton received from Wolseley, Lansdowne and Chamberlain were reinforced with other interviews with only slightly lesser, or fading, luminaries such as Cambridge (now chief personal ADC to the Queen and Colonel-in-Chief to the forces), General Sir Richard Harrison, Inspector-General of Fortification, Major-General Sir Coleridge Grove, Military Secretary at the War Office, his old patron Evelyn Wood and Sir Edward Wingfield, Undersecretary of State for the Colonies. Wingfield, on 10 August, gave his own endorsement of Hutton's plan for a New South Wales–type military system in Canada and for the reduction of political interference in the militia. Hutton was further influenced by letters from Canada, such as those from Lieutenant-General Lord William Seymour, commanding British troops in Halifax (and the senior British commander in Canada), who wrote in September 1898 noting that 'the Canadian Government has procrastinated in accepting your name from the Home Government', in a typical 'example of what I fear your will find touching all military affairs' – politics.[54] Another old friend and current Commandant of the Royal Military College of Canada, Colonel Gerald Charles Kitson, warned him: 'The position will never be granted you, except in name and when they want to throw the blame on you. Otherwise, you are merely the mouthpiece of the Minister' – another red flag to a rather easily provoked bull.[55]

The important point here is that, on the eve of his departure to Canada, Hutton felt he had a clear mandate from home. His views with respect to the necessity of imperial defence cooperation were well known, at least in British military circles. Indeed, to him such ideas 'were held by those responsible for Imperial Defence to be a special qualification for the task at hand'. This was even more so in context of emerging tension in South Africa. 'If Canada were to play her part as the eldest daughter of the Empire', Hutton later wrote, 'no time must be lost in undertaking the military reforms which were well known to be so urgently required.'[56] A triple agenda was therefore clear and not overly dissimilar to that which he had taken to New South Wales. He would aim at transforming the Canadian militia into an efficient and effective force for Canadian defence. This meant remoulding it along the lines of a self-sufficient army complete in all arms and administrative services. The task also implied the removal of what was widely perceived in British defence circles as undue political interference in Canadian military affairs. In the process, both objectives would fit into his wider long-term designs for a cooperative imperial defence system. In his paper, 'Comrades of Greater Britain', for example, Hutton had pointed explicitly to a general want of administrative and support services in the colonial militaries, which, were they better provided for, would allow them to operate as coherent formations in the field abroad.

As a mark of his growing self-confidence, in his pre-embarkation interviews Hutton seemed keener than he had been in 1893 to air his own views rather than to seek advice. The feedback he received with regard to his first two aims in Canada was reasonably clear and aligned with what he already thought was needed. Guidance regarding imperial cooperative defence, although still unspecific, was much stronger and more consistent than had been the case before his appointment in New South Wales. There is little doubt, for example, that Hutton had more than once told Ardagh of his wish to introduce 'a co-operative system of defence into Canada, based on the re-organisation of her militia upon the sound lines as those in Australia', and Ardagh had raised no objections.[57] Overall, Hutton's interviews affirmed in his mind importance of the job and, crucially, the reliability of support back home. He intended to work with the Canadian Government to bring serious reform. Should it block him, however, again on the basis of a misinterpretation of his 'success' in New South Wales, he had decided to appeal to the public (on the grounds that all they needed was to have his ideas explained in order for right-minded people to support them) and the militia itself. Feckless politicians would then act out of public pressure. Hutton felt he had the right to make use of all means at his disposal to make sure his aims were met.

Never in any doubt as to the wisdom and importance of his own ideas, Hutton never expected anything but success in Canada. He had paid close attention to speeches advocating closer Empire ties by colonial figures during the Jubilee celebrations, including Laurier's promise that if Britain's existence were threatened the colonies would not stand idly by.[58] So too he was convinced that the fear aroused in Britain over the Venezuelan Crisis of 1895 must have been felt even more in Canada. Surely, he thought, all and sundry would welcome his ambitious plans. Shortly before leaving for Canada, Minto's appointment was announced, which gave Hutton 'unqualified satisfaction and pleasure'.[59] Even if there were obstacles, he felt certain his old friend would support him, come what may. 'The principles and opinions of the new Governor-General', he wrote, 'were in all essential points identical with those of the Wolseley school.' 'Associated together in Eton days, congenial in our many tastes', he continued, 'we were of one mind upon military reform and had been brought into particularly intimate relations by all that was involved in the much discussed Mounted Infantry movement.'[60] On the eve of his departure Hutton wrote to Minto, suggesting that the two men shared a mission in Canada. Minto did nothing to dissuade him.[61]

Edward and Eleanor, their household and Colonel Hubert Foster (specially selected by Ardagh to act as Hutton's chief staff officer) at last embarked for Montreal on Saturday, 11 August 1898. The new General Officer Commanding the Canadian Militia was at the height of his professional career and the peak of his reputation in London. He was also happy, in a manner of something of a zealot who believed he had a mission of true imperial importance and one worthy of his talents. Time and circumstance would shake his contentedness – if never his self-belief – but for now Hutton relished the thought of his arrival on Canadian shores.

Photo 10 Eleanor Hutton prepared once more in August 1898 to accompany Edward to the edge of the Empire, this time to Canada. (Library and Archives Canada, PA-057332)

CHAPTER 6

'MAKING SOLDIERS OF THEM RAPIDLY'

REFORMING THE CANADIAN MILITIA, 1898–99

Canada in 1898 was in the midst of a period of industrialisation, economic growth, immigration and optimism concerning the nation's potential. Many aspects of Canadian society were transforming, from market structures to lifestyles, with literacy levels and media access rising rapidly as the nineteenth century drew to a close. Sir John Macdonald's forty-year public career had ended with his death in 1891, bringing on a period of difficulty for Conservatives, culminating in electoral defeat in 1896. From this point Sir Wilfrid Laurier, a French Canadian with a political power base in Quebec, led a new Liberal government that, despite its rhetoric, did not change existing policy directions in any significant way. Laurier did, however, recognise the wave of confidence buoying the country, declaring that while the eighteenth century belonged to Britain and the nineteenth to the United States, the twentieth was Canada's.[1] Such sentiment marked an important sense of emergent national consciousness. This was not so much the assertion of Canadian nationalism – if this meant a self-identity that stood outside the Empire – but rather a newfound self-belief and willingness to emphasise Canadian domestic prerogatives and preferences in both the political and public spheres. Growing Canadian power came with a growing assertion of Canada's aspirations, desires and its rightful place *within* the Empire, not in place of it.

In fact, despite Canada's rising sense of self as a nation, fashionable imperialism, or rather Empire nationalism, remained a powerful social and intellectual force. Canadians dined on the same diet of Kipling, Henty and Ballantyne as their cousins in South Africa and Australasia. Similar social, church and educational structures, for example, promoted the idea of Empire, and the same range of patriotic and imperially oriented organisations such as the Navy League, the Empire Loyalist Associations and even the Boys' Brigades drove the message home in Canada, as they did in all of the self-governing colonies. The Imperial Federation League maintained a small but influential branch founded in Montreal, providing a platform for such vocal imperial advocates as Colonel George Taylor Denison of the militia, George Monro Grant of Queen's University, George Robert Parkin of Upper Canada College and the prolific writer John Castell Hopkins. Jubilant Empire Day celebrations affirmed Canadian imperial sentiment as representative of the idea of a strong nation within a strong and united Empire. Yet Canadian imperialism, particularly on a political level, was layered. Canadian politicians of the late nineteenth century were even more jealous of their hard-earned political autonomy, perhaps as a consequence of growing feelings of national power, than their counterparts in the other self-governing colonies. Canadian politics roundly resented, for example, anything perceived as unwarranted external interference in domestic affairs.[2]

For a military perspective, traditional Canadian indifference to defence matters continued into the late 1890s. People still rarely thought of war and, if they did, it was as something far away and fought by British soldiers. The economic development of the nation in a prosperous time occupied the centre of attention. So too the majority of French Canadians were, in the main, neither conscious of nor interested in events beyond their borders. Moreover, Canada was perceived to be in no real danger, protected as it was by the Royal Navy and to some extent by its large southern neighbour. There was therefore little perceived need to spend or focus too much on defence.[3] Laurier told Hutton's predecessor, Major-General William J. Gascoigne: 'You must not take the Militia seriously ... the Monroe doctrine protects us against enemy aggression.'[4] This pattern was partially interrupted by the Venezuelan Crisis, which inspired a spark of limited and *ad hoc* reform by the new Liberal Minister for the Militia, Dr Frederick William Borden, who increased the number of militia trained at camps in 1896–97 from around 10 500 to 35 000 and who imposed a five-year limit on the tenure of militia unit command at a time when thirty-seven of ninety-three commanding officers averaged eighteen years in the appointment.[5] Along with the Spanish–American War of April–August 1898, such developments caused a limited and short-term revival of military interest. This included a spurt of complaint by a small but vocal section of public opinion temporarily aroused by the poor state of Canadian defences. Most Canadian politicians and the public, however, far more than observers in London, understood President Cleveland's sabre-rattling to be for domestic consumption. Nevertheless, some 40 000 new Lee–Enfield rifles were ordered for the militia, along with several batteries of 12-pounder artillery. Such developments were in themselves, however, in many ways more reflections of the state of feelings about national maturity than they were purely military considerations in that, in Wood's words, 'maintaining a national army was simply something that "grown up" nations did'.[6] At the same time there was little appetite for any type of imperial defence or cooperative military arrangement with London, or anyone else. There seemed to be no obvious benefits, so long as Britain continued to guarantee Canadian security.[7]

In any case, on 25 April 1898 Laurier told parliament that 'General Gascoigne has offered his resignation and it has been accepted'.[8] Canadian eyes turned towards his replacement. There was some debate in parliament and the press, led by the Member for Victoria North, Sam Hughes, as to whether the new General Officer Commanding (GOC) the Militia ought to be a 'Canadian', rather than a British officer, but such arguments, at this stage, found little traction.[9] Hutton was on his way with all the baggage, motivations and imperatives developed in his early career, in New South Wales and most recently in Britain. So too, packed among Hutton's luggage, was his refined plan for a cooperative system of imperial defence, itself dependent on the reorganisation of the Canadian militia into a complete army and shaped by the dubious lessons he had taken from his time in New South Wales. The difference in Canada was the scale of the task and the commensurate risks it bore.

During his voyage from London, Hutton learned that Laurier and members of his Cabinet (apart from Borden, who was absent in Nova Scotia) were at Quebec preparing for a conference with US statesmen. He arranged to disembark on 19 August to meet them while his entourage went on to Montreal. Here Hutton recalled a 'very chilly reception', which contrasted sharply with 'the warmth of feeling shown at our departure from Sydney'.[10] He later wrote to Minto, who assumed his duty as Governor-General in Canada on 12 November 1898, that he felt it 'very evident that my arrival was not welcomed by the Government'.[11] In this regard Hutton's reputation as a man of action, along with an obvious sense of purpose, seemed to have won few friends. The militia department was of little relevance within a Cabinet that saw itself as having nothing to gain through the agency of an energetic GOC. The following day Hutton left for Montreal and arrived at Ottawa on 23 August to take up temporary residence in a house near Government House provided by Lord Aberdeen, before relocating to Earnscliffe on the Ottawa River. Despite the cold political shoulder he had received in Quebec, there was yet a spring in Hutton's step, buttressed by the knowledge of sure support from home. He was 49 years old and at a high point in his career. Hutton wore the prestige of his rank as a British officer, his connections with the British Commander-in-Chief, which still carried weight in Canada thanks to Wolseley's role in suppression of the Riel Rebellion, and his position as an aide-de-camp to the Queen, on his sleeve.

Photo 11 Major-General Hutton (third from right) in Canada not long after his arrival. Lieutenant-Colonel W.D. Otter is third from left and Hutton's aide-de-camp, Captain A.C. Morrison-Bell, is first left. (Library and Archives Canada/ C-031371)

Hutton's first task, and one he wasted no time beginning, was to assess his new command. Nevertheless there is ample evidence to suggest that many of his subsequent conclusions especially regarding the overall poor state of the militia, had been reached well before sailing from England. At the 1897 Colonial Conference, Borden had invited the British to send a committee to examine the state of Canadian defences.[12] The composition of this Defence Commission had been discussed between Hutton and Major-General Sir John Ardagh, Director of Military Intelligence at the War Office, early in 1898. According to Hutton, the purpose of the commission was to strengthen *his* hand when appointed GOC in Canada. Reform and reorganisation of the Canadian militia had already been decided upon in the War Office as necessary. Whether Hutton should lead the commission had been discussed between Wolseley, Ardagh and Sir Richard Harrison (president of the CDC). Togther these men decided, however, that the commission would be more effective if its recommendations were perceived as completely independent. The Canadian Government was assessed at the time as 'lukewarm' or even antagonistic to the idea of the serious reform that War Office wanted. Hutton was happy to be separated from the commission, 'provided always that the main principles ... were identical with my own views and accepted by the Commission beforehand'. He anticipated, before leaving England, that: 'The annual Report which I, as General, would submit to the Government pointing out the reforms necessary, would thus receive the powerful support of the Report of the Defence Commission ... so that it would be difficult, if not impossible for my recommendations to be ignored.' The commission, headed by Major-General Edward Leach as President, left England in July for Canada.[13]

The preordained nature of the 'need' for reform in Canada, as understood by the War Office and Hutton, did not of course mean that it was not required. Nor did it mean that Hutton was any less energetic in ensuring that he got a first-hand feeling for militia shortcomings as soon as possible. One initial and rather foreboding problem was Borden's avoidance of a meeting with his new GOC from 23 August to 3 October, under the flimsy excuse of personal business in Nova Scotia. Borden was perhaps intimidated by Hutton's reputation and the obvious conclusion that he would likely demand some significant and immediate reorganisation of the militia. Before his appointment as minister, Borden had never been an active participant in defence debates, although he was an avid and enthusiastic militiaman. Nor did Borden consider himself to be a military expert.[14] Be this as it may, such a snubbing must have reminded Hutton of his treatment at the hands of Dibbs. It was an inauspicious beginning to a key relationship.

Nonetheless, in the absence of any discussions with his minister, Hutton set out in the first few weeks after his arrival to assess his command, with the exception of the Prairie States and British Columbia. Such touring had an additional purpose: 'to establish direct and personal relations with the Forces under my command' – and to cement his authority and reputation.[15] The reflection here of Hawley's personal touch was clear. Hutton knew he needed to win over the militia if his plans for reform were to take root, and they were no easy target. His first official duty was open range at Rockcliffe, and his speech was received in silence. Hutton was then to fire the first shot on the new range, but someone had loaded his rifle with a blank.[16] Not to be deterred, Hutton went on in the next two months to visit every major militia centre from Halifax to London (Ontario). Where he stopped he summoned senior militia officers to discuss their commands and his ideas, all the while building a personal empathy. Along the way Hutton put his flair for public speaking to good use. On 11 October 1898, for example, he gave an address to the Canadian Military Institute, informing his audience, rather misleadingly: 'I am ready to accept criticism and am always ready to consider it.'[17] The speech was well received and widely reported. He made a similar address with similar positive outcomes to the militia Field Officers' Association, focusing on 'the necessity for cordially sympathetic relations between the general officer commanding and all the officers of the force'. He 'took care to inspire' the men by 'candidly assuring the officers of his own efficiency in the profession of arms and placing it unreservedly at their disposal'.[18] 'I know my business', Hutton told them. 'I expect you to do your duty and as a brother officer I shall help you all I can.'[19]

Hutton worked fifteen-hour days during this period – and he succeeded.[20] Lieutenant-General Seymour at Halifax wrote to Minto in November 1898 that 'since his arrival two months ago', the new GOC 'seems to have already obtained a personal influence amongst the Officers of the Force many of whom were hitherto lukewarm'.[21] The *Globe* reported Hutton as 'popular with all ranks'.[22] The *Canadian Military Gazette*, the mouthpiece of the militia, noted that Hutton's approach 'in moving about and becoming personally acquainted' was one considered 'extremely satisfactory to the militia' and in stark contrast to his predecessors, who had remained in Ottawa the whole year round. 'Canada has at present an enthusiastic, capable and hard-working militia officer', the *Gazette* concluded, 'Major-General Hutton really commands the militia' and his efforts were 'bound to produce beneficial results'.[23] By the end of November Hutton himself felt had had a good 'grip' of the force.

The second purpose of Hutton's touring was to assess the state of military efficiency of his new command. In an administrative sense, as GOC he headed one of the two branches of the Department of the

Militia. The other 'civil branch' comprised public servants under the Deputy Minister and was responsible for money, stores and property. Hutton's 'military branch' was linked directly to each of the country's twelve Military Districts. Each district was itself divided into 'brigade divisions', each covering a number of counties and the militia units within them. As was largely the case for British auxiliary forces, all these arrangements were purely administrative and the force had no tactical structure at all. Around 36 000 militiamen in disparate infantry, artillery and cavalry units were scattered across city and rural areas, representing a type of 'ancient auxiliary' thinking whereby the militia would plug into a British force landed for Canadian defence if needed.[24] Much to the War Office's continuing chagrin, there was no standing plan to defend Canada beyond this vague conception.[25] Like similar military forces throughout the self-governing colonies, Canadian society remained enthralled by the amateur volunteer tradition, despite a small nucleus of poorly paid permanent soldiers used in the main as instructors and small British regular garrisons still stationed at Halifax and Esquimalt. Not even the Venezuela scare shook faith in the innate qualities of citizen soldiers – there was no room here for expensive rigid structures, organisation, discipline or realistic training of the professional. If some militia officers thought differently, they were in the minority. For many volunteers, soldiering 'remained primarily a social rather than military occupation'.[26]

Recent history had not been kind to the force Hutton had inherited. The militia was in many ways 'the Cinderella of the public services'.[27] The prestige of the soldier ranked low in Canada, lower even than in New South Wales. Previous governments of all persuasions had voted money to militia with reluctance: £300 000 pounds in 1898, the smallest spent per capita within the Empire. Three years earlier serious cuts to budget had seen the cancellation of all training for rural corps (66 per cent of force) and a one-third reduction in pay for urban units. In 1898, 30 per cent of the militia received no training at all. Efficiency varied from bad to worse as a result, depending on local enthusiasm.[28] Colin Campbell, secretary to a committee appointed by the Canadian Government to examine the question of coastal defence, had concluded a decade before that 'it takes a strong wrench to turn the key of the Canadian cash-box when money is wanted for the Military service beyond matters of political, personal or local interest'.[29] By the time Hutton arrived very little had changed.

Nor had Hutton's immediate predecessors achieved much of note. Sir Frederick Middleton, GOC from 1884 to 1890, was never considered an effective officer and retired after parliamentary criticism over the misappropriation of furs during the North-West Rebellion. He was replaced by Colonel Ivor Herbert, who found stagnation, not to mention 'incompetence, patronage and theft', and who attempted reform, particularly of the full-time militia component.[30] Herbert soon clashed with Sam Hughes, who used his paper, the Victorian *Warder*, to complain that Herbert was favouring the regular force. For his part Hutton's immediate predecessor, Gascoigne, was an indolent, ageing, unimaginative, lazy and conventional soldier guided by a strong desire to be accepted by Canadians and to defer to local authority. Within months of his arrival Gascoigne concluded that his position had no real power and was happy to leave it that way.[31] The Canadian Government remembered Gascoigne as a failure – but a compliant failure.

Hutton's own opinions on the state of his new command were predictable but accurate. In November 1898 he told Ardagh that 'the militia of Canada for offensive-defensive, or even for defensive purposes is, under existing conditions, worthless! ... the Canadian Force generally is in the lowest depths of military inefficiency.'[32] In the same month he warned Borden that 'the militia is in a state of paralysis and chaos'.[33] The artillery, in particular, was 'insufficient for modern military conditions' with officers too ignorant to train their troops.[34] In February the next year he wrote to Sir Bevan Edwards further decrying the state of Canadian military efficiency.[35] To Evelyn Wood he similarly lamented a 'low state of discipline, of organisation and of efficiency'. 'As for stores ... I may say at once, that except blankets and tents none exist!'[36] To Chamberlain, Hutton concluded that 'for years the question of Canadian defence has never received any attention'. Moreover, what was true in general terms, he concluded, was worse in the French Canadian militia units. Hutton complained that there were no trained staff officers, that troops never exercised in anything other than basic drill and practised little, if any musketry, that there were no supply, medical or pay departments and next to no engineers. Even the thousands of rifles purchased after the Venezuelan Crisis could only be held in cities, as rural regiments had no means of caring for them. Quebec, Montreal, Kingston and Toronto, Hutton continued, were 'without any modern armament of any kind'.[37] He concluded that, since the withdrawal of imperial troops, 'no serious effort has been made by Canada to place her defences upon a footing worthy of a Nation'.[38] True to form, it was not long before Hutton was airing such sentiments in public.

Although the loudest, it is noteworthy that Hutton was never the only voice crying for radical militia reform in Canada from 1898. Many militia officers, for example, watched the chaos of US mobilisation in the war with Spain and were convinced of need for change in their own organisation well before Hutton arrived. One described the force as 'literally in the position of an undressed man liable to be suddenly thrust out into the midst of an Arctic winter to battle with the elements in a condition fit only for the warmth and comfort of his own room'.[39] Hutton's own aide-de-camp, Captain Arthur Clive Morrison-Bell, in a personal letter to his twin brother and with no agenda of his own to run, complained: 'Clerks, politicians and civilians seem to do everything, without the knowledge of anybody . . . The stores are full of the funniest old guns (on old wooden step carriages) and boarding pikes . . . Chaos is the word for everything.'[40] It is true that Hutton needed to paint the militia as a largely broken organisation in order to enact his pre-prepared plans for reorganisation. It was also true, however, that his conclusions were sound.

As Hutton was busy touring and sketching his outline of all that was wrong with the militia in late 1898, the Leach Defence Commission was busy compiling its own reports. Many of the shortcomings already identified by Hutton were reflected by Leach's committee, in particular in its third report, drawn up for the information of the War Office and sent to that office on 30 November, not the Colonial Office as the previous two reports had been. This final report was blunt. Leach's terms of reference had included making recommendations with regard to the defence of the Canadian frontier but this, his committee concluded, was impossible owing to the existing condition of the militia.[41] Any real prospect of the landward defence of Canada therefore depended entirely on Hutton's efforts at reform. There is little question that Hutton had been directly involved with the Leach Commission's third report as much adverse criticism of the militia came from interviews he must have had a hand in arranging. To this end, as Hutton had hoped, it strengthened his hand – but back in Britain rather than in Ottawa. At the same time Hutton's influence was not complete. He bristled at Leach's notion that Lieutenant-General Seymour at Halifax might have a 'closer connection' to the Canadian militia in peacetime and was annoyed that none of the three reports made any reference to Canadian contributions to imperial defence.[42] Yet he still assured Minto confidentially that 'all the important recommendations were made in direct collusion with myself'.[43]

Hutton's next step, based on his preconceptions, the picture of the militia he had gained while touring, his 'unofficial' knowledge of the contents of Leach's reports and the nervousness engendered by the most serious stages of the current British Fashoda Crisis with France from November 1898 to March 1899, was to draft his first annual report. For three weeks in December, Hutton took himself to the New Brunswick forests to hunt moose in the snow by day and construct his report by campfire at night. This seminal document collected and collated Hutton's opinion of the deficiencies in the present militia organisation. These included all the necessary components of his plan for Canada, a trained nucleus of a general staff through the establishment of a staff course at the Royal Military College and a clear definition of his own role and powers as a commander-in-chief. Hutton was careful, as ever, to identify problems with the militia *system*, not with the troops themselves.[44]

Other elements of Hutton's professional and personal outlooks and the consequences of his experiences in New South Wales also manifested themselves in his report. He recommended, for example, raising a two-battalion regiment of mounted infantry in Manitoba and the north-west provinces and increased training in dismounted duties for militia cavalry units. Underscoring his belief in military service as an important part of citizenship, he also argued for a cadet corps to help Canadian boys 'realize that among the obligations of citizenship, the defence of their country is, above all, a national duty and a sacred privilege'.[45] No doubt with Colonels Spalding and Airey in mind, Hutton was scathing in his criticism of the standard of Canadian artillery officers and requested that a British officer be appointed for three years to command the militia artillery. Lieutenant-Colonel F.G. Stone, Royal Artillery, subsequently took on this role from 1 June 1899. Crucially, Hutton also called for the establishment of two key principles with regard to the role of the militia, in the defence of Canadian soil *and* the ability to participate in the defence of the Empire more broadly. Troops, Hutton argued, might be deployed to wherever 'it might be the desire of Canada' to send them.[46]

Hutton knew the risks in writing such a forceful report, which, according to Mowbray, 'amounted to a revolution in the military institutions of the first Dominion'.[47] Yet it was a calculated gamble. He felt it needed to be 'truthful and yet not discouraging or offensive' to the troops.[48] At the same time the report needed to be pointed enough to grab the attention of the government. Conscious of the importance of the press, Hutton also felt that the report 'should not be dry, but should attract the interest of the general public'. 'I was compelled to lay down in clear terms the policy which I recommended to the Government for adoption', Hutton later reflected, 'yet by doing so I was rendering myself liable to the criticism that I was encroaching upon ground which was more appropriate to the statesman than to the soldier.'[49]

Conscious of Dibbs' reaction to a similarly critical report in 1893, Hutton was surprised to find that it was digested and accepted by Borden and the government with minimal fuss. Criticisms raised in parliament when the report was tabled were few, and the only eyebrows raised regarding his 'principles', including the potential of an overseas role for the militia therein, 'of really vast Imperial moment', was from the English-language press.[50] Aside from some murmurings in a few rural newspapers, press coverage was also positive, and the militia response was equally supportive.[51] The key issue here was that such endorsement was understood by Hutton as a wider sanction for his plans. He had tested the limits and found them spongy. He wrote to Ardagh that his report was 'well received by the Press and by both political parties.[52] 'It augers well for the future', he told Seymour.[53] The reception of the report spurred Hutton on to continue with his plans with more self-belief than ever before, doubly so when he received glowing CDC approval, especially with regard to the development of administrative services.[54]

Typically, however, Hutton was blind to the political currents that had shaped the government's response to his report. His understanding of what such acceptance signalled was far removed from reality. In the first instance, not arguing with the contents of the report was one thing, implementing it quite another. As his report was tabled, the risk of war between Britain and France grew less likely and the government could once more afford pay lip service to the militia – and its GOC. Borden had additional reasons to acquiesce. Hutton's report and that of the Leach Committee coincided in many ways. The minister had sat on the latter and could hardly argue against his own findings.[55] Borden was also safe in the knowledge that a critical report might encourage Cabinet to take his department more seriously, which might mean more money, while blame for the state of the militia would rest with the Conservative Party, who had brought it to this point.[56] The sum of these factors, however, did not represent the level of universal backing for his reforms and wider plans that Hutton took away from the process.

So inspired by a false interpretation of his government's commitment to military reform according to his model, Hutton pressed hard from early 1899 to implement the changes he had flagged. Most of his structural reorganisations revolved around the idea of re-creating the militia as a national army with all supporting arms and service corps. Yet Hutton knew that the Canadians spent only 32 cents per head on defence (half that of New South Wales), so he went public once more in an attempt to ensure that the national army concept would be supported and funded by the government. He had already told Ardagh the previous November that he considered 'public opinion was ripe for accepting the proposal of putting one militia, at present existing in an inchoate and in an atomic condition, upon a national footing'.[57] Consequently, at such public events as his March 1899 speech at a Toronto Garrison dinner, Hutton argued for a 'complete military machine' with not only a combat force but also 'the brain power to deal with it, the administrative department to supply it with food, to move it from one point to another, to treat it in sickness and disease, to pay it in the field, to supply it with arms and equipment'. 'None of these departments', he reminded his audience, 'yet existed in Canada.'[58] At another banquet in the same month he called on the government to provide the means to raise a national army, tying the issue to emerging Canadian national pride. 'We must not lean on the strong arm of the Empire', he warned, 'but depend on ourselves as soldiers of a young and vigorous country.'[59] Hutton confided in Minto that if only he could get Canadians to look on the militia as a 'national army', then the 'remodelling and reconstructing necessary for enabling a Defence Force thus designated to perform its role will become comparatively easy'.[60]

At the same time the continuity of thought behind Hutton's national army concept was about much more than an effective and self-contained militia force, or mobilising the public and political will to implement it. Above all, for example, the idea embraced his professional ethos. No matter the bravery of the man, Hutton consistently argued, it meant nothing without 'measured organization and matured by scientific preparation for war'.[61] The notion was also a deliberate rejection of Herbert and Gascoigne's earlier attempts to integrate local permanent troops into the British Army, an imperative that had been endorsed by Chamberlain at the Colonial Conference 1897. Further, it was a conscious attempt to embrace the French Canadian population and encourage the militia in French-speaking Quebec. Last, the national army idea represented an authentic attempt to engage with the emerging Canadian sense of national identity and to instil Hutton's own deep belief of a key role of the military in society and the fundamental, racially based idea that 'British' citizen soldiers were the best form of defence.

In practical terms the national army concept underpinned a host of militia initiatives in 1899. By the end of the year Hutton had overseen the creation of a medical corps, including bearer companies; the beginning of field hospitals and the raising of two field engineer companies to form the nucleus of an engineer corps; and had gained approval for the establishment of four service corps companies. To this point he had failed to establish an ordnance corps, a pay department or a veterinary department – but not through want of effort.[62]

The imperative to build a militia army that could actually be mobilised to fight also implied a restructure of existing units. To this end, in mid-May 1899 Hutton drew up a paper, 'Mobilization for Defence', which sketched the required changes. He was quite clear that mobilisation was impossible unless existing small units of varying sizes were increased in strength up to uniform establishments. Hutton planned for 'gentleness' and a gradual implementation with weak and variable battalions combined, in the first instance, into 'provisional regiments without interfering with their present identity' or 'much-prized historical and local tradition'.[63] Units thus organised with fixed establishments could then be formed into brigades and divisions along British lines. The system would take the existing militia organisation and give it the capacity to expand to 50 000 troops grouped into viable field formations in time of war, with the same number again in the course of formation at various depots, once more on the Swiss model. Inevitably, some commanding officers resented the changes and complained long and loud. Hutton, just as inevitably, was intolerant and silenced such dissenters summarily. He expected complaining senior militiamen to behave according to his own professional code, never truly grasping that a sizeable proportion of citizen officers rejected the rigidity of that code.[64]

In the process of establishing administrative arms and rationalising the structure of militia fighting units, Hutton's vision for the defence of Canada gradually came to the fore. Again replicating his scheme of defence for New South Wales and in line with the broader principles of his wider cooperative imperial defence scheme, Hutton drafted a General Order in May 1899 dividing the militia into garrison forces designated for 'the defence of certain given strategical centres' and a Field Force 'for the active operations which are of primary importance in the defence of an extended frontier'.[65] Hutton envisaged a total militia force, built from existing units, of two infantry divisions, two cavalry brigades and two independent brigades of all arms and support services on War Office patterns. The lack of complaint by Borden or the government once more signalled to Hutton an acceptance of his militia army concept, structure and scheme of employment.[66]

Hutton's other substantial reform of 1899 was a dramatic improvement in militia training standards. He first focused on arranging fewer but larger summer camps of instruction. The first of these was held at London, Ontario, in May. This was the first time militia units had ever assembled into tactical formations, with staffs, in accordance with modern practice, and the first time senior militia officers experienced command of large formations. During the year virtually all the rural corps were mobilised for twelve days annual training at camp, were formed into brigades and took part in tactical exercises. City corps generally participated but were, in some cases, unable to take part in field training. Hutton further pressed for an increase to sixteen days camp training time each year, and was supported by the CDC but stonewalled by Borden.[67] Discipline was also much tighter than in the past under Hutton's supervision and, in line with his personal convictions, there was a 'new concern for the amenities of soldiering' during militia training camps.[68] Such developments won Hutton further public acclaim. The 1899 Niagara camp, for example, attracted such newspaper headlines as 'Volunteers have now begun work in earnest', 'Making soldiers of them rapidly', 'Wonderful progress at the Big Niagara Camp' and even 'Pointers for Tommy Atkins'.[69]

Aside from a focus on tactical training at continuous camps, Hutton instituted a number of other important training initiatives, such as a Staff Ride system for militia officers, akin to that he had raised in Ireland. He boasted to Minto of the success of such activities, 'an experiment which many considered too ambitious for Militia officers'.[70] By the end of 1899 Hutton was talking of a 'very satisfactory improvement' in artillery training and was impressed that infantry training standards had reached the point where brigade manoeuvres could be attempted. He was equally pleased with the work and zeal of permanent Canadian troops, who had been transformed into an effective instructional organisation, as well as the standards of training at the infantry and cavalry schools.[71] Hutton further praised the graduates of his new staff course run at Kingston 'who now form the nucleus of a General Staff'.[72]

Photo 12 Officers of the Staff Ride, Niagara Peninsula, May 1898. Fourth from the left, front row, left to right: Lieutenant-Colonel Sam Hughes, Lieutenant-Colonel Hubert Foster, Lieutenant-Colonel W.D. Gordon, Lieutenant-Colonel Gerald Kitson, Major-General E.T.H. Hutton, Lieutenant-Colonel W.D. Otter, Lieutenant-Colonel James Mason, Lieutenant-Colonel Francois Lessard. (Library and Archives Canada/C-31361)

Unsurprisingly, Hutton was careful as always to report his training 'successes' back to England. He wrote to Redvers Buller, for example, now a full general and in command at Aldershot, to this end in June.[73] The message reached the right ears. Wolseley wrote to Minto in December 1899 noting how well Hutton had done and was doing.[74] Interestingly, news of Hutton's training innovations and wider reforms also reached southwards. The British Military Attaché in Washington, Lieutenant-Colonel Arthur Lee, wrote to Hutton about Theodore Roosevelt's desire to visit one of the new-style Canadian military training camps. Roosevelt was presently reorganising the New York State Militia and, according to Lee, 'is quite your counterpart in energy!' Hutton invited Roosevelt and was told in reply: 'The idea is most attractive and if I possibly can go, I will.'[75] In the end Roosevelt could not attend and Lee reported him 'genuinely disappointed'.[76]

Overall, Canada's new GOC had accomplished much thus far. His reforms, although drastic, were generally well received by the militia itself and the wider public, and were noticed even outside the British sphere. In October 1901 Roosevelt, now President, expressed his 'high appreciation of a really first-class volunteer force' that Hutton had built.[77] There is no question the militia was set on a path of greater efficiency, and Hutton's reforms became a blueprint for future development. There is also no question that, as had been the case in New South Wales, a more efficient militia was a key ingredient of Hutton's wider plans. Once more there was no real conflict, at least in Hutton's mind, in this regard. A strong, professionalised, well-trained, militia army of all arms and services, capable of independent action, was surely in the best interests of Canada. It was also, according to Hutton, and as will be examined in following chapters, in the best interests of the Empire. Yet even as Hutton was making his improvements and reaping praise from his patrons in London for them, darker and more worrying signals were appearing. His reorganisations of the militia had been accepted, in the main, by a minister and a government happy to let the GOC have his head so long as his program did not interfere with departments, activities, agendas and prerogatives that were held to be politically important. But it was a truce destined to falter. Hutton had come to Canada fired with a passionate belief, shared by his predecessors and many fellow officers and at home, that real military effectiveness could only ever be attained by removing the influence of politics from the militia. The difference was that Hutton had the courage of his convictions and was forced by the nature of his own outlook and personality to try to confront and destroy what he saw as a malignant type of cancer in Canadian military affairs. It was this agenda, along with his plan to find a place for the Canadian militia within the wider defensive potential of the Empire, that would slowly but surely pitch him against his political masters. It was at once a battle he could not win and one he could not help but fight.

CHAPTER 7

'I AM HERE AS ONE OF YOURSELVES'

POLITICAL DIFFICULTIES AND IMPERIAL IMPERATIVES, 1898–99

Despite Hutton's successful militia reforms in the first year of his appointment in Canada, or perhaps to some degree because of them, friction between the GOC and the Canadian Government had begun to simmer under the surface. Matters finally came to a dramatic head in the latter part of 1899, in the context of events unfolding in South Africa, and they need to be understood as the logical endpoint to a process that was already in train. There were two layers to the problems that eventually drove Hutton and the Laurier government to loggerheads. The first, as much a catalyst as a cause, was Hutton's predetermined mission to rid the militia of what he and many others considered to be undue political influence. On a second level, as important as this 'crusade' was in framing mutual distain, it was in some respects a symptom of a more significant issue – one of power and control. Hutton coveted it, Canadian politicians jealously guarded it.

Before Hutton sailed for Canadian shores he was convinced, as were many of his patrons, superiors and colleagues in Britain, that the root cause of Canadian militia inefficiency was political interference and 'jobbery'. In 1885, after the North-West Rebellion, the Secretary of State for War, Lord Lansdowne, complained that political intrusion was 'the secret of the rottenness which one encounters again and again whenever one is tempted to force one's penknife into the political fabric of this country'.[1] Lord Minto, with his experience as Military Secretary to the Governor-General in Canada in the 1880s, agreed, arguing that the 'whole Militia system is saturated with political influence, which is the ruin of its efficiency'.[2] Indeed, much of the reason why a British GOC to command the militia was originally agreed upon by John A. McDonald in the first Militia Act was so that the incumbent would be placed beyond local political intrigue. In the early 1890s Colonel Herbert had tried to curb political appointments of unqualified officers but found he had in the process alienated Canadian politicians and was forced to resign. Hutton's predecessor, Gascoigne, promised the War Office he would do what he could to 'obstruct, if I can do no more, the political interference which is the Curse of the Force'.[3] By spring 1898 Gascoigne, in middle of political manoeuvring over participation in the Jubilee celebrations (a political plum Borden looked after with great care), felt his position was untenable and resigned. By June 1899 Gascoigne was busy expressing his distaste of serving ministers 'who have only their own little pettifogging ambitions and axes to grind and not the good of the country nor the Militia'.[4]

Hutton knew these feelings, opinions and stories well and, predisposed to think poorly of politicians at the best of times, swallowed them whole. He was convinced that up to his appointment the Canadian militia had been wholly neglected, except as a 'dumping ground' for political purposes.[5] Those he respected drove home the point; both Wolseley and Redvers Buller sternly criticising political interference in militia matters.[6] Hutton therefore assumed command at Ottawa with an earnest and forgone conclusion that the militia was infected with political intrigue and that it stood as the first obstacle to military efficiency.

Hutton's experiences in Canada in autumn 1898 did nothing to disavow him of his beliefs in this regard, and he went on the offensive. 'We think that some practical attempt should be made to divorce politics from the militia service', he argued in the *Canadian Military Gazette* in September.[7] 'If politics can only be kept out of the Militia Department', noted the *Montreal Gazette*, 'or rather that superabundance which marks it at present, the force in Canada must certainly receive the widest benefit from having such a man [as Hutton] at its head.'[8] At his first meeting with Borden on 3 October, Hutton told his minister, in tones that bordered on insubordination, that he hoped that no politics or political influence would be allowed to interfere with his military administration. He later claimed that Borden urged caution as, under existing circumstances, 'special advantages as regards contracts, supplies, military works, must be given to friends of his party'.[9] But in the main Borden seemed to acquiesce and, according to Hutton, with his political master suitably compliant, things began well. Thus encouraged, Hutton spent the rest of 1898 hammering the message. To loud applause he told the Canadian Military Institute, Toronto, a fortnight after his meeting with Borden, that the 'military force of Canada, the national army of Canada, should be put upon a national basis and as a national institution should, in every respect, be above party questions of all kinds'.[10] Privately, Hutton bombarded Minto with similar sentiments and received in return nothing but echoes of agreement.[11]

It was not long before Hutton's rhetoric was tested by real events. In mid-November 1898, for example, the paymaster of the 9th Battalion left his duty with the Yukon Field Force on what were to Hutton trivial and unsatisfactory pretexts and was ordered back to work. This officer was, however, brother to a Liberal MP for Quebec, and Hutton was pressured to reverse his order. 'In deference to political pressure which I then did not feel equal to stem I yielded', he admitted, only to discover subsequently the officer had been drawing two rates of pay. The incident 'opened my eyes to the system of party-political influence', Hutton wrote, and he grew determined not to let such a transgression pass in future.[12] A minor run-in with Borden followed in late January 1899 when the GOC blocked the inappropriate promotion of an unqualified officer despite Borden's advocacy. This time, Borden knew he was on tenuous ground and gave in. These were relatively trivial issues, however, and despite some early friction the relationship between minister and GOC endured, while the government cared little.

Hutton, however, grew ever more militant. By February 1899 he was writing to Chamberlain that the militia was 'entirely governed by political intrigue and party influence such that military discipline and soldierly discipline have been sacrificed'.[13] He argued that senior officers could not enforce their authority for fear of losing their positions to competitors with political influence. Even promotions and appointments and the allotment of military contracts, he continued to the Colonial Secretary, were 'reserved for political adherents'.[14] Similar sentiments were penned to most of his patrons and senior contacts back in Britain. Thus primed, the scene was set for a showdown. All it took was for an issue to arise in which both Hutton and real political agendas had a stake. This came in the person of Lieutenant-Colonel James Domville, Commanding Officer of the 8th (Princess Louise's New Brunswick) Regiment of Cavalry and a Liberal parliamentarian.

Photo 13 Frederick William Borden, Minister for Militia and Defence, 13 July 1896 – 6 October 1911. (Topley Studio, Library and Archives Canada/PA-025988)

The Domville case was a complicated but illustrative affair. As a former Conservative, Domville had won his seat of New Brunswick in 1896 for the Liberals, replacing the previous incumbent and Minister of Finance, George Eulas Foster, who was elected to the Opposition in an alternative seat. The two had a bitter history of rivalry, and it rankled with Foster that Domville had been returned for New Brunswick. Foster bided his time. Meanwhile, Domville's specified period of command of his militia regiment ended in July 1898, and Gascoigne had called for his resignation. Domville, however, refused. He had little time for Borden and, worse, his second-in-command and likely successor, Lieutenant-Colonel Alfred Markham, was a Conservative Party member who had used his newspaper to oppose Domville's election two years before. Further, Domville did not want to see the votes associated with the regiment switch sides with a provincial New Brunswick election looming. Domville appealed to his friend Laurier, and he remained in command. When Hutton reviewed the case he saw no reason – because there was no military reason – to extend Domville's tenure. This was doubly so given unfavourable reports he had received on the choleric officer, who had not called his unit to drill for more than a year. Hutton wrote to Domville to this effect in November, suggesting he submit his resignation, and informed Borden. Domville was at this point absent in Britain, on leave until 26 November, and asked Hutton to delay the transfer of command until he could write to him on the matter. Hutton agreed, but Domville outstayed his leave until the end of December. In the meantime, Hutton began the process of replacing him.[15]

By early February politics began to intrude further. Domville again wrote to Hutton claiming that in his discussions with Borden the minister had told him that regulations would not be used against him – contrary to Borden's apparent support for Hutton's decision. Hutton resented the tone, 'wanting in discipline from junior to senior officer', and prepared the Gazette notice retiring Domville.[16] Borden, however, now requested that it be deferred until after the New Brunswick elections, and Hutton complied. Hutton again placed Domville's name in the Gazette on 18 February, and again Borden requested it be withdrawn for no specified reason. Again Hutton consented. Next, on 7 April, Domville applied to Hutton to have retirement suspended pending the inquiry into his accounts initiated by Foster, who had attacked Domville in the House of Commons over the misuse of militia funds. Hutton initially refused, but Borden persuaded him once more to suspend action until after a parliamentary investigation.[17] Domville, however, failed to appear, trying to forestall the committee. A few days later, annoyed and conscious of the damage the delayed decision was having in Domville's regiment, Hutton placed Domville on leave, pending his retirement. Publicity about the order, 'misconstrued in local New Brunswick press' according to Hutton 'for political reasons', raised a howl of protest.[18]

In late May Borden wrote to Hutton demanding he withdraw the leave order, which 'should not have been issued under the circumstances', as the two had agreed to do nothing until the Public Accounts Committee had reviewed the charges against Domville. Hutton believed he had every right to follow military procedure here, but that Borden had discussed the issue with his Cabinet colleagues and they had ruled against him. Hutton responded with an 'outspoken' letter of his own, claiming that Borden's order was 'unprecedented' and that the 'reversal of orders will, in this case, assuredly lower, if it does not wreck, the discipline and subordination to orders throughout the forces under my command'. He told his minister: 'I understood from you, when assuming command, that political influence would not be allowed, under the new Government, to weigh against the discipline and good order of the Force.'[19] Hutton concluded that he had no choice but to obey, but asked for an official order to this effect so that he could resign his command. The relationship between Hutton and Borden degenerated, as also did Hutton's relationship with Cabinet since Borden had showed this letter to his colleagues.

At this point Minto became involved, after Hutton presented Borden's 'order' to him. Hutton began to see the issue more and more as a line in the sand and told the Governor-General: 'I have to put my foot down firmly.' He called Domville a 'notorious wire-puller' and that if he gave way to his 'immoral political pressure' then he had no hope of implementing his wider reforms.[20] Minto encouraged Hutton, affirming his right to 'retire' Domville 'when the regulations were so direct' and called it a 'battle of "right and principle" against "wrong and corruption"' – a challenge to Hutton's authority and ability to cut through the politics both men saw as bedevilling the militia.[21] Minto's support hardened Hutton's position and soon placed him in the centre of the storm, trying to broker a solution. On one hand he listened to Borden's complaints over the improper tone of Hutton's letters, the GOC's rash threats to resign and the fact that Domville had been placed on leave despite the agreement with Hutton to wait until the financial investigation was over. On the other he listened to Hutton (despite Minto's urging of caution and compromise), talking of a need for 'victory' to remove 'their interference as regards discipline'.[22] By the end of June, however, encouraged by Minto, Hutton accepted a compromise from Borden in that he would allow Domville to resume command until August, to allow him to be able to clear his name. Domville subsequently retired as planned after the Accounts Committee found irregularities but cleared him of personal guilt. Markham took over his regiment for a week before himself reaching the age limit and handing the regiment to another. The affair was at an end, although the acrimony between Borden and Hutton continued regarding Domville's appointment on the Reserve of Officers list.

At one level Hutton and Minto were correct. Strict letter of military law should have seen Domville retired. This was not a ministerial or political issue but a matter, in Hutton's words to Borden, of 'conforming to regulations which are equally applicable to Colonel Domville as to all other members of the Force'.[23] There is also no question that the affair developed owing to wider political considerations. Wolseley wrote to Hutton 17 March 1899 reminding him: 'Politicians influence army efficiency in this country as you know', but 'in Canada they can not only do so far more, but the patronage of militia appointments is used for the purposes of party jobbery'.[24] This was plainly true. The notion of rampant politicking concerning the militia and militia affairs that so offended Wolseley, Minto, Hutton and their like was a fact of life in Canada. Political patronage *was* part of the Canadian political system and therefore part of the militia. Borden had set about, as soon as he was appointed as minister, dispensing 'favours' for the good of his party. No less than ten of his letter books for the period 1896–99 were devoted to tracking and dispensing political favours. This from a minister more circumspect in this regard and more restrained than many. One type of log-rolling in the militia was financial and consisted in the main of letting contracts for government business to political friends and supporters. Another concerned key military appointments. These were occasionally presented as 'gifts' from the minister. Even as late as choosing men for first contingent to South Africa in 1900, Borden told the Attorney-General in Ottawa the selections were made with consideration not only to suitability but also 'men who are friends, or endorsed by friends'.[25] As even Borden's forgiving biographer, Carmen Miller, admitted: 'Hungry and often demanding were his Liberal friends.'[26]

Beyond the Domville affair there were countless other examples of overt political patronage that confronted Hutton in 1899. When he tried to transfer the Royal Canadian Dragoons from Winnipeg to Toronto, for example – a reasonable decision on military grounds – the Minister for the Interior, Clifford Sifton, concerned about the political fallout, told Borden in May 1899 to reverse the decision. Borden obeyed.[27] A similar situation arose with regard to Hutton's proposed reorganisation of certain Quebec regiments. On another occasion Hutton was pressured by Borden to promote the son of Sir Richard Cartwright, Minister for Trade and Commerce, as a political favour.[28] On yet another, one C.F. Gildersleeve, general manager of Richelieu Navigation company and a long-term dedicated Liberal, described by Laurier to Borden as an 'old friend', wrote to Borden seeking employment for his son-in-law as a staff officer on Hutton's headquarters.[29] Gildersleeve even suggested an appropriate salary level. With pressure from Laurier, Borden was happy to comply. Other examples were legion. Perhaps Hutton's biggest 'failing' in this regard – and one shared with Minto – was to disregard or believe he might change in an instant an essential reality of the system in which he was placed.

Yet the Domville affair also showcased many aspects of Hutton's character that were destined to bring him into increasing conflict with his political masters from the autumn of 1899. As he told Lady Minto, the 'storm had been brewing for some months and must, I knew, inevitably break'.[30] The inflexibility with which he applied regulations, for example, was to Hutton a mark of professionalism but to others a petulant, unnecessary and destructive stubbornness. Nor did his self-righteous arrogance underscored Hutton's ability to interpret events unfolding around him according to how he wanted to see them, rather than how they were. He told Buller he had 'just emerged from a desperate battle',[31] and described the outcome of the affair to Minto as 'a great victory and one that will do more to raise the discipline of the militia than anything that has been done since the Dominion was formed'.[32] In truth, the only 'victory' won was in Hutton's mind, the only 'test case' for the demise of log-rolling one of his own construction. He had in fact consistently acceded to Borden's demands. The political aspects of the Canadian militia carried on as before.

The real outcomes of the Domville affair were more prosaic. The relationship between Hutton and Borden never recovered. Moreover, Hutton had come to the notice of Cabinet, and its members had little patience for what had unfolded. Indeed, many Liberals thought Hutton guilty of pushing Conservative interests thanks to the affair. Moreover, Hutton had courted political resentment that he was 'interfering with the natural process of replacing Conservatives with Liberals'.[33] His extreme position, in Wood's words, 'entailed stepping on the toes of elected officials who regarded the militia primarily as a tool for the dispensing of government patronage'.[34] For his part Hutton's 'win', particularly as it had demonstrated to him that the Governor-General was at his back (despite clear signs that Minto's efforts quickly transitioned to finding a solution rather than blindly backing the GOC) made Hutton bolder still. He told Borden he planned to recommend the next year that militia officers who became MPs ought to resign their military positions – Borden, of course, was one such officer.

For all the professionally inspired pride, egotism and obstinacy of Hutton's approach to the Domville affair and the broader issue of 'political interference', it is well to remember those who continued to stoke his fires from afar. Throughout his appointment Chamberlain, Wolseley, Buller, Evelyn Wood, Ardagh and General Sir Richard Harrison, Inspector-General of Fortifications in Britain and President of the CDC, all encouraged Hutton to speak and act against political interference and to support him in this campaign. Even non-military figures, such as Gilbert Parker, Canadian novelist, imperialist and future British politician, encouraged Hutton's struggle towards 'ridding the military life of the country of all political [unknown] and interference'. 'It will be a fight', Parker warned, 'but it can be won and one is inspired to believe you will do it.'[35]

It was not only Hutton's direct and indirect challenge to Borden over Domville and other cases of log-rolling that began to draw the government from its apathy towards him into active antipathy but also Hutton's determination, as in the past, to make use of the press. Just as he had used public forums to garner support for his structural reforms, so too he used them to champion the idea of a politics-free militia and boasted to Ardagh that he had consistently 'made the speeches with that object in view'.[36] He told Harrison: 'No colonial government, however strong, will undertake reform unless outside opinion presses it upon the area of practical politics.'[37] In his Toronto speech in October 1898, Hutton called for a militia 'above party politics'.[38] The message was received well by the press, and the pattern continued. 'By private and personal explanation to leading members of the press', Hutton later admitted, 'I endeavoured to enlist their support' for a military organisation 'above party politics'.[39] As Hutton's efforts to woo the press gained ground and his public messages gained traction, his stocks with ministers fell. The more he spoke to the press about political interference, the more they felt the impression 'of a subordinate too masterful for safety'.[40]

The crux of the issue then, beyond catalysts like Domville or inflammatory remarks to the press, was a struggle for power and authority. To accomplish his aims and to satisfy the requirements of his own personality, Hutton felt he needed a free hand. He wanted the authority he mistakenly assumed Wolseley possessed in the War Office. He needed his word, unchallenged, to rule supreme in militia-related affairs. Conversely, as he began to encroach on turf and issues Canadian politicians had a vested interest in preserving, they became increasingly determined to keep the GOC in the entirely subordinate position they ascribed to him.

An early manifestation of this friction was Hutton's attempts in August 1898 to press Borden for a clear definition of his responsibilities and duties. He did so again in October, suggesting that the position of GOC be brought into line as equivalent to the British Commander-in-Chief. In November 1898, Hutton again asked for clarity. He told Ardagh that the lack of military authority in the face of the minister had been the 'rock upon which all my predecessors have split ... the Minister has usurped most of the functions of the General Commanding ... I must be given the military command contemplated by the Canadian Militia Act and defined by the Queen's Regulations.'[41] In his 1898 annual report, Hutton repeated the call to make his duties with respect to his military command 'clear and definite'.[42] Again, his position was strengthened by Minto, who agreed with and supported his ideas of the role and authority of the GOC. Like Lansdowne and Chamberlain, Minto believed the GOC held a unique position and deserved special consideration and independence as an expert and British representative.

Borden, however, avoided the issue. He had no intention of codifying the powers for the GOC. To do so was unnecessary and dangerous. Ambiguity meant freedom to manoeuvre and a free hand to check his general. For Borden and Laurier the GOC was merely a civil servant with military skills who had no authority for independent action outside ministerial and parliamentary control. Borden naturally blocked Hutton's attempt to repeat his efforts in New South Wales to usurp responsibility from the civil branch of the Militia Department in late 1898. The rebuff was in Hutton's eyes a consequence of yet more patronage in that '[c]ivilian storekeepers and pay-masters [within the Department of Militia] were unblushing political appointees and their force of clerks, labourers and caretakers came and went with a shift in party fortunes'.[43] Hutton's efforts in this regard took a further hit when Louis Felix Pinault, prominent Quebec Liberal, newspaper manager and major in the militia, became deputy minister in November 1898. With such ill-defined lines of authority in the Militia Department, Pinault became an alternative source of advice and assistance for Borden.

Photo 14 Sir Wilfrid Laurier, Prime Minister of Canada, 11 July 1896 – 6 October 1911. Laurier never accepted the notion that Hutton possessed any special authority beyond that of a civil servant. (C.T. Desjardins, Libraries and Archives Canada/ C-001968)

Central to the difficulties regarding the power and authority of the GOC was the ambiguity of the position in constitutional terms. The Militia Act charged the GOC 'under the order of Her Majesty with the military command and discipline of the Militia' while 'the Minister of Militia and Defence shall have the initiative in all Militia affairs involving the expenditure of money' – which was, of course, everything.[44] The trouble for men like Hutton and Minto was that it was tempting to make a direct link with the Crown, thereby investing a level of authority in the GOC that was abhorrent to Canadian parliamentarians. No constitutional conventions had ever been established in this regard, as defence was traditionally so unimportant. Hutton was in fact the last of a string of GOCs who had demanded, unsuccessfully, for their powers to be clarified. The government never did so, preferring the situation 'where a misstep might be used as an excuse to dismiss a recalcitrant general'.[45] When Hutton tried to claim the authority he believed was his due, he met the opposition of a minister protecting what he believed to be proper constitutional practices.

Again, however, it is important to note that Hutton's own personality framed the struggle for authority and power in the Canadian militia. Many of the same insecurities and motivations that set him to push the limits with Borden were just as surely aimed at anyone, or anything, that threatened to reduce or intrude upon the level of authority in Canadian defence affairs that Hutton believed he was owed. In parallel with his more visible clashes with Canadian politicians, for example, Hutton waged a bitter war from August 1898 to February 1900, out of public view, with his old friend Lieutenant-General Seymour, commanding British troops stationed at Halifax. The issue at hand was essentially whether Seymour, as the senior British officer in Canada, had any authority over the militia (and therefore Hutton). The dispute once again dragged Minto in as a mediator, although one again predisposed to support his fellow Etonian. The messy and acrimonious affair bounced around the Canadian Militia Department, the War Office and Colonial Office and eventually came down in Hutton's favour. Seymour's claims for authority over the militia were always spurious, and were accepted and described as such by Hutton's patrons in the War Office. They were rejected out of hand by Lansdowne, who described Seymour as an 'infatuated ass'.[46] As a consequence of the War Office position, Seymour resigned in 1900, although a later military inquiry upheld some of his grievances. The affair earned Hutton an influential and life-long enemy, who went on in 1901 to be appointed to the influential position of Military Secretary. Lansdowne perceptively commented to Minto that 'no definition of duties will make up for absence of tact on either side and I fear the trouble has been due to this'.[47] The irony is that Hutton was never under threat by Seymour and knew it, but could not resist rising even to the suggestion of a challenge to his authority.

One final piece of the puzzle remains with respect to Hutton's struggle for power and authority in Canada and that is the context of a wider battle still simmering in London, one of which Hutton was well aware, between military 'reformers' and politicians over essentially the same issues. The old system of amateur officers, with no deep sense of career commitment, as part of a system of shared connections to amateur politicians was eroding thanks to professionally oriented officers like Wolseley, Kitchener and

Roberts and the rise of the importance of 'party politics'. Gentlemen's agreements were no longer sufficient. By 1898 there was a growing consensus among reformers in the British Army that real efficiency could be achieved only by removing questions of national security from party politics. For Wolseley, 'government' now meant *following* public opinion, not *leading* it. The trouble was that any move to hand more power to professional soldiers rather than to politicians or civil servants was seen as an attack on parliamentary principles. Military dissatisfaction with politicians was thus increasingly evident in the closing years of the century, thanks to the latter's focus on cost combined with a tendency not to yield, as in the past, to military expertise. Many officers remembered the old system and looked back longingly. This type of conflict was embodied, for example, in the feuds between such men as Buller and Sir Arthur Haliburton in the War Office (and later with Milner in South Africa) and Kitchener's attitudes in Egypt. Hutton and his difficulties in Canada were part of this milieu – a symptom of a wider ailment.[48]

Although it is certainly true that the more Hutton focused on 'wire pulling', the less able he was to perceive the political subtleties and requirements of his position, it should not be forgotten that he was not the only GOC who had found difficulty with politics Canada-style and its relationship with the militia. Gascoigne had retired not only for personal reasons but also after serious feuds with politicians, including Sir Charles Tupper, Leader of the Opposition, who believed he had disgraced his office. After Hutton, Major-General Richard Hebden O'Grady Haly simply marked time as a 'safe' seat-warmer. The next reforming general, Lord Dundonald, shared many of Hutton's difficulties. He was just as controversial in his public pronouncements, appeals to public opinion, clashes with Borden over the state of the militia and his condemnations of political influences. 'I have a dreadful pariah to deal with in Borden', wrote Dundonald. 'He lies and lies.'[49] By June 1904, amid controversy, Dundonald was removed. In fact, of all the British GOCs in Canada from 1874 to 1904 only one left Canada at the end of his term with both the Canadian and British governments pleased at his performance. Of the remainder, one was dismissed, three resigned before they were sacked, two others in frustration and a seventh left by British pressure. Nor was Borden blameless. He knew as little of the military as Hutton did of domestic politics and too often failed to communicate his wishes, as *orders*, to the GOC. Borden tried to avoid quarrels and only after a confrontation was underway, when pushed, did he make use of the chain of command that was his to wield. Hutton read this as weakness, describing Borden to Major-General Sir Coleridge Grove, Military Secretary at the War Office, as 'very pliant'.[50] The fact was that any GOC in Canada at the turn of the twentieth century had a choice of two distinct paths, with no chance of straddling both at once. He might, with tact, fill the position without friction. Alternatively, he might commit to improving militia efficiency. In the context within which the GOC operated he could not do both. Moreover, a general intent on harmonious relations could not hope to bring about a grand plan of cooperative imperial defence, and this agenda was always in the background for Hutton.

Hutton played a clear game of doublespeak in regard to his imperial defence aspirations in Canada until the autumn of 1899. His feelings regarding the subject were well known from his address at the Royal Colonial Institute in April 1898 and, if anything, his desire to see his scheme implemented only grew stronger as he sailed for Canada and in his first twelve months as GOC. He later reflected on an 'intense feeling of conviction' to this end during this period, which 'impelled [him] to adopt whatever course seemed to conduce towards the above end'.[51] Yet it was a different program from that followed in New South Wales. There Hutton worked towards what he thought to be the vague principles suggested to him by his superiors and in accordance with his own coalescing but indistinct ideas. In Canada, however, his scheme was more concrete and his methods more independent of any guidance from London. His goals might well have aligned with the hopes expressed by senior figures at the War and Colonial Offices, but Hutton followed *his* plan to achieve *his* conception of 'that larger federation for defence of the whole Empire'.[52] While Chamberlain struggled against entrenched liberalism and looked to unify the Empire in the closing stages of the nineteenth century in a wide and general sense, with defence cooperation as a potentially useful wedge with which to open the door, for Hutton imperial defence was the beginning and end of the argument. It was an important distinction. The two were playing parallel to each other – not in concert.

Hutton knew full well that no scheme of imperial defence cooperation would stand a chance given the jealously guarded political prerogatives and local sensitivities in Canada, if it was perceived that it had been developed in Britain and was to be implemented by a British general. This was a real danger. Soon after his arrival in August 1898, for example, the *Globe* told its readers that Hutton 'already has had his share in the evolving of a definite constructive scheme of defence' and reminded them of his recent speeches in England.[53] Hutton therefore set out to distance himself from his scheme and his connections back home. On 6 August 1898 he told the Field Officers' Association of Canada: 'I am here as one of yourselves and not as an imperial officer', and in April the following year he declined to have his name added to the Council of the British Empire.[54]

Thanks to concerns raised by the Liberal press that he and Minto intended to cooperate to impose a scheme on the militia, possible contrary to Laurier's avoidance of imperial commitments at the 1897 Colonial Conference, Hutton was also always forced to play down the important connection between himself and the Governor-General. Shortly after his arrival in Canada he was interviewed by the *Mail and Empire* and asked whether his and Minto's appointments were 'due to the desire on the part of the British authorities to develop the scheme of imperial defence in Canada'.[55] Minto's early naivety did not help in this regard. Only a month after his own arrival December 1898 he was supporting publicly Hutton as an old friend (after privately reassuring Hutton he could 'depend on me to back you heart and soul in whatever line we decide on').[56] Minto shared Hutton's belief that the militia could and should contribute to an imperial strategy and subsequently declared himself a supporter of imperial federation, which might 'make the involvement of Canadian troops to assist the old country in case of war obligatory'.[57] Liberal journalists worried that Minto and Hutton were too close and in danger of overstepping their duties and responsibilities. It was in part to prevent any idea of joint action between the two in connection with defence questions that Hutton took himself hunting for three weeks to write his first annual report.

It was with this report, drafted in late 1898, that Hutton tested the water with respect to his imperial ambitions in Canada. As noted previously, the report laid down two clear principles upon which the militia should be built: the 'defence of Canadian soil' and the 'power to participate in the defence of the British Empire'. 'Canada is, moreover', he continued, 'a part of that larger empire which has given her birth ... there is, at the present time, a universally held determination to uphold at all costs the integrity of the Empire and at all hazards to maintain its interests against hostile aggression or foreign interference.' Further, Hutton was clear in that his proposed 'Field Force' could be made 'quickly and readily available' for operations 'undertaken conjointly with other British troops in whatever part of the Empire it might be the desire of Canada to employ them'.[58]

Just as Hutton's shock at how smoothly his report was accepted by the government spurred him to pursue the structural reform of the militia, so too it convinced him that the 'psychological moment' was ripe for 'pressing the question of cooperation for defence upon imperial lines had arrived so far as Canada was concerned'.[59] Hutton sent copies of his report to George Sydenham Clarke, George Parkin and Bevan Edwards. To the latter he suggested that it embodied 'the system of co-operative Defence which you so heartily support' and that 'if you approve, you can give our efforts here your valuable and widely influential support'.[60] He also wrote to Evelyn Wood that 'the principle of Canada co-operating with her Militia in the defences of the Empire if need be is indicated upon the same lines as those proposed for Australia in the Scheme of Australian Federal Defence',[61] and assured Chamberlain that there was 'good ground for the hope that Canada purposes to take a foremost part in solving the question of a Co-operative System of defence for the Empire'.[62] He was further encouraged by the CDC remarks on his report that commended his suggestion of a militia 'able to supply out of Canada a complete and well-equipped force of all arms to give full expression to the loyalty of the country'.[63]

Hutton had, of course, misjudged the government once more. Unlike Dibbs in New South Wales, Borden and the Canadian parliament took Hutton's report as an expression of his own opinion – not as government policy. This had always been the convention in Ottawa. Borden saw the report before it was tabled, showed Hutton where he disagreed, then gave him permission to table the document as his own. It cost the government nothing to let the GOC state his mind and, moreover, such principles as Hutton advocated would likely keep Britain happy; a sentiment the government was keen to encourage given the recent Venezuelan scare, continuing border disputes with the United States over Alaska in which British diplomatic help was essential, and given the renewed realisation of the importance of British trade since the McKinley tariff of 1890. Passive governmental acceptance, once again, indicated neither official agreement nor any willingness to act. Hutton never understood this. He wrote excitedly to Ardagh that the government 'would declare with a policy having its object – active cooperation with the Mother Country . . . to take an active part in a cooperative defence of the Empire'.[64]

Aside from, or perhaps as a result of, his official opinion as stated in his 1898 report and its reception, Hutton dropped plenty of hints to a wider public audience when he judged it beneficial. Initially this was tentative, but it grew increasingly audacious throughout 1899. In March, at the annual dinner of the sergeants of the Toronto Garrison, Hutton gave a speech, reported in the press, in which he gave the militia a role 'not only of the defence of Canadian soil, but of participating, when necessary in the defence of the Empire'.[65] In August, at his opening speech at the Canadian National Exhibition, Toronto, he reiterated that the Canadian militia's role, if need be, was to protect the wider interests of the Empire. This was a calculated ploy. Hutton had previously explained to Captain J.E. Clauson, Secretary of the CDC, how he had deliberately engaged Canadian newspapers in order to get his principles accepted in the public sphere.[66] The difficulty, he admitted to Seymour before their relationship broke down, was 'to go in advance just so far as to lead so as to be followed and not so far as to frighten and bewilder those who should follow!'[67] Hutton's messages to Borden also grew steadily more direct. In November 1898, he told his minister that 'a properly organised system is required to place your troops in a foremost position as regards their responsibilities to Canada and to the Empire'.[68] In May the next year he decried the Leech Commission's reports to Borden in that 'no reference is made to any possible effort on the part of Canada to contribute towards the defence of the Empire, of which she forms a part'.[69]

Hutton's private correspondence with his patrons and contacts in Britain revealed a degree of commitment to and confidence about his chances of implementing his cooperative scheme in Canada, far in excess of his official or public utterances. In the first half of 1899, he told Buller (and Evelyn Wood) of his determination to place 'the Canadian Militia upon a footing as will not only satisfy Canadian defence, but be able if need be, to afford assistance the Empire in case of need'.[70] Late that year Hutton informed Ardagh in detail of the actions he had taken and planned to take in this regard, and he reported to Wolseley that soon the militia would be 'ready to accept a defined place in a cooperative system of defence embracing Great Britain and her Colonies'.[71]

As a consequence of Hutton's reports, speeches and correspondence in Canada up to October 1899, it has been tempting for a number of authors to describe him as once more little more than a perfidious agent of Empire, running a simple 'programme of military imperialism'.[72] Hutton is portrayed as the villain, the natural agent of British policy.[73] He came to Canada, a puppet of Chamberlain and Lansdowne, for the purpose of 're-establishing British influence in Canadian defence'.[74] His clashes with politicians up to the autumn of 1899 were then reflections of the clash between British and Canadian interests. It was no coincidence that Minto and Hutton were appointed at the same time, so the charge runs, as their intention to collaborate to this end was present from the beginning. The militia, for Hutton, was never a 'Canadian military organisation but . . . a district of the British military command system'.[75]

Although there is no question that Hutton carried an imperial agenda with him to Canada, such interpretations fall well short of the mark.

Hutton's attempts at reform were genuine, and some initiatives, such as his support for a cadet scheme and a naval reserve for the defence of the Great Lakes, had no imperial aspects at all. Moreover, his aims should not be seen as being split between building an effective militia and fostering the ability for it to be used to defend the Empire. Rather these two aims were never mutually exclusive. The truth was, despite how much more modern nationalist Canadian authors, like their Australian counterparts, might wish otherwise, that late nineteenth-century Canadian and imperial interests *were* meshed together. It was in both imperial and Canadian domestic interests to field an effective militia for Canadian defence, just as it was in wider Canadian and imperial interest for the Empire to be preserved from external threat.

It should further be noted that it was certainly not only Hutton and Minto who saw the issues at stake in these terms in 1898–99. Such ideas were shared with the small segment of the Canadian community that was interested in defence. Hutton's predecessor, Colonel Herbert, had argued for the possibility of Canadian regulars fighting alongside British regulars. His successor, O'Grady-Haly, hoped that the militia would be 'a real and most important factor in maintaining and solidifying Canada's important position in the British Empire'.[76] The militia itself hardly needed convincing. Similar views were also being aired elsewhere in the Empire. In September 1899 a New South Wales parliamentarian and volunteer officer, Kenneth Mackay, with George Reid's and his Governor's blessing, proposed to raise 5000 auxiliary cavalrymen in Australia for use anywhere London might decide.[77]

Elsewhere in Canada, the British Empire League advocated defence policies entirely in line with Hutton's thinking. At its annual meeting in Ottawa in 1899 George Denison argued: 'If we Canadians desire to be free and safe it must be in that empire to which we are attached by every tie and to which we must be ready to give our strength for the common defence.'[78] Even Borden shared many of these sentiments. He was never against the idea of intra-Empire defence cooperation: for him, Canadian autonomy and wider imperialism were complementary (not contradictory), although like many colonial politicians he baulked at the idea of British control. At a dinner given by officers of the Montreal garrison in July 1899, Borden told them: 'I feel absolutely secure that the land and naval forces of the Empire will take care of me and take care of every part of the Empire.'[79] Furthermore, pressed by Minto on the question in early 1899, Laurier, Borden and the Minister for Justice, David Mills, were all of the opinion that language of the Militia Act enabled Britain to move forces outside the dominion wherever it saw fit.[80] So too the continuing, widespread and deep imperial sentiment in Canada was an all-important context for Hutton's plans and actions.

Nor does the idea of Hutton as imperial agent hold up well when placed in the context of events unfolding in London. There simply was still no wider, definite plan for imperial defence in 1898–99 at the War Office or the Colonial Office. Certainly, recognition of the need for one was gaining momentum, particularly under Chamberlain's influence, but British reactive defence decision-making 'by crisis' continued as it had done for decades. Meanwhile, simmering rifts in military and civilian relationships within the War Office ran deeper than ever as the cumulative results of Wolseley's well-known frustrations, reluctance by a string of governments to define a role for the army in the defence of the Empire and civilian disparagement of senior officers from making their own views on these key issues public. In this environment high-level work at the War Office remained swamped under a mass of routine administration. There was still little time, inclination or pressure to devote energy to large problems such as imperial defence. Even the CDC at this stage was only grappling with the problem and was unable to formulate a coherent imperial defence scheme; not that it ever had a mandate to develop such a scheme in any case. Any suggestion that the combination of Minto and Hutton was part of Chamberlain's long-term plans is equally unsustainable, given that the Colonial Secretary's first vice-regal choice had been the Duke of Connaught, but the Queen had disallowed it. Several other candidates declined the post before Minto was suggested by Wolseley.

Nor, in Canada, aside from the ever-present careerist desire to please his patrons, which was never far from his mind, was Hutton controlled by anyone or anything but his own convictions. The 'guidance' he had received before sailing for Canada was entirely in accordance with his own agenda, and there is no evidence that he ever acted in any way that diverged from his own personal wishes. On the contrary, there are plenty of examples of his deviating from what he knew to be London's short-term goals. He systematically sunk, for example, Wolseley and Chamberlain's efforts to station a British regiment in Canada, or to raise an exchange scheme with British and Canadian units, as these were initiatives that might undermine his own project. He was equally dismissive of Lansdowne's ideas of raising a regular regiment in Canada for imperial purposes.[81]

Overall, in the first year of his appointment Hutton's imperial defence and other plans were, in his mind, on track. His militia reforms were considerable and had been accepted, by and large, by a generally apathetic government. These reforms were important both on their own terms as long-overdue boosts to militia efficiency and inasmuch as they were a vital precursor for Hutton's cooperative imperial defence scheme. For Canada to contribute to the type of Empire-wide volunteer, part-time citizen force Hutton saw as the only answer to the imperial defence dilemma, the nation needed a balanced, all-arms, deployable and properly trained military organisation. Yet this was not, in his mind, any subservience of Canadian interest to the greater imperial good. A more efficient militia would be just as valuable for the defence of the Canadian frontier as it might be for defending other portions of the Empire if called upon to do so. This was never a case of the Empire *or* Canada. For Hutton, as for most Canadians of the era, these were not separate entities.

Twentieth-century critics of Hutton's time, policies and plans in Canada were never wrong in concluding that he always regarded the militia as having an imperial role. Rather, they have erred in the inference that this essentially demanded some sort of betrayal, some sort of subjugation of local interests. Assertions, for example, that it imposed 'too great a strain on most men reared in the service of the Crown to ask them to serve the Crown solely through the Canadian Government, rather than in the wider and more imperial sense' highlights the misunderstanding.[82] Hutton felt no strain in this regard. He did not need to choose sides. His efforts were aimed at serving both interests at once. They were not split. Moreover, any potential conflict between what he thought best for the Canadian militia and what he felt the Canadian Government, or London, desired was equally reconciled by his unerring self-belief. Hutton did exactly what Hutton wished, no more and no less.

At the same time the relatively smooth ride, with all the real and perceived successes Hutton had enjoyed in his first twelve months in command in Canada, was drawing to a sharp close. The slow but sure degeneration of his relationship with Borden and the Canadian Government caused thus far by his difficult, impulsive, vain, arrogant, outspoken and even dictatorial manner, combined with his steady encroachment on turf of real interest and sensitivity to Canadian politicians, was about to burst into something much more serious. The fuse had been lit in South Africa. The descent to war between Britain and the Boer Republics both interrupted Hutton's plans and represented an opportune time to test and perhaps cement them into place. At the same time and for the first time since coming to power, the Laurier government was forced, despite its inclinations, to focus its attention on Canadian defence policy, and in particular on the doings of its GOC. It was a recipe for a set of social, military and political events the likes of which Canada had not previously witnessed.

CHAPTER 8

'Pregnant of great results'

Canada and an imperial war, 1899–1900

The sharp decline in Hutton's fortunes in Canada and a commensurate increase in interest in military affairs throughout the Empire corresponded with, and was dramatically hastened by, the outbreak of the Second South African War. The causes of the tensions between Britain and Transvaal that eventually led to war were long-running and numerous, including the lingering grievances and consequences of the war of 1881 and the ill-fated Jameson Raid of 1885–86, global alliance politics, the continuing 'scramble' for Africa and the economics of the diamonds and gold of the Witwatersrand. Sir Alfred Milner arrived as High Commissioner for Southern Africa and Governor of Cape Colony in May 1898 determined to further the British agenda of a union of southern African states under its control. He therefore took a hard line, determined to break Afrikaner power and aspirations. The catalyst for war was the issue of 'uitlander' rights. President Kruger feared that granting a full franchise to these expatriate immigrant workers, whose numbers were almost double those of Boer burghers in Transvaal, would threaten Boer independence. Chamberlain and Milner knew it, too – and pressed their diplomatic attack.

Throughout 1899, particularly in autumn, press outcries around the Empire concerning Boer 'injustices' inflicted upon the uitlanders gathered momentum, as did calls for the British Government to act. Tensions and discontent mounted on the Rand, mines closed and talk of war filled the air.[1] A meeting between Milner and Kruger at Bloemfontein in early June 1899 solved none of the issues at hand. Three days later the decision was made in London to despatch an expeditionary force. Chamberlain admitted to Minto privately that with 'the influence of Great Britain' at stake, war was inevitable.[2] Faced with a shifting balance of military power as British troops under Redvers Buller steamed towards Africa, Kruger issued his famous ultimatum to Whitehall demanding a recall of the ships, the removal of British troops already landed and the submission of the dispute to arbitration. In less than forty-eight hours the British answered in predictable fashion, and early on the morning of 11 October, Boer troops crossed into British territory. Transvaal and its ally, the Orange Free State, were at war with Britain. The War Office, politicians and the wider public expected no serious resistance from two tiny Boer republics. The true military potential of the Boers was badly misjudged, despite the fact that Milner knew the size of the Boer citizen armies and had in fact learned of the Boer campaign plan as early as June 1899, yet he failed to pass this information on to London.[3] Under such circumstances began the largest British military effort since the Napoleonic Wars.

As the crisis in South Africa deepened, Chamberlain sought to harness the imperial sentiment he had been shepherding so assiduously. A few hundred militiamen around the Empire had already offered service, including a detachment of New South Wales Lancers training at Aldershot. As Wolseley noted after the Bloemfontein Conference, as preparations for a British expeditionary force proceeded, 'It would create an excellent feeling if each of the Australian Colonies, Tasmania and New Zealand, furnished contingents of mounted troops' and if Canada offered 'two battalions of foot'.[4] Certainly the idea of colonials fighting beside British regulars had been Chamberlain's vision at the 1897 Colonial Conference. Hence, on 3 July, without any thought at the War Office of what to do with any colonial contingents that did appear for service in South Africa, he cabled Minto in Canada and the governors in New South Wales and Victoria asking whether their governments might make formal offers of troops for 'a military demonstration against the Transvaal'. Only the self-governing colonies were asked since the use of non-white troops from New Zealand, India or Africa was out of the question. Their victory over white Boer soldiers risked a bad precedent for future governance in non-white areas of the Empire. 'Such an offer', he continued, 'spontaneously made', 'would be welcomed here & might have a great effect in South Africa'.[5] The 'effect' referred to was the sense of imperial unity they would symbolise rather than the military power they represented. Meanwhile, offers of service from British militiamen were refused. There seemed, as yet, no real need for them.

Chamberlain received a reply to his initial request from the Queensland Premier, James Dickson, only a week later with an offer of a 250-man mounted contingent. Dickson, seeking to raise the profile and stamp the imperial 'loyalty' of his colony at little cost to itself, in the process laid down the gauntlet for his fellow premiers in an atmosphere of perpetual inter-colonial rivalry. The other Australian colonies were, however, initially more guarded. Charles Cameron Kingston, Premier of South Australia, told Chamberlain, without giving any precise commitment, that members of its defence force would no doubt volunteer if needed. In New South Wales the push was led by Major-General French, who had already, on 27 June, written on his own initiative to the War Office with a plan to send 2500 men 'to be of use in South Africa in the next few months'. 'To my mind', French explained, 'it is highly important for Imperial as well as Colonial reasons that such an excellent spirit should be encouraged.'[6] French also thought to advise Wolseley as to how his government might be encouraged; explaining that all the War Office had to do was to let it be known that it would bear the costs of any contingents. 'The average Colonial Government', French continued, 'has usually not got backbone enough to offer the services of their men who volunteer, if they have to bear the cost and defend their actions in Parliament when asking supplies to be voted.'[7] He was right. Correspondence between 5 and 14 July from the governors of New South Wales and Victoria informed Chamberlain that their governments would likely support the enlistment of volunteers, yet they baulked at bearing the cost of sending and maintaining such contingents – not least when there did not seem to be much pressing military need to justify such expenditure. Meanwhile, French had lists of volunteers drawn up, continued to press his Premier and even called for a federal contingent. Eventually, under such pressure, Reid cabled Chamberlain on 21 July noting that some 1860 men had volunteered, although his government would not bear the expense of sending them.

Further south, the Victorian Commandant, Major-General Holled Smith, a Wolseley protégé and a veteran of the humiliation at Majuba Hill, publicly declared his support of the idea of an 'Australian' force and lobbied his government hard to make such an offer to London. By mid-September, with the strength of public opinion in support of not only the war but also colonial involvement in it growing stronger than ever, the Victorians began enrolling volunteers and called for a commandant's conference in Melbourne to discuss the federal idea. Despite considerable and continuous colonial jealousies, the conference went ahead in late September, as Boer the commandos were mobilising. It managed, in the face of Queensland hopes that its contingent might stand alone in distaste from New South Wales of any Victorian-led initiative, to cobble together a plan for an Australian expeditionary force of more than 2000 men.[8]

Meanwhile, across the Tasman, the New Zealanders might have been beaten to the punch by the Australians, but here there was perhaps more chance than in any other self-governing colony that Chamberlain's hopes would be answered. On 28 September 1899, Premier Richard Seddon moved in parliament to raise a force of mounted rifles to be offered for service in South Africa, at his colony's expense. The atmosphere was emotional, and the motion passed overwhelmingly with loud applause followed by three cheers for the Queen. 'We belong to and are an integral part of a great Empire', announced Seddon. 'The flag that floats over us and protects us was expected to protect our kindred and countrymen who are in the Transvaal.' As in all the Australasian colonies, however, self-interest was always at play thanks to 'a connection so closely interwoven with our interests, so inseparably bound are we together'.[9] Developing Australian and New Zealand plans were, however, halted in their tracks on 3 October by another cable from Chamberlain.

On the other side of the Empire, the largest of the self-governing colonies followed a path to war that was, in many respects, more complex than elsewhere. There is no question that the idea of imperial service should the Empire face real danger, by official or unofficial contingents, was lauded by the majority of Canadians. Non-French-speaking Canadians at the end of the nineteenth century shared the same ever-growing fascination with the Empire and spirit of imperialism – 'the growth of Imperial sentiment' as Borden called it – the same self-interested ties of economics and the same ties of history, ethnicity, culture and shared identity with all things 'British' as their Anglo-Saxon cousins elsewhere.[10] This was mixed, in Canada, with the idea of a new and more active cooperation with Britain, perhaps on more equal terms, thanks to stirring local aspirations. Yet the question was, for a larger proportion of Canadians than Australians (and certainly New Zealanders) at this early stage, did the trouble brewing on the Rand really threaten the Empire to an extent that warranted Canadian involvement? In July 1899, with press reporting subdued, even though the balance of opinion was in favour of British policies, in general terms traditional Canadian military apathy dominated. Hutton's description to Evelyn Wood of an intense sympathy for the uitlanders spoke more to his social circles and personal outlook than anything else.[11]

In Canadian politics, with a Liberal Prime Minister sensitive of his French Canadian power base, which was not in the main much interested in British imperial scheming in southern Africa, things seemed clear-cut. Laurier told Minto on 20 July 1899 that neither he nor parliament supported the notion that Canada should offer material assistance in case of war as Chamberlain had implied in his 3 July cable. With no real danger posed to the Empire by two small agrarian Boer republics, Laurier felt that the 'present case does not seem to be one in which England, if there is war, ought to ask us, or even to expect us to take a part'.[12] Ten days later the furthest Laurier was prepared to go was to secure a parliamentary expression of sympathy towards the uitlanders. It would not do well, he told Minto, to 'assume the burdens of military expenditure, except – which God forbid – in the case of pressing danger'.[13] The message was repeated privately by Borden to Hutton. Laurier and his government were quite happy to follow the previous practice of allowing Canadians to volunteer if they so wished, at British cost, but this was not the same as the type of official offer Chamberlain sought. Minto told Chamberlain the disappointing news.

The Governor-General, however, was convinced from his correspondence with Chamberlain that war was on the way and that at some point troops would be despatched from Canada. He therefore sent for Hutton and asked him 'privately' to prepare a plan for a contingent 'Canada might reasonably contribute towards military operations in South Africa'. Hutton immediately wrote to Chamberlain to tell him, despite it being in contradiction to Laurier's known public position, yet too excited by his task to still his pen, that nothing would be more 'enthusiastically received by the Militia generally and by Canada generally, except perhaps by parts of French-Canada, than such an opportunity for showing loyalty and determination to uphold Empire and Imperial interests'.[14] Hutton subsequently prepared a detailed plan for a self-contained, all-arms contingent of 1209 men. This was the sort of self-contained colonial militia force Hutton had always envisaged under his cooperative imperial defence scheme. At this point, however, cognisant of the government's position, Minto and Hutton kept this 'contingency' plan to themselves.

In August and September, Hutton distanced himself from Ottawa with a short holiday in the United States, then went on to attend training camps in the eastern provinces. He trusted that the degeneration of the situation in South Africa and commensurate rise in press reporting and public feeling in support of the British cause would soon encourage the government to change its position. Hutton was conscious at this point not be seen as overtly leading the push for a Canadian expedition as 'any appearance of an Imperial Officer such as myself having a hand in such coercion . . . could only be much detrimental to its successful issue'.[15] He was pleased to find at this stage that Borden, for one, was of the opinion that if war was declared a contingent must follow. Moreover, he informed Minto on 3 September that as soon as such an offer was made he intended to cable Wolseley, Chamberlain and Buller offering his services to lead it. Unable to contain himself, only the next day he made such an offer to Chamberlain, who replied that he was needed in Canada. Minto wrote back the following day to cool Hutton's fires, saying that he saw no immediate prospect of the government 'changing their decision' and echoing Chamberlain's advice that he would do more good remaining in Canada.[16] Hutton would have none of it, fretting that continuing delay might see Canadian troops arrive too late to see any fighting, and suggested that Minto exert his influence directly on Laurier.[17]

Meanwhile, trouble was brewing on another front. From late July a rift had opened between Hutton and Sam Hughes over the issue of a potential 'unofficial' contingent to South Africa, which eventually became more controversial than even the Domville affair and more damaging to Hutton's relationship with the government.[18] Hughes, an ardent imperialist and philosophical supporter of Hutton's imperial ideas, wanted to raise and lead his own volunteer force in South Africa. He initiated a lengthy debate on the issue in parliament in early May, subsequently informing his parliamentary colleagues of his intention to raise 5000 troops for this purpose. In late July, to Hutton and Minto's dismay, Hughes made his offer in writing to Hutton, Borden and Chamberlain.[19] Previously Hutton had intended to give Hughes a place in an official force, should one be authorised, but no more. Not only was Hughes committing a grave breach of military protocol in Hutton's eyes but also such an offer stood in direct opposition to his (and Chamberlain's) hopes for an *official* contingent. Hutton's response was quick and harsh. Hughes 'struck back like a doomed man', and what followed was a vitriolic personal and, to some degree, public slander campaign by both parties against each other.[20] Hughes' outlandish letters to Hutton bordered on maniacal, calling him not only wrong but also 'ridiculous', convincing Hutton that he was dealing with 'a species of lunatic'.[21] On the other hand, Hutton's accusations and provocations, including threats to suspend Hughes from his militia command – although most often from a position of technical correctness – were little better.[22] In September the press began reporting the feud. The government soon entered the fray, dismissing Hutton's notion that Hughes had no right raise a force, as this type of offer well suited its purposes and the controversy helped mask its own inaction.[23]

By September, however, Hutton's predictions of mounting press and public pressure on the government were coming to pass. Canadian pride was touched by the idea of being forestalled while other colonies made their commitments. Sir Charles Tupper returned from a visit to London where Chamberlain had been careful to let him know that Britain would gladly accept any offer made by the Canadian Government. Tupper henceforth put himself and his party at the head of a movement for sending a contingent. The press, pro-war and dominated by the Conservative Party, was militant and brutal in its attacks on Laurier and the government. With a growing sense that Laurier's administration was not responding to public will, feelings became more fervent still. Ethnic tensions were excited, cries of loyalty and disloyalty abounded. Initially the French Canadian view was mostly ambivalent. It was less accepting of British decision-making than Anglo-Canadians but, as the pressure mounted, grew generally more stridently against what it saw as a strictly colonial war. Other opposition voices, including classic liberals, sections of the Irish and German Canadian communities, some in the labour movement and pacifist religions like Mennonites and Doukabors, were small and ineffective. The almost unanimous English-speaking public position gave Laurier very little political room to manoeuvre. Cabinet opinion hardened in the opposite direction under the influence of Joseph Tarte, Minister of Public Works and a French Canadian, with a temper that made it difficult to predict his position on any given issue, and Richard William Scott, Secretary of State and an Irishman with clear anti-British attitudes. Laurier, all too aware of such feelings in his Cabinet, continued his policy of delay. Meanwhile, Chamberlain continued to press Minto about the chances of an official offer, but received no favourable replies.[24]

Hutton returned to Ottawa from New Brunswick and Nova Scotia on 25 September to find the question of a Canadian contingent had become a pressing public issue. In Borden's absence, he was summoned to speak with Scott, who asked whether a few volunteers might be gathered together to go to South Africa. Hutton replied 'not a few but 5000 men without any difficulty', to which Scott rejoined that 'he did not agree' and that Hutton 'did not know the feeling of the Country'.[25] Hutton went further and told Scott that, in the event of war, public opinion would force the government to send troops. Scott was furious. It was a meeting that would return to haunt Hutton as his inferred knowledge of the upcoming war and Canada's place in it undermined his efforts to appear uninvolved.[26] Two days later Hutton departed again, this time on an extended tour of the western provinces and prairie towns, convinced once more that the crisis in South Africa was close to breaking point and of the surge of public opinion that must follow.

Hutton certainly *was* involved, despite his careful efforts to absent himself from Ottawa. The public speaking noted in chapter 7, which helped to turn government attitudes against him from mid-1899, was to some degree designed, in his words, 'to raise military enthusiasm and active patriotism' to a 'white hot' level – just as Laurier sought to cool it.[27] Few direct references to South Africa were made, but the looming war, particularly from August, was the clear context. The French Canadian press accused him in early September of deliberately arousing the press to 'influence the policy of the Government', despite his absence in British Columbia.[28] For his part Hutton blamed French Canadian influences in the government for its continuing reluctance, despite the clear majority public view. Hutton was also involved at a practical level. He told Borden of the plan he had developed at Minto's suggestion in September. Borden was not displeased.[29] Without publicity the minister instructed Hutton to 'place the Canadian forces in a state of readiness, pending a call to arms'.[30]

The bombshell dropped in Canada on 3 October with the receipt of another message from Chamberlain. It read: 'Secretary of State for War and Commander-in-Chief desire that you express high appreciation of signal exhibition of patriotic feeling of people of Canada shown by offers to serve in South Africa.'[31] It was a circular memo, with similar versions being sent out to the various self-governing colonies. Borden's deputy minister, Pinault, made an unauthorised press release of the contents of the cable, but even had he not done so, it would soon have been public news as the message was published in the British press soon after the event. The Australians were surprised by the cable, whose immediate effect was to end the continuing commandants' conference and any chance of a federal contingent. All six Australian colonies then got on with planning contingents in accordance with London's request and initiating parliamentary debates to authorise their despatch. Laurier's government was somewhat more perplexed, however, given that no official offer of any type had yet been made. The wording of the cable to the Canadians might well have been the result of confusion between the War Office and the Colonial Office, or else it might have been taken to refer to the individual or non-government offers of service already received from various Canadians. Certainly, Chamberlain was well aware that there was still no official offer from the Canadian Government. Two days later he noted: 'From Canada no definite offer has yet reached Lord Lansdowne.'[32]

Surprise in Ottawa gave way almost immediately to suspicion and then fury, largely because on the same day the cable was received the *Canadian Military Gazette* published the Borden–Hutton plan for a contingent. Moreover, the *Gazette* claimed: 'If war should be commenced in the Transvaal – which seems most probable – the offer of a force from the Canadian militia for service will be made by the Canadian Government.'[33] Readers were left to conclude that the choice must already have been made by Laurier, which was not at all the case. The coincidence seemed more than suspicious; it smelled like a conspiracy to force the government's hands. This was doubly so in that special efforts had been made to publicise this article with advance proofs being sent to various newspapers, which published the story simultaneously with the *Gazette*.

The obvious culprit was Hutton. The *Gazette* had close ties to him and Militia Headquarters. He had the motive (the article's ridicule of private efforts at recruitment was noteworthy given Hutton's continuing conflict with Hughes) and the means. Cabinet members began to wonder, especially after his confrontation with Scott only a week earlier, whether Hutton had taken active steps and, if he had not actually offered Canadian troops to the War Office behind the back of his minister and government, then at the very least had used the *Gazette* to back them into a corner. Hutton had, of course, made no such secret offers. The closest he had come were letters to Minto, Chamberlain and Buller in early September telling them Borden believed that if war broke out the government would despatch troops. On the other hand, although there was no direct or circumstantial evidence that ever connected Hutton to the article, it is possible he had a hand in its instigation. If this was so, it was a daring risk – but one not beyond his character. At the same time, however, Hutton's correspondence showed him to be convinced that the government must soon yield, especially if war was declared. If Hutton was involved with the article it was a gamble, in this regard, without much of a purpose. Nonetheless, appearances and passions, at this heated moment in Canadian political history, well and truly trumped balanced analysis. Hutton was in trouble.

Laurier and his government were already feeling the public and political heat before Chamberlain's cable and the *Gazette* article, but from 3 October even more serious pressure was applied. Laurier used the Liberal-oriented *Globe* to call the inferred claims of both 'pure invention', but this did not stop a large section of the pro-war lobby interpreting Chamberlain's thanks to the 'people of Canada' as censure of the lack of government action. Agitation rose to new heights.[34] On 5 October Tupper made speeches urging a contingent, and on the same day news arrived of the official British acceptance of troops from Queensland and New Zealanders. Formal offers had also been made by Jamaica, Trinidad, Malaya, Hong Kong and Lagos. The *New York Tribune* reported Canada as 'the one important British colony which makes no offer of martial aid'.[35] According to Hutton, 'Anglo-Canada rose like one man and the whole press of Upper Canada and the Eastern Provinces, New Brunswick and Nova Scotia, took up the cudgels by means of headlines and leading articles which no government could withstand'.[36] The *Ottawa Citizen*, for example, ran letters complaining: 'After all our protestations of Imperial loyalty, our parliamentary resolutions on the Transvaal question and singing of God Save the Queen, the government crawls into its shell and refuses to do anything.'[37] Representations by militiamen themselves were just as stinging.

Laurier and his government were now caught in an inescapable quandary. With the contents of Chamberlain's cable being open knowledge, private non-official volunteering was no longer a viable alternative. The government could now reverse its position and raise a contingent, decline to do so in the face of crushing public opinion, or resign. Pressure continued to mount on Laurier from Chamberlain through Minto and from Lord Strathcona, Canada's High Commissioner in London, reminding him on 11 October, the day war was declared, that the Colonial Office had now announced it had accepted contingents from Western Australia and Tasmania, that the Victorian Government had the previous day voted to send its men and that similar outcomes were expected at any moment from New South Wales and South Australia.[38] *The Times* noted that such announcements 'give most gratification to all who have rightly apprehended unity sentiment and interest upon which the Empire depends' and continued that, if Canada had not yet offered anything, it was not for want of public opinion but 'solely on account hesitation on part of Government'.[39] The same day the *Globe* ran a story that troops were ready to go to South Africa. Hutton believed that it had been leaked by Borden.[40] Yet still Laurier held out.

By now, with war declared, Laurier's position was no longer sustainable. Hastening back from a conference in Chicago, the Prime Minister, faced with the prospect of being forced to change policy by the sheer weight of public opinion, had a meeting with his Cabinet. A stormy six-hour session ensued. Tarte and Scott opposed involvement and attacked

Chamberlain, Hutton and Minto. Borden and William Mulock, the Postmaster General, declared for a full national contingent. Other members of the Cabinet vacillated between these two positions. No result was obtained, and a new meeting was scheduled for the next day. Laurier then passed a message to Chamberlain, through Minto, that his views had not varied and, moreover, in sharp tones noted that 'the clandestine attempt which is made to force our hands must unavoidably result in impeding rather than in facilitating whatever action we may have to take'.[41] Chamberlain replied next day that he had had only two offers of Canadian service in South Africa, one from Sam Hughes and one from British Columbia, and made it clear, once more, that an official offer would be appreciated. The next day, 13 October, Cabinet voted in favour of sending troops. Minto informed Chamberlain, and the decision was announced to the press. The Canadian contingent was on its way. Chamberlain subsequently wrote to Minto that 'All's well that ends well' and that 'very few people here have any idea of the hitch which took place in the course of the arrangement'.[42]

For his part, Hutton had been under siege. His chief staff officer, Colonel Foster, warned him on 7 October that an 'astonished' Cabinet believed he had offered Canadian troops to London, hence Chamberlain's cable. Hutton was further forced to reassure Minto two days later that he was not the source of the *Gazette*'s information. Foster was summoned by Borden on 12 October and told to try to get from Hutton 'some denial of the possibility of you having communicated to London' the offer of Canadian troops. Borden did not believe it, but wished for something concrete with which to reassure his colleagues.[43] Rather than giving Borden what he needed, however, Hutton replied to Foster that the idea he offered the contingent was 'too absurd' for a strenuous denial.[44] Angry that such a message had come through Foster and not directly to him, Hutton declined to respond to Borden's request. Meanwhile, *La Patrie*, Tarte's newspaper, directly accused Hutton of 'trying to force the hands of the Government', and hinted at his removal.[45] Although the government could do nothing immediately against him, from this point there was an open antagonism between it and its GOC. Even those willing to accept that Hutton had not made direct, unauthorised offers of troops to Chamberlain remained bitter that he had nonetheless, in their eyes, engineered the demonstration of public feeling that had arisen. Laurier in particular began to criticise Hutton whenever an opportunity presented.

Meanwhile, Hutton's inspections in the west continued, all the while plagued by the issue of Sam Hughes. After the contingent had been announced, Minto stepped back from his original position and tried to persuade Hutton to compromise by finding Hughes a place within it. Borden also applied pressure, but Hutton would have none of it. Never one to forgive easily, for him Hughes was the epitome of unprofessionalism, 'ignorant of real discipline' and possessed of 'an unsound military judgement'.[46] Hence, as a consequence of his continuing hardline stand, on 26 October, the day after returning to Ottawa from his western tour, Hutton was summoned to a Cabinet meeting to explain his position regarding Hughes' potential employment. Laurier was absent, and the meeting was chaired by Scott, who berated Hutton before he could even speak. Here was a chance to exact a little revenge. Scott asked Hutton whether he thought he governed the country and accused him of trying to assume governmental functions. Scott also claimed that Hutton had been forced to leave Australia, was a martinet and had driven Hughes into insubordinate conduct. Hutton simply bowed, gave his opinion of Hughes and produced all his correspondence on the matter. Much to Scott's chagrin, Hughes' inappropriate letters ensured that Cabinet could do little to argue with Hutton's decision. Nonetheless, the next day Hutton was twice more summoned to Cabinet to discuss Hughes, but refused to withdraw his objections.[47]

The problem for Hutton by this stage, however, although he did not yet realise it, was that after the controversies of 3 October he no longer worked under the lax supervision of Borden but under the watchful, shaken and suspicious eyes of a hostile Prime Minister and Cabinet. The militia had now become central to Canadian political calculations. What Hutton had previously got away with on account of parliamentary apathy towards military affairs now came under close scrutiny. Laurier began to complain directly to Minto of Hutton's speeches on political issues, which he argued were 'absolutely out of place'.[48] At the same time Hutton himself became more uncompromising. Increasingly convinced that Cabinet was now set against him, he perhaps felt there were few reasons left to soften his polices. He was further frustrated by 'missing' the war and his correspondence to Buller begging for active service in South Africa continued, to no avail.[49] All the while Hutton's language and attitude to Borden grew more insubordinate. From this point Borden, now caught between pressures from his senior Cabinet colleagues and irritated by Hutton's new approach, took a much firmer stand on his GOC's attitudes. Not only was trust broken between the two men but also they were now on a collision course.

With no time to rest, the night following his Cabinet interviews Hutton joined the entourage of officials bound for Quebec to farewell the first

Canadian contingent for South Africa. *En route*, Borden entered Hutton's carriage, and the two reached a compromise in that Hughes would be permitted to sail with the contingent as a passenger but not in uniform. Hughes was initially grateful (although he did not stay that way for long) and apologised to Hutton for his past correspondence – an apology accepted rather ungraciously by the GOC.[50] Subsequently, in Quebec, on the night of 28 October, Borden and Hutton were guests at a banquet given by the Garrison Club to officers of the contingent. Both delivered speeches. Hutton, intoxicated by the spirit of the moment and his own rhetoric, predicted that Canada would send 50 000 to 100 000 men to defend the Empire's integrity if required.[51] This declaration directly repudiated the government's public promise that the 1000-man contingent constituted no precedent for the future. Hutton further chastised the government about its continuing efforts to interfere with the militia, this time with regard to the selection of officers for South Africa. Borden was incensed and later, drunk, after verbally abusing Hutton, got into a 'discreditable' fracas over the contents of the GOC's speech with a former militia officer before retiring to bed 'in a helpless state'.[52] The whole messy business made it into the newspapers. The following evening, this time at a reception hosted by Minto, Borden again managed to become intoxicated and arrived very late at the next day's review of the contingent. Hutton asked him to address the officers who were embarking about their pay, a provocative move given that the two had argued on the issue at the previous evening's event. Borden replied, recalled Hutton, 'in the most offensive and insolent tone that I had no business to interfere in any such matters and that I was always interfering etc, etc'.[53] Believing him drunk once more, Hutton turned away.

Laurier soon became aware of events in Quebec and moved quickly to support Borden against Hutton. The Prime Minister complained to Minto that Hutton's remarks were inappropriate and insubordinate and, moreover, that it was 'not in the traditions of the British Army ... [that] ... soldiers of high or low rank should ever venture onto political ground'. Hutton's comments on government policy, Laurier warned, brought him perilously close to breaching 'the duties entrusted to the General Commanding the Militia'.[54] Clearly Laurier was unaware that the 'tradition' in London was, if anything, the reverse. The Prime Minister wrote again the next day, concerned that the press had picked up Hutton's remarks about 100 000 Canadian volunteers and was making it a political issue. By this stage Hutton was convinced that the tide of political opinion was now actively set against him and that it had been decided, 'tacitly or otherwise, that I must be got rid of' by making his position uncomfortable to the point of being intolerable such that he would either resign or perhaps abandon his command for a position in South Africa.[55]

On 2 November 1899, after witnessing the swell of Canadian opinion in support of the first contingent and with some early Boer military success stirring the public mood further, the Laurier government offered a second contingent to London. The offer was politely refused, much to Hutton's disappointment, as the gesture to imperial unity had already been made in the initial contingent and there was as yet no perceived military need for more colonials. By mid-December this British position had been dramatically reversed thanks to the deep shock and humiliation of 'Black Week'. When Buller had arrived in South Africa he had immediately embarked upon three simultaneous offensives in Natal, the Eastern Cape and to the west. All three were defeated within a week at the Battles of Colenso, Stormberg and Magersfontein (10–17 December 1899). The disaster was as 'incomprehensible' to men like Borden as it was throughout the Empire.[56] In the wake of the crisis Hutton appealed to the War Office once more to be allowed to serve in South Africa, but again he was refused. For Hutton and many throughout the Empire, defeat at the hands of Boer farmers was bad enough, but even greater was the concern that such a display of British weakness would invite European intervention and a general war, a prospect no less fearful in the colonies than in Britain. Support for the war was thus sealed in both English-speaking and French-speaking Canada and elsewhere in the Empire. Any lingering cries of opposition fell silent. An air of crisis and seriousness took hold. In Australia, even the radical and irreverent *Bulletin* now declared: 'The Empire right or wrong.'[57]

On 16 December, in the context of Black Week disasters, Chamberlain informed the colonies that he would now 'entertain favourably' further offers of troops.[58] The Empire heeded the call. In the Australian colonial legislatures no more than four votes in total were recorded against making such offers. In New Zealand only four parliamentarians voted against a 266-man second contingent. Chamberlain was also now pleased to accept Canada's earlier offer of its own second contingent.[59] Its subsequent recruitment, however, widened the gap between Hutton and Borden even further. Appointments soon became an issue and, although Hutton won his refusal to accept Borden's 'political' nominees, more damage was done. So too many large contracts for equipment, forage and horses were needed, which increased clashes over patronage. 'General, I ask myself this question', an angry Borden responded to Hutton's urges to model the new contingent on a mounted infantry plan he had already developed. 'Is it worth Canada's while to remain part of an Empire, which can suffer disasters such as those of Methuen, Gatacre and Buller?'[60] Hutton responded with the veiled threat that 'the Canadian public would see to it'.[61] All the while Hutton still pined for active service. He wrote to Colonel William Dillon Otter, commanding the first Canadian contingent in South Africa, of 'how anxious I have been and are to join you all in this campaign'.[62] He had Foster, then in England, raise the issue directly with Wolseley, who suggested Hutton would be welcomed but doubted the Canadians would let him go.[63]

Photo 15 Hutton in Ottawa in late 1899 where the attitude of Cabinet had turned as cold as the weather. (Topley Studio, Library and Archives Canada/e011083962)

From this point the rapidly degenerating relationship between Borden, the government and their GOC was punctuated and accentuated by a series of incidents that were in themselves of little consequence. Each took on an undue significance, however, making a difficult situation untenable. The first such incident involved the purchase of horses for the second contingent. Hutton was initially informed that such horses were to be bought from Robert Beith, a Liberal parliamentarian and horse dealer. Hutton did not approve, correctly sensing political patronage, and directed they be bought by Colonel Kitson, under his orders, on the open market. On 5 January Borden ordered Kitson to Ottawa with his purchase book and accused both him and Hutton of giving preference to a Conservative dealer. Borden further ordered Kitson to allow Beith to inspect the horses he had bought and chastised Hutton for 'interfering' with his ministerial representative.[64] Hutton returned to Ottawa on 12 January complaining how offended he was that Beith had been despatched. Borden sent another sharp minute the next day with more questions about the purchase, felt by Hutton to be outlandishly and deliberately offensive. For his part, Borden considered Hutton's reply 'unsatisfactory if not intentionally rude'.[65] Hutton took Borden's actions as a vote of no confidence in him and born of Liberal log-rolling. Borden saw Hutton's treatment of Beith as yet more insubordination. Both men were influenced by emotions and growing personal antipathy. Both appealed to Laurier, who predictably judged in favour of Borden. Borden laid out his case against Hutton to the Cabinet, which had, by now, grown receptive ears. The Prime Minster told Minto that Borden and Hutton were at an impasse, which he knew not know how to solve. Hutton complained to Wolseley, with some justification, that Borden's actions were 'intentionally meant to insult myself' and that he was supported by a Cabinet 'determined to see me removed from the command'. Subject to 'every kind of petty annoyances and discourtesy', he saw no alternative but to ask for permission to resign his appointment.[66] Wolseley refused.

There was, of course, far more afoot than horse contracts. By mid-January Borden was exhausted. Departmental correspondence in the last three months of 1899 had averaged seven times the amount in the previous nine months. Meanwhile, Hutton's ongoing string of imperially oriented speeches continued to annoy him. On top of this, Borden's private business ventures were failing such that the minister was in debt and facing legal action. Meanwhile, on 12 January, Strathcona advised his agent in Canada to ask Hutton to take direct control of raising a force of mounted troops for South African service, privately funded by Strathcona himself. The next day Strathcona informed Laurier of his plans, including those to give Hutton control of its financial accounting, in order to avoid 'political' appointments and to select horses and equipment. This was unacceptable to both Laurier and Borden in its implied censure and that it would remove contracts worth $260 000 that might otherwise be used to political advantage. Indeed, in an example of outright corruption, Borden's financial problems led him to secretly arrange for his own company in Nova Scotia to supply meat to

Strathcona's force. If Hutton had control of its procurement and finances he would have discovered the truth. Further, Strathcona's plan would allow Hutton to assume the functions of the civilian branch of the militia department, even if only temporarily and for a specific purpose. Neither politician could accept this new role for the GOC. The solution then lay in 'exploiting the tension that already existed';[67] that is, there was a degree of collaboration between Laurier and Borden at this point to see Hutton removed, which to some extent explains the rapid hardening of attitudes of both men from mid-January. Laurier moved quickly to pressure Strathcona to reverse his decision to place Hutton, outside normal departmental chains, in charge of overseeing his force. He disingenuously assured Strathcona that there had been no 'politics' in the raising of either contingent so far.[68] By 17 January Strathcona had conceded the issue to Laurier.

In the wake of such issues, Hutton went to Halifax to oversee the departure of the second Canadian contingent, leaving Minto to negotiate with Laurier about the problem of the ever-deepening rift between the GOC and his political masters. Minto's plan to deal with the government's clear desire to remove Hutton was to delay and to consult London. A subsequent series of interviews between Minto and Laurier were heated. Laurier complained that Hutton was meddlesome and insubordinate. Minto defended his old friend to the hilt, telling the Prime Minister that political interference in the Militia Department prevented Hutton from doing 'good work' and that if compelled to ask London for his removal he would place his own official opinion on the matter before the Colonial Secretary.[69] Such an action, Laurier retorted, might compel his government to resign. Escalating the situation, Minto wrote to Chamberlain that in such circumstances he would accept its resignation. After a further interview between the two men on 20 January, Minto wrote a memo protesting against both political interference in military affairs and Borden's discourtesies towards Hutton. This memo, according to Minto, fell accidentally into Cabinet hands rather than into the possession of a Cabinet committee as he had intended.[70]

Meanwhile, Hutton, anxious about his fate, continued to pepper Minto with his own perspective on events, complaining of ever more offensive communications by Borden and guessing correctly that the government wanted to force him to resign or, failing that, demand his recall. 'I suppose that Sir Wilfrid has seen you about myself', he wrote. 'I have been distant with Dr Borden and by the wild look of the gentleman I gather that he is in a suppressed state of indignation and whisky.'[71] At the same time Hutton appealed to his patrons back home for support and prepared them to accept his version of the unfolding crisis. To Evelyn Wood he explained that the Laurier government had 'credited me with having forced their hands and aroused public opinion' and that as a result 'I am viewed with jealousy and suspicion'. 'For this reason', he continued, 'I am now the victim of petty unpleasantness and discourtesies, which if they are seriously augmented may make it almost impossible for me to remain.'[72]

Photo 16 Major-General E.T.H. Hutton in Canada in early 1900, busy, as always, with his pen. (AWM, P03875.002)

A week later Laurier again had a meeting with Minto, bringing with him the Governor-General's earlier memo and pointing out that he and his colleagues believed Minto to have misunderstood the relative position of the minister and general and that 'supreme authority rested with the civil power'.[73] Minto nonetheless again warned that he would write a protest if Laurier demanded Hutton's recall and see it placed on the official record. Laurier was unimpressed, hoping to keep matters confidential, but he would not be deterred. Two days later, on 29 January, despite Minto's threats, Laurier wrote his own note to Council, initiating Hutton's recall. It described conditions within the Department of Militia as 'very unsatisfactory by reason of the attitude of Major-General Hutton towards the Minister of Militia and the Government' and that 'he should not be retained as General Officer commanding the Canadian Militia'.[74] Laurier requested that the Colonial Office expedite his immediate recall via the War Office. The next day Minto told Laurier that, given 'the present anxious condition of the Empire', he was considering refusing to sign the Prime Minister's order, 'even though my refusal might be unconstitutional'. Minto also told Laurier that even though he had not spoken to Chamberlain, he believed it possible that the Imperial Government might refuse to consider the request for Hutton's recall, in order to avoid removing a 'most capable officer' at such a critical time.[75] Minto warned Laurier that his government was taking on a grave public and political risk in its course of action and suggested rearranging Cabinet. Laurier retorted that no minister would serve with Hutton. The meeting closed with the Prime Minister leaving his Order-in-Council with Minto. Hutton's spirits sagged. He wrote to the Military Secretary at the War Office, Major-General Sir Coleridge Grove, on 1 February, this time not to plead for service in South Africa but rather about the possibility of ending his appointment in Canada. Grove replied that he was quite aware of 'the extent to which politics permeate the military administration in Canada', but that Hutton would have to resign if he wanted to come home.[76]

Meanwhile, Borden maintained the pressure on Laurier to see Hutton removed. On 3 February, in a rage, he sent Laurier a new set of accusations regarding a system of 'secret orders' he had discovered that morning in Hutton's headquarters. It appeared the GOC had directed that his subordinates were not to respond to any correspondence from the minister, or meet him directly if possible, without first getting Hutton's permission and thereafter reporting back anything that had transpired. Such conduct on the part of the GOC was, according to Borden, 'unprecedented in our history, is unsupported by the rules and practice of the English War Office and is ... certainly is opposed to common sense and the efficient working of the department'.[77] Worse, Borden had become aware of this 'system' as a consequence of reviewing a list of names of militia officers to attend a staff course. On the list he found two officers whom he thought should not have been included owing to their age and health concerns. The two officers were subsequently informed that they would not be participating in the course. One of them inquired why not and was informed through Hutton that his name had been removed on the grounds that 'he had of late taken some active part in politics on behalf of the opposition'.[78] There is no evidence that this was Borden's motivation for having the names removed. Borden was convinced that Hutton had provided this misrepresentation with 'a deliberately mischievous intent'.[79]

Although Hutton might well have been guilty of attempting to stir up trouble for Borden over the staff college issue, the idea of a 'secret orders' scandal was an invention of the minister for his own purposes. Indeed, Borden's claim that Hutton had contravened War Office practice proved only his own ignorance of the way things worked in London. Wolseley, for one, had never accepted the principle that his subordinates should have direct access to the Secretary of State for War. Indeed, he openly directed that all correspondence to his minister would go through him, exactly as Hutton implemented in Ottawa. The chain of command was sacrosanct for Hutton in his own branch, and this practice was especially appropriate in his view given his strained relationship with Borden.[80] Nonetheless, Borden's 'secret orders' storm in a teacup swept away any remaining political sympathy for Hutton.

All that now stood between Hutton and an embarrassing official recall to London was Minto's intransigence. Both Ottawa and London would have avoided the awkwardness of a scandal if they could and seen Hutton unofficially recalled, but the Governor-General would have none of it, determined to use the crisis to force a showdown. Minto wrote to the Privy Council the day of Borden's exposure of Hutton's 'secret orders', suggesting that the Canadian Government possessed a 'mistaken view of the relative positions of the Minster of Militia and the General Officer Commanding'.[81] Moreover, Minto declared, Hutton's attempts to eradicate 'political influence' in the militia was the true reason for problems between himself and the government, just as it had been with the GOCs who had preceded him.[82]

Temporarily buoyed by Minto's position, Hutton found courage in his desperation and told his old friend he had 'made up my mind to fight and to fight *à l'outrance*', in order to eliminate party politics and party-political interference with the functioning of the military'.[83] He prepared a very long minute to Laurier outlining his grievances in three parts: cases of party-political influence 'exerted to the detriment of discipline'; cases where he had been subjected to 'ungenerous and discourteous treatment'; and deductions from both calling for a royal commission.[84] '[I]n no single instance', Hutton declared, 'have I over-stepped the limits of my jurisdiction, but on the other hand have experienced constant interference.'[85] For the time being Minto persuaded him not to send it.

Cabinet responded to Minto's 3 February memo with a long constitutional rebuttal of his first charge and with accusations of its own in that Hutton had looked to 'establish for himself a position in the public service wholly independent of all Ministerial control'. It is not the minister who was in 'want of appreciation for Hutton'; rather it was Hutton who 'under the delusion' that he was not under Borden's control.[86] It was a clear sign that the government would not back down. Over the next few days, Hutton, ill in bed with a cold, busied his pen explaining to Chamberlain all the failings of the Canadian Government and his own never-ending patience in dealing with 'every sort of discourtesy' heaped upon him as a consequence of the effectiveness of his reforms and attempts to remove political interference.[87] Minto's temper now began to cool and the reality of his untenable position began to dawn. The Governor-General began to slowly back-peddle and withdraw some of his earlier sting. On 7 February Laurier called on him again, once more bringing the Privy Council Order for Hutton's recall with him. This time Minto signed. The order was sent to Chamberlain the next day with Minto's cover sheet putting his opinion of the whole affair on the official record, not that the Colonial Secretary appreciated the official vice-regal 'complaint' any more than Laurier. The GOC himself, never one for humility, could hardly have penned a more supportive note to the Colonial Office.[88] Hutton called on Minto that afternoon and received the news, once again very much dispirited.

The next day, furious and embarrassed in equal measure, Hutton assured Minto that 'the Can. Govt shall pay my passage and I shall fire a parting shot when my Canadian military mantle has been dropped'. In desperation more than hope he also began to talk once more of using the limited time he had left to instigate a royal commission 'which shall carefully and publicly enquire into and report upon the administration of the Department of Militia and Defence'.[89] It was, however, a path left untrodden for at the moment of Hutton's deepest despair, as he set himself to wait for the order directing him home, Hutton received instead cable from the Adjutant-General in London on 9 February telling him: 'You have been selected for special service in South Africa ... proceed at once and acknowledge receipt.' Hutton replied by telegram same day, noting: 'Honour of selection for active service much appreciated' and resigned his Canadian appointment the next day.[90] The impasse was broken. Borden wrote back the same night that Hutton's resignation was accepted and that an Order-in-Council to that effect had already been passed and forwarded to Minto for approval. It was a remarkable forty-eight-hour turnaround of fortunes.

Three factors had saved Hutton's career and reputation and at the same time granted him his fondest wish of serving in South Africa. Foremost, the decision to send him on active service was a Colonial Office effort to avoid the controversy of a recall. Chamberlain had become all too aware of the crisis and Minto's efforts to force the Canadian Government into a public position rather than facilitate a quiet recall. By the time Minto signed the Order-in-Council for Hutton's recall, therefore, Chamberlain had hit on his own solution. It was not so much that the Colonial Secretary agreed with the Canadian Government's position as an understandable desire to preserve London's relationship with Ottawa. Without Minto's determination to support his friend and to make a stand on principle, Hutton would have been as quietly recalled as his predecessors.[91] The other two key considerations were the persistent influence of Hutton's War Office friends and Minto's consistently strongly worded communications home praising the GOC's achievements while denigrating those of his government. 'Whatever small mistakes he may have made here', Minto assured Chamberlain, for example, 'his great energy and ability under difficult circumstances deserve recognition.'[92]

Hutton's considerable ego, however, and his resentment towards the Laurier government prevented him quietly thanking his good fortune and sailing for South Africa. The problem was that he worried that the press and public in Canada would assume he was leaving *only* for active service, with no knowledge of the government's 'conspiracy' against him. Hutton therefore used two banquets given in his honour, one at the Rideau Cub in Ottawa on 13 February and another given by Ottawa District Troops the next evening, to provide a thinly veiled account of his view of the Canadian political situation and the issues between him and the government. Even more unnecessary offence was thus caused to the government when the speeches were reported in the press. The *Military Gazette* responded, for example, with a claim that Hutton was forced out because he was a 'standing menace and a continual source of discomfiture to the wire pullers and managers who manipulate the militia' and because of his role in 'making a Canadian contingent to South Africa an accomplished fact'.[93]

Hutton's actual departure from Canada belied the circumstances of his leaving. He and Eleanor left Ottawa in a special carriage decked with flowers on 15 February. The *Ottawa Citizen* reported a crowd of 2500 to see him off. 'All ranks and classes were there', it noted, 'including many women who formed part of the Soldiers' Wives league [who] presented Mrs Hutton with two bouquets.'[94] The 43rd Battalion provided an escort accompanied by a regimental band. At 4.00pm a militia artillery detachment provided a final salute, signifying the end of Hutton's time in Canada. Although he later reflected fondly upon his departure and despite the fact he had agitated long and loud to be released to go to South Africa, Hutton never forgave those he though responsible for his removal. 'I have the deepest and most profound contempt for the present Canadian Government', he later wrote, 'and have the worst opinion of their integrity and honour.'[95] 'No man of independent value or of any manly individuality as a soldier', he spat to Minto, 'would ever consent to accept the position of GOC as it exists at present in Canada.'[96]

Meanwhile, Hutton's departure and his parting speeches caused much less public outcry than Laurier had feared, as the war had tarnished British military reputations and quarrels with such men as Hughes and Domville had cost Hutton a large measure of his popularity. Hutton's words did, however, also ensure that the Laurier government gave official and public voice to its own grievances after he had departed. Laurier told the House that the GOC had been recalled due to his being consistently 'insubordinate and indiscreet and [having] deliberately ignored the authority of the minister'.[97] For his part Borden reflected, 'Since the time of Alexander I doubt if a more ambitious and unscrupulous warrior ever lived. He was always playing to the galleries, always thinking about the possible effect of any move upon his own name and fame. It was Hutton first and the devil take whoever came afterwards.'[98] The trauma had cut both ways. It was not by coincidence that after Hutton's departure the Canadian Militia Act was soon revised to allow for command of militia to go to a Canadian. None were appointed, however, as shortly afterwards the position of GOC was replaced with a Militia Council under which the powers of the minister were made clearer and many command ambiguities removed.

So what can be said of Canada's path to war, Hutton's role in it and the wider issue of imperial defence? It is clear that following the disappointment of the 1897 Colonial Conference Chamberlain continued to hope for and work towards a closer unity throughout the white Empire. This imperative continued during Hutton's tenure in Canada and, for the Colonial Secretary, the worsening situation in South Africa seemed to offer an opportunity. Following the breakdown of the Bloemfontein Conference on 9 June 1899, for example, Chamberlain drafted (but never sent) a note to Minto suggesting that in the event of war, 'the colonies should join with the mother country in a show of imperial loyalty'.[99] Three weeks later he renewed the suggestion in a secret communication explaining that he felt the mounting crisis was an 'opportunity of showing the solidarity of the Empire'. Chamberlain asked Minto whether an offer of troops was 'probable', but reminded him that 'I do not desire that it should be the result of external pressure or suggestion' – as this would defeat the purpose of creating an appearance of imperial unity with which to help coerce the Boers.[100] The object here, however, was not to build any form of imperial defence arrangement as such. The point was not to secure the services of colonial troops, but rather to garner official colonial support. The small numbers suggested by Wolseley for the initial contingents – sufficient to achieve symbolic value and small enough not to cost too much – were further evidence of this.

This is the context within which Hutton has been accused, over time, of 'every kind of Machiavellian plot' to draw Canada into the war, often as part of a wider imperial defence conspiracy involving Chamberlain and Minto.[101] He was the mastermind of 'an effective campaign to push the government into sending a contingent'.[102] Yet there was no secret accord between these men. Such individuals certainly shared a wish to see Canadians in South Africa, but in this they were hardly alone. Hutton's attempts to explain and justify his actions to Chamberlain in October would hardly have been necessary if he was simply following the Colonial Secretary's instructions. The closest Hutton ever came to conspiracy was telling Wolseley in August of the plan he had developed at Minto's suggestion for such a contingent should it be approved by the Canadian Government.[103] He received nothing in reply. This 'secret' plan, it should be noted, initially drafted without Borden's knowledge, certainly had his blessing from September. Hutton is far less 'guilty' here than many of his fellow commandants, such as George Arthur French (in New South Wales) and Joseph Maria Gordon (in South Australia), who actively, openly and unashamedly tried to pressure their governments into committing troops, in public as well as privately, and who corresponded directly with the War Office concerning the issue to a far greater extent than Hutton ever did.

Complicating the issue were Hutton's own self-delusions regarding his role in bringing Canada to the war and his subsequent writings in this regard. In March 1900, after returning to England, he boasted to Lansdowne that it was owing to his influence 'that the French Canadian element in the Cabinet was over-ridden and troops sent'.[104] He similarly argued to Wolseley and Evelyn Wood of the importance of joint action between himself and the Governor-General. As Hutton later reflected to Minto: 'As years pass we shall both of us (you and I) more clearly realize the importance of our successful action in indirectly in forcing the weak-kneed and vacillating Laurier Government with their ill-disguised French and pro-Boer proclivities to take part.'[105] Hutton's correspondence to all and sundry crediting himself and Minto with forcing the Laurier government to war continued for the rest of his life.

Hutton's personal role and influence in bringing Canada into the war was, in reality, much less than either he or many of his subsequent critics would have it. Hutton blatantly and consistently misunderstood Minto's position and his own influence, while underestimating the role of other key figures and forces. In the end, the decision to send troops was a reluctant, politically motivated capitulation by the government to the strident demands of Canada's pro-war advocates – the overwhelming majority position by 13 October – measured against the risk of domestic disharmony and a mounting state of British expectancy. Hutton's touring and public-speaking played some part in stirring militia and public feelings towards the imperial cause, but his was but one voice within a much wider swell of support for the war that engulfed Canada in the autumn of 1899. Hutton was a tiny part and by no means a prime mover of the spirit of imperialism in Canada at this time. This was the same spirit that animated pro-war movements throughout the self-governing colonies; in the words of the Prime Minister of New Zealand as his first contingent sailed: 'for one flag, one Queen, one tongue and for one country – Britain'.[106]

There is no question that Chamberlain consistently attempted to use the march to war to further his goal of increased imperial unity, and one important technique was his leveraging off the issue of imperial defence. The colonies, however, showed little interest. In fact, although their offers of contingents made it obvious that they might be willing to send troops to Britain's aid in any future conflict, ideas of formally codified, standing imperial defence arrangements remained a long way from reality. Colonial enthusiasm was born of Empire nationalism, not of a desire for closer standing defence ties. Nor, although such notions might have bounced around the Colonial Office and sections of the War Office, was there any truly unified British position on the issue in the lead-up to and early phases of the war in South Africa. Thinking of cost and their negligible military value, Lansdowne was, for example, unenthusiastic about accepting the initial colonial offers. The British Treasury, for its part, initially recommended against paying for them. Imperial defence principles were hardly foremost in the mind of the British Government. The lead-up to and commitment of the first Canadian contingent to South Africa represented therefore less than might be expected with regard to the development of philosophies and structures of imperial defence. What remained to be seen was whether anything more concrete might be born in the aftermath of war – but this was yet a long way off as Hutton sailed from Canadian shores.

Importantly for Hutton, during the voyage back to Britain his misinterpretations of his role in bringing Canada to war began to merge with thoughts regarding his Empire-wide cooperative defence scheme. Somehow his helping to 'force' Canada to war, Hutton concluded, was in itself an important step in successful implementation of this grand scheme.[107] 'The Canadian public had gradually been led up to accept as a matter of course the principles thus indicated', he later wrote, 'which, inferentially understood, meant a share in the defence of the Empire.'[108] In Hutton's mind, the system of cooperative imperial defence sketched in New South Wales and published in England was now implemented, more or less, in Canada and would be tested on the veldt. The subsequent conduct of the war was thus for him 'more pregnant of great results than any event in the last half century'.[109] This was especially so as Hutton remained, like many of his contemporaries, convinced that this conflict was itself only a prelude to the far greater European struggle. All that remained was to see whether his white, colonial, volunteer, citizen-soldiers could prove his faith in them in battle, and circumstances had transpired to allow him to assess this first hand.

CHAPTER 9

'QUITE AS MUCH POLITICAL AND IMPERIAL, AS IT IS MILITARY'

HUTTON'S WAR IN SOUTH AFRICA AND RAISING AN AUSTRALIAN ARMY, 1900–03

When Hutton returned to London he was terrified that events in Canada might have sullied his reputation and thereby ruined his future prospects. He need never had worried. Lansdowne and Chamberlain assured him that not only was his work in Canada highly valued but also that they well understood the great 'difficulties' under which he had laboured.[1] His spirits buoyed, Hutton chose this moment to address the issue that had been forefront in his mind since leaving Canada, namely, his ideas of a 'Militia System of Co-operative Defence'. Chamberlain was interested and asked Hutton whether he thought a militia system on the Canadian or New South Wales model might be applied in Britain. Hutton assured him it could. The present 'fragmented' auxiliaries in Britain, in that they still consisted of infantry units without field artillery, mounted units or military departments, could and should, Hutton argued, be restructured as a self-contained army. Chamberlain initially doubted the quality of such a militia, but Hutton assured him that 'with a good system of organisation and a good set of experienced officers it mattered little if the men were at first somewhat ill-trained'.[2] Chamberlain was so impressed that he took Hutton at once to see the First Lord of the Treasury and future Prime Minister,

Arthur Balfour, who was deeply alarmed by the British military weaknesses exposed in South Africa. To Hutton's delight, Balfour reiterated the government's satisfaction with his service in Canada. Hutton then once more outlined his idea for a British militia, based on his Canadian and New South Wales model and its potential to fit into his wider ambition of a cooperative imperial defence system. Balfour explained that his senior military advisers had told him militia artillery regiments were impractical, but Hutton countered by arguing that what had been possible in the colonies was possible in Britain. Balfour seemed impressed.[3] It was an important moment, the first time Hutton had openly pitched his grand scheme to those in a position to do something about it.

Hutton was further heartened by a subsequent series of informal meetings with Wolseley, who also assured him that his 'successes' in Canada were obvious and that those in positions of responsibility in London knew better than to take Laurier's public pronouncements of Hutton's 'insubordination' at face value.[4] Other patrons and sponsors offered similar messages of support and encouragement. Most significant, however, was a second interview with Lansdowne, on 2 March, where Hutton was told he would likely command a body of imperial troops in South Africa.[5] Lansdowne wrote to Minto that he trusted Field Marshal Lord Roberts, now in command of British troops in South Africa, would see this done.[6] It was with high optimism, sharpened ambitions and renewed self-confidence that Hutton bade farewell to Eleanor and set sail bound for Cape Town on the afternoon of Saturday 3 March 1900.

Hutton arrived in South Africa a little over a fortnight later. After a brief stint in command of a brigade of militia at Kimberley with the local rank of major-general, he was summoned to Bloemfontein to take charge of one of the two brigades of the newly formed Mounted Infantry Division, under Major-General Ian Hamilton. Hutton's new command was organised into four mounted corps, each made up of two or three Australian, Canadian or New Zealand mounted units, with the addition of a regular British mounted infantry battalion. These regular battalions had been drawn from the mounted companies of various British infantry regiments, men who had often been trained under the mounted infantry system Hutton had set up at Aldershot.[7] Hutton set to organising his brigade with gusto, typically impatient with anything perceived as standing in his path.

Photo 17 Major-General E.T.H. Hutton, commanding the 1st Mounted Infantry Brigade, South Africa. (Author's collection)

In addition to a natural desire to prove himself on operational service after the humiliations of 1884 and the positive influence on his career this would have, part of Hutton's enthusiasm was also a consequence of the personal and professional significance of commanding a composite 'Empire' formation of mounted infantrymen. First, if successful, Hutton's brigade would place the value of mounted infantry, the lifelong focal point of his professional endeavours, 'above all cavil of argument'.[8] More importantly still, already concerned with British military ineffectiveness and imperial defence arrangements more generally (fears only accentuated by Black Week), here was an opportunity to test his cooperative imperial solution. Hutton's grand vision of a white, Empire-wide (predominantly mounted) volunteer militia of citizen-soldiers was almost perfectly represented by his brigade, even down to the scattering of British regulars to stiffen colonial inexperience. This was a force born of the Empire, deployed far from home, for the purpose of defending the greater whole.

'I must make my command a success under Providence', he wrote home, describing his responsibility as 'quite as much political and Imperial, as it is military'.[9] To Chamberlain, Hutton mused, 'this happy association of selected representatives from the self-governing Colonies . . . will exercise no small effect upon the future military consolidation of the defences of the Empire'.[10] He predicted to Minto 'the success which it achieves will to a very great extent depend on the feeling of the Australian and Canadian Troops and through them the Colonies whom they represent towards a Military Co-operative system of Defence for the Empire'.[11] Here was the wider context and lens that guided Hutton's hand throughout his time in South Africa.

The significance Hutton attached to his command also puffed his pride, not a trait that ever needed much encouragement. He corrected his wife sharply, for example, for the grave error of addressing him as a brigadier, rather than a major-general. He was also sure to write to the Australian premiers and to Laurier, to let them know who now commanded their troops abroad and how relieved they ought to feel that it was an officer with his colonial empathy and experience. The Australians and New Zealanders were polite, Laurier was furious. Hutton was deliberately provocative, to the point of vindictiveness, to the Canadian Prime Minister. '[O]nly in October last I was accused in Canada by those who did not then share your present opinions', he wrote, 'of endeavouring to "force a policy upon the Government which was opposed to the interests of the people".' 'It is satisfactory indeed', he went on, 'to find that the sentiments which I was in October last accused of fostering' were now 'applauded to the echo by both sides of an enthusiastic Canadian House of Commons'.[12] Doubly galling for Borden was that his son, a young Canadian volunteer officer, was now part of Hutton's brigade and entrusted to his care. To Hutton's pure delight he later discovered that his appointment was 'taken as a slap in the face' by Laurier's government, 'so much so that it was proposed to send a remonstrance' back to Whitehall.[13]

As happy as Hutton was at thumbing his nose at Canadian politicians now he was in South Africa, he was less pleased to realise the potential influence of current British Army politics on his future prospects. Hutton was a Wolseley protégé, but Buller's 'Black Week' disgrace and Roberts' subsequent appointment had fundamentally altered the balance of power. Roberts led a coterie of officers that had vied with Wolseley's circle for many years. The fortunes of the Roberts Ring were now on the rise, just as Wolseley's star was falling. The mix was complicated further by

Kitchener, not aligned with either (although closer to the 'Indians' (Roberts) than the 'Africans' (Wolseley), with his own smaller patronage circle of Egyptian veterans. 'I quite realize that I am received with extreme jealousy by the Roberts clique of which my Divisional General Ian Hamilton is a prominent member', Hutton complained in April. 'As for Kitchener', he continued, 'he is to me a sort of Sphinx.'[14] For so long protected and promoted by his Wolseley patrons, Hutton was now on his own, in somewhat hostile territory, and he knew it.

In late April Roberts' long-expected advance to Pretoria began. Hutton and his brigade, most often in cooperation with Major-General John French's cavalry division, fought well in a number of notable actions during the advance at such places as Brandford, Coetzee's Drift on the Vet River, in the Kamelspruit valley, defending the Witpoort–Reitvlei area (and thus foiling General Louis Botha's attempt to retake Pretoria) and in the capture Kaapsche Hoop plateau, which helped open up the Eland Valley. At last, on 24 September, as British infantry entered Komatipoort and seized its stores, the President of the Transvaal, Paul Kruger, slipped across the border into Portuguese East Africa and sailed for Europe. Exhausted and ragged, Botha dispersed most of the commandos into the mountains to the north. At this point and despite his earlier fears, Hutton and a great many other British officers concluded erroneously that the war was won and all that remained was to form an army of occupation. 'Everything now seems to point to a speedy conclusion of active hostilities', he wrote to Eleanor, 'and ere long, please God, I shall be on my way home to join you.'[15] He had already told Kitchener he was anxious to get home. 'In fact the rules as regards local rank make my employment almost impossible', he wrote to Minto, 'even if I wished to remain, which I do not.'[16] With there being no further role for large field formations, Hutton's brigade was broken up in early October, and he was told by Roberts that he could return to England. 'I can hardly express of how happy I feel', he told his wife, and expected to be back in London in the first week of November.[17]

Taken in total, Hutton's time on the veldt was a seminal period for him on both personal and professional levels. He had succeeded in a military sense and was mentioned in despatches, and his professional competence was well recognised by his subordinates. Lieutenant-Colonel James Macarthur-Onslow, Hutton's aide-de-camp, for example, recalled of the action at Witpoort: 'His command was outnumbered, almost surrounded. Through a long and anxious day he showed no sign of discomposure, not even haste. Clear, terse orders, quietly dictated, a calm somewhat stern face and a cold resolute demeanour inspired confidence wherever he went on a six-mile front with one flank turned and the other heavily attacked.'[18] Moreover, Hutton *believed* himself to have triumphed in a physical and professional sense, further erasing the scars of Egypt and vindicating the very high regard that he placed on his own abilities. Although he never shielded his men from danger, the casualties suffered by his brigade, for example, were very small – in more than thirty engagements Hutton lost twenty-one killed. This result he put down to his own professional competence, with a dash of divine Providence.

There is no question that in South Africa Hutton put into practice the tenets of professionalism he had previously preached. Subordinates, for example, were routinely informed of his plans in order to secure 'the intelligent co-operation of everyone'.[19] Hutton was equally conscious and conscientious of transport and logistics issues. Typical of the polarising effect of his personality, his brusque manner, lack of tact and insistence of the outward signs of professional standards certainly annoyed many of his subordinates. Just as many, however, recognised his ability and were more than happy to serve under him, if not as delighted as Hutton might have thought.[20] In any case, Hutton was clear in his own mind, at least, that had he only been given more latitude he would have accomplished even greater things, going as far as suggesting that had this been the case the war might have been brought sooner to a close.[21] The net result was a man with more self-confidence and with more self-belief than ever. Given his consistently high opinion of himself, this was no mean feat.

The only burr in Hutton's hide as he sailed back to England was his belief that the injustice of intra-army politics had and would continue to prevent him receiving the accolades that he thought his due. He grumbled to French that 'the very least possible has been said as to our part in the triumphant advance', and he saw conspiracy at work when he could find no thorough press coverage of his defence of the Witpoort passes.[22] Hutton also resented Roberts' public praise of the mounted infantry without direct reference to himself. Hamilton, previously an aide-de-camp and military secretary to Roberts, came in for particular scorn in that he was given command of the mounted infantry division, which Hutton believed should rightfully have been his, and consistently detached several of Hutton's corps during the advance to Pretoria apparently in an effort to undermine Hutton and aggrandise himself. 'I knew very well that he [Hamilton] would [do] all in his power to put me in the wrong and get me sent away', he wrote to Eleanor in August. 'They call it being "Stellenbosched" here'.[23] Hutton had, of course, conveniently forgotten that the knife cut both ways. Just as Hutton had been coming to the notice of the Wolseley Ring in Egypt in 1884, for example, Hamilton was a victim of it. 'Nothing could have been more inhospitable or forbidding than the response from the special preserve of the Wolselyites', Hamilton wrote at the time. 'I was an intruder; I was alone in this hostile camp.'[24] Besides, Hutton had enough jealousy to go around – even French, by no means a Roberts man, came in for his share of abuse from Hutton's pen. Yet to some degree he was correct. Hutton was not promoted and, despite his clear success, was passed over by many of his better-connected contemporaries. This would not have occurred if he had possessed the sympathy of the Roberts' coterie or the public fame of French.

Just as Hutton believed in the imperial significance of his mixed colonial and British mounted infantry brigade in South Africa when he took command, so too the experience of leading it in combat further shaped his long-standing cooperative defence scheme for the Empire. His column had represented a physical embodiment of the essential characteristics of his scheme writ small. The brigade was a collection of white, volunteer, citizen soldiers from across the Empire, fashioned as mounted infantry. Moreover it had formed and fought, to protect imperial (and therefore local) interests as two sides of the same coin. The supremacy of the Anglo-Saxon race and Empire and British military prestige – by even the harshest means if necessary – was the common goal. The success of the 1st Mounted Infantry Brigade was for Hutton proof, then, of the correctness not only of his personal and professional outlook and philosophies but also of his larger project.

The war also further cemented Hutton's commitment to mounted infantrymen as soldiers and as an operational concept. South Africa had been a chance, as he told French, to put 'into practice before a worthy foe those very principles of tactics for which we had both contended 12 years ago at Aldershot in the teeth of bitter opposition'.[25] By June he was arguing that 'men on foot are perfectly helpless ... It is the difficulty of comprehending this fact and accepting it which has caused all our disasters in this war.'[26] He preached to Minto that the advance to Pretoria was 'a most complete illustration of the power of Mounted Troops in war ... in fact the whole campaign is corroborative of the fact which Your Excellency and I have been preaching for the last

20 years.'[27] Indeed, in the end for Hutton it was mounted infantrymen who 'won the campaign in South Africa'.[28] The flip side was that the war equally demonstrated for Hutton all the weaknesses of traditional cavalry. On the advance from Johannesburg to Pretoria he lamented that the cavalry 'effect upon the enemy is purely moral as they rarely if ever dismount to fire and as for their swords and lances . . . they are less than a good riding cane would be'.[29] Falling back as always on the insecurities of his middle-class background and foundation of his professional outlook, Hutton complained of the incompetence and timidity of cavalry officers as 'the result of a century of a mischievous system which has made our Cavalry the dumping ground and the play ground of the aristocracy'.[30]

Of his wider solution to the Empire's military dilemma, Hutton took his brigade's achievements as more evidence of the potential and appropriateness of the system he had devised – and of his own brilliance in conceiving it in the first place. He praised the manner in which his disparate colonial troops worked 'cordially and in unison with each other', for example, and 'upon cordial and equal terms with the regulars as brothers in arms'.[31] Reflecting an opinion of politicians only hardened by his time in Canada and echoed among much of the senior British officer corps, Hutton felt all that stood in the way of the reform required to bring such a scheme to fruition, even as the war raged, was the continuing inability of the British Government first to lay down the '[p]rinciples governing the Defence of the Empire and then leave us soldiers to prepare the scheme'.[32] The answer for Hutton, even as he marched and fought, he explained to Minto and Chamberlain, was again the shaping of public opinion; a idea itself based on an exaggerated notion of his influence in this regard in New South Wales and Canada. So too his experiences on the veldt, of dealing with colonial troops and officers, reconfirmed in Hutton's mind that any system of imperial defence cooperation must rely on ties 'of silk and not of steel'. He condemned those 'misguided people' in London 'who imagine that our Colonies with their strong feelings of independence and individuality can be bound by treaties and half concealed coercion'.[33] In South Africa, as in his previous colonial appointments, Hutton believed earnestly that the time was nearing 'when the whole Defence System of the Empire will require to be placed upon a basis of co-operation or mutual aid'.[34] In his mind the 1st Mounted Infantry Brigade was a template solution. All that was needed was a wider canvass – an environment and circumstances where it might be put into effect on a much grander scale.

As Hutton marched to Pretoria, then east to Kaapsche Hoop, he had thought constantly of what might come after his service in South Africa. Indeed, as early as July, aware of developments towards federal union in Australia, he wrote to Minto of 'the presentiment that I shall go to Australia and complete my work done in '93 and organize the Commonwealth Army'.[35] It was the beginning of a campaign to this end by Hutton, partially motivated by the belief that the change of guard at the War Office would rule out future career prospects if he stayed in England, set to continue, with fluctuating intensity, for the next eighteen months. Hutton went as far as telling Eleanor in August that he had received 'many letters from Australia and our return is pretty well accepted as certain'.[36] Moreover, he told her he would gladly go, if asked. On 5 October, Hutton made a tentative official approach, writing to Lansdowne that 'there is, I understand, some talk in Australia I believe and among the Australian troops here of my being offered the command of the Federal Army of Australia'. If the 'opportunity presented itself of being called upon to put into practice the particulars of the Federal Defence Scheme which I drafted in the Australian Colonies in 94–96', he continued, 'I should certainly feel it my duty to accept'.[37] With previous experience in Australia and Canada and of commanding colonial troops in South Africa, Hutton thought himself in a unique position to make a success of such a posting. More to the point, he began to see the potential of a stint in Australia to forward his grand imperial defence project.

Hutton returned to England in early November 1900 to a disturbing set of circumstances. In addition to the lack of public or official recognition of his success on the veldt (although an appointment as a KCMG soon followed), what remained of his ring of patronage, already badly damaged by the war, was soon to be smashed with Roberts set to replace Wolseley as Commander-in-Chief. No plum, full-time military posting followed, and Hutton worried about being sent back to South Africa. At the same time, he was even more determined to further his ideas of cooperative imperial defence, and his imagination had been fired by talk of a possible return to Australia. Hutton now set his considerable energies towards achieving these two outcomes.

Fortunately for Hutton, political currents were moving in his favour. As a consequence of the 'khaki election' of October 1900, Salisbury was returned and Lord Lansdowne, exhausted and fed up with his position as Secretary of State for War, was moved to the Foreign Office. He was replaced by the young (at forty-four years of age) and ambitious St John Brodrick, who had had previous experience at the

War and Foreign Offices. In the context of difficulties in South Africa, army reform was now a pressing political issue and one Brodrick planned to use to make his name. From December 1900 the new War Secretary started seeking advice on military improvement from such key figures as Kitchener.[38] Meanwhile, Hutton was advocating his own ideas to all who might listen. The Empire's only salvation, he argued long and loud, 'is in the development of the Militia system and its reorganisation in conjunction with the Militia systems of Australia and Canada upon the principle of cooperation'. He complained further of the continuing and dire need for the new government to lay down tangible principles for the land defence of the Empire so that a system based on them, something like his scheme, might be implemented. 'All the thinking soldiers agree with me', Hutton was sure, 'but none will speak out.'[39]

Hutton's own 'speaking out' soon attracted Brodrick's attention. On 30 January 1901, he later reported, 'we had a long talk upon the lines on which military assistance to the Empire might be obtained from our self-governing Colonies'.[40] Hutton pressed his cooperative plan onto Brodrick, providing details of how many troops might be furnished 'upon the necessity arising and upon the Colonial Governments in question desiring to offer'.[41] This included a full mounted brigade from Canada of 2700 men, two brigades from Australia and a half-brigade from New Zealand. Only the cadres of such formations would exist in peacetime, to be filled in wartime by volunteers. This was predicated in Hutton's mind, as in the past, on colonial cooperation, not compulsion or subordination to the War Office. His scheme depended on volunteerism and eager colonial governments, and he advised Brodrick that no imperial defence system should be tabled for consideration except through means of a collaborative 'Defence Conference' in which colonial representatives were present.[42]

On 8 March Brodrick unveiled his plan of army reform to the House of Commons, arguing that he could not rule out, as Stanhope had done, British military involvement on the continent in the event of a calamitous general war. Brodrick continued that, in this context, 'the day is not far distant when some of our colonial brethren who gave us mounted assistance during the war will be willing, subject to the consent of their own Governments, to keep up mounted contingents ... who, when occasion demands, will be available to join our own Yeomanry should they volunteer to go abroad'. 'If the Australian Mounted Infantry could be strengthened and be regarded as a possible source of supply of troops for overseas service in time of war', Brodrick continued, 'Australia would be contributing to the Imperial forces on active service abroad in precisely the same manner as the United Kingdom.'[43] Hutton was thrilled and invigorated, seeing his scheme in Brodrick's words.

By the end of the month details of Brodrick's proposed reform were becoming known. His 'solution', at almost £5.5 million above the standard army vote, was to enlist 11 500 more regulars and to reorganise the British army into six self-contained corps of 40 000 men each, three regular and three made up of auxiliary troops. The plan was attacked in parliament by a young Winston Churchill, among others, on various grounds including the difficulty of finding recruits and that such formations were an illusion given the lack of administrative and support services in the militia, yeomanry and volunteers. Naval authorities also opposed it, fearing a reduction of their own estimates. Nor was it long before Brodrick faced the same strength of recalcitrance by Roberts' new guard at the War Office as Lansdowne had battled against when the Wolselyites had been dominant.[44] Hutton was himself indignant, primarily because the details of Brodrick reforms looked nothing like his scheme. He 'has completely lost the whole point of the requirement of the Empire', Hutton fumed to Minto, 'and he has lost the golden opportunity which this great crisis which we have just passed through has given him and the Salisbury Government'. Hutton's main complaint was that Brodrick presented no new plan to defend the Empire, merely increasing the size of the force available to defend Britain. Always ready to conclude that those not of like mind were his intellectual inferiors, Hutton thought Brodrick had 'not the grasp of mind, nor the personality to carry through any strong measure of reform' and therefore 'our funny, quaint, out-of-date Army' would stay that way a while yet.[45]

It was not all bad news, however, for Hutton and his cooperative scheme. He was encouraged, for example, by a CDC report that aligned much more closely with his vision than the Brodrick reforms. 'It is in any case evident', ran the report, 'that the whole of the Imperial army, using the term in its widest sense ... at home and in the Colonies, must now be regarded ... as a training ground for the men who will form the nucleus of that greater army which it may be necessary to put into the field.'[46] At the same time Hutton was forced to fight his natural and 'learned' urges to speak out to public opinion to win support to his cause, unless he chose to abandon all idea of future employment, which he would not do while the prospect of a posting to Australian lingered. 'My future is very uncertain', he wrote. 'If I do not go to Australia and if the new regime assign me some uncongenial and humdrum job, I shall give up the active list and go into Parliament, or endeavour to do something and make some use of the experience and knowledge of the Empire and of Imperial questions I have gained.'[47]

Despite quips to friends in late 1900 that he could not decide whether he ought to remain in London to assist in the 'Sisyphus task' of military reform, or to go Australia to command the new federal force when the colonies finally united, there was, in reality, no vacillation in Hutton's mind.[48] As he had already told Eleanor, he would jump at the appointment if it was offered, especially as he assumed that the new Australian federal government would be free from the political intrigue that he was convinced had made his position in Canada untenable. The problem was that no such offer had been made. The best and only semi-official indication that Hutton might be offered it had been an indirect query from Sir William Lyne, Premier of New South Wales, as to whether he would consider proceeding to New South Wales to 're-arrange their military affairs ... and then take up the Federal reins later'.[49] Hutton replied that the federal job would be a great honour, but this was a tentative Australian approach, not a War Office order.

The whole issue of the appointment of a General Officer Commanding (GOC) for the new Commonwealth of Australia, which came into being on 1 January 1901, and its federal military force, gained impetus in April 1901. The inaugural Australian Minister for Defence, Sir John Forrest, pressed the Prime Minister, Edmund Barton, to ask the War Office for a suitable general to act as GOC. A cable was subsequently sent through the Colonial Office asking Roberts to make his confidential recommendations.[50] As Hutton had feared, Roberts favoured Lieutenant-General Sir Reginald Pole-Carew, a member of his coterie and personal friend of Lord Hopetoun, the Australian Governor-General, who described him to Barton as an 'enthusiastic soldier of varied experience and with knowledge and sympathy for the citizen soldier'. On 11 June Barton replied to the Colonial Secretary that his government would pay a salary of £2000 plus passage for the position. Roberts replied, fearing that 'neither Pole Carew, nor any other officer without independent means would be willing to accept the appointment on bare terms offered'.[51] Barton upped it to £2500 (any more would put the GOC on a considerably higher salary than his minister), but Pole-Carew still refused, hoping for twice that amount. Other names were canvassed, but the low salary remained a stumbling block. By now it was August, and still no GOC had been decided upon.[52]

Photo 18 The Barton Ministry, 1902. The Hon. Sir John Forrest is on the far right, standing, and Edmund Barton is second from the left, seated. (National Archives of Australia, A1200, L13365)

On 20 September 1901, the *Daily Telegraph* in Sydney reported some good news for Hutton in that with the first four candidates for the Australian GOC position no longer under consideration, the Federal Government would now be glad of the services of either him or Major-General Horace Smith-Dorrien. 'Sir John Forrest, Sir William Lyne and other members of the Cabinet', it continued, 'are believed to be favourable to the appointment of General Hutton.'[53] Running out of options and with pressure mounting, the War Office officially wrote to Hutton on 2 November 1901 asking whether he would accept the position with the rank of major-general and on £2500. With a degree of independent means at his disposal and hence less need to quibble over his salary than others, Hutton confirmed that he would. Chamberlain passed Roberts' recommendation to Barton on 14 November, and the Australian Prime Minister agreed. The War Office announced Hutton's appointment a week later, and on 3 December he received formal orders from Roberts, along with directions to report to the Colonial Office for further instructions.[54]

Once sure of his appointment, Hutton wasted no time putting pen to paper. He assured Barton that he well realised 'the grave responsibility that will rest upon me' and that the Prime Minister 'may in all respects rely upon it that I will do all in my power to loyally and truly carry out the instructions I may receive from your government, yourself and my respected Minister'. With some irony Hutton claimed that his 'sole desire' was to assist Forrest in 'perfecting such measure of defence as your policy may deem desirable'.[55] Hutton also sought to mend some bridges, writing disingenuously to George Dibbs that if he had in 1894 'ventured, at some points, to differ upon your views upon Military questions', he did so 'only from a strict and over-powering sense of duty and in opposition to my personal feeling of cordiality to yourself'.[56] Cordiality had, it was clear, been the last thing present between the two.

Before Hutton departed England for Australia, he once again attended the round of obligatory official interviews. He had a meeting with Chamberlain on 19 December and was reminded by the Colonial Secretary, conscious of accusations of collaboration with London when he was in Canada and Hutton's over-active pen, that 'it must never appear that he was acting as the Agent of the Imperial Government, or in any way being in collusion with him'.[57] Hutton assured Chamberlain that he sought no instructions tying the Colonial Office into declaring a policy to be followed in Australia. Rather, Hutton suggested that the path he intended to tread was that outlined in 'Part 3' of his Annual Report for Canada of 1 January 1899, which 'contained the exact principles' he proposed for his coming command.[58] This, in a nutshell, was the dual aim of improving the force he found, particularly in its ability to field self-contained militia formations, for the purposes of both strengthening Australian defences and for facilitating the use of such forces for the wider defence of the Empire should the Australian Government deem it appropriate – the essentials of his cooperative scheme. In Hutton's own words, 'a Militia Army, which after satisfying the requirements of local defence, should be available for offensive operations outside the local area, as is the most suitable form of defence, if Parliament so asked it'. Further influenced by his *perceptions* of the difficulties faced during his Canadian appointment and a number of personal letters from Australia along the same lines, Hutton stressed his determination to make such a force truly national and above party politics. Dangerously, he added a determination to act as a 'true' GOC, with his opinions not to be vetoed 'by an interested and relatively ignorant majority'.[59]

Hutton reported that Chamberlain was quite in accordance with his views during the interview between them – with the exception, perhaps, of Hutton's prediction that his greatest problem would be the fact he might be too popular! In truth, however, despite all the assurances given on his return to England from Ottawa, Canada had left its scars. Chamberlain had hardly championed Hutton during the selection process and had in fact told Hopetoun the appointment 'is not in my opinion the best that could have been made'.[60] It was not Hutton's ends that worried the Colonial Secretary, rather his abrasive, unsubtle and controversial means of chasing them. Hopetoun replied hoping the new GOC would avoid controversial speeches and engagement with the press.[61] Even Minto wrote to Hopetoun, before Hutton arrived, warning of the GOC's tendencies.[62]

On 26 December 1901, Hutton was made a substantive major-general and on the same day, with Eleanor, left England for Marseilles, bound for Australia. He set sail with the knowledge that this was to be his most important command and his best chance yet to implement his long-standing professional aspirations and deep personal convictions regarding the security of the Empire. Hutton was outwardly happy, radiating a renewed self-righteous zeal.

As Hutton had fretted in London over his military prospects and laboured to secure his new appointment, much had been unfolding in Australia pertinent to his future role. By far the most urgent concern of the new Federal Government, for example, and one that stood at odds with Hutton's grand plans, was the issue of finance. The Governor-General had confirmed at the opening of the first parliament that 'extravagant expenditure will be avoided'.[63] Moreover, in its first decade of existence, thanks to Barton's pledge of no new federal taxation, the government's main source of income was restricted to customs and excise duties. Even then, thanks to the 'Braddon Clause' of the Constitution, the Federal Government was required to allocate to the states three-quarters of this revenue for ten years from 1901. A devastating drought, which began during Hutton's tenure in New South Wales and which did not break until 1903, further ensured that economic frugality was the order of the day. In the first decade of the new nation's history, expenditure on defence averaged a total of only 0.42 per cent of gross domestic product. Across the Empire only Canada spent less per person on defence than Australia. Nor, after the end of the Second South African War in 1902, was defence much of a public issue.[64]

At the same time those politicians and members of the public who maintained an interest in military affairs expected Federation to bring increased military strength and security, at reduced cost, with minimal trauma imposed on long-standing colonial units. All of this at a time when the prestige of senior British officers was at a low ebb in Australia, with losses in South Africa peaking just after Federation. Major-General Stuart Beatson's description of Australian soldiers after the disaster of Wilmansrust in June 1901 as 'a fat-arsed, pot-bellied, lazy lot of wasters' and 'a lot of white-livered curs' certainly did not help in this regard.[65] Such were some of the challenges facing Hutton on his arrival in Melbourne on 29 January 1902.

The state in which Hutton found his new command, the first 'Australian' army, was confused, at best. Although Forrest's fledgling department had begun to carry out its functions from Victoria Barracks, Melbourne, from March 1901, staff members were not transferred to it until late July. Even then the department consisted only of the minister, Captain Robert Henry Muirhead Collins (the shrewd and sharp-minded former Secretary of the Victorian Defence Department) as his civil adviser, a chief clerk with six subordinate clerks, two messengers and a caretaker. Until federal legislation was enacted, the department was little more than an administrative post office. Forrest's first priority therefore was to draw up and pass the federal Defence Act, for until this was done he had no legal control over the military forces he presided over. Indeed, without proper legislation military personnel could not even be transferred between military districts without the individual's own consent![66]

In March 1901 Forrest had directed the Federal Military Committee to draw up such a bill. The subsequent draft, formulated in the context of CDC advice on the matter, confirmed an 'active' force containing serving part-time militia and volunteer troops and small numbers of permanent soldiers and made provision for a 'reserve' of men who had served in the active force at some stage. The Bill also sanctioned rifle clubs and a cadet organisation for boys. It further allowed for compulsory military service in times of 'emergency' and, similar to Canadian legislation, the power to call out the Commonwealth military forces for active service anywhere, inside or outside Australia, at any time deemed necessary, 'for its defence'. Although careful to ensure that the minister (and therefore parliament) rather than the Governor-General or a GOC had final authority over the forces, Forrest accepted these principles and as matter of urgency introduced the first Defence Bill to Parliament in June.[67]

Forrest's presentation of the Bill, however, was clumsy, and his defence of it reflected its hasty revision and his own lack of confidence. His initial speech reaffirmed his intention to keep military costs down and his commitment to a citizen force. Forrest then departed for Perth for a family funeral, leaving Barton to fend off the many critics. Debate raged with forty-one of seventy-five members of the House of Representatives speaking. Parliamentarians expressed fears that the Bill's provisions for compulsion might lead to standing permanent forces and even continental-style conscription. Such anxieties increased Labour's apprehension that a standing army might be used for quelling domestic disturbances. There were also concerns about the active forces in that a partially paid militia might destroy the finer spirit of volunteerism. Others argued in favour of a purely militia organisation on the basis of its greater efficiency. Although few disagreed with the Bill's provision for voluntary overseas service, some worried about its power to compel such service 'in defence of the nation' and what that might actually mean. A few members, infatuated with Boer success on the veldt, advocated dismantling traditional military structures entirely and extending rifle clubs to become the backbone of the forces. Alternatively, William Morris Hughes, a loud critic, advocated a national militia something like the Swiss model of compulsory yearly training for all males.[68]

By the time of the Bill's second reading not only were its compromises now criticised by the state commandants who had drafted it (especially those adding restrictions for troops to be deployed outside Australia) but also further complications had been added by emerging aspirations and agitation for an Australian navy, led by Captain William Rooke Creswell, Commandant of the Queensland Naval Forces, an issue that crossed over into debates concerning the Defence Bill. Thus, with no hope of its passing and with the government now preoccupied with framing tariff legislation, on Barton's motion the Bill was discharged. As a result of the Defence Act debacle, Barton asked the state premiers to direct all defence-related inquiries through him rather than the Defence Department. It was therefore Barton and not Forrest who announced Hutton's appointment.[69]

With no Defence Act, Hutton assumed command of the Commonwealth Military Forces with no strategic or policy legislation to guide him. For a man with very fixed ideas this was as much an opportunity as an impediment. He was encouraged in this regard, immediately upon his arrival, by the Prime Minister. Hutton was naturally critical of the failed Bill's restrictions on overseas service, inasmuch as they might limit the application of his cooperative scheme of imperial defence. He at once began stressing to Barton and Forrest the 'erroneous strategical assumption' of the Bill in that 'the defence of Australia was to be narrowed down to the defence of Australian shores'.[70] He pressed the case that real security could be ensured only by the capacity for 'a strong and vigorous offence'.[71] The result was spectacular for Hutton. On 15 February, at a banquet given by the government at Parliament House to honour his arrival, Barton argued for a wider interpretation of Australian security imperatives that seemed to support the notion of Australian troops being used for imperial defence. Furthermore, during the speech Barton quoted directly from Hutton's *Our Comrades of Greater Britain*.[72]

The new GOC, however, took too much away from the Prime Minister's words. Having just passed the Immigration Restriction Act (or White Australia Policy), effectively restricting immigration from non-European countries, Barton was unsettled at hearing, two days previously, of the ratification of the Anglo-Japanese Treaty and had perhaps spoken rashly. He had also, it seems, momentarily forgotten the Labor Party's dominance in the Senate and its less than enthusiastic support for anything that hinted at compulsory military overseas service. Further, while Barton and Forrest were personally comfortable with the principles of imperial defence, others in the Cabinet such as George Turner and Charles Kingston were not. Knowledge of the executions after court martial of Lieutenants Harry ('Breaker') Morant and Peter Handcock in Pretoria on 27 February followed. Barton had not been informed by the British beforehand of these sentences and faced questions in parliament he could not answer, highlighting concerns about Australians abroad under British authority. Barton never again gave his public support for this idea of compulsory overseas service in support of the Empire. For Hutton, however, it was but one more indication that he was free to push on with his planned reorganisations. He boasted to Brodrick that he felt he could secure agreement for 20 000 mounted troops, if need be, 'organised for service <u>wherever Australian interests are threatened</u>'.[73]

Before Hutton could begin his work he needed to take stock of the military forces now under his command. In total the Commonwealth Military Forces consisted of around 27 300 officers and men out of an establishment strength of just over 30 000. These were split, in terms of roles, between manning static fortifications and forces that saw themselves as acting in the field. Out of this total the permanent force numbered around 1400 men, 1000 of whom were artillerymen and the remainder staff troops and engineers. Part-time infantrymen dominated with nearly 18 000 troops, followed by almost 5300 mounted men (formed as cavalry or mounted infantry units). All the state's volunteer forces were a mix of part-paid militiamen and non-paid volunteers, except for South Australia and Western Australia, which had by this stage converted all volunteer troops to militia status.[74]

This newly combined 'federal' force was, however, national in name only. Even within the states and certainly across them, there was a marked lack of uniformity, just as Hutton had found in Canada. Both the nomenclature and the size of various state units, for example, had little in common. Many of these shortcomings were outlined to Hutton, even before he inspected the units and troops for himself, in the Finn Report, an account of the state of Australian defence forces provided by the Federal Military Committee to Forrest, in 1901. This report had also accurately identified a lack of ammunition and small arms and unserviceable or incompatible warlike stores and equipment.[75] Thus, 'thrown upon my own initiative', he later reflected, 'I had no recourse but either drift along with a slow tide and with a certainty of failure, or act upon the lines which I knew would achieve the result desired and desirable'.[76] He naturally chose to act and the place to begin was at the top.

Between March and April 1902 Hutton built the administrative and command structure for the new Australian Army. His first general order named the officers appointed to his staff as the 'Military Branch' of the Department of Defence and described their duties. This initial 'headquarters' numbered only eight (not including Hutton's aide-de-camp and personal secretary), all Australians. This was actually two less than the pre-Federation military headquarters of New South Wales alone and five less than that the thirteen recommended by the CDC (which had included three imperial officers). Despite this skeleton staff Hutton still found himself under attack from the outset over the size of his headquarters. Indeed, the government decided that the offices of Deputy Adjutant General and Deputy Quartermaster General would not be filled once their original occupants retired. Always under pressure to keep defence costs down, Forrest complained to Hutton that he needed to show to parliament not only how the new headquarters would function efficiently but also how it saved money.[77]

Photo 19 Major-General Hutton (front, centre) surrounded by the Australian state commandants, 17 July 1902. (Australian Army Infantry Museum)

As Hutton was establishing his headquarters he simultaneously struck upon his line of action insofar as the wider restructure and reform of the Australian military was concerned. In late March 1902, he drafted his famous *Minute Upon the Defence of Australia*. The purpose of this seminal document, in the absence of any government guidance, was nothing less than to set the military policy for the new nation. Hutton defined within it the military threat faced by Australia and his solution to it. The general idea, in his words, was to sketch a scheme to 'provide a military system which shall be elastic, capable of expansion and which shall form a carefully constructed framework into which the fighting material of this nation can be fitted when the emergency arises'.[78] Once again Hutton's dual aims were apparent. He openly planned for a force capable of providing effective local defence while at the same time tailoring it to fit into his wider imperial cooperative plan should the need arise.

Two central factors, therefore, were to govern the future organisation of the federal force: the 'defence of Australian soil' and the 'defence of Australian interests wherever they may be threatened'.[79] Hutton confessed to Minto that he would be 'somewhat amused to see how closely it [the minute] follows the lines of my first Report to the Canadian Government'.[80] Further, borrowing from his colonial scheme of organisation for New South Wales and a recent CDC memorandum, Hutton again prescribed 'Garrison Troops', to protect 'certain pre-determined strategical centres' and made up primarily of non-paid volunteer units and a 'Field Force' for mobile and 'active' operations, built from militia units. It was this Field Force that must be kept 'not only well trained, carefully organized and well equipped' but also capable of undertaking military operations in whatever part of the world the Australian Government chose to employ them; that is, in accordance with the grand cooperative imperial militia he envisaged.[81] Further, again as had been the case in Canada, if this force was required to conduct independent operations in the field, it needed to be an 'army', a 'thoroughly complete military organisation' with a well-trained staff, modern equipment and all departmental services.[82] The GOC had laid down a brief but clear blueprint.

Hutton knew there was risk in putting such a sketch-plan to paper, especially given parliamentary reactions to the first Defence Bill. Yet those objections had primarily been about the spectre of militarism in the form of a standing army or potential conscription for foreign service. Hutton's minute skirted such issue entirely, ignoring the potential for compulsory service and leaving the decision as to when and where Australian military forces might fight to the Australian Government. Nonetheless, Hutton was relieved, then '[e]ncouraged beyond measure' when his minute was privately endorsed by the Prime Minister in a 'warm-hearted letter', 'tacitly accepted by the Cabinet, printed and laid upon the Table of the House of Representatives' on 23 April 1902.[83] Indeed, Barton praised Hutton's plan as 'lucid and most able'.[84] Hutton was similarly surprised and encouraged by the lack of serious criticism his minute elicited in parliament and the public arena. The *Sydney Morning Herald* predicted that under the scheme Hutton would, before the end of his term of office, have established 'a service equal to our requirements and worthy of our respect and confidence'.[85] The *Register* (Adelaide) was relieved that there was no hint of conscription in Hutton's minute and, although worried about cost, concluded that the scheme was 'in accord with popular sentiment'.[86] Meanwhile, the Tasmanian press was concerned only that there was no explicit mention of their island.

The press was not, however, wholly without suspicion. The *West Australian* noted that the notion of a 'Field Force capable of undertaking military operations in whatever part of the world it may be desired by Australia to employ them', was in itself a seemingly innocuous idea, but it looked 'suspiciously like a feeler, thrown out, possibly under Imperial direction, to provoke an expression of Australian sentiment in regard to Imperial, as distinct from national, defence'.[87] The complaint here was not over the idea of Australian troops defending the Empire but that such service should be made *voluntarily* by individuals to the government and by the government to the Empire. Such sentiments were entirely in accordance with Hutton's own. The chief political sceptic was Sir William Lyne, Minister for Home Affairs, who in Forrest's absence in London had taken on his portfolio. Lyne instructed Collins to make it clear that the 'Minister does not agree with any proposal to give control, or implied control, over Australian troops to any but the Commonwealth authority'.[88] Lyne accepted that situations like the war in South Africa might arise where voluntary forces might be sent but that current *financial* factors mean Hutton was not to maintain an establishment based on 'any considerations of undertaking such external operations'.[89] Hutton shrugged off Lyne's first charge as, once again, it had never been part of his wider plan to remove the decision to despatch Australian troops from the Australia Government. As for Lyne's instructions against maintaining a structure to facilitate such a use should the Commonwealth deem it necessary, Hutton chose not to respond.

Aside from its key organisational principles, Hutton's minute also set out his plans to raise the training standards of the Australian military forces, once more following the lines used in Canada. He flagged his intention to establish schools of instruction for militia and volunteer officers where permanent officers and soldiers would instruct, 'Staff Rides upon Field Service conditions' and the establishment of a military college modelled on a cross between the Royal Military College in Kingston, Canada, and 'the Great Public schools of England'. Across the board Hutton recommended sixteen days training for infantry and mounted troops, with twenty days for engineers and artillerymen, conducted as long annual camps in country areas or as afternoon and evening training (with short camps) in the cities. Hutton further indicated his support for military assistance to rifle clubs, on the proviso that shooting was conducted along military lines and that members of the clubs were 'prepared to undertake in some definite form a direct share in the defence of the country', probably as a 'reserve' attached to military units. Last, Hutton recommended a national system of cadet training along the Victorian colonial model, attaching 'great value to the military training thus taught and discipline thus impressed upon the rising generation'.[90]

Hutton was so pleased at the general acceptance and publication of his minute that he followed it in May with a treatise, *The Defence and Defensive Power of Australia*, which contained three chapters on the value and capability of Australian troops and (not coincidentally), a version of his imperial defence scheme in the form of the paper he had given before the Royal Colonial Institute on 19 April 1898, 'A Co-operative System of Defence for the Empire'. He was also sure to write of his 'success' to those back home who mattered. He predicted to Sir Arthur Bigge, private secretary to the Prince of Wales, that Barton and Forrest were likely to advocate the recommendations and principles laid down in his minute when they arrived in London for the Colonial Conference scheduled for June.[91] The Prince of Wales replied that Hutton's proposals 'all seem excellent ... but I suppose you will be confronted with the old difficulty of money, or rather, the lack of it'.[92] Hutton explained to Field Marshal Prince Arthur, the Duke of Connaught, Commander-in-Chief of Ireland, that it would 'require much patience and persistence to get all the recommendations carried through but I feel sanguine of success in the end'.[93] The only obstacle Hutton could yet foresee was the extra cost of implementing the scheme sketched out in his minute.

By mid-April, aside from his frustration at early limitations placed on his staff, the continuing refusal of the War Office to promote him to lieutenant-general despite the much wider responsibilities he now held than he had as a major-general in New South Wales in the 1890s and the refusal of the Australians to allow him to secure the services of his own British aide-de-camp, Hutton felt satisfied. The first few months of his command, as had been the case in Canada, had been largely free of problems. He had been warmly received and Barton seemed happy, like Laurier in early 1898, to support his proposals, postponing any further work on the Defence Bill until Hutton could redraft it. He had also successfully overseen the organisation and despatch of the first Australian federal contingents to the war in South Africa, which departed between February and June 1902. All the while the GOC worked to flesh out the blueprint presented in his minute, despite not having formal government approval for his scheme of reorganisation. Once more repeating the performance in Canada, from May he personally visited troops in each state in turn, sure to make direct and personal appeals to senior officers concerning his reorganisation plans and taking special care to enlist 'the sympathy and good-will of the press'.[94]

In early December 1902 Hutton managed to win Forrest's provisional consent for his new peace and war establishments, so long as any changes would be 'effected with as little inconvenience or hardship to Corps as possible'.[95] This was followed, in late July 1903, by formal approval for his reorganisation plan. It was 'sound and thorough organisation', Hutton boasted to Sir Montagu Ommanney, Permanent Undersecretary of State for the Colonies, 'based on definite defence principles'.[96] From this point, in Hutton's mind, subtlety was no longer required, and he accelerated the remoulding of existing military forces into his planned Field Force and Garrison Troops. In reality, however, the implementation of Hutton's new scheme was bound to affect the existing forces a great deal more than paper tables might have suggested and certainly more than Forrest had hoped. All his planned six 'light horse' regiments (a rather anachronistic designation for what were always envisaged to be mounted infantrymen) in New South Wales, for example, were all to be created from a mix of cavalry, mounted infantry and foot infantry troops that already existed in the state. Similar trauma was to be inflicted on infantry, artillery, engineer units and service units in order to comply with Hutton's plan. This example was reflected in the other states, the only real difference being the number of units involved. As will be discussed in chapter 10, Hutton's drive for restructuring as quickly and, on occasion, as ruthlessly as possible had serious ramifications.

There is no question, however, that Hutton's administrative zeal and skill in the first eighteen months of his appointment forced through a number of important reforms. By late July 1903 he had formulated and gained political approval for a national force that in his mind suited both Australian needs and the requirements of his vision for imperial defence. That the physical restructuring of the federal force, in many ways nothing more a collection of colonial forces under a federal banner, lagged behind his paper plan was not of significant concern for Hutton as yet; he felt he just needed to work harder. Meanwhile, he had raised the Royal Australian Artillery in mid-1902 out of various artillery detachments while a number of submarine mining and field/electric companies in each state were made into the Corps of Australian Engineers in July 1903. Reflecting the lessons Hutton had absorbed from operational service throughout his career, administrative and supporting services were a priority. A medical corps was formed at the same time, followed by a military nursing service.[97] For the most part, with some notable exceptions, by mid-1903 all states possessed elements from all of the military arms and services.[98] Despite some setbacks, therefore, Hutton was reasonably content. He told Bigge that he had thought 'the development of things military and of the present Scheme of Organisation has been unexpectedly rapid'.[99] Forrest too seemed reasonably satisfied with Hutton's efforts.

Despite this success, it is possible to trace a sort of tipping point in Hutton's fortunes in the first half of 1903. Once again, this was intimately connected to his absolute single-mindedness and inability to entertain, let alone tolerate, any idea or person that stood in his way. Such radical reforms as those Hutton had set in train for the Australia Army would invariably draw scepticism and resistance, yet the ability to respond to criticism and to compromise accordingly were no more a part of Hutton's constitution now than they had been in the past. It was, as always, the human aspect to which Hutton remained blind, and in the process his boundless energy began to work against him. From the second half of 1903 Hutton's ship began to run aground, and his only response was to press on, full steam ahead. Thus began the second and much more difficult phase of his Australian appointment.

CHAPTER 10

'UNFORTUNATELY NOT IN TOUCH OR SYMPATHY'

DIFFICULTIES AND DISAPPOINTMENTS, 1903–04

In mid-December 1903, Hutton wrote to Lord Northcote, soon to be appointed Australia's third Governor-General, to introduce himself. He claimed that his success as GOC thus far in forging an Australian federal army and the radical restructuring it entailed had been 'very remarkable'. Few could have anticipated so little friction, Hutton continued, in effecting 'so many and such vital changes'.[1] It was a similar message to many others Hutton had been sending home to friends and patrons back in Britain, yet it smacked more of wishful thinking than reality. The truth was that from mid-1903 Hutton faced a slowly rising tide of resistance and antagonism towards his sweeping reform plans and, in some quarters, against his person. It began to feel no doubt like a version of Canada all over again. Many of the drivers were in fact similar, especially those connected with Hutton's methods and personality. Others were quite different. The net result, however, was hauntingly familiar.

To begin, in the wake of the war in South Africa, the colonies watched with interest continuing turmoil at the War Office, especially the submission of the Elgin Report, weeks before Brodrick left office on 6 October 1903. His successor, Hugh Oakeley Arnold-Forster, took the Elgin recommendations regarding War Office reform and established the Esher (War Office Reconstitution) Committee to oversee them. Hutton, like other senior British officers in the colonies, was increasingly identified with what was seen from afar as rank War Office incompetence, which itself was understood to have contributed to difficulties in South Africa. At same time the Norfolk Commission, appointed in spring 1903 to investigate

British auxiliary forces, was brutal in its criticisms. Questions began to be asked in Australia. Was it not the same 'British' system, for example, that Hutton was trying to impose? The fact that the GOC was already advocating many of the commission's recommendations was less important than perceptions. Arnold-Forster was assailed on all sides over the proposed Norfolk Commission reforms by supporters of the British militia and volunteers and in the British Parliament, and the fall of the Balfour government in December 1905 ended any prospect of the scheme being implemented in full. Such was the reward for attempting too much too quickly in the face of determined opposition in Britain.[2] What unfolded at the centre was reflected at the edges.

Overlaying these events and attitudes was the post-war self-perception in Australia (and the other colonies) that South Africa had shown its own military men to be equal, or superior, to British regulars. The perception had ironically been encouraged by consistent British hyperbole as to the innate martial ability of colonial soldiers, often designed with political outcomes in mind rather than as an objective assessment of colonial battlefield performance. It encouraged a pre-existing notion that cheap, barely trained citizen soldiers, or even rifle club members, might be all the defence Australia needed. British-style regulars, discipline, organisation and staffs had 'proven' themselves lacking. British officers were no longer objects of legend.[3] Such ideas dovetailed nicely in Australia with concerns over costs. The point was that all of this contextual 'tinder' was in place, just as Hutton began to impose his scheme more seriously in 1903. It would never have taken much to spark them into flames.

Meanwhile, Hutton worked to shape a revised Defence Bill that Forrest was determined to table in parliament – under significant political pressure, with an election looming and against Tennyson's advice to wait for the next parliamentary session.[4] Importantly, while the 1901 Bill had contained provision to despatch Australian troops overseas if they volunteered, or to compel them to do so in 'defence of the Commonwealth' if directed by the government, the new version allowed only for the despatch of permanent troops without express consent. Otherwise, part-time citizen military forces were not liable to serve overseas unless they volunteered. To this, with his imperial defence scheme no doubt in mind, Hutton registered his 'gravest apprehension', pointing out: 'It would be difficult to point out any single instance in history in which a purely passive defence had been successful.' He used the British Isles as an example: 'In every instance in which British arms had been successful and the invasion of British territory been avoided, it had been with offensive combined with defensive operations ... forcing the enemy to fight on territory other than Great Britain.'[5] He further cited the potential need for 'external service' due to the rise of Japan and Russia, and France in the Pacific, and that (borrowing from an old CDC argument) Australia must be prepared to act offensively. Forrest, however, was not swayed this time around. Moreover, the minister knew full well, thanks to recent clumsy and ill-conceived representations from London attempting to codify colonial military commitments to the Empire in peacetime (see chapter 11), that the mood of the House ran contrary to Hutton's preferred clauses.

It is important to note, however, that Forrest's position was still neither anti-imperial nor anti-imperial defence. When tabling the new Bill he announced: 'I am proud to say I am imperialistic, in the sense that I believe in binding Australia as closely as possible with the mother country.' Echoing the prevailing sentiment of the government, he argued that 'we may be able, in case of need, or our own free will to assist in maintaining the integrity and the power of our empire ... we are under an obligation to assist in maintaining it, not in the interests of others, but in our own interests, which I hold, are identical with the interests of the British race.'[6] This must come, however, through individual volunteering, as had been the case in South Africa. It was on this point that minister and GOC diverged. Hutton did not believe in conscription. Rather, he valued volunteer forces. Yet once an individual had volunteered his services, Hutton saw it as both right and necessary that the Australian Government, if it so desired, should be able to send this individual and his unit abroad. Not only was this vital in his eyes for capitalising on peacetime training and organisation but also it was a fundamental building block in his system of cooperative defence.

With Hutton's potentially controversial suggestions ignored, Forrest did not expect many problems this time around and hoped that the new Bill might be passed the night of its introduction. There was 'nothing very novel' about it, he claimed, in that the defence forces would be citizen-based and that 'the primary duty of such forces is to defend Australia from invasion or attack'.[7] Provision remained for a permanent force only sufficient for manning forts and ships, working submarine mines and instructing the citizen army. Forrest's optimism, however, was misplaced. He was forced to reassure parliament once more that permanent troops were not the precursor of a standing army. Unconvinced, the House inserted a new clause whereby no permanent force could be raised except for administrative or instructional purposes. Further, although provision for conscription in the event of an attack on Australia was maintained, so strong was opinion against compulsion that the section allowing permanents to be forced to fight overseas was removed without dissent.[8]

Despite another rough passage, this time the amended Bill was passed, and the Defence Act was proclaimed on 1 March 1904. Military regulations and seniority lists followed. Importantly, following events in Britain and seemingly rather innocuous to Hutton at the time (given that he had suggested it), the Act also made provision for the establishment of a Military Board of advice intended to discuss matters referred to it by the minister.[9] This board was not formed initially, and defence matters continued to be discussed by the minister directly (and usually separately) with Hutton and Creswell (recently appointed Naval Officer Commanding the Commonwealth Naval Forces). Meanwhile, many parliamentarians, still annoyed with the provisions of the original Bill, and those dissatisfied with the subsequent Act, saw the hand of Hutton rather than Forrest. The GOC was known to have drafted it and, as a uniformed senior British officer, remained for some the visible representative of what they had argued against.

Ironically, Hutton himself was more unimpressed by the Act than any members of parliament. He told Ommanney that despite his best efforts it was 'much to be deplored'. 'I did my utmost, directly and indirectly', he continued, to encourage 'a broader view of the necessities and the strategical and political situation in Australia as it appears to those of us who consider the question from a broad imperial standpoint', but was foiled in his view by the 'ignorance and self-interest of politicians', particularly those of a labour persuasion.[10] Nonetheless, Hutton was correct in his assurances that in an emergency the British Government 'might rely with absolute certainty on the assistance of at least one portion of the Commonwealth troops': those willing to volunteer as individuals.[11] Hutton never really resigned himself to reality on this issue. Throughout 1904 he was still lamenting to friends and patrons the failure to carry the principle that Australian standing units, formed in peacetime, could be utilised outside Australian soil and was still doing so well after his appointment in Australia had ended. The problem was that to accept the situation in Australia meant acknowledging that his cooperative scheme of imperial defence could not be implemented. In private moments Hutton glimpsed the truth, writing to Major-General Lord Dundonald, commanding the militia in Canada from 1902, that there 'was a time when I hoped I should someday have an opportunity with 10 000 mounted men in single rank meeting an equal number of a European Power's Cavalry in two ranks. I am getting, I fear, too old now, for such a chance.'[12] But such sentiments did not last; better for Hutton to work on the principle that the Act and the political will behind it might change. Meanwhile, the Act was Forrest's cue to depart, and on 7 August it was announced he was to be appointed Minister for Home Affairs. On 23 September Barton left politics for the High Court. Hutton thus lost two ardent imperialists in key positions.

When the murmurs of dissatisfaction and complaint began to emerge, they did so in many cases from the grassroots upwards. Hutton's accelerating attempts to implement his extensive reforms in 1903 placed the physical structure of the army in a state of flux that outlived his appointment. Forrest's impossible instruction to him – that any changes made were to cause as little inconvenience to existing corps as possible – illustrated the minister's ignorance and naivety. The lack of attention Hutton paid to it, on the other hand, reflected his own self-assured conviction. For many part-time soldiers, not being privy to Hutton's master plan, it seemed that military units were being established and disbanded at regular and random intervals. Worse, it was clear that Hutton was privileging the militia over volunteer units, in accordance with both his long-standing professional convictions and advice given by the CDC to Australian authorities as early as March 1901 advocating part-paid in preference to non-paid troops in the new federal army. Overall, almost 1500 volunteers were converted to militia status, whether they liked it or not, under Hutton's scheme.[13] The officers and men of these volunteer units were commonly from the wealthier and more influential segments of the community, thanks to the very nature of their seeking social capital from their non-paid services, and were also those best placed to turn public and political opinion against Hutton and his system. Even outside volunteer drill halls, many citizens with no direct connection to the forces found that their community no longer supported a military unit, or that their local force had been so changed in role that they could no longer be a part of it. This was an issue that *mattered* to small Australian towns in the early part of the twentieth century.

More to the point, Hutton's scheme required a preponderance of mounted infantry units, which were created at the expense of the many small infantry formations that had existed throughout the new nation. Often town dwellers could not afford the horses required to convert to light horse and, as noted by the *Sydney Morning Herald*, there were many cases 'of suitable men who are deterred from ... taking up a commission by the expense they will have to incur'.[14] One result was a growing antagonism between the mounted and non-mounted arms. Jealousy and friction therefore grew in direct proportion to Hutton's efforts to raise these light horse units, so much so that it became a divisive issue in many rural areas. This type of resentment was evident in the Monaro district of New South Wales, for example, when the local infantry company at Cooma was replaced by a light horse squadron. Residents complained to their member and future Minister for Defence, Austin Chapman, while local papers claimed Hutton was attempting to exclude the lower classes by replacing 141 foot soldiers with a troop of eighteen horsemen.[15] Similar indignation was expressed elsewhere. Examples were legion. In Queensland the member for Moreton, James Wilkinson, expressed his concern that two well-established infantry companies at Ipswich could not continue to function owing to the cost of mounts.[16] In Victoria, Allan McLean, member for Gippsland, drew attention to the plight of the Victorian Rangers, who were disbanded despite their long history and consistently high numbers.[17] It was a loss of close on 300 men and, as a result of McLean's complaining, allied to that of the *Kerang New Times*, the whole issue was examined by Victorian military headquarters.[18] It was to no avail and, as was the case in Cooma, the locals could do nothing but grow bitter at the closure of the Ranger companies.

This type of friction, especially aspects related to identity and perception, also involved units already mounted but forced by Hutton's plan to alter roles. Two prime examples involved the New South Wales Lancer Regiment and the Melbourne Cavalry. The former fought hard to retain its cavalry function, uniform and even its traditional weapon, the lance. What followed was a running battle between the unit's influential commanding officer, James Burns, and Hutton. In this case the GOC could not lose (even if he felt insecure enough to seek advice on the issue from Roberts). Burns quit his post in disgust, and ill-feeling festered.[19] The Melbourne Cavalry similarly fought hard to retain its identity. Originally established against the wishes of the Victorian commandant and without any consideration of its relationship to other Victorian forces, Alexander Rushall, a businessman, built up the unit believing it 'would be attractive to huntsmen and gentlemen in the city'.[20] In 1903 Rushall resisted the order become a light horse squadron, went public and demanded ministerial confirmation of the unit's independent nature and cavalry status, as well as the retention of its distinctive uniforms and weapons. Eventually, like Burns, Rushall was forced to submit, but his experience again illustrates the chagrin felt by such units. Hutton's will won out, but his reputation was damaged further.[21] Of course this type of confrontation was symptomatic of similar quarrels over the role of auxiliary cavalry units in Britain, and *The Times* was used in this regard to great effect. Unaware of such a context, however, Hutton seemed to the Australian rank and file little more than a bully.[22]

Aside from resistance associated directly with Hutton's plan to physically reorganise the forces, additional tensions sprouted from a range of other sources. Many of these were either inevitable or not strictly of his making. The obvious need to standardise dress and equipment across the federal army, from the wide variety that existed within and between the colonial defence forces Hutton inherited, offended feelings of pride and independence, even in units not otherwise unduly affected by his scheme. Colonial units had often grown from men of like interests, and their individual customs and traditions grew with them. They were used to running their own affairs with minimal interference. Such traditions were bound to clash with new requirements for federal regulation, regardless of who might be the GOC. Of course Hutton's professional insistence on real military order and discipline, something entirely foreign to many Australian part-time soldiers, exacerbated the issue and gave it a 'face' for a growing number of malcontents.[23]

Further, the issue of pay and conditions became a sore point with many and one for which Hutton often bore the blame, despite his complete lack of power to change any financial arrangements. The result, thanks to the interim need before the passing of the Defence Act to continue with old colonial arrangements, was officers and men on different scales of pay for equal services rendered, depending on the state in which they were based. Behind the scenes Hutton argued vigorously to his minister against a system he called 'manifestly unfair'.[24] This was, of course, not known to those who riled against it. As reported by the Adelaide *Advertiser*, a 'general feeling of dissatisfaction amongst both the officers and the men' mounted.[25] Problem associated with pay degenerated further when Hutton began imposing his scheme. The plan was that Field Force militia units would receive pay, but those who were allocated to the garrisons would remain unpaid volunteers. What happened in practice, however, was that all Garrison Troops immediately ceased to be paid whereas previously unpaid units now assigned to the Field Force and entitled to payment did not receive it. The result was chaos, especially in Western Australia, South Australia and Tasmania, whose citizen soldiers had *all* previously received either pay or allowances. This naturally created a serious morale problem and howls of protests from both the state commandants and local members of parliament.[26] Forrest, in a scramble, restored temporary payment to two garrison units in Queensland but nowhere else.

The problem was at its worst in Tasmania. On 6 February 1904, 500 out of 750 soldiers in Hobart refused to parade in protest over receiving pay levels, still based on state scales, lower than the rest of the army. It was a deeply humiliating experience for Hutton and the new minister, Chapman, who were both present. Hutton exploded in a fit of rage, and the senior officer on parade wept openly. The story was well covered by the press, and Hutton's credibility, along with military morale, plummeted further.[27] The unit that had refused to parade was disbanded by Hutton, to whom the mutinous parade represented the gravest affront to his professional convictions, provoking a remark by a Tasmanian parliamentarian that 'Hobart is defenceless'. To this the Prime Minister replied pathetically, 'I can say nothing to that.'[28] The ever-irreverent *Bulletin* concluded that 'practically the only means of fending off an attack would be to mobilise General Hutton, armed with adjectives, and launch him against the foe'.[29] Hutton was sure to write to both Northcote and Roberts to give his version of events and to justify his actions, the former warning him not to act out of 'personal irritation'.[30] For Hutton, however, the issue was black and white. He saw no reason for leniency. News of the incident eventually reached the King, who began to hint to Arnold Forster of a possible recall of the GOC.[31] Individually, complaints over pay issues meant little, but together they suggested inept administration. Hutton might not have been entirely responsible for this, but he certainly wore the blame.

Hutton's popularity was further and consistently undermined by his involvement in pubic conflict with a number of prominent individuals, just as had been the case in Canada. During the Victorian Easter Camp of 1903, for example, for justifiable military reasons, he replaced the most senior but incompetent militia officer, Lieutenant-Colonel William Braithwaite, with a more junior regular officer, Lieutenant-Colonel George Lee. Both Barton and Forrest were forced to intervene when Hutton attempted to discipline Lieutenant-Colonel William Reay, a fellow militia officer and state politician, for an inflammatory article in Melbourne's *Herald* (of which Reay was news editor) that criticised Hutton's actions. Reay refused to resign as Hutton demanded and continued to libel his GOC in print, calling Hutton a military dictator and challenging Forrest to protect the interests of citizen soldiers.[32] Hutton, typically, missed the point. What was for him an issue of professionalism was for others a question of primacy of part-time volunteer soldiers in Australia. Public interested skyrocketed, especially when the correspondence between Barton and Forrest was leaked, much to Hutton's embarrassment. Yet Hutton was unrepentant, telling Forrest on 25 March 1903 that 'if the Cabinet decide against the appointment of Lieutenant-Colonel

Lee ... I shall ask Sir Edmund Barton or Mr Kingston to come and command the Light Horse'.[33] It took advice from the Governor-General to calm Hutton down. Hutton had his way, but again the price was high, even if he failed to see it.

Hutton's most dangerous opponent in this regard, however – his Australian Domeville – was a federal conservative senator and Commanding Officer of the volunteer St George's English Rifles, John Cash Neild. As an officer, Neild was incompetent and petulant, and had run afoul of a succession of New South Wales military commandants since he raised his notoriously inefficient regiment in 1896. Major-General French in fact had recommended his forced retirement in 1900. Neild was routinely ridiculed by Labor parliamentarians, politicians of his own persuasion and the press. A board of inquiry of 1899 concluded that he lacked the judgement to command an efficient regiment.[34] Yet Neild endured. As a natural opponent to Hutton's plans to restructure the army, to privilege militia units and to standardise discipline, Neild was tireless in his efforts to use his Senate platform to deride the GOC and the state of the forces. In early March 1904, for example, he roundly criticised the military regulations Hutton framed from the Act of 1903 and lambasted the GOC's reorganisation as nothing more than disorganisation. Chapman asked Hutton to respond to such criticisms. True to form and managing not only to offend Chapman but also to insult a whole host of other parliamentarians to boot, Hutton responded: 'I find it difficult to reply to the comprehensive criticism by ill-informed Members of Parliament who have neither the training nor possess the Military instincts to qualify them as critics.'[35] Unable to tolerate continued taunting from Neild, Hutton removed him from command on the grounds of incompetence. Neild played it up to the Labor Party in that his sacking was not about his military ability but rather an attempt to silence an elected representative. He was supported, of all people, by Dawson, deeply resentful of any implication that a senator was being coerced. A Senate Select Committee appointed to investigate Neild's charges found that although the dismissal 'may be regarded as an attempt to interfere with Senator Neild in the discharge of his duties as a Senator', Neild's military failings had nonetheless fully justified his removal from military office.[36] Again, being technically correct did not save Hutton the damage to his reputation, or improve parliament's attitude to him.

There were a host of other cases in which Hutton's determination to see his version of 'professionalism' and correct military procedure followed at all costs, regardless of consequence or context, added ever more names to the set of political, military and community adversaries arrayed against him. Senior militia officers resented his attempts, for example, to have regulars placed in command of the battalions of Commonwealth Horse bound for South Africa in 1902. So too Hutton's arbitrary retirement of one Major J.W.M. Carroll on the grounds that the GOC thought him incompetent in South Africa brought a Senate committee investigation that overturned Hutton's ruling.[37] Similarly, his inability to accept the sharing of power with Collins as the civil head of the Defence Department (reflecting similar intolerance in New South Wales and in Canada over this issue) earned Hutton a subtle but persistent enemy. To be fair, in this case Collins was equally unenthusiastic about losing what had been a near-monopoly of control of the department, including the usurpation of military roles, before Hutton had arrived. Hutton intended to use his 1903 Report, to be tabled in parliament, to criticise Collins' civil branch as 'detrimental to the best military interests of the Commonwealth'.[38] Collins complained to Forrest, who warned the GOC against such 'circulating vague and unsupported charges' and ordered Hutton to withdraw the offending cause in his report – a directive with which Hutton only partially complied.[39]

Meanwhile, the mounting backlash to Hutton's reorganisations (in addition to a natural post-war drawdown) began affecting military numbers, which in turn provided more ammunition for his critics. It was soon apparent that the 26 000 personnel called for by his scheme was well beyond what could be easily or immediately raised. In June 1903 there were 3600 too few soldiers to fill Hutton's planned units, and numbers were falling. By 30 June 1904, troop levels in Australia had plummeted to under 20 000.[40] In the words of the Member for Wentworth, William Kelly: 'Everyone who has studied the question knows that, for some reason or other, there is the gravest lack of confidence through every rank ... We have seen officers resigning and giving up the sword for the ploughshare.'[41] Neild and others of like mind took every chance to point this out. Not that Hutton could to do much, in the short term at least, to reverse the flow. Driven by the need to save money, Forrest had already ordered troop strengths in Tasmania and Western Australia temporarily frozen, despite already approving the GOC's new, larger establishments in those states.

Hutton's reaction to the range of criticism mounted against him in 1903 and into 1904 continued to highlight the arrogance, intolerance and inability to self-reflect that had so consistently bedevilled his career and undermined his efforts. He was simply unable to brook the notion that anyone might have a valid reason to complain with the wide-ranging changes he wrought. Critics were therefore written off as radicals, malcontents, those with vested interests, or of a type who 'object to all changes'.[42] In responding to his minister, Chapman, over a critical article in the *Age* in November 1903, Hutton declared: 'I am not prepared to make a categorical reply ... I have neither the time, nor do I consider it within my duty to reply to all irresponsible newspaper criticisms.'[43] The rifts grew ever wider.

Much less visible than public and military resistance to Hutton's plans, but no less dangerous to them, were continuing financial restrictions. Before arriving in Australia Hutton had assumed that he would receive the equivalent of all colonial military expenditure combined, some £937 000 in 1900. Conversely, as noted, the new government expected the cost of defence to be reduced as a function of federal union, and Forrest got the original defence estimates past the Committee of Supply only by initially reducing this figure by almost £176 000, with the promise of a further reduction of £84 524 in the 1901–02 estimates and £130 000 in the next year. Less than two weeks after submission of his 1902 Minute, Hutton therefore found himself fighting planned spending cuts for 1902–03. His mood was not improved by Wolseley's dry observation that the colonies 'can find money to build monuments to one another, but when asked to put their hands in their pockets to support Military Institutions they do not feel so anxious to spend'.[44]

With Forrest absent at the colonial conference in 1902, Lyne went further, submitting further reductions to parliament worth £175 000. With parliamentary debates focusing on how well colonial detachments had performed in South Africa with little training or infrastructure, and under political and press pressure, Lyne also agreed to an additional £35 000 of cuts aimed squarely at Hutton's administrative staff. Hutton was furious with Lyne, pointing to his being 'influenced by the Labour Section', a 'want of confidence in himself' and damning his failure to explain 'in the smallest degree to the House the lines which the Government proposes to adopt'. These arbitrary reductions, Hutton soon concluded, 'made solid re-organization and re-construction almost impossible'.[45] Hutton delayed any compliance with Lyne's cuts until Forrest's return. Once back in Australia, however, Forrest rebuked Hutton for warning in an official minute that Lyne's reductions were 'imperilling the security of Australia'.[46] The wish of the House, the minister reminded him, must be complied with. Forrest insisted Hutton reduce his staff; Hutton resisted and threatened resignation, claiming that no satisfactory defence force (i.e. his scheme) could be built without investment in a permanent nucleus and specialist departments. Forrest, however, stood firm and the GOC eventually complied, primarily as he saw no alternative. The trend continued. Military estimates for 1903–04 amounted to a little over £581 000, a reduction of some £300 000 from 1901–02.[47]

Moreover, these figures referred only to the general and ongoing annual defence budget. Greater expenditure still was required for Hutton's reorganisation. The GOC requested a total of £486 000 over a four-year period from 1903 to 1907 to implement his Field Force and Garrison Troops system, but received no extra money in order to do it. The entire defence budget in 1903 was a mere 0.38 per cent of the year's Gross Domestic Product.[48] The Postmaster-General's Department alone received an average of three times the amount spent on defence at the time. In addition, in May 1903 Hutton was ordered to reduce his staff once more and once more threatened to resign, informing Forrest: 'I am not prepared to continue efforts which must be necessarily doomed to failure ... and to continue responsibilities which I am unable to vindicate.'[49] He carped to Tennyson that he 'must fail unless I have assistance ... I am justly entitled to a minimum number of officers to help me.'[50] Hutton voiced his official opinion on the cuts in his report for 1903, viewing them with 'gravest apprehension'.[51] Embarrassed, Forrest initially refused to publish the report and urged Hutton to amend it. Hutton only ever partially complied, provoking more disputes over money and initiating a series of clashes with Collins over civil branch 'interference' in minor expenditures. In his May 1904 report Hutton complained that another proposed reduction of his headquarters staff from seven to six members would 'if carried out, render it impracticable for the General Officer Commanding to accept the responsibilities'.[52] It was 'only a question of time', Hutton warned, under such conditions, 'for chaos and disintegration to replace the military order and system which is now being introduced'.[53] Hutton was still complaining about this issue in October 1904. He never received an official response.

It was not just reductions to permanent and headquarters staff in the name of saving money that frustrated Hutton and acted against the implementation of his planned reorganisations. Similar government parsimony saw only £75 000 released by Treasury in 1903 with which to purchase warlike stores for the federal force, despite the fact that more than £480 000 had already been approved over four years (a figure itself £45 000 less than Hutton's conservative estimation of what he needed, which included the continuing use of obsolete equipment).[54] Indeed, up to 1909 only £370 000 was ever spent on rectifying appalling shortages of guns, arms, equipment and ammunition. In some states there was a complete lack of artillery carriages, which would have been more pressing still had the permanent artillery force not been reduced by 39 per cent! Hutton warned that this particular reduction would 'seriously compromise the security of the Commonwealth'.[55]

The overall level of federal defence expenditure did not, in fact, exceed the combined colonial total until 1906–07. The net result of such a shortage of funds was that Hutton's reorganisation was never able to be properly implemented. In the words of Sir George Clarke, they remained 'largely of a paper character and therefore illusionary'.[56] The GOC, however, cannot bear responsibility for the fact that his costs were not met. The government had, after all, approved his plan.

Largely oblivious to mounting discontent brought on by his radical structural reforms and public confrontations, and despite the prevailing financial circumstances, Hutton followed his instincts in 1903 and 1904 and pushed ever onwards. Some of his successes, in this context, were remarkable, particularly with respect to training. As was the case on assuming command in Canada, Hutton found standards of military instruction and professional competence in Australia to be far lower than he required. Such conclusions were to some extent forgone; an observation that all was well was not the platform required to launch his planned reorganisations. At the same time Hutton did not need to over-embellish the issue.

Across the board, while a number of militia and volunteer units were reasonably competent and took training seriously, a larger proportion were little more than gentlemen's clubs and were unprepared for any sort of military action, a situation compounded the erroneous lesson that South Africa had apparently proven the military worth of 'untrained' troops. Overall, training, where it was conducted, was mostly confined to elementary drill parades of a ceremonial nature with little attempt being made to give advanced instruction. Few attempts had ever been made to exercise them in mobile columns, for example, and part-time field artillery batteries had typically done little, if any, tactical or battle-firing practices. Indeed, as late as 1904 'live' practices over land targets had still not been attempted in some states. In particular, the efficiency of the citizen forces depended directly on the efficiency of citizen officers, which was in a very precarious state. Part-time officers were accused of an inability to apply drill to any situation, but the parade ground and training was too often devolved directly onto the permanent instructional staff. This in part explains Hutton's bitter complaints about the 1903 reductions in the numbers of permanents and simultaneous advocacy for a military college.[57] It also underwrote his support for a pension scheme for permanent officers to avoid, as he had seen in colonial New South Wales, the retention of ageing or incompetent officers on 'charitable grounds'.[58]

Against this backdrop professionalism and realism was the order of the day for Hutton – Colonel Hawley's influence never left him. Among his innovations and successes in 1903–04 was the beginning of a system of exchanging permanent officers to Britain and India to be trained, while gaining admission for others to the British Staff College. Hutton also instituted a Staff Ride system – the first in Australia – on a model similar to that he had established in Canada in 1899.[59] So too he set up a system of Schools of Instruction, again as he had done in Canada, for infantry, mounted infantry, artillery and supporting troops. Furthermore, Hutton laid down a systematic scheme of training at the annual field camps and exercises, which usually took place over the Easter period, as they had done in colonial times, to minimise the number of lost work days for part-time soldiers. In keeping with Hawley's theory that 'those who lead should be those who instructed', these annual training camps on Hutton's orders were now carried out by the officers of the units, assisted where necessary by the Instructional Staff.[60] Across all of these initiatives Hutton ensured that the emphasis was slowly shifted from parades and ceremony to field training. Musketry regulations, for example, were formulated in 1904 focusing on 'battlefield' practices with moving targets and rapid aiming, and a compulsory annual shooting course was carried out for all arms from this time.

At the same time Hutton's training initiatives were neither perfect nor perfectly carried through. His schools, for example, suffered from the difficulty faced by those of the citizen forces with full-time work to find time to attend them and by the reduction of the numbers of permanent instructors. Equally, his annual camps were spasmodic in that troops could not be compelled to attend (55 per cent of volunteers participated in 1904 and 82 per cent of the militia). At the same time, in a general sense there is no question his training reforms improved standards throughout the army not only during his tenure but also well after he had left Australian shores.[61]

Photo 20 Major-General E.T.H. Hutton (front, centre) photographed with the students of the first Commonwealth artillery course. (Australian Army Infantry Museum)

As Hutton focused on his plans for training and restructuring the army, he continued to fail to see, or understand, the forces building against him. For his political masters, however, the 'problem' was becoming clearer. The relationship between Forrest and Hutton had been deteriorating for some time, particularly over issues of staff reductions and financial stringency. Forrest was succeeded by Senator James Drake on 7 August 1903, much to Hutton's relief. 'Sir John Forrest is even more weak than his colleagues', Hutton told Brodrick. To Ommanney, he claimed his former minister 'was never in sympathy with the troops . . . and had no real interest in the success of any military scheme'.[62] For his part, Forrest (like Borden before him) came to bristle at Hutton's manner, reprimanding him through Collins in August 1903, for example, for applying the term 'unwarranted assumptions' to official ministerial correspondence.[63] After only forty-five days in the job, Drake was himself replaced on 24 September 1903 by Chapman in Deakin's new government.

In early 1904 the relationship between Hutton and Chapman began to sour thanks to the Neild affair, the Tasmanian parade debacle, disagreements over senior officer appointments, continuing friction between Hutton and the civil branch of the department and a host of other minor niggles. Chapman's growing impatience with Hutton reflected the parliamentary mood. Into this mix was added a showdown of personalities, with Chapman much more sensitive to Hutton's pushing of the boundaries of his authority than Forrest had been. In March 1904, for example, Hutton was upset about press reports of his new regulations, which suggested they had come from Collins with no recognition of him. Chapman pounced, rebuking Hutton that his complaint was 'written under a misapprehension of the responsibilities and position of the General Officer commanding'. 'Information to the Press is given by me under my direction as I may consider advisable', continued the minister. 'I am the sole judge.'[64] The Governor-General, a friend and confidant to Hutton, knew where the relationship was headed. He wrote to Chapman suggesting that the only real problem with the GOC was that 'he is over-energetic and expects the Government to keep pace with him'. 'If any friction arises', Tennyson, urged, 'pray always see Hutton yourself and do not write.'[65] A much more serious crisis arose when Chapman requested a copy of a ciphered message from Hutton sent to the Secretary for War in London. Hutton refused to divulge its contents as the original, if provided with a transcript, would decrypt the code in which it was written. Chapman was astonished and requested it again. The Deakin government fell in April and with it Chapman's time as minister was at an end, leaving the issue unresolved.

The return of the first Labor government in Australia under John Christian Watson, with Senator Andrew Dawson as the new Minister for Defence, was a disaster for Hutton. The two men were equally strong-willed and predisposed to antagonism. Hutton, like most with his background and social pretensions, had no time for the labour movement, which threatened to 'engulf this fine country'.[66] He was an Etonian, a senior British officer, on the periphery of the aristocracy, with an outspoken imperial perspective. He was, in political terms, every inch a conservative. Dawson, in stark contrast, was 'a hard-drinking, poorly educated orphan'.[67] He had been a miner, bullock-driver and republican journalist who had opposed the dispatch of Queensland's first contingent to the war in South Africa. Moreover, like many in his party, Dawson scorned military pomp, saw the forces as being in disarray and was intent on 'fixing' them. It was all too easy for Dawson to see Hutton as the personification of the problems at hand and for Hutton to write Dawson off as a 'total illiterate' who could 'barely sign his own name'.[68]

Photo 21 Members of the Labor Party, first Australian federal Parliament. The return of the first Labor government in Australia in 1904, with Senator Andrew Dawson as the new Minister for Defence, represented a serious challenge for Hutton. (National Archives of Australia, A6988, 30)

Dawson did not have to look far to find issues on which to challenge Hutton. In early May he silenced Hutton's continuing agitation over senior military appointments and his potential successor, warning him that the whole issue 'will require careful consideration by Government'.[69] Subsequent meetings made it clear that Labor liked the idea of the military forces being controlled by a board, rather than by a GOC. Meanwhile, Dawson picked up the cipher issue and pursued it. The minister demanded to see a transcript. Hutton was considering how to respond when the story broke in the press, and he was directed back to Melbourne to see both Dawson and the Prime Minister.[70] Hutton subsequently provided a decoded copy of the offending but quite innocuous message. Watson was satisfied. Hutton less so, first at the Prime Minister's inference of undue subterfuge on Hutton's part and second as to how the incident had been leaked to the press. Hutton blamed the 'malicious misrepresentation of Captain Collins ... [and] some person in the Civil Department ... who purposefully gave a pressman access to confidential official papers'.[71] Again Hutton's reputation in parliament and in the press suffered. So too, in this case, his stocks with Arnold Forster, who had become aware of the cipher issue and who recorded in his diary that Hutton 'cannot keep his mouth shut' and would likely 'talk us into difficulty every week'.[72]

From here one point of friction and frustration followed another between Dawson and Hutton, which again must have reminded the GOC of his final months in Canada. Many of them revolved around the ever-present issue of authority. At one point, for example, Hutton requested a paltry total of £15 to have a pistol prototype built for his light horse troops. A strained exchanged followed in which Hutton felt his professional judgment was in question. Dawson requested an explanation of why the pistol was required. Hutton gave it. Dawson then decided to seek imperial advice on the matter. Hutton, furious, informed his minister on 21 June: 'I am not prepared to submit further recommendations on this subject.'[73] Dawson responded angrily to what seemed to be an attack on his authority, reminding Hutton that 'the GOC, whilst under engagement by this Government, will be expected to furnish such reports and information as may be called for by the Minister, as may be in his power to supply'.[74] 'I wish it clearly understood', he went on, 'that, in future, any minutes furnished by the GOC which appear to be studiously discourteous will be returned with a view to further action.'[75] By August the minister and GOC were in an open war of words in official correspondence and in the press. The situation was relieved only by the fall of Watson's government and the appointment of the Reid–McLean ministry on 18 August 1904. Dawson subsequently wrote of his 'happy relations [with] Collins and his civilian departmental staff' but that he and the GOC 'were, unfortunately not in touch or sympathy' and that the military branch was in 'discord'.[76] It was a suitably bitter ending to an acidic relationship.

Despite his short tenure as minister and in the context of his feuding with Hutton, Dawson had initiated a key reform of his own (with considerable assistance from Collins) that haunted the GOC for the rest of his appointment and well after he left office.[77] The minister had set up a committee, with himself as chairman, to investigate command and administration of the military and naval forces. Its findings were stark. The committee rejected the whole idea of a GOC as 'the sole responsible adviser of the Minister on all Military questions'. A change was proposed therefore to allow for more varied input, to encourage decentralisation and to bring together the military and civil branches of the department. This would be achieved through the raising of a Council of Defence to 'collate information and afford the Government advice on all questions of policy'. A Military Board and a Naval Board would also be raised to administer the military and naval forces respectively, while an Inspector-General would be appointed, separate from the Military Board, to 'ascertain and report upon the condition of the Military Forces'.[78] Such an organisation had been partially provided for in the Defence Act of 1903, but had not been acted upon. The Dawson Committee's report was released just as the Watson government fell.

It would be a mistake to conclude that frictions between Hutton and Dawson were the sole motivation for the raising of Dawson's committee, or the substance of its report. Rather, such recommendations had important international contexts. The Elgin and Esher reports in Britain had important roles to play here. The Esher Committee, among other findings, recommended the abolition of the post of Commander-in-Chief in favour of a 'Chief of the General Staff' and the establishment of an Army Council as a formal advisory and executive committee responsible to parliament. These were, in themselves, not necessarily new ideas; the Hartington Commission of 1890 had, for example, recommended the creation of a 'War Office Council' to replace the position of Commander-in-Chief, but in the wake of South Africa they had a new urgency. The British Government accepted Esher's recommendations, despite resistance by such key military figures as Kitchener. The seven-member Army Council, a conglomerate of soldiers and politicians, was raised in February 1904 (along similar lines to the Admiralty Board), the post of Commander-in-Chief abolished and Lieutenant-General Sir Neville Gerald Lyttelton appointed as the Chief of the (new) General Staff department. Meanwhile, the Duke of Connaught was made Inspector-General of the forces.[79] Little did Hutton realise that Sir George Sydenham Clarke, formerly of the CDC, Victorian Governor from September 1901 to November 1903 and a member of the committee that issued the Esher Report, had been advising Australian officials to adopt a similar system.[80]

So too the serious personal enmity and public feuding in Britain between the Commander-in-Chief and his responsible minister that helped lend impetus to War Office reform paralleled many of Hutton's difficulties in Australia. Such disputes reached a peak in autumn 1900. The Queen asked Wolseley to draw up a memorandum giving his views on this issue. Wolseley recommended the appointment of a supreme commander with full responsibility to control the army – free from ministerial interference. Lansdowne and Wolseley subsequently fought a major debate launched in the House of Lords regarding the division of civil and military authority. Throughout, Wolseley maintained that he had the right to appeal directly to the press on issues of significance. Roberts was no less determined than his predecessor to challenge civil influence and just as appalled at the idea that his authority might be questioned by the War Office Council. Broderick rejected his complaints, and Roberts appealed directly to Cabinet. By September 1901 he was considering resigning over the issue; he would not be a figurehead. From 1902 Kitchener followed Wolseley's and Roberts' examples and used the press to pressure politicians and policy-making.[81] There is no question that Hutton knew of these arguments and developments. In fact, at one point he congratulated Wolseley for holding the line on such issues that threatened 'the very existence of the British Empire'.[82]

The pattern was reflected elsewhere in the Empire. The removal of Dundonald in Canada in June 1904, for example, again due largely to friction with the government and confusion over his authority relative to his minister, paved the way for a new Canadian Militia Council of civil and military figures to advise the minister and led to the appointment of Major-General Sir Percy Henry Noel Lake, a Canadian officer, as Chief of the General Staff. Dawson therefore had plenty of 'templates' from which to work. So too, a little later in 1906 in New Zealand, on the departure of the last Commandant of local forces, Major-General James Melville Babington, once more with unanswered questions of his authority, heralded with the establishment of a Defence Council, which finally removed friction between Commandant and civil department. The point was that Dawson's committee and the forces and ideas that drove it were Empire-wide and his conclusions were entirely in line with those reached elsewhere. There is no question that difficulties surrounding the person of Hutton had a role, but the board and council system in Australia was also an answer to a long-standing institutional problem associated with the position of GOC or Commandant throughout the Empire.

On 17 August 1904 the Reid–McLean government assumed office, and a militia officer and lawyer, James Whiteside McCay, assumed the post of Defence Minister. Two weeks later he asked Hutton for his thoughts on Dawson's report and for his confidential opinion as to which officers now in Australia might be fit for duties on the proposed council and board. By now, at last becoming aware of mounting public and political criticisms of the state of his reorganisations, Hutton began by reminding McCay that owing to financial stringency and reductions in his staff it had 'become impossible for the General Officer Commanding to fulfil the responsibilities laid down and further he is powerless to arrest the progress of chaos and disintegration which has now already set in'.[83] Yet Hutton, predictably, found serious fault with Dawson's 'solution'. He argued that such a drastic change would destroy all he had managed to build and that the tried experience of a senior British officer was indispensible.

Hutton further argued, not unreasonably, that Dawson had been watching the War Office too closely. The removal of the Commander-in-Chief position in London, he suggested, was a consequence of the vastness of his responsibilities, which had grown into too much for one man. This argument, he contended, 'does not apply to the comparatively diminutive forces in Australia'. It was also too early to know whether Esher's reforms had actually worked. In the context of his rivalry with Collins, Hutton worried that the proposed Military Board would invariably be controlled by the Secretary of Defence as the representative of the minister. The Secretary, who also administered the financial branch, would 'thus practically assume all the administrative powers and executive functions of the present General Officer Commanding and of the Minister combined'. 'I can conceive of no system which is more certain to be fatal to the efficiency or well-being of the Military Forces of the Commonwealth', predicted Hutton, 'than one which will place control, administration, and, indirectly, command, of the troops in the hands of a civilian.' Aside from the board, Hutton was comfortable with the idea of a Council for Defence 'to decide upon questions of policy and to discuss the same'. Reflecting his professional prejudices and colonial experiences, however, he was hostile to the suggestion of an inspector-general, arguing: 'The Australian Forces require a Leader and Instructor, far more than a mere Inspector who would have no executive functions or powers of command.'[84] Moreover, such a post would require the qualifications, skills and experience of a senior British officer, not an Australian.

Hutton's protests were as predictable as they were in vain. McCay, like his government and parliamentary colleagues, was convinced by Dawson's arguments. Not only would the proposed administrative and command rearrangements bring Australia into line with Britain and Canada but also they would in the process remove the perpetually fraught position of an imperial GOC and the troublesome personality of Edward Hutton. The Defence Act of 1904, an amendment to the act of the previous year, was framed, presented, passed in July and assented on 9 December 1904.[85] The position of GOC was no more.

Towards the end Hutton had finally seen the writing on the wall and actively sought out an 'acceptable' end to his appointment. He wrote to Arthur Lee (Military Attaché in Washington when Hutton was in Canada) congratulating him on his appointment as Civil Lord of the Admiralty and volunteering to return home to help reform at War Office.[86] He similarly wrote to Lieutenant-General Thomas Kelly Kenny, Adjutant-General in Britain, suggesting his experiences in the colonies might be useful in helping to implement reform in Britain.[87] Hutton's friend and confidant Lord Tennyson departed in January 1904 to be replaced by Lord Northcote, not nearly the ally for Hutton his predecessor had been, which further encouraged him in this direction. Moreover, by the middle of the year, Hutton later reflected, it was 'abundantly clear' that feelings in the press and parliament were 'gradually overpowering my personal popularity'. Unable to see, or accept, that the turning of opinion was in many ways a function of difficulties associated with his reorganisations and the manner in which he carried them out, Hutton concluded that the true cause of angst against him was the very strength and foresight of his scheme in that he 'had laid down a policy for Australia and had built thereupon – almost before they were aware – an edifice which was likely to stand'. As a result, he beleived, 'I became the butt of continuous attacks by politicians of the Labour and "Free Lance" class ... [who] spared no pains to belittle my efforts and to impugn my judgement'. By now Hutton knew he 'could only look forward to a repetition of the difficulties and troubles which I had experienced at the hands of the Laurier government in Canada'.[88]

Hutton duly wrote to Collins on 20 August 1904 asking that McCay inform the War Office 'of the termination of my command of the Military Forces of the Commonwealth on December 26th next' and that he planned to depart Australia on 15 November.[89] In communicating the message to Prime Minister, George Reid, McCay referred to his 'appreciation of services rendered'; faint praise indeed.[90] Reid passed the request on to Government House the same day, omitting McCay's polite words altogether. As had been the case in Canada, on the eve of his departure Hutton chose to vent his frustrations, this time at the King's Birthday Banquet at the Melbourne Town Hall. The barbs flew thick and fast. 'The difficulties with which I had to contend no man knows except myself', Hutton began. 'There are more tests of courage than the test of a battlefield', he continued. 'I could not say anything for a soldier's hands are tied ... If I have been silent it has not been for want of courage or love of fighting ... I fearlessly look Australia in the face, to the Press, Parliament and Public and say that I have done my utmost.'[91] On 2 November 1904 McCay announced the formation of the Military Board and the end to the position of GOC. Thirteen days later Hutton and Eleanor departed 'with heavy heart', although, Hutton admitted, 'perhaps without that feeling of relief which not unnaturally accompanies the termination of a period of great difficulty and strain'.[92] The pair arrived in England on 17 December.

Back in Australia military affairs without Hutton moved on, although stability and efficiency proved not to be the products of the departure of the man many believed to have been at the root of military problems. In January 1905 the Military Board and Council for Defence began operations. The council's impotence was obvious from the beginning, as Cabinet was not obliged to heed its recommendations and rarely did. Its meetings – and there was a grand total of two in a decade – often bogged down in administrative details. McCay's vision of a Military Board with an informal atmosphere, no military pecking order and members free to dissent was also largely a failure, thanks to the military mindset and efforts of Hutton's chief Australian protégé, Lieutenant-Colonel William Throsby Bridges. Moreover, when it met, Major James Gordon Legge reported to Hutton in January 1908, it 'did nothing but quarrel over their relative spheres of influence and draw fine distinctions as to the design of new badges'.[93] In a similar vein the Surgeon-General, William Williams, told Hutton in 1908 that 'the Board system for Australia is a failure and must be a failure'. 'The Minister is practically GOC', he continued, 'pulled here and there by first one adviser then another.'[94]

Nor was the public or the government any more satisfied with the post-Hutton army than it had been with him at the helm. In October 1905 Deakin, again Prime Minister, wrote to Clarke of his desire to see 'the completion of the Defence of Australia'. The work done by Hutton, although necessary, argued Deakin, was 'too isolated an effort'.[95] Deakin flagged his own preference for a complete overhaul of the army and the adoption of a system of compulsory military training on the Swiss model. In December 1907 he announced such plans to the House, but was temporarily foiled in this long-term ambition by an election loss in November 1908. In 1911, however, a Labor government adopted a scheme for the compulsory military training of males between 18 and 26 years of age.

As Hutton sailed from Melbourne he knew his tenure in Australia had failed to achieve what he had hoped. His grand scheme of a white, Empire-wide, volunteer (predominantly mounted) militia was perhaps now further from reality than it had been when he had arrived in early 1902. Australian legislation expressly forbade the despatch of the whole or part of his beloved Field Force in support of the Empire, an integral aspect of his vision of its purpose. Certainly the option for Australians to volunteer as individuals for imperial expeditionary forces still existed, and it remained an article of faith for the vast majority of Australians that this course of action would be both appropriate and automatic if the Empire were truly threatened. This, however, was not Hutton's scheme. There was no point organising and training part-time military units in Australia, Canada or anywhere else if they were not permitted to be deployed, as units, when and where their governments decided. In an unsigned article published in the Melbourne *Life* magazine, the day he left Australia, Hutton claimed that if the new nation was invaded its military forces would be worse off than the French Army before the Battle of Sedan in 1870 and, if some other part of the Empire was attacked, the value of Australia's army would be practically nil.[96]

It was just as impossible in 1904 for Hutton to countenance a professional failure for all but the briefest periods as it had been throughout his career. He set about convincing himself and those around him that he had, in fact, met his aims. 'I had achieved all that I had laid myself out to do in the three short years that had passed', he later mused.[97] In less than three years, Hutton wrote in 1905, a military system had been put in place 'out of the motley defence forces previously existing in the six States of Australia, in spite of drastic retrenchment and in spite of the halting administration of three successive Governments so widely divergent in their views'.[98] There was something to this argument, even if his legacy was by no means the military edifice Hutton came to think. Leaving aside his plans for a 'co-operative system' and the turmoil created by his restructuring, there can be no question that Hutton's drive and energy left a federal military force in Australia more organised, better administered and more highly trained than the disparate colonial groupings he had inherited. All of this was done under crippling restrictions. So too many key figures in the subsequent development of the Australian Army – such men as Cyril Brudenell Bingham White, Harry Chauvel, John Antill and William Bridges – were fundamentally shaped by Hutton in the post-Federation period. As George Reid predicted on the eve of Hutton's departure in 1904: '[T]he people of this nation will see more and more clearly the results of the invaluable service that have been rendered to us, in the infancy of this nation, by General Hutton.'[99] In 1921 Charles Bean described him, not unreasonably, as 'a soldier of a brilliance only too rare' and that his 'mark will always be deeply pressed on the Australian Army'.[100]

Such praise does not, however, lessen the bitterness, confrontation and enmity that Hutton left in his wake in Australia. As always, where conciliation, compromise, moderation and tact were needed, Hutton presented stubbornness, arrogance and intolerance. The issue was especially acute given that he was forced to serve five ministers in three years, each with a different style and policies to match. The result was predictable. Again, however, it should be noted that this was the lot of reforming

British generals throughout the Empire when thrust into such appointments. Those quick to condemn Hutton have often been less inclined to contextualise his problems. Reformers caused trouble in Canada and New Zealand as well, while compliant GOCs failed at reform. The system was that it was very rare to have it both ways. As Major-General Smith-Dorrien told Hutton in mid-1903, 'there are not many men who have got that form of ability which enables them to combine diplomacy with soldiering, hence you have to suffer'.[101]

So too it is worth bearing in mind that Hutton's reforms were attacked as much for social, financial and personal as for military reasons. Any GOC who sought to fuse the Australian colonial forces into a federal system required a degree of centralised control that inevitably aroused resentment in the states and at a local level. Cooperation was always at a premium across the gambit of Australian defence in the post-Federation period. Regulars clashed with part-time soldiers, militiamen fought volunteers, commandants fought the centre, the civil and military branches within the department struggled with each other, while politicians traded insults with military figures. In any case critics – and there was no shortage of them by 1904 – saw the military as disorganised and unsatisfactory for the nation's defence. Whether this was true or not was almost beside the point, for it was the impression that they held. Impressions meant votes then, as they do now, and the vulnerable parliamentarians responded. If Hutton had not resigned at the end of his allotted three years, he would have been pushed.

CHAPTER 11

'Hopelessly ignorant of our self-governing Colonies'

The New Australian Army and Imperial Defence, 1902–04

Any investigation of the issue of imperial defence at the turn of the twentieth century must begin with the conflict in South Africa. In the first instance, the war crystallised anti-British feelings throughout Europe. The hostility of the great powers, with the exception of Japan and the United States, was clear in Britain and in the colonies. This was especially the case in Germany, where press attacks against British policy and the Empire in a wider sense were vehement. The spectre of European intervention in South Africa and a wider war (perceived dangers exacerbated by the shocking revelations of British military weakness of Black Week) were causes of significant political and public concern. Pre-existing, long-term feelings that the Empire was under siege were reinforced. The 'blanket of public enthusiasm that had enveloped Britain's imperial enterprise during the 1890s' was replaced by a drive for imperial consolidation and security.[1] Men like Chamberlain embodied this sentiment; the Empire was the defining characteristic of Britain and things British, and its very existence depended on its being strong and unified. This atmosphere of fear partially accounts for the continuing failure of a Liberal vision in Britain, despite the efforts of such groups as the Fabian Society to use the war to advocate a revision of the imperial idea to include social and domestic reform. The conservative picture of Empire, even if it had transitioned from imperial celebration to imperial protection, was more dominant than ever during the war years, in the centre and in the colonies.

Under such circumstances many leading advocates of imperial unity saw both an opportunity and evidence in support of their arguments for more extensive intra-Empire connections. From South Australia, for example, Lord Tennyson, as Governor, wrote to Chamberlain in April 1900 that in his opinion 'most prominent Australian statesmen' saw the war as proof that the Empire should be 'more firmly and formally federated than it is now'. Tennyson argued that the war made imperial political union not only possible but also urgent and that any federated Australia would henceforth demand a voice in the settlement of imperial questions. What was required, in Tennyson's mind, was action 'before the present sentiment wears off'.[2] This is not to suggest that Tennyson's conclusions were correct; rather they illustrate a mode of thinking, particularly by political elites already predisposed towards imperial unity. Chamberlain himself wondered to Minto in March 1900 whether, in the context of war, there might be a chance of 'harvesting some permanent results from so verdant a field of imperial sentiment' and whether 'something practical' might be affected to bring about that 'closer union which we have constantly kept in view'.[3] He had told the House of Commons in January that 'we are advancing steadily, if slowly, to the realisation of that great federation of our race which will inevitably make for peace and liberty and justice'. The theme was echoed by Brodrick in 1902: 'The dream of Colonial Federation ... had been made a reality by the Boer War.'[4] Unsurprisingly, the same was true of like-minded military figures. In March 1900 Wolseley claimed: 'This war has federated the Empire.'[5] For Hutton, Chamberlain's policy of unifying and solidifying the imperial edifice had already proven successful, by all portions of the Empire springing forward to assist the Mother Country in South Africa.[6]

The general feeling of *opportunity* felt by advocates of imperial unity during the war years was reflected in attitudes towards the question of imperial defence. Before the war defence policy in London was consistently subordinated to the idea of constitutional and economic progress, as the basis of Britain's status as a world power. The game, however, had changed: more and more importance was now attached to defence and strategic power. The Empire was fundamentally a part of that. Overall, therefore, in the context of the crises of the war's early stages, various colonial contributions alerted defence policy-makers to the Empire's military potential more than ever before. The numbers were simply too great to ignore. New Zealand contingents alone, per capita, were the equivalent of a force of 102 000 men from Britain. Moreover, as late as January 1902 the Australian parliament was passing resolutions in support of imperial activities in South Africa and ending them with three cheers for the King. Nor was the South African example the only such message it sent to London. Australian contributions to the Boxer Rebellion in June 1900, which exceeded British requests as the Australian colonies fell over themselves to offer assistance, again signalled an apparent willingness to assume a far greater share in imperial defence burden. The fanfare surrounding the departure of the expeditionary force to China and the public outcry in Adelaide, for example, when it appeared for a time that the colonial ship *Protector* might not sail as part of it, *seemed* a clear indication of public and political attitudes above and beyond the false start of the Sudan in the 1880s.[7]

For many in London therefore the rush of colonial volunteers to the veldt ushered a new era of imperial defence cooperation and solidarity, which implied the possibility of a level of real organisation not previously seen. The Undersecretary of State for War, George Wyndham, concluded that the colonies 'may play a very great part in the future evolution of the Empire and will seek, not indeed to perpetuate these splendid efforts they have made from year to year, but to render their repetition more easy by adopting some kind of organization on prearranged lines'. *The Times* reported that the war had raised the 'possibility' of such standing arrangements 'to the rank of probability' and looked forward to 'some wide and far reaching plan for welding together the indissoluble bond the might of the British race' to capture 'the worth of the resources it has to draw upon in the days of its trouble in its strong sons beyond the seas'. Even Cabinet member Sir Michael Hick Beach, by no measure an ardent imperial federationist, confessed on 19 April 1900 that he saw potential for a common system of defence organisation 'in which all of us might take our fair and equal share in the responsibilities of the defence of the Empire at large'.[8] The day before sailing for South Africa, Hutton himself wrote that 'the Imperial Government are quite determined to have a consistent and properly organised military system in which the Colonies shall be invited to take part at the end of the present war'.[9] He was right, but at the same time such feelings represented a line of thinking in Britain that was neither grounded in nor responsive to the colonial sentiments it sought to capitalise upon.

As had been the case in 1885, in many ways those in London inclined to interpret colonial commitments to South Africa as a watershed moment in the long-running saga of imperial defence saw only what they wanted to see. There was plenty of evidence that precious little had actually changed at the periphery. Barton warned at a banquet hosted by the British Empire League in April 1900, for example, that it was dangerous to formulate proposals that acted too strongly as obligations. Here he was referring to the same message that had been sent from the colonies to London for the last twenty years; that is, there was no question that in Britain's hour of need the colonies would be there, but volunteerism in a crisis was a far cry from standing formalised commitments in peacetime. Indeed Australian ministers, like their counterparts in Canada and New Zealand, refrained assiduously during the war years from codifying even their own actions. The colonial legislatures all avoided addressing the issue, let alone constructing any policy of when, where and how their troops might be used when the Empire called. The parliamentary debates that unfolded in the colonies were about the war at hand, not a war of the future. The point is that the sense of 'opportunity' in London brought about by South Africa was not reflected in the colonies. Opinions to the contrary, from those British military and diplomatic representatives on the spot such as Hutton, Minto and others, failed to impress.[10]

These trends continued in the immediate aftermath of the war. Although the majority of military attention in London soon switched to War Office and British Army reform under the idea that 'the heart of the Empire had to be cared for before attention could be paid to the greater use of the limbs', that strand of thought focused on imperial defence continued to draw conclusions based on desire, not evidence.[11] The shock of post-tallying in London, showing that the war had cost a quarter of a billion pounds and required 400 000 troops 'to subdue a Boer male population which did not outnumber that of Brighton', was considerable.[12] Such imperial federationists as George Parkin lobbied for post-war military reform to include 'the whole colonial problem of military preparation as well as with the mother land'.[13] At the same time influential military writers such as Colonel G.F.R. Henderson found it incomprehensible that 'no effort had been made so to organise the Forces of the Empire that each portion might be mobilised and the whole rapidly assembled'.[14] Such men were aghast that the war years were 'wasted' and that no attempt had been made to capitalise on imperial sentiment by framing an imperial defence policy. Their lobbying continued in the aftermath of the conflict, an important context to the next Colonial Conference, held on the occasion of the coronation of King Edward VII, in London, from June to August 1902.

Again, however, this was a line of argument about the Empire raised in Britain for British ears, with little account taken of the opinions of the actual subjects of the debate. In the colonies the war's conclusion marked no more of a change in thinking about the principles of imperial defence than had its course and conduct. If anything, the message was exactly the opposite in that final victory confirmed that existing arrangements, or the lack of them, were fine as they were. On top of this, and in light of the outcomes of the various British inquiries into the war, there was a lingering feeling in the colonies that British military institutions had failed. In 1903 the Victorian Governor, Sir George Sydenham Clarke, told Arthur Balfour, the British Prime Minister, that the effect of such revelations was 'deplorable' and that 'the imperfections of the War Office were a potent source of imperial disintegration'.[15] The message was reinforced by Minto in Canada, who reported a growing contempt in the militia of imperial military officers and administration. Such feelings, in turn and as noted in chapter 10, encouraged a focus on domestic defence issues, a misreading of military 'lessons' and the rise of colonial notions of their innate martial superiority, which trumped the need for British-style administration and organisation. In Clarke's words, 'Australians, many of them, believe they were the only real soldiers and the belief is not good for them. They are quite unfit, in training & discipline to meet good regular troops.'[16] Nonetheless, the consequent rise of a nascent 'Militia Myth' in Canada and similar sentimentality in Australia did nothing to move the colonies closer to formal imperial defence arrangements. In this context Brodrick's testimony to the royal commission on the war in South African was sage. 'We cannot press for anything', he noted, 'they are not prepared to tender.'[17] The problem was that such advice did not align with emergent British thinking, particularly Chamberlain's thinking, on the issue. It was therefore ignored.

Such were some of the forces and factors in play when Hutton was sent to Australia. Certainly, opinion in London was firming with regard to the need to formalise defence arrangements with the colonies, but there was as yet still no plan for how this might be achieved, nor any thought to gauge the opinion of the colonies themselves in such matters – so much for the notion that Hutton arrived as an agent of a coherent British imperial defence plot designed to manipulate the newly federated nation into subordinating its interests to those of the Empire. Yet claims to the contrary have persisted, and Hutton was, once more, a Trojan Horse in the Australian defence system. In particular, so the charges run, Hutton's Field Force was itself proof of the plot. With a 'clandestine relationship' with Chamberlain, Hutton was, by disguising the force as a mechanism to defend Australia, 'attempting a grand deception of the Australian Government and people'.[18] Surely he must have known that with no truly national rail system in a country of such size his Field Force would never be mobile in any true sense. But this was hardly the point if London's agent was secretly arranging an expeditionary force on its behalf. This is in fact why Hutton never planned for a formation higher than a brigade, not, as Hutton claimed to Lieutenant-General W.G. Nicholson, Director-General of Mobilization and Military

Intelligence at the War Office, that there were no officers to command it, but because it was intended these brigades would fit seamlessly into larger British formations. '[T]his and not the defence of Australia was the determinant of force structure.'[19]

Like all good conspiracies, this one is based on a partial truth, yet in its overall conclusions it is fundamentally mistaken. As has been discussed, Hutton certainly *did* have a scheme in mind whereby Australian troops might be used to defend the Empire, if and when the Australian Government wished to deploy them to this end. His message to Forrest in August 1902 that his reorganisation was, from beginning to end, based only on what was 'necessary for "The Defence of Australian Soil"', was a manifest mistruth.[20] This scheme was behind his boasts to his superiors in London that an expeditionary force of 20 000 Australian mounted troops was possible. The plan behind the boast, however, was his, not Chamberlain's, not Balfour's and certainly not the product of coordinated instructions from the War Office – if for no other reason than such plans still did not exist in April 1902. As will be seen, when Chamberlain and the War Office at last came upon a scheme to codify colonial imperial defence commitments later in 1902 it stood in *opposition* to Hutton's long-standing plans. Moreover, beyond such obvious counter-points the simplistic reductionism of Hutton as imperial agent also fails on many other grounds. It was true, for example, that the Field Force from 1902 to 1904 could never hope to be a truly mobile national force and that brigades composed of units from smaller states would be very difficult to mobilise or concentrate, let alone train as formations, yet there were few real alternatives. To have left post-Federation Australian units unbrigaded, or restricted to garrison roles, would have made them no better suited to defending Australia. Indeed, the absence of the higher command and administrative structures, technical and supply units demanded by Hutton's Field Force would likely have made them considerably worse.

Above and beyond the details of Hutton's plans for the Australian Army, any suggestion of a conspiracy beyond his personal agenda also fails to grasp (as was the case with similar suggestions connected to his time in New South Wales and Canada) the true nature of Australian identity of the era. The dominant nationalism was imperial, not Australian. Australian interests, in sentimental terms and to a large degree in material terms as well, *were* those of the Empire. To base historical interpretations of this period as a conflict or competition between imperial and national ideologies is to describe a mirage. Even had there been a conspiracy, it would have been a conspiracy of conspicuous agreement! This is not to suggest that Australian politicians, the press and elements of the public were not concerned about Hutton's activities and motives. Rather, to posit such friction as a clash of imperial versus Australian loyalties is a fundamental misreading of the reality of imperial identity of the era.[21] Hutton's actions need to be understood on their own terms and in their own context. The institutional culture of the officer corps of which he was part, the influence of the Wolseley Ring, his life-long professional preferences, which fed into his own sense of self, his operational experiences, prevailing financial circumstances, even his Eton inheritance and self-perceived social standing, for example, all informed, fed and shaped the attitudes brought back to Australia in 1902. In truth, complicated and prosaic reality emerges above exciting ideas of imperial plotting in 1902–04.

At the same time, throughout his tenure Hutton was careful, as he had been in the past, to cautiously shepherd his connections with London. The voluminous correspondence it generated and the messages therein certainly fuelled subsequent notions of imperial conspiracy. Before setting sail for Melbourne, Hutton had promised Chamberlain that he would attempt to help frame a Defence Act that would admit 'use of Australian Troops outside Australian Waters in case of a National Emergency'.[22] He wrote to Roberts in July 1902 that he would try his best to ensure the adoption of a Defence Bill that would 'realise the wishes and hopes of Mr Chamberlain, Mr Brodrick and yourself'.[23] In February 1902 he told Brodrick that his promise of mounted horsemen for service wherever Australian interests are threatened 'was perceived with a most satisfying acquiescence' and that he felt sure clauses in the existing Defence Bill precluding overseas service would soon be withdrawn. In April, the same day he finished his famous *Minute upon the Defence of Australia*, not only did Hutton send a copy to Brodrick but also he explained that he had been 'careful to avoid any direct reference to assistance of the Empire in time of war except inferentially'.[24] He went on to explain to Ommanney, Permanent Undersecretary of State for the Colonies, later that year that his Field Force was serving not only in protection of Australian soil but also 'outside their own waters, if need arise'.[25] The force was 'as easily concentrated in South Africa or in the Persian Gulf', he explained to Tennyson, 'as in Northern Ireland or Western Australia'.[26] Even once it became clear that the Defence Act of 1903 precluded the despatch of militia units outside Australia, Hutton continued to remind those in positions of power in London that the bulk of the Field Force would no doubt volunteer in a crisis for 'service abroad'; indeed he had always intended that 'this spirit shall be the guiding principle' within this force.[27]

The key to understanding the significance of Hutton's voluminous correspondence is in the context of his personality and professional circumstances. His busy pen was never indicative of personal or imperial scheming. His stream of letters to London, as it had been in each colonial appointment, and as was common among all colonial GOCs in the period, was about maintaining personal contacts (and therefore career prospects) often concerned with big-noting his perceived and actual successes. More to the point, when Hutton referred to the service of Australian troops outside Australia he was invariably talking about *his* ideas for cooperative defence, *not* any schemes coming out of the War or Colonial Offices. In fact, when such plans were eventually developed they were at odds with Hutton's objectives, not synchronised with them, which at once frustrated him and further belied any notion of imperial plotting.

Photo 22 Major-General Edward Hutton, General Officer Commanding the Military Forces of the Commonwealth of Australia, by Thomas William 'Tom' Roberts (1856–1931). (Royal Military College, Duntroon)

When the move to formalise imperial defence arrangements was finally initiated in Britain, it took the form of an 'Imperial Reserve' scheme. In the context of an exploding deficit thanks to the war in South Africa, pressure from Treasury to reduce expenditure and reports from the Navy that it was overstretched, something had to be done. Momentum in this direction had in fact been building for some time. It originated not with Hutton but with Major-General George Arthur French in New South Wales who, in May 1900, devised his own plan for an imperial reserve of mounted troops from Australia. French's contention was that the war proved that 'the defence of the British Empire in the future is not a question to be left wholly to the people of the British Isles'. His scheme envisaged 10 000 troops earmarked from those 'who have passed through the ranks of the Defence Forces' to form a reserve to serve within or outside Australia as required and paid for by London.[28] While French's proposal gained no traction in New South Wales, Prime Minister Seddon in New Zealand became infatuated with the idea (especially given that Britain was to foot the bill). Seddon saw 'direct advantages to the Imperial authorities and the Empire in having a reserve force established ready for any contingency that might arise'.[29] It might also be said that he saw votes in the scheme and perhaps even a way to increase New Zealand's influence in the Pacific. In any case, by the end of the month he was writing to Chamberlain of the need for a 'real plan for Imperial Defence'.[30] Seddon had French's plan reprinted and submitted to his parliament in July 1900, where it was received favourably. The scheme was subsequently refined to suit New Zealand circumstances and passed into legislation in October.

Seddon subsequently sent the 'reserve' plan to the Colonial Office with the suggestion that copies might be forwarded to the War Office and the other self-governing colonies. Lansdowne, however, was uninterested, seeing practical problems and wishing to wait until the war in South Africa was over before judging what might be asked of the colonies. Despite this temporary postponement, the New Zealanders had taken an important step. The CDC, for one, recognised its significance. This was the first time a colonial legislature had enacted any formal scheme for imperial service that aimed to make its military resources explicitly available for imperial service outside that colony. The committee praised the 'promise of a real strengthening and knitting together in the future of the organized land forces of the Crown'.[31] Yet the CDC also recognised a danger of trying to 'press for any formal agreement at the present time' on the other self-governing colonies.[32]

Developments in New Zealand soon became a topic of discussion at the War Office. As Seddon's legislation was being passed, Lieutenant-Colonel E.A. Altham, Assistant Quartermaster General, urged Major-General Ardagh, now Director of Military Intelligence, to view French and Seddon's 'imperial reserve' scheme with 'something more than of academic interest'.[33] Up to this point the War Office had never given serious consideration to the systematic use of colonial troops outside their own borders – this was a British responsibility with a 'pious hope' that colonial volunteers would come forward if needed. There had never been any formal arrangements made, nor even serious enquiries as to whether and in what strength such reinforcements could be expected. Indeed the necessity of such aid was by no means obvious and its reliability more than doubted within the War Office. South Africa, however, had suggested the British army was too weak to meet imperial needs and that the colonies were willing to offer aid. 'The establishment of these two points', Altham argued, was 'an extremely important factor in the future consideration of problems of Imperial Defence'.[34] Moreover, returning to a familiar argument, and contrary to CDC advice, Altham suggested that real plans might be drawn up if a formal agreement was made and numbers were guaranteed. Such forces might then be the basis of an imperial military strategy. Ardagh listened.

From this point the 'imperial reserve' idea bounced around the War and Colonial Offices, slowly gathering momentum. Ardagh wrote to Wolseley in March 1901 advocating the cost-benefit of a system based on the New Zealand model, and Altham was subsequently directed to prepare a formal scheme to this end. Meanwhile, Chamberlain wrote to the Governor in New Zealand, Lord Ranfurly, describing the Seddon's legislative provisions as 'sound and weighty' and hoping his government would enact the necessary laws 'at an early date'.[35] Altham completed his task in November 1901. His system envisaged a war between Britain and a European state that must be fought by 'white subjects of the King', meaning troops from Britain and the self-governing colonies of Australia, New Zealand, Canada and South Africa. In a great war, Altham insisted, the Empire 'must stand or fall as a whole'. Therefore, in assisting the Empire, wherever assistance is needed, 'the Colonies will but be defending themselves'. Altham called for a force of specified strength and structure, established in peacetime, to be automatically available for defence or offensive operations anywhere in the world. Australia would provide 9000 such troops, New Zealand 4000, only 3000 from Canada (given the need to protect the frontier with the United States) and a number from

South Africa to be set a later date. 'Unless such preparations were made', Altham warned, 'the continuance of the Empire is doubtful, if not improbable'. The key point was that, although the numbers involved in Altham's scheme were relatively small, the principles involved, and what they might mean for the future, were momentous. Altham understood that the subject of defence cooperation was to be discussed at the upcoming 1902 Colonial Conference and suggested that this might be 'an admirable opportunity for the free exchange of views' with respect to his plan.[36]

Altham's proposal was submitted initially to Roberts in December, who recommended it to Brodrick as a low cost/high return solution, his only worry being that the colonies might baulk at entering into a definite engagement without a say in the setting of imperial policy. Brodrick harboured more doubts than Roberts that the colonies would agree, and in February he sought discussions with Chamberlain ahead of the Colonial Conference scheduled for June.[37] Chamberlain, however, looked kindly on Altham's proposal as it coincided in form and timing (not accidentally) with a separate proposal from Seddon to discuss at the forthcoming conference an 'Imperial Reserve Force', based on the New Zealand Defence Act amendment of 1900. The two proposals, from the War Office (Altham) and from New Zealand (Seddon), were not identical, but neither were they substantially different. Brodrick and Chamberlain agreed that both should be examined together by the CDC, which met in early June 1902. By now the CDC was more enthusiastic than had been the case in 1901, describing itself as 'in entire accord' with the proposed schemes and urging that they receive 'the most favourable consideration' by the governments of the self-governing colonies. Such pre-organised expeditionary forces, the committee noted, would be especially valuable as 'no European Power other than Great Britain is in a position to draw on large communities of white subjects outside Europe for military assistance'. Such a system was, moreover, an important step 'towards facilitating the conception and execution of comprehensive schemes of Imperial Defence'.[38] Much depended therefore on the looming conference.

Unknown to either Brodrick or Chamberlain, attitudes towards any formal imperial defence arrangements in Australia and Canada were certainly not the same as those in New Zealand. Hutton had long argued that such binding agreements in peacetime would be rejected in the two largest self-governing colonies if they were pressed and certainly would have said so again, had he been asked, or even warned of what was to be tabled at the conference. In Australia, during parliamentary debates on the first defence estimates in early 1902, clear hostility was evident from the Labor Party against Seddon's publicly announced plan to raise the issue of an 'imperial reserve' while in London, predominantly for fear of any costs involved. Forrest and Barton left for the conference well aware of the parliamentary mood, with the Prime Minister assuring the House he was not prepared to 'take any important step, except with the approval of Parliament'.[39] In Canada, Minto had consistently warned the Colonial Office that Laurier expected more imperial good to come from sentimental connections than from participation in official imperial schemes and that Canadian politicians did 'not anticipate that in the varying conditions of the colonies there can be any scheme of defence applicable to all'.[40] Indeed, the Prime Minister wrote to J.S. Wilson of the Toronto *Globe* in April 1902 that 'this is a thing as to which I have my mind firmly made up'.[41] For all of Altham's work, Seddon's advocacy and Chamberlain's hopes, no one in London, it seemed, had thought to test the mood in Ottawa or Melbourne.

Nonetheless, Chamberlain's opening address at the conference, which ran from 30 June to 11 August, described his 'paramount object' as being 'to strengthen the bonds which unite us'. This was to be done, in part, 'by considering the question which arises out of Imperial Defence'. 'Gentlemen we do want your aid', Chamberlain continued. '[T]he weary Titan staggers under the too vast orb of its fate.'[42] When subsequent discussions turned to the issue of imperial defence, Chamberlain began by pointing out relative expenditure on defence between Britain and the self-governing colonies. In this regard Britain's 29s 3d per head (for the year 1898–99) dwarfed Canada's 2s, or expenditure hovering a little over the 3s mark for the Australasian colonies. 'Now, no one, I think, will pretend that that is a fair distribution of the burdens of Empire', noted Chamberlain in his speech. 'While the colonies were young and poor [it was] perfectly right and natural that the Mother Country should undertake the protection of her children', he continued, 'but now the colonies are rich and powerful.'[43] Laurier and Barton were not particularly impressed. Brodrick followed by referring to Seddon's motion for an Imperial Reserve, which he wholeheartedly endorsed. Brodrick also presented Altham's paper and the CDC's report on it. Other War Office representatives continued the pitch to the colonial delegates, and Chamberlain closed the argument noting that the contingents sent to South Africa were evidence of 'our whole progress in this country for the last twenty years' with respect to imperial defence.[44] Moreover, while the Boers had been a difficult foe, Britain now faced much more dire European threats. The whole Empire would be needed to counter them, and London *must know for certain* what help would be available in a crisis.

Predictably (given the recent war), Natal supported Brodrick's and Seddon's proposals. So too, in principle, did the Cape Colony, although with a small proportion of white inhabitants any unreserved commitments were worrisome.[45] In the context of purely voluntary offers of troops, which had seemed to work adequately for South Africa, however, the Canadian and Australian representatives were uninterested. For Laurier, there seemed no pressing need to risk the goodwill of Francophile politicians and voters bound to be unimpressed by such a standing imperial commitment. In addition, Canada's only danger came from a foreign navy as no land defence could really be mounted against the United States, and the Royal Navy remained responsible for countering this threat. Laurier also contended that any proposal to raise an 'alternate' force in Canada risked degrading the Canadian militia. Most of all, despite the strategic logic involved, the removal of the right to decide whether, when and where Canadians might be sent to fight represented a grave 'departure from the principle of self-government'.[46] Barton's sentiments were similar. He feared parliamentary and public reactions to a standing arrangement that involved the loss of Australian control over Australian troops, 'a thing which is foreign to the sentiment of the colonies at the present time'.[47] Like Laurier, he also feared that the formation of such a force might impede the general improvement in training and organisation of the new Australian Army. Faced with such an impasse, Seddon withdrew his motion.

In the aftermath of such a blatant rebuff, Chamberlain's subsequent and equally fruitless discussion of the wider issue of political federation throughout the Empire seemed hollow. The most significant resolutions actually reached at the conference included a commitment to hold future meetings at intervals not exceeding four years and an Australian concurrence to renew the 1887 Naval Agreement. This was a meagre return for Chamberlain's high hopes. Disappointed, the Colonial Secretary reflected at the conclusion of formalities: 'I have no doubt many outside, who know nothing of our difficulties, will be disappointed with the results we have achieved.' Brodrick too was deflated. 'I can only express the pious hope', he offered, 'that the two great continent authorities will find themselves, some day or another ... able to consider something along similar lines.'[48] For his part Roberts was 'not altogether sanguine' that this might happen soon.[49] Of all those involved in framing the abortive attempt to impose the imperial reserve scheme it was Altham, ironically, who most easily accepted and understood the outcome. 'One can', he later wrote, 'sympathise with the sensitivities of a young community, which comparatively only recently has secured self-government, to any sort of interference by another authority over which they have no control.'[50]

Photo 23 At the Colonial Office on the last day of the Colonial Conference, 1902. Joseph Chamberlain is front, centre, with Edmund Barton to his left and Wilfrid Laurier to his right. Richard Seddon of New Zealand is seated next to Laurier. (National Archives of Australia, A8139, vol. 5)

Not that it lifted Chamberlain's immediate mood, but one important longer-term outcome of London's disappointment regarding the defence outcomes of the 1902 conference, combined with pressure brought to bear on Balfour from both Brodrick and Lord Selborne, First Lord of the Admiralty, was to forge substantive links between the British government departments concerned with defence issues through the creation of the Committee of Imperial Defence (CID), as a reconstitution of the lapsed Defence Committee of Cabinet. Even this new committee, however, which met for the first time under Balfour's chairmanship in December 1902, had its limitations. It was, to begin, intended as a small advisory committee with responsibilities for collection of information from the Empire rather than devising and implementing imperial strategy. Although it soon expanded its membership to include foreign, colonial and treasury ministers, the committee still had little executive authority, and departmental cooperation remained *ad hoc*. In this way the CID initially resembled a higher-level version of the CDC, which ultimately became one of its subcommittees. There were no arrangements at its inception to pass on its conclusions or see them implemented. In 1904, on the recommendation of the Esher Committee, the CID was given a permanent secretariat under Sir George Sydenham Clarke, and from this point its work became slowly more concerned with coordinating the defensive resources of the Empire.[51] This gradual change of tack, however, came well after Hutton's time in Australia had come to a close.

Back in Australia, the fallout of the failed imperial reserve proposal at the 1902 conference and a subsequent memorandum published by the CDC on Hutton's *Minute upon the Defence of Australia* was considerable. The personal and professional damage these two issues caused the GOC was a revealing insight into the continuing lack of coordination, let alone collaboration, with regard to imperial defence between London and its military representatives in the colonies. In the first instance Hutton had no idea what Chamberlain and Brodrick had planned, beyond a solitary quip from Roberts in late 1901 that imperial defence issues would likely by discussed at the forthcoming conference.[52] Hutton first heard about the 'imperial reserve' discussions at the conference from Forrest in August and was aghast. Why, he not unreasonably asked Nicholson at the War Office, if Altham's scheme was published confidentially in November 1901 (before his appointment to Australia) was he not informed of its existence or the War Office's prevailing views? Surely this information was relevant to his future task.[53] Moreover, Hutton knew full well how such proposals would be received in Australia. 'Brodrick's ill-considered quite hopeless scheme for creating a Colonial Reserve', he fumed to Minto when he received the news, 'has made my hopes for a sound military and political system of defence in Australia immeasurably harder to carry into effect.' With some truth in his words, he continued, 'The War Office ... is hopelessly ignorant of our self-governing Colonies.'[54] 'How unfortunate it was that Mr Brodrick did not consult someone who really understood our self-governing Colonies', he lamented to Lieutenant-General Sir Thomas Kelly Kenny, as it was always an 'absurd proposition that our Colonies would accept any definite military contribution to the military strength of the Empire without due representation'.[55] The attempt, he warned the Duke of Connaught, 'can only end in a disastrous conflict of opinion'.[56]

Hutton was right. By November 1902 news of British proposals for the imperial reserve was public and roused general disapproval. As a result the principles of his seminal Minute also began to be scrutinised and questioned. Hutton had been urging the acceptance of the idea that his Field Force ought to be able to serve outside Australia at *the discretion of the Australian Government*. The imperial reserve plan contravened this important principle and made his assurances seem inconsequential or misleading. From this moment, Hutton argued to Tennyson and to Sir Frederick Darley, it was 'doubtful' that Cabinet would agree to 'any clause enabling Australian troops to be used outside Australasian waters'.[57] Of course news of the War Office's promotion of Altham's plan was also a bitter pill for Hutton's considerable pride. After all, he had submitted details of his own cooperative imperial defence scheme to Brodrick in early 1901, which, it was now clear, had been pigeon-holed.[58] In any case, once more underscoring the absence of any coordinated policy in London, Ommanney agreed wholeheartedly with Hutton's complaints. 'I have always regarded the WO schemes for using the Australian Colonies as a recruiting ground for a Reserve as quite impractical', he told Hutton, 'and on being based on a complete ignorance of the Constitutional position of our Self-governing Colonies and a most extraordinary failure to appreciate the trend of public opinion in those Colonies.'[59]

If public knowledge of the presentation of the imperial reserve scheme at the Colonial Conference was not bad enough for Hutton, what followed was worse. The CDC's response to his Minute of April 1902, drafted in October, was for all intents and purposes a further attempt, after the conference's failure, to press for an imperial defence agreement. It challenged the idea Australia could be invaded without the knowledge and decisive intervention of the Royal Navy (thereby removing impetus for domestic defence reform) and argued that in such circumstances it was all the more important for Australia to think in terms of providing the Empire with well-prepared expeditionary forces. Echoing Altham's point, the CDC further described it as 'clearly essential that the forces likely to be available should be known quantities'. If such was the 'settled policy' of the country, British authorities could assign such a contingent a 'definite role in those initial strategic dispositions on which success in war so largely depends', and it would represent 'a real accession to the military strength of the Empire'.[60] To this end, and in order to bring Hutton's proposed structure closer to that advocated by Altham, the CDC recommended that the Field Force be reduced by a third with peacetime enrolments closer to war establishments. That way, if half of it could be fully manned on mobilisation, it would yield two mounted and one infantry brigade, exactly as Altham and the War Office recommended.

In February 1903 the CDC's memorandum on Hutton's Minute, with a copy of Altham's scheme and the CDC's favourable comments upon it, was received by Tennyson to be forwarded to the government. Tennyson knew as well as Hutton the potential impact of such official documentation. The Governor-General first cabled Chamberlain seeking to suppress the report. At present, he noted, such information was shared between Hutton, Barton and Forrest where it 'may cause not a little friction'. He assured Chamberlain that if the principles therein made their way to Cabinet or the press the consequences would be significant, if for no other reason than it would seem as though the CDC was advocating retrenchment just as Hutton fought to preserve his shrinking budget and planned restructuring. Moreover, the Defence Bill would have much less chance of passing if fears of compelling Australians to fight overseas were stimulated. 'It is clear to me', Tennyson continued in pointed language, 'that the writers do not understand that they cannot make Australia a recruiting ground for the Reserve ... the attitude of the War Office has been one of entire ignorance with regard to Australian sentiment.'[61] In frustration, Tennyson implored Barton and Forrest to keep the report quiet, for which he later received a rebuke from the Colonial Office. For the moment, however, Barton and Forrest complied. For his part Hutton was shocked. These documents, he wrote, gave him 'no little concern and indeed, grave embarrassment', especially as he had previously received 'semi-official' praise from Nicholson and from John Clauson, Secretary of the CDC, for the reorganisation plan embodied in his Minute.[62]

Despite Tennyson's efforts and Hutton's hopes, the contents of the CDC memorandum eventually leaked. Hutton did his best to preserve his scheme in the face of a growing crop of questions raised by the CDC's comments, dodging Forrest's probes about expeditionary forces as a matter 'outside my province' and questions about the Field Force being in excess of requirements by suggesting that he could only address this issue if the government accepted the principles on which it was based;[63] that is, if Forrest agreed with the CDC's expeditionary assumptions, then discussions might be had about reducing the Field Force. He could not, however, prevent a spreading awareness of the CDC's comments, particularly in parliament, leading to greater and greater scrutiny of his planned federal force and the Defence Bill.

It was not long before Hutton began blaming his building frustrations, particularly the government's determination to legislate against the possibility of Australian solders being 'sent' overseas as opposed to volunteering for overseas service, almost entirely on the imperial reserve plan and the CDC's comments on his Minute. He could not help but confront those he deemed responsible. He wrote to Nicholson in March 1903 condemning Altham's proposals as 'impractical' and 'too hasty', going as far as suggesting they were received in the same way 'that the Americans viewed the policy of the North Administration in 1776'. Hutton was free with his language with Nicholson, especially given that he was very much a Roberts man in a key War Office appointment. It was 'all very well', he continued with regard to the criticism of his Minute, to 'take exception to what is recommended by those on the spot and conversant with local conditions'. Hutton argued that the CDC and War Office should have 'strengthened my hand by a general concurrence', not contradict him. He wrote to Nicholson again a week later, once more lecturing him on colonial political and public sensitivities and the inappropriateness of what had been proposed as 'neither possible nor desirable'. 'This is not England', he correctly, yet condescendingly, pointed out.[64] Nicholson, whom both men knew had supported the imperial reserve idea, did not take Hutton's inferred criticism well. He replied in June attempting, unconvincingly, to rebuff Hutton's charges. All Hutton had achieved in venting his spleen was to create a powerful enemy within a new War Office coterie that already considered him an outsider.

Hutton subsequently wrote to Brodrick in August 1903 making the case why he had no intention of following the CDC/War Office advice to modify his Field Force. He explained that his scheme had at last been 'officially approved and published' and that to attempt to amend it risked serious dislocation and 'a feeling of a want of confidence among the troops and Australian public'. Hutton noted once more that the whole affair had caused him irrecoverable embarrassment and, more importantly, his promise in December 1901 to create a force available to assist the Empire in a crisis had been critically undermined by the War Office and CDC. 'If I am not able to make good on that promise, it is not, as I have shown, altogether my fault.'[65] Distracted by difficulties associated with his own efforts at reform at the War Office, Brodrick conceded that the attempt to press the imperial reserve idea had probably done more harm than good to the cause of a coordinated plan of imperial defence.[66] Similarly distracted, even Roberts was prepared to concede to Hutton: 'I regret that this should have been the case and can only imagine that our proposals have been somewhat misunderstood. They were carefully considered here and certainly not intended to arouse the not unnatural susceptibilities of a self-governing community.'[67]

Despite Roberts' concessions and the abject failure of the imperial reserve scheme, throughout Hutton's remaining time in Australia there were plenty of indications from War Office officials that little had been learned. In December 1903, for example, Major-General Sir Ian Hamilton, now Quartermaster-General to the forces, wrote to both Hutton in Australia and Colonel William Otter in Canada suggesting that a few thousand horsemen from each might be deployed to assist the Japanese against the Russians if and when a war broke out.[68] At the same time the CDC could still see 'no reasonable objection' to what had been suggested in 1902.[69] For his part Hutton never forgave the War Office for its reserve scheme and what he saw as its destructive effect on his own plans for Australia and the Empire. He was still lamenting to Clark, his friend and first Secretary of the CID, in 1906: 'I was justified in believing that the military authorities in London would endorse my schemes, or that if they did not do so, they would at least have the courtesy and consideration to inform me of their change in policy and even invite my views.'[70] He was still fuming at Nicholson in 1915 over his 'ignorance and callousness of the political considerations which govern all measures of military defence in our democratic communities'.[71]

Aside from removing any lingering notion of covert imperial defence collusion between the War Office and Hutton in Australia, the friction between the centre and the periphery brought about by the imperial reserve debacle illustrates two further key and related points. The first is that refusal by Australia (like Canada) to participate in a formalised imperial defence scheme was a consequence of various shared domestic pressures, not a rejection of the imperial idea or a lessening of the Empire nationalism that underwrote it. Certainly, desires to further local interests remained, but these existed on a different plane from the links that bound the Empire. There remained throughout Hutton's time in Australia, as had been the case in the past, no real conflict between the two. Indeed feelings of 'Australianness' in the early years of the new century drew strength from imagery of youthful vigour at the extremity of the Empire revitalising the core. Deakin, at the 1907 Imperial Conference, for example, declared: 'We propose a closer partnership ... the blood which goes from the heart here in the United Kingdom to the furthest extremities of Empire and returns again does so, not debilitated, but invigorated by hope and faith in our national stock and national life.'[72] Meanwhile, the republican leagues had withered and even such organisations as the Australian Natives Association had moved towards positions of strict imperial loyalty.

All the while the symbols of Empire grew more powerful. Empire Day in 1905 was a case in point. Introduced in Australia a decade before it was celebrated in Britain, this 'sacred occasion' was closest thing to a national day.[73] As far as most Australians were concerned, to celebrate the whole 'was to automatically praise the part'.[74] Even from a material or practical point of view the links that bound endured. Australian independence was, after all, premised on the maintenance of the Empire. White Australia at its heart really meant a British Australia.[75] Moreover, at Federation, 98 per cent of Australians were of British descent, with almost one in five being born there. Some eight of every ten grocery lines were British, and it was Britain that took most exports and provided most investment. Such material dependence on Britain 'could well have been resented by Australians if they were not so British themselves'. As Labor parliamentarian and future Prime Minister William Morris Hughes explained, once more: 'A man may be a very loyal and devoted adherent to and worshipper of, the Empire and still he may be a very loyal and patriotic Australian all the time.'[76] Kipling's poem 'The Young Queen' provided an apt analogy. Australia aspired to grow from 'daughter' to 'sister' to Britannia in order to strengthen the family, not leave it.

The second point is that Australian and Canadian reticence reflected the long-term and continuing question of spontaneous volunteerism versus standing imperial defence arrangements. Barton and Laurier favoured the former on domestic political grounds. Both young democracies felt uncomfortable with assigning troops in peacetime, which was felt to be an abrogation of hard-won political autonomy. In an Australian context, similar sensitivity was seen in discussions in London in 1900 regarding the draft Australian constitution. The result of the 1902 conference was, for the Brisbane *Courier*, 'recognition of the political rights of the self-governing colonies'.[77] It also hinted at a potential for military compulsion outside national borders that contravened long-held military-political philosophies, many of which had been originally imported from Britain. Moreover, a formal defence scheme seemed to imply increased expenditure, something neither Prime Minister was prepared to countenance. Further, any formal defence commitments were likely to arouse innate suspicion and hostility from such important parliamentary groups as Labour in Australia and a proportion of French Canadian parliamentarians in Ottawa. All of this in the context of a war in South Africa that had so recently 'proven' the existing (non)arrangements to be sufficient, and without any obvious new existential threat, aside from dire predictions occasionally emanating from London. On the other side of the ledger stood Chamberlain's politics of imperial union – of which he always considered defence to be a useful thin edge of the wedge – overlaid with the sensible, logical, strategic calculations of the War Office. Fears of a cataclysmic European war had been brewing in Britain for years and were made more acute by difficulties in South Africa. The imperial reserve was thus a pragmatic solution to a problem the self-governing dominions had the luxury of ignoring. These were the mismatches. Yet they embodied a misalignment of temporary prerogatives, not a lasting divergence of intentions.

The point is that all and sundry, from Chamberlain to Brodrick, Barton to Laurier to Seddon and all those political elites in between, assumed, as did the wider imperial public, that if the Empire was truly under threat then its constituent parts would rise to its aid. This had been the message from the colonies to the centre for decades, and nothing had changed. In the context of a faraway, messy, dubious war on the veldt in 1902, colonial contingents still had more volunteers than spaces available for them. The self-governing parliaments still rose as one to declare their support. There was no precedent, nor any serious suggestion that this would not be repeated, *en masse*, in a real crisis. Indeed this line of argument was used, in part, to justify the avoidance of peacetime commitments. As Barton himself made clear at the 1902 conference, 'they will do much in time of warlike emergency which in time of peace they would decline to bind themselves beforehand to accomplish'.[78] The conference proceedings confirmed this sentiment in that there was 'no room for doubt that such assistance would be given readily and effectively and to the utmost of their ability in any future emergency'.[79] 'We think what does attach us to the Mother Country is the link of relationship and affection', Barton continued, 'and the affection wells with overwhelming strength whenever any question of defence of the Empire, whether at our own doors or anyone else's, arises.'[80]

Importantly, Barton's sentiments reflected the general Australian parliamentary position, even from those who most sharply criticised Hutton and the various Defence Bills. Forrest told Hutton in April 1902, for example, that 'we must get rid of the idea that we have different interest to those of the rest of the Empire and we must look at the matter from a broad common standpoint'.[81] Both 'duty and stern necessity', Forrest told the Prime Minister, 'require that we stand shoulder to shoulder with the motherland in the determination to maintain inviolate the integrity of the British Empire'.[82] 'If the British nation is at war', Forrest continued, 'so are we; if it gains victories or suffers defeats, so do we.'[83] The idea of voluntary service in support of the Empire was similarly supported by Labor's Andrew Fisher, who asked, 'Has an appeal for volunteers ever had to be repeated in a British community when danger has appeared on the horizon? Happily it is characteristic of the British people that twice as many as are wanted always respond to such an appeal.'[84] Even George Reid expressed his absolute loyalty to the physical preservation of the Empire. Newspapers of the era reflected such assumptions. The *Sydney Morning Herald* told its readers in July 1902: 'Everything really important in the request of the Minister [Brodrick], however, will be fully secured if the local forces are trained and equipped [and] Imperial authorities will continue to trust the self-governing dependencies as before.'[85] The issue in Australia arising out of the 1902 conference, debates surrounding the Defence Bills and throughout Hutton's tenure, was never *whether* Australians would fight for the Empire but rather *how* that support would be framed.

No one more clearly understood that in a time of imperial peril Australians would flock to the colours than Hutton, and no one was more cognisant that it was 'at the present moment and under existing conditions impracticable to propose any scheme which will bind the Commonwealth Government to maintain a Military force' for imperial use without representation on the decision-making bodies that would use them.[86] The weight of this understanding, so clear in his eyes, underpinned his frustration with War Office officials who seemed so consistently ignorant of it. He told Sir Frederick Darley of the Boer War Commission in 1903, with considerable forethought, for example, that a binding scheme would not be accepted by the self-governing colonies without representation on imperial councils, but that, in an emergency that menaced the unity of the Empire, Australia 'would be determined at all hazards to take a foremost part'.[87] He repeated the message, *ad nauseam* to Tennyson, Roberts, Brodrick, Nicholson, Ommanney and anyone else who might listen. Hutton's disgust at the imperial reserve scheme and the Defence Act of 1903 was based in the fact they ensured that, when the day of reckoning finally came, the inevitable flood of volunteers would be unorganised, *ad hoc* and untrained as coherent units, an anathema to his own plans and professional instincts. There would, or could, under such circumstances be no easy deployment of his well-planned, well-organised militia units. In this way Hutton sought to shape the fundamental imperial reliance of volunteerism, whereas the War Office had sought to replace it with impossible formality.

What threads then might be drawn from Hutton's tenure in Australia as regards the wider issue of imperial defence up to 1904? First, he, like his fellow GOCs and commandants throughout the Empire, was no agent of imperial defence-plotting coordinated from London. No such coordination existed. Even outside Australia, British attitudes and positions were inconsistent and in flux. On one hand Brodrick was pressing Canada to contribute troops to India, for example, while the Navy was admitting that it could no longer control the Western Atlantic to reinforce Canada in a war with the United States. Rather, Hutton had his own scheme in front of mind, from beginning to end. To some degree his aspirations, or desired outcomes, were shared with such men as Chamberlain, but never the detail and never to a script. Hutton's scheme reflected the fruits of his own intellectual and professional labour, not those of the War Office. In this regard British officers in London did more to harm his ambitions in Australia than did Australian politicians. Moreover, the rejection of London's attempt to codify imperial defence arrangements in 1902 was not, as some have seen it, a statement of burgeoning local nationalism. It was, as Hutton well knew, a predictable colonial rebuff to a clumsy British overture, based primarily on domestic colonial political imperatives and sensitivities. These, again as Hutton recognised, had nothing to do with a lack of any commitment to defend the Empire when and if it was under real danger. This was an assumption so ingrained in the colonial psyche, in sentimental and pragmatic terms, that to question it is to fundamentally misunderstand the nature of Australian (and imperial) identity of this era. The 'silken cords of kindred, tradition and self-interest' made the colonies into reliable, if poorly organised, defence partners whatever ill-conceived notions sprouted from the War Office.[88]

Meanwhile, his plans blocked in Australia for the moment, Hutton's irrepressible ambition began to focus once more on home. Unable to give up his scheme of cooperative imperial defence just because it was now legislatively impossible in Australia, he invested more and more energy thinking about the situation in Britain. Frustrated with the limbs of the Empire, perhaps he could reach its heart. After all, in his mind, as the embodiment of a life's work (and still the grand solution just waiting for those of a sufficient intellect to grasp its importance), practical difficulties ought not to stand in the way of powerful ideas. To this end, Hutton began a campaign to persuade the new Secretary of State for War, Arnold Forster, to cast off Brodrick's limited vision in favour of 'the cause of a co-operative system of the Empire, towards the consummation of which I have for the last ten years, been working'.[89] This time the pathway was to reorganise the British volunteer forces as a national militia army on his model. Colonel Sir Edward May, Assistant Director of Military Training at the War Office, warned Hutton in September 1904 that such ideas 'will find no favour as yet', but such advice was a red rag to a bull.[90] The irony was, of course, that with Hutton *en route* back to London, the gap between his ambition and his real professional circumstances was opening to breaking point. It is therefore to the tragic conclusion to his career that attention, for the last time, must turn.

CHAPTER 12

'HOW FAR HIS VISION RANGED'

THE TWILIGHT YEARS, 1905–23

Hutton returned to England on 17 December 1904 and a few days later visited the War Office. The reception, this time around, was not as it had been after his return from New South Wales, Canada or South Africa. Although military figures received Hutton with courtesy, the environment had changed. A new guard with new ideas had taken over. Moreover, Arnold-Forster, as Secretary of State for War, gave a 'coldness' of reception that disturbed Hutton, despite the long pseudo-friendship between the two. He refused Hutton an official audience and ensured that he never officially received the Australian Government's formal thanks for his efforts. Nor, for that matter, did Hutton receive any formal honours for his services in Australia. In Hutton's mind such a rebuff was a consequence of Arnold-Forster's support for the failed imperial reserve scheme of 1902. Hutton was received well by Sir Montagu Ommanney at the Colonial Office and with civility by Alfred Lyttelton, Chamberlain's successor as Secretary of State for the Colonies. In truth, however, Hutton had risen on the stars of Wolseley and Chamberlain. Without such men there was little to shield him from the controversies that had stalked him for the last decade or from his reputation at home and abroad as an outspoken and difficult martinet.

As a consequence, once back in London Hutton had difficulty securing an active appointment of significance. On 1 July 1905 he was given temporary command of the 3rd Division at Aldershot (subordinate to the now General Sir John French) and, soon after, concurrently took up responsibilities as the officer in charge of administration within Eastern Command under the command of Lieutenant-General Lord Methuen. Neither role satisfied

Hutton's ambitions, and he chaffed at working under officers he considered from his time in South Africa to be his equals, if not his inferiors. Winning no friends in the process, he complained to those around him that more was his due thanks to 'twelve years of Independent Command under diverse and difficult circumstances in various parts of the Empire'.[1] Hutton, of course, was convinced that he knew best. So too, in typical fashion, blinded by self-confidence, he failed to read the changes in the military and political landscape. In May 1906, for example, he confided to Methuen that he was confident of a promotion to lieutenant-general 'at no distant date'.[2]

It was, in the end, this state of mind that effectively ended Hutton's career. From 6 to 16 August 1906 he led his division in a series of training manoeuvres under French's supervision. The trouble began when French began critiquing the performance of the division and suggesting improvements, as he was required to do. Hutton, however, could not bear anything that felt like professional criticism from a man whose tactical decisions he had so often questioned on the veldt and one whose star had skyrocketed on the back of the war in South Africa just as Hutton's was stalling. The result was a serious confrontation that Hutton could not win. French made an official complaint to the War Office about Hutton's insubordination, his 'taking up an attitude not conducive to discipline' and his 'wilful misconception of instructions'. Hutton was 'an impossible subordinate', French argued, with a 'personal influence over those serving under him [that] does not make for good'. The whole exercise, French declared, 'was useless because at meetings with senior officers of the division no lessons could be brought home owing to General Hutton's opposition to any line of thought but his own'.[3] At last realising the seriousness of such accusations, Hutton flew into a sycophantic rearguard action, pleading with French that he had misunderstood, while never really acknowledging he had done any wrong. In one letter Hutton told French: 'No one is more alive to his weaknesses than I am. I am unfortunately – yet fortunately – independent-minded and impulsive; these two qualities lead one into many conflicts and friction, – yet they prompt initiative, and, if wisely directed, beget great deeds! I must pray my friends and those under whom I serve to balance the evil that is in me with the good I would fain achieve.'[4] French, however, never the forgiving type, would have none of it. With this blight brought to the attention of the new Secretary of State for War, Richard Haldane, Hutton was finished. After his term of temporary command concluded in September 1906, Hutton found no further active military employment. In November 1907, after forty years since first commissioning, he was at last, as a courtesy, promoted to lieutenant-general, before being placed on the Retired List on 26 December that year.

Photo 24 Field Marshal Sir John French wearing full dress uniform and holding his field marshal's baton, 24 February 1914. Hutton's arguments with French in August 1906 ended what was left of his career. (AWM, P02419.001)

After retirement Hutton was at a professional loose end. He took over as Colonel Commandant of his old battalion, King's Royal Rifle Corps, wrote profusely and spoke often at informal gatherings, reliving his time in colonies and continuing to preach his solution to the imperial defence quandary. After flirting with, then rejecting, the idea of a political career, he gave public addresses, for example, on topics like the 'Military Power and Organization of our Colonies' in which he returned to the 'National Militia Army' idea as 'the basis of cooperation between Great Britain and her Dependencies'.[5] Other military-oriented conversations continued in private, such as his arguments over tactical issues with J.F.C. Fuller. Hutton generally made the old points that the defence of Britain was tied up with defence of the Empire, that such a defence demanded an offensive capability, that the force required could never be met by a regular army due to cost and recruiting and that a volunteer imperial militia army was the only answer. He also argued in print that his cooperative imperial defence model was, in his own mind at least, not only possible but also imperative for the survival of the Empire. Predictably, his lifelong association with the mounted infantry remained part of this 'solution', and Hutton also placed himself once more in the centre of mounted infantry/cavalry debates; arguments he and other advocates of the mounted infantry arm, such as Colonel Alexander Godley, were destined to lose as men like French and Douglas Haig rose to prominence. Appointed KCB in 1912, which only ever partially removed a strong sense of his being unfairly unrecognised for a career of struggles by jealous rivals and fickle politicians, Hutton never tired of claiming colonial expertise, advocating the merits of colonial militia and their inherent advantages of 'individuality and self-reliance' and reiterating his essential professional philosophies of technical competence, effective administration and officer-led training.

Meanwhile, from early 1906 Lord Haldane began his own military reforms in Britain. Building on the creation of the CID and General Staff for peacetime planning and in light of the Entente Cordiale and growing recognition of the likelihood of a war in Europe, Haldane planned to reshape the British Army.[6] The regular component moved towards what would become the British Expeditionary Force and the auxilliaries were remodelled into a Territorial Force, to be complete in all arms and services and able to be mobilised, if not compelled to fight overseas. Despite financial and other limitations, real fears of Germany allowed Haldane to succeed in these regards where Brodrick and Arnold-Forster had failed. Inasmuch as these reforms aligned with Hutton's own ideas, he misinterpreted them as not only justification of his agitations in this direction over an extended period but also a *consequence* of them, as if somehow he had been the only voice crying for reform along the lines taken. Hutton thus strove to stay in the debate, mistakenly thinking himself central, as forces and factors well beyond his control pushed past and around him.

Many such factors related directly to the theory and, to some degree, the application of imperial defence arrangements, and they were proceeding apace. At the Colonial Conference of 1907 the War Office announced the creation of an Imperial General Staff (IGS) to lay down elements of strategic doctrine and the provision for common training, organisation and equipment for all land forces throughout the Empire. Branches were to be established in each self-governing colony (henceforth to be known as dominions). Haldane explained the benefits of the new body to colonial representatives, urging for a united defence of the Empire (while wisely and assiduously avoiding any idea of standing peacetime commitments) and suggesting that colonial members could possibly sit on the IGS and offer advice on military matters. This was, at its heart, 'a request for cooperation, not commitment'.[7] The dominions, this time, were on board, and such branches were established in Canada, Australia and New Zealand in the period 1909–11.[8] The 1907 conference was itself followed two years later by a special defence-themed conference in the wake of a deteriorating global strategic situation. This meeting, among other issues, confirmed the need for imperial standardisation. Borden, for his part, agreed to the concept of a Canadian expeditionary force if required for a major war, so long as there were no binding peacetime obligations. The result, according to the British Prime Minister, Lord Asquith, was 'a plan for organising the forces of the Crown wheresoever they are, while preserving the complete autonomy of each Dominion'.[9]

The next Imperial Conference of 1911 continued the trend. It referred defence questions to a special meeting of the CID, confirming the notion that each dominion would be willing to make its preparations on such lines that would enable it, should it so desire, to take its share of the general defence of the Empire. Further practical steps were also to be taken by local sections of the IGS under local governments, in communication and consultation with the War Office. The pathways were thus being set that would allow for the integration of the inevitable thousands of dominion volunteers should the long-expected European war break out. The dominions themselves were both party to and advocates of this movement. All this was done without standing peacetime arrangements and without any undertaking to deploy complete trained units or formations from the dominion volunteer part-time armies. Aside from this important caveat, the basic elements of Hutton's grand scheme were playing out at the very time his ability to influence or participate in the process had ebbed.

As was the case with Haldane's domestic military reforms, Hutton's retirement and removal from the practical course of imperial defence developments did not, however, mean that he did not credit himself with them. From the day he returned to London, and especially once he had retired, Hutton had continued to advocate his imperial defence system and to ascribe any move that looked like it was headed in this direction as a product of this vision, arguments and enterprise over the proceeding decades. In January 1906, for example, put out that no one had thought to keep him abreast of military developments in Australia, he argued to Prime Minister Deakin that his cooperative scheme was already in place in Australia and in Canada, and would soon be implemented as part of the current military reforms in Britain.[10] Hutton was still repeating the message to Edmund Barton a decade later.[11] This was, of course, manifestly untrue, but the details of his failure were unacceptable and they paled before conceptions of success in his eyes. For Hutton the progression was clear. It was his grand scheme 'initiated in New South Wales in 1893–96, elaborated in Canada in 1898–1900 and perfected for the Commonwealth of Australia in 1901–04, which, offered in vain to Arnold Forster and the Conservative Government in 1904 to 1905, became the Territorial Army Scheme of Lord Haldane and the Liberal Government in 1906'.[12] In fact, for Hutton, the Territorial system was a direct 'copy of the Australian scheme' and 'proof of the soundness of my work!'[13] 'My wildest dreams in 1893', he went on, 'never pictured a result so improbable of attainment in thirteen short years.' Not only that but also the fruits of his scheme were, apparently, 'gathered ten months later upon the South African Veldt in 1899–1902' and afterwards.[14]

Conveniently ignoring the original provisions against service by formed volunteer Territorial units abroad (which was always part of his grand scheme), Hutton later lamented that had the British Government only funded *his* Territorial Army system properly, then it would have met the challenge of 1914.[15] Reliance on that 'hasty and improvised system which had, at the eleventh hour, to be created for the raising of the so-called "Kitchener armies"' would thus have been avoided.[16] In the process, as World War I approached, Hutton was forced to abandon his lifelong commitment to volunteerism. In the decade up to 1914 men like Roberts and Brigadier Henry Wilson had mounted campaigns through the press, for both conscription and a commitment to the continent. So too, giving evidence to the Norfolk Commission, patrons like Wolseley, Kelly Kenny and the Duke of Connaught all supported some form of compulsory military training.[17] Hutton, however, had held his line and had been equally active arguing against such policies. In 1908 he wrote repeatedly to John Forrest decrying Australia's movement towards universal compulsory military training. In 1913, as war loomed, Lord Haldane, now Lord Chancellor, wrote to Hutton 'anxious that your name should appear in connection with the new organisation for making intelligible to the public the case for Voluntary Service'. By this late stage, however, the looming crisis had forced a change of heart and with 'the greatest regret' Hutton felt 'compelled to give up my advocacy of the defence of the United Kingdom upon a voluntary basis'.[18] It was more than a change of heart. The concept of a *voluntary* Empire-wide white militia army had been at the heart of his life's vision.

When the war he had long feared finally broke out in Europe, its scale and Britain's desperation gave Hutton one last chance at military service. When his old protégé, now Major-General William Throsby Bridges, was raising the Australian Imperial Force in 1914 he suggested that it be led by Hutton.[19] The Australian Government rejected the idea, however, and Hutton was instead recalled to service to organise and command the British 21st Division. For one last time his fires were temporarily fanned, and Hutton wrote to Field Marshal French, hoping to erase past injury and to find himself soon 'serving in a less humble capacity than the command of a Division and under your command'.[20] A heart ailment, however, removed the need for French to decline, and Hutton was forced to retire once more. With little sign of sympathy Kitchener gave his regrets that Hutton could not deploy with his division and in same breath told him he would be replaced immediately.[21]

In stark contrast to the low regard in which the ailing Hutton was held by the prevailing military authorities in London, as a mark of the esteem by which he had been held in *military* circles in Australia, or in the eyes of those connected with Australian troops, Hutton spent the remainder of the war years in constant correspondence, providing advice and encouragement, to many senior Australian officers. Men like Colonel (later General) Cyril Brudenell Bingham White assured him that any laurels won by the Australians at the Dardanelles were 'really only the fruits of the seed sown by you during your periods of command'.[22] Major-General (later General) Henry George 'Harry' Chauvel wrote to him in 1916 as 'one who had had such a lot to do with our early training and to whom we owe so much'. 'The older soldiers', he continued, 'and better school of younger ones and all thinking men . . . fully appreciate all you did for us in the past and the sound foundation you laid, upon which everything which has since been accomplished has been built.'[23] 'In no way', Chauvel later wrote, 'have we departed from your maxims and teachings.'[24] Lieutenant-General Sir Alexander Godley, on taking command of the ANZAC Corps from Lieutenant-General William Birdwood, in December 1915, wrote to Hutton: 'Knowing, as I do, how much the very existence of the Australian Imperial Force and this Army Corps is due to what you did for the Commonwealth . . . I hope you will be glad that one of your MI [mounted infantry] disciples has succeeded to such a command.'[25] Birdwood himself, when commanding I ANZAC Corps in 1916, sought Hutton's counsel and praised his 'Herculean work' as the seeds that sprouted a decade later with 'the result that Australia was able to put into the field such a magnificent force as she did'.[26] All the while, Hutton saw his own hand at work. 'I have worked long and consistently', he told Deakin in 1916, at a scheme if imperial defence at once 'now definitely accepted' and, simultaneously, 'bearing rich and lasting fruit – not only for giving us victory over our German foe, but by consolidation the Empire as its final result'.[27] Retirement was one thing; irrelevancy was simply not an option.

Lieutenant-General Sir Edward 'Curley' Hutton passed away on 4 August 1923 at Fox Hills, his home in Chertsey, and was buried in nearby Lyne, leaving Eleanor but no children behind him. He died, as he had lived, convinced of the importance and absolute correctness of his own convictions. Even leaving aside the fantasy not only that his imperial defence scheme had been implemented in Canada, Australia and Britain (through the Territorial system) but also that it had gone a long way towards the outcome of the European war he had always feared in 1918, the basic ingredients of his sense of self had remained constant. He preached to such men as Birdwood and White when they visited him after the war the same messages in the same way he had lectured his subordinates in Canada and Australia years before. The year before his death Hutton wrote: 'We owe our stupendous success during the late Great War to the characteristics of the British Soldier . . . manliness, honour, devotion to duty and a fixed determination to "play the game".'[28] He took to his deathbed the same attitudes that had shaped his life: the same brilliance, determination, conviction, arrogance, blindness and self-delusion.

What can be said, then, about Hutton and imperial defence in the later-Victorian era? He was, of course, never of the stature or military significance of the giants of his age – such men as Wolseley, Buller, Roberts or Kitchener. So too he was, in so many ways, simply a man of his time and but one of a set of British regular officers who spent their careers and made their names, predominantly in the service of the self-governing colonies. Yet in other ways Hutton was both unique and significant, certainly more than the historiographical record attests. Although he was by no means without his critics, there were voices that recognised Hutton's contributions and what he represented in the aftermath of his passing. Charles Bean, the Australian Official Historian of World War I, for example, called him 'a soldier of a brilliance only too rare'. Leo Amery, former First Lord of the Admiralty and Secretary of State for the Colonies, recalled in 1931: 'I knew him well and I know how keenly he felt about the efficiency of Armies of the outer Empire, how intensely he believed in them and in their future and how far his vision ranged.'[29] It was a vision 'born in the British army, in his relationships with Warre and Wolseley, it was given direction from Seeley; but, ultimately, it was his own'.[30]

Amery had the measure of it. It was Hutton's vision that offers an important keyhole into the wider issue of imperial defence in the 1890s and early years of the twentieth century. He was placed by serendipity and the efforts of his patrons at the coalface of imperial defence at key times and in key places. This was as true of an important self-governing colony like New South Wales in 1893 as it was in Canada, South Africa and Australia. The successes, achievements, trials and tribulations suffered by Hutton in all of these appointments, most often products of his own strongly held ideas rubbing up against colonial political and financial realities in the face of War and Colonial Office clumsiness, brought out all the essential characteristics of the imperial defence dilemma of the era. Close study of his career shows, for example, why formal arrangements were impossible. All of these impediments and all of the potential of a functional system of imperial land defence were highlighted by Hutton and his ordeals.

Here is Hutton's true historical worth. Imperial military defence was not a structural or administrative reality up to Hutton's return from Australia in late 1904 in the sense of a prearranged and Empire-wide coordinated strategies, mobilisation plans and troops assigned to task. Only with the increasing importance of the CID from 1906, particularly under the guidance of Maurice Hankey as its Secretary from 1912, were statesmen and military experts from across the Empire able to meet and plan in a truly systematic manner. Yet the significance, scale and nature of imperial assistance to Britain during World War I did not spring from a vacuum; rather it was the product of more than twenty years of thought, discussions, frustration, misunderstandings, failed experiments and incremental advancement. Hutton remains, in so many ways, a crucial window through which to make sense of this very important landscape.

Notes

Introduction

1 Horne, *Source Records of the Great War*, p. 404.
2 Lehane, 'Lieutenant-General Edward Hutton and "Greater Britain"', pp. 1–2.
3 Burroughs, 'John Robert Seeley and British imperial history', p. 204.
4 Trainor, 'British policy', p. 251. See also Porter, *Critics of Empire*.
5 Burroughs, 'John Robert Seeley', p. 191.
6 Dilke, *Problems of Greater Britain*; Dilke & Wilkinson, *Imperial Defence*; Froude, *Oceana*.
7 Lehane, 'Lieutenant-General Edward Hutton and "Greater Britain"', pp. 2–6.
8 Robinson & Gallagher, *Africa and the Victorians*, pp. 20–6.
9 Knaplund, 'Intra-imperial aspects of Britain's defence question, 1870–1900', p. 120.
10 Darwin, 'Imperialism and the Victorians', pp. 614–42.
11 Cain & Hopkins, *British Imperialism*.
12 Gillon, 'The triumph of pragmatic imperialism', p. 10.
13 Knaplund, 'Intra-imperial aspects of Britain's defence question, 1870–1900', pp. 120–3.
14 Burroughs, 'John Robert Seeley', p. 191.
15 Penlington, 'General Hutton and the problem of military imperialism in Canada', p. 156.
16 Gordon, *The Dominion Partnership in Imperial Defense, 1870–1914*, p. vii.
17 Lehane, 'Lieutenant-General Edward Hutton and "Greater Britain"', p. 14.
18 Darwin, *The Empire Project*, pp. 92–101.
19 Lehane, 'Lieutenant-General Edward Hutton and "Greater Britain"', pp. 3–6.
20 Thompson, 'The language of imperialism', pp. 147–50.
21 Kennedy & Neilson, *Imperial Defence*, p. 6.
22 Lehane, 'Lieutenant-General Edward Hutton and "Greater Britain"', p. 142.
23 Thompson, 'The language of imperialism', pp. 154–5.
24 Spiers, *The Late Victorian Army*, pp. 59, 180.
25 Burroughs, 'Imperial defence and the Victorian army', p. 58.
26 Knaplund, 'Intra-imperial aspects of Britain's defence question, 1870–1900', p. 126.
27 Graham, *The Politics of Naval Supremacy*.
28 Kennedy, 'The concept of imperial defence, 1856–1956', p. 2.
29 Ibid.
30 Ibid., p. 1.

31 Clarke, 'Marching to their own drum', p. xix. Unfortunately, Lehane's quality work, which focuses on Hutton's career in depth, remains unpublished.
32 Morton, 'Authority and policy in the Canadian militia, 1874–1904', p. 360.
33 Buchan, *Lord Minto*, chapter 6.
34 Adams, 'The military view of the Empire, 1870–1899'.
35 'Notes for lecture on "Personal Recollections of the Zulu War"', 1880, Hutton Papers (HP), Reel F-1, UNSW Canberra Library.
36 Morton, *Ministers and Generals*, p. 134.
37 Aubrey, 'Major-General E.T.H. Hutton', pp. 7–8.
38 Hutton to Alderson, 3 June 1902, HP, A-6.
39 Hutton to Reid, 10 February 1916, HP, A-4.
40 Clarke, 'Marching to their own drum', p. xix.

Chapter 1 Developments in the imperial defence idea, 1848–92

1 Clarke, *Imperial Defence*, pp. 167–8.
2 Tucker, 'Army and society in England, 1870–1900', pp. 110–41; Gordon, 'The Colonial Defence Committee and imperial collaboration', p. 526.
3 Gordon, *The Dominion Partnership*, p. 1.
4 Durrans, 'Imperial defence', pp. 4–5.
5 'Defence as an impetus to Federation', National Archives of Australia (NAA) 5954, 794/2.
6 Schuyler, 'The recall of the legions', pp. 18–36.
7 Mowbray, 'Militiaman', pp. 2–3.
8 Wilcox, *For Hearths and Homes*, pp. 1–2.
9 Inglis, *The Australian Colonists*.
10 Wilcox, *For Hearths and Homes*, pp. 3–4, 10–12.
11 Wood, *Militia Myths*, pp. 3–5.
12 Wilcox, *For Hearths and Homes*, p. 31.
13 Ibid., pp. 3–6, 17–18.
14 Clarke, 'Marching to their own drum', p. 3.
15 Durrans, 'Imperial defence', p. 34.
16 Wood, *Militia Myths*, pp. 5, 49–50.
17 Knaplund, 'Intra-imperial aspects of Britain's defence question, 1870–1900', p. 127.
18 Gordon, *The Dominion Partnership*, p. 28.
19 Wood, *Militia Myths*, p. 20.
20 Durrans, 'Imperial defence', p. 6–7; Mowbray, 'Militiaman', pp. 2–3.
21 Hamer, *The British Army*, p. 9.
22 Gordon, *The Dominion Partnership*, pp. 119ff.
23 Hamer, *The British Army*, pp. x, 9–13.
24 Harries-Jenkins, *The Army in Victorian Society*, pp. 195–6.
25 Spiers, *The Late Victorian Army*, pp. 156–7.
26 Badsey, *Doctrine and Reform in the British Cavalry 1880–1918*, p. 68.
27 Strachan, *The Politics of the British Army*, p. 25; Harries-Jenkins, *The Army in Victorian Society*, p. 6.
28 Harries-Jenkins, *The Army in Victorian Society*, pp. 104–5.
29 Ibid., p. 197.

30 Janowitz, *The Professional Soldier*, passim.
31 Spiers, *The Late Victorian Army*, p. 181.
32 Maxwell, *The Ashanti Ring*, passim.
33 Hamer, *The British Army*, pp. 31–2.
34 Clarke, *Imperial Defence*, p. 173.
35 Gordon, *The Dominion Partnership*, p. 31.
36 Knaplund, 'Intra-imperial aspects of Britain's defence question, 1870–1900', pp. 132–3.
37 Gordon, *The Dominion Partnership*, pp. 58–9.
38 Knaplund, 'Intra-imperial aspects of Britain's defence question, 1870–1900', pp. 133–4.
39 Spiers, *The Late Victorian Army*, p. 157.
40 Trainor, *British Imperialism and Australian Nationalism*, p. 22.
41 Gordon, *The Dominion Partnership*, p. 71.
42 Clarke, 'Marching to their own drum', p. 32.
43 Durrans, 'Imperial defence', p. 8.
44 Gordon, *The Dominion Partnership*, p. 65.
45 Clarke, 'Marching to their own drum', p. 241.
46 'Defence as an impetus to Federation', NAA 5954, 794/2.
47 Porter, *Oxford History of the British Empire*, vol. 3, pp. 334–5.
48 Trainor, 'British policy', p. 249.
49 'Scratchley's Report', NAA B3778, 1883/1; 'Defences: Preliminary Report', State Records of New South Wales (SRNSW) NRS 906, 4/906.1; Jervois to Scratchley, 12 May 1880, HP, A-4.
50 McGibbon, *The Path to Gallipoli*, p. 26.
51 Sanford Evans, *The Canadian Contingents and Canadian Imperialism*, p. 2.
52 McGibbon, *The Path to Gallipoli*, pp. 3–4.
53 Sanford Evans, *The Canadian Contingents and Canadian Imperialism*, p. 32.
54 Knaplund, 'Intra-imperial aspects of Britain's defence question, 1870–1900', p. 131.
55 Gordon, *The Dominion Partnership*, p. 68–9.
56 Clarke, 'Marching to their own drum', p. 238.
57 Knaplund, 'Intra-imperial aspects of Britain's defence question, 1870–1900', p. 124.
58 Lehane, 'Lieutenant-General Edward Hutton and "Greater Britain"', p. 72.
59 Gordon, *The Dominion Partnership*, pp. 76–7.
60 Trainor, 'British policy', p. 33.
61 Thompson, 'The language of imperialism', pp. 162, 175–6.
62 Souter, *Lion and Kangaroo*, p. 22.
63 Ward, *Concise History of Australia*, pp. 90, 187.
64 Such local figures included Dalton McCarthy in Ontario, a Conservative MP and one of the founders of the League. In Victoria, Henry D'Esterre Taylor, a Free Trade politician, was instrumental in keeping his branch alive after 1894.
65 'Speech delivered by Colonel George Denison, 19 March 1890', Libraries and Archives Canada (LAC), George Denison Fonds, MG29-E 29, vol. 19.
66 Trainor, 'Convenient conflict?', in Dennis & Grey, *The Boer War*, p. 226.

67 'Offers by the Colonies of Troops for Service in the Soudan', NAA B3756, 1885/3424.
68 Ibid.
69 MacDonald to Minto, 10 February 1885, The National Archives (UK) (TNA), WO 32/6367.
70 Durrans, 'Imperial defence', pp. 27–30.
71 Hutton, 'Our comrades of Greater Britain', p. 27.
72 Mordike, 'The origins of Australia's army', p. 8.
73 Trainor, *British Imperialism and Australian Nationalism*, p. 26.
74 Knaplund, 'Intra-imperial aspects of Britain's defence question, 1870–1900', p. 135.
75 Clarke, 'Marching to their own drum', p. 35.
76 Wilcox, *For Hearths and Homes*, p. 24.
77 McGibbon, *The Path to Gallipoli*, pp. 49, 3–4.
78 Durrans, 'Imperial defence', p. 30.
79 MacLean, 'The imperial federation movement in Canada, 1884–1902', p. i.
80 Wood, 'The Sudan Contingent of 1885 and the anti-war movement', p. 53.
81 'Colonial Defence Committee: Constitution and Work, 1885 to 1904', NAA A5954, 1707/6.
82 'Local preparations to be made in anticipation of war', 46M, 1 November 1886, TNA CAB 9/1.
83 'Colonial Defence Committee: Constitution and Work, 1885 to 1904', NAA A5954, 1707/6.
84 Clarke, 'Marching to their own drum', pp. 14, 26.
85 Trainor, 'Convenient conflict?', p. 226.
86 Ibid., pp. 113, 114.
87 'Means of Dealing with Questions of National defence', NAA B3756, 1892/1628.
88 Gordon, *The Dominion Partnership*, p. 118.
89 Hamer, *The British Army*, pp. 91–2.
90 Strachan, *The Politics of the British Army*, pp. 64, 122.
91 Hamer, *The British Army*, p. 26.
92 Stanhope to Wolseley, 18 July 1892, Wolseley Papers, National Library of Australia (NLA), MFM G 10279.
93 Harries-Jenkins, *The Army in Victorian Society*, p. 165.
94 'Defence as an impetus to Federation', NAA 5954, 794/2.
95 Knaplund, 'Intra-imperial aspects of Britain's defence question, 1870–1900', p. 136.
96 Hutton, E.T.H., 'A Co-operative System for Defence of the Empire', Selected Papers, No. 1/05, Royal Canadian Military Institute, Toronto, 2005, p. 1.
97 Clarke, 'Marching to their own drum', p. 243.
98 Ibid.
99 Clarke, *Imperial Defence*, p. 194.
100 Durrans, 'Imperial defence', p. 13; Knaplund, 'Intra-imperial aspects of Britain's defence question, 1870–1900', p. 136.
101 Shields, 'Australian opinion and defence of the Empire', pp. 44–5; Gordon, *The Dominion Partnership*, p. 88.
102 'Imperial Defence Act, 1888', NAA B3756, 1889/2258.

103 'Defence forces and defence, no. 254M', NAA CP601/2, vol. 1.
104 'Defence as an impetus to Federation', NAA 5954, 794/2.
105 Clarke, *Imperial Defence*, p. 194.
106 Shields, 'Australian opinion and defence of the Empire', pp. 47–9, 50.
107 Mordike, 'The origins of Australia's army', p. 9.
108 Shields, 'Australian opinion and defence of the Empire', pp. 47–8.
109 Trainor, 'British policy', p. 394.
110 Beckett, 'The South African War and the late Victorian army', in Grey & Dennis, *The Boer War*, p. 42.
111 Harries-Jenkins, *The Army in Victorian Society*, pp. 171–2.
112 Hamer, *The British Army*, p. 32.
113 Trainor, 'Convenient conflict?', p. 228.
114 'Proposed organization of the military forces of the Australian colonies', 9 October 1889, NAA B3756, 1889/3614.
115 'Imperial Inspecting General Officer for the military forces in the Australasian Colonies', 1 March 1889, NAA B3756, 1889/2258.
116 Clarke, 'Marching to their own drum', p. 190.
117 'Proposed organization of the military forces of the Australasian colonies', no. 40R, TNA CAB 9/1; 'Australian defence', 29 September 1959, NAA A5954, 1211/3.
118 'Defence as an impetus to Federation', NAA 5954, 794/2.
119 Clarke, 'Marching to their own drum', p. 40.
120 Ibid., pp. 245–6.
121 Trainor, 'Convenient conflict?', p. 227.
122 Clarke, 'Marching to their own drum', p. 47.
123 Preston, *Canada and 'Imperial Defense'*, p. 95.

Chapter 2 Hutton's formative years, 1848–92

1 'Draft Memoirs of Lieutenant General Sir Edward Hutton' (hereafter 'Memoirs'), HP, F-2.
2 Ibid.
3 Lehane, 'Lieutenant-General Edward Hutton and "Greater Britain"', chapter 2.
4 'Memoirs', HP, F-2.
5 Ibid.
6 'The Rev. Edmund Warre, DD', HP, F-1.
7 Crotty, *Making the Australian Male*, pp. 221–2.
8 Lehane, 'Lieutenant-General Edward Hutton and "Greater Britain"', p. 40.
9 'Memoirs', HP, F-2.
10 'Our recent campaigns', HP, F-1.
11 'Memoirs', HP, F-2.
12 Ibid.
13 Lehane, 'Lieutenant-General Edward Hutton and "Greater Britain"', p. 41.
14 Ibid., p. 39.
15 'Memoirs', HP, F-2.
16 Ibid.
17 Hutton to Lawrence, 1868–69, HP, B-1.

18 Gillon, 'The triumph of pragmatic imperialism', p. 222.
19 'Memoirs', HP, F-2.
20 Strachan, *The Politics of the British Army*, pp. 96, 200.
21 'My visit to the Franco-Prussian War, 1870', HP, E-1.
22 'Memoirs', HP, F-2.
23 Ibid.
24 Ibid.
25 Lehane, 'Lieutenant-General Edward Hutton and "Greater Britain"', p. 48.
26 Ibid.
27 Hutton to Hinxman, 27 March 1877, HP, C-1.
28 'Memoirs', HP, F-2.
29 Ibid.
30 Ibid.
31 Ibid.
32 Ibid.
33 'Notes for lecture on "Personal recollections of the Zulu War"', 1880, HP, F-1.
34 'Record of service, Edward Thomas Henry Hutton', HP, C-1; *Mercury* (Hobart), 12 February 1894, p. 3.
35 'Memoirs', HP, F-2.
36 Hutton to Lawrence, 30 April 1879, HP, B-1.
37 Hutton to Lawrence, 3 May 1879, HP, B-1.
38 Ibid.
39 Wolseley to Stanley, 4 July 1879, Wolseley Papers, NLA, MFM G 10279.
40 'Memoirs', HP, F-2.
41 Hutton to Lawrence, 23 July, 7 June and 15 September 1879, HP, B-1.
42 Hutton to Clifford (various), May 1879, HP, C-1.
43 'The Operations of the 1st Division', HP, F-1.
44 'Lieutenant-General Edward Hutton and "Greater Britain"', p. 49.
45 'Memoirs', HP, F-2.
46 Crealock to Hutton, 7 May 1880, HP, C-1.
47 'Notes upon the Evolution of Mounted Infantry in the British Army', HP, F-1.
48 *Mercury* (Hobart), 12 February 1894, p. 3.
49 Hutton to Lawrence, 19 May and 17 June 1881, HP, B-1.
50 Hutton to Lawrence, 18 April 1881, HP, B-1.
51 'Memoirs', HP, F-2.
52 Hutton to Lawrence, 4 June 1881, HP, B-1; Barrow to Hutton, 10 August 1881, HP, C-1.
53 Hutton to Lawrence, 17 June 1881, HP, B-1.
54 'Memoirs', HP, F-2.
55 Ibid.
56 Ibid.
57 Strachan, *The Politics of the British Army*, p. 101.
58 Hutton to Lawrence, 16 July, 22 June, 29 July and 5 August 1882, HP, B-1.
59 Hutton to Lawrence, 5 August 1882, HP, B-1.
60 'Memoirs', HP, F-2.
61 'Lieutenant-General Edward Hutton and "Greater Britain"', p. 67.

62 Hutton to Lawrence, 27 September 1882, HP, B-1.
63 Radcliffe to Hutton, 19 September 1881, HP, C-1.
64 'Memoirs', HP, F-2.
65 Hutton to Lawrence, 27 September 1882, HP, B-1.
66 'Memoirs', HP, F-2.
67 'Despatches to the Secretary of State for War by Sir Archibald Alison', HP, C-1; Hutton to Lawrence, 20 November 1882, HP, B-1; 'Campaign – 1882', HP, C-1.
68 War Office to Hutton, 21 March 1883, HP, A-2.
69 Buller to Hutton, 29 April 1884, HP, A-5.
70 'Selection of confidential notes', February 1884, HP, A-5.
71 'Mounted Infantry in Egypt', E.T.H. Hutton, HP, F-1.
72 Hutton to Lawrence, 29 June 1884, HP, B-1.
73 Ibid.
74 Kochanski, *Sir Garnet Wolseley*, p. 59.
75 Hutton to Lawrence, 6 and 20 July 1884, HP, B-1.
76 'Memoirs', HP, F-2.
77 Hutton to Lawrence, 7 August 1884, HP, B-1.
78 'Memoirs', HP, F-2.
79 'Lieutenant-General Edward Hutton and "Greater Britain"', pp. 69–70.
80 'Memoirs', HP, F-2.
81 Buller to Hutton, 19 February 1885, HP, A-5.
82 Hutton to Lawrence, 30 November and 20 December 1884, HP, B-1.
83 Phipps to Hutton, March 1885, HP, C-1.
84 'Extract from Corps Orders', March 1885, HP, C-1.
85 Hutton to Lawrence, 12 April 1885, HP, B-1.
86 'Scheme for raising a brigade of mounted infantry volunteers', 7 March 1885, HP, F-1.
87 Hutton to Lawrence, 12 April 1885, HP, B-1.
88 'Memoirs', HP, F-2.
89 'Lieutenant-General Edward Hutton and "Greater Britain"', pp. 60–1.
90 'The 4th Earl of Minto – An appreciation', HP, A-1.
91 Hutton, 'Mounted infantry', pp. 696–703, 705–8, 720.
92 Bou, 'Modern cavalry', in Grey & Dennis, *The Boer War*, p. 99.
93 Hutton, 'Mounted infantry', p. 695.
94 Ibid., p. 734.
95 'Memoirs', HP, F-2.
96 Hutton, 'Mounted infantry', pp. 722–37.
97 'Memoirs', HP, F-2.
98 Ibid.
99 Ibid.
100 Ibid.
101 Harries-Jenkins, *The Army in Victorian Society*, p. 151.
102 War Office to Hutton, 1 September 1887, HP, C-1; Aubrey, 'Major-General E.T.H. Hutton', p. 5.
103 Notes on 'Mounted infantry', 18 August 1887, HP, F-1.
104 Alison to War Office, 13 December 1887, HP, F-1.

105 Bethune, 'The uses of cavalry and mounted infantry in modern warfare', pp. 628–9.
106 Kochanski, *Sir Garnet Wolseley*, p. 163.
107 Badsey, *Doctrine and Reform in the British Cavalry 1880–1918*, pp. 62–3.
108 Badsey, 'Fire and sword', pp. 94–6.
109 'Memoirs', HP, F-2.
110 Hutton to Burgess, 13 April 1889, HP, C-1.
111 'Memoirs', HP, F-2.
112 'Lieutenant-General Edward Hutton and "Greater Britain"', p. 90.
113 Wood to Hutton, 20 May 1899, HP, A-5.
114 'Copy of memo upon the mounted infantry organisation', December 1891, HP, A-5.
115 'Memoirs', HP, F-2.
116 'Lieutenant-General Edward Hutton and "Greater Britain"', p. 88.
117 Notes on 'Mounted infantry', 18 September 1912, HP, F-1.
118 'Memoirs', HP, F-2.
119 Hale to Hutton, 13 April 1889, HP, C-1.
120 Hutton, 'The Territorial Army and its field artillery', p. 1586.
121 Badsey, *Doctrine and Reform in the British Cavalry 1880–1918*, pp. 63–4.
122 Spiers, *The Late Victorian Army*, p. 113.
123 'Memoirs', HP, F-2.
124 'Lieutenant-General Edward Hutton and "Greater Britain"', p. 99.
125 Paulet to Lawrence, 7 March 1889, HP, B-1.
126 Buller to Hutton, 5 March 1889, HP, A-5.
127 'Memoirs', HP, F-2.
128 Clarke, 'Marching to their own drum', p. 78 fn.
129 Memoirs', HP, F-2.
130 Hutton, 'The art of marching', p. 626.
131 'Memoirs', HP, F-2.
132 'Notes for lecture on "Personal Recollections of the Zulu War"', 1880, HP, F-1.
133 Seeley, *The Expansion of England*, pp. 8, 14, 31; 'Lieutenant-General Edward Hutton and "Greater Britain"', pp. 12, 101–2.
134 'Memoirs', HP, F-2.
135 Dilke & Wilkinson, *Imperial Defence*, pp. 22, 34, 177–8, 198, 233–4.
136 'The 4th Earl of Minto – An appreciation', HP, A-1.

Chapter 3 A colonial commandant, 1893–96

1 'Memoirs', HP, F-2.
2 Ibid.
3 Walker to Hutton, 20 June 1893, SRNSW NRS 985, mfm Reel 2875.
4 'Memorandum of conversation', Meade and Hutton, 9 March 1893, HP, A-2.
5 'Memoirs', HP, F-2.
6 'Memorandum of conversation', Meade and Hutton, 9 March 1893, HP, A-2.
7 Hutton to Bridge, 14 November 1894, HP, C-2.
8 'Memorandum of conversation', Bridge and Hutton, 18 April 1893, HP, C-2.
9 Edwards to Hutton, 22 March 1893, HP, C-2.

10 Wood to Hutton, 9 March 1893, HP, A-5.
11 Clarke, 'Marching to their own drum', p. 152.
12 Meaney, 'British and Australian identity', p. 79; Wilcox, *Australia's Boer War*, pp. 1–3.
13 Macintyre, *A Concise History of Australia*, pp. 41–2, 129–30.
14 'Defence as an impetus to Federation', NAA 5954, 794/2.
15 Clarke, 'Marching to their own drum', p. 189.
16 'Defence forces and defence', no. 254M', NAA CP601/2, vol. 1; 'Australian defence', 29 September 1959, NAA A5954, 1211/3.
17 'Defence as an impetus to Federation', NAA 5954, 794/2.
18 Perry, 'Military reforms in the colony of New South Wales, 1893–96', Papers of Warren Perry, NLA MS 8655, pp. 2–3.
19 'Report on Royal Commission of 1892', 67R, 25 October 1893, TNA CAB 9/1.
20 Trainor, 'British imperial defence policy and the Australian colonies, 1892–96', p. 210.
21 'Notes of a conversation', Reid and Hutton, 6 August 1894, HP, A-4.
22 Hutton to Hampden, 4 July 1894, HP, A-3.
23 Hutton to Parkes, 27 June 1893, State Library of New South Wales (SLNSW), Henry Parkes Correspondence, mfm V53 A923.46.
24 Hutton to Cambridge, 18 September 1893, HP, A-2.
25 'Memoirs', HP, F-2.
26 Hutton to Cambridge, 18 September 1893, HP, A-2.
27 Hutton to Peacocke, 19 May 1894, 7 April 1899, HP, A-5.
28 Hutton to Parkes, 26 October 1893, SLNSW, Henry Parkes Correspondence, mfm V53 A923.21.
29 'Memoirs', HP, F-2.
30 Hutton to Buller, 13 November 1893, HP, A-5.
31 Clarke, 'Marching to their own drum', p. 21.
32 Hutton to Cambridge, 18 September 1893, HP, A-2.
33 Hutton to Cambridge, 22 April 1895, HP, A-2.
34 Hutton to Cambridge, 18 September 1893, HP, A-2.
35 Hutton to Peacocke, 19 May 1894, 7 April 1899, HP, A-5.
36 'Defence scheme of September 1894', 104R, 28 February 1895, TNA CAB 9/1.
37 Local Defence Minute Book, NAA MP481/2, vol. 1.
38 'Summary of Proceedings of Military Conference, 22 December 1890', HP, A-3; Hutton to Peacocke, 19 May 1903, 7 April 1899, HP, A-5.
39 *Sydney Morning Herald*, 10 June 1893, p. 7.
40 Wilcox, *For Hearths and Homes*, pp. 27, 44–5.
41 Walker to Hutton, 27 May 1893; Hutton to Dibbs, 16 June 1893; correspondence (various), Hutton to Walker, 25 January 1894, all at SRNSW NRS 985, mfm 2875.
42 Clarke, 'Marching to their own drum', p. 124.
43 Bou, 'Modern cavalry', pp. 106–07; 'Cavalry in New South Wales', Australian War Memorial (AWM), Series 1, 17/1.
44 Clarke, 'Marching to their own drum', p. 124.
45 Walker to Hutton, 4 July 1893, SRNSW NRS 985, mfm 2875.

46 Hutton, *The Defence and Defensive Power of Australia*, p. 9.
47 'Memoirs', HP, F-2.
48 Hutton, 'The tactical and strategical power of mounted troops in war', p. 16.
49 Hutton to Edwards, 3 June 1895, HP, C-2.
50 Hutton to Cambridge, 29 August 1894, HP, A-2.
51 Hutton–Windeyer (various), 1894–95, HP, C-2; 'Memoirs', HP, F-2.
52 Walker to Hutton, 23 August 1894, SRNSW NRS 985, mfm 2875.
53 Hutton to Cambridge, 29 August 1895, HP, A-2.
54 Perry, 'Military reforms in the Colony of New South Wales, 1893–96', p. 33.
55 Hutton to Cambridge, 18 September 1893, HP, A-2.
56 Hutton to Buller, 13 November 1893, HP, A-5.
57 Walker to Hutton, 4 November 1893, SRNSW NRS 985, mfm 2875.
58 Clarke, 'Marching to their own drum', p. 154.
59 'Notes of a conversation', Reid and Hutton, 6 August 1894, HP, A-4.
60 Hutton to Buller, 13 November 1893, HP, A-5.
61 Hutton, *Defence of New South Wales*, NLA, Npf 355.4509944 H984, p. 1; 'Observations by the Military Commandant on Colonial Defence Committee's Remarks Nos 133 R and 143 R', 97M, NAA CP601/2, vol. 1.
62 Strachan, *The Politics of the British Army*, p. 96.
63 'Memoirs', HP, F-2.
64 'Resume of a personal interview' between Dibbs and Hutton, 13 November 1893, HP, A-4.
65 'Memoirs', HP, F-2.
66 Hutton to Parkes, 17 December 1895, SLNSW, Henry Parkes Correspondence, mfm V53 A923.38.
67 Davidson to Hutton, 10 December 1893, HP, C-2.
68 Hutton, 'The tactical and strategical power of mounted troops in war', pp. 22–4.
69 'Memoirs', HP, F-2.
70 'Notes of a conversation', Reid and Hutton, 6 August 1894, HP, A-4.
71 Hutton to Brunker, 27 September 1893, HP, A-4.
72 *Daily Telegraph* (Sydney), 4 November 1893, p. 9.
73 Hutton to Buller, November 1893, HP, A-5.
74 'Notes regarding my interview with Sir George Dibbs, Premier of NSW Nov. 13. 1893', HP, A-2.
75 'Résumé of a personal interview between Sir George Dibbs and Major General Hutton', 13 November 1893, HP, A-4.
76 Ibid.
77 Ibid.
78 'Notes regarding my interview with Sir George Dibbs, Premier of NSW Nov. 13. 1893', HP, A-2.
79 Mordike, *An Army for a Nation*, pp. 35–6.
80 Clarke, 'Marching to their own drum', p. 156.
81 Hutton to Cambridge, 22 April 1895, HP, A-2.
82 'Memoirs', HP, F-2.
83 *Daily Telegraph* (Sydney), 15 March 1894, p. 4.
84 Walker to Hutton, 17 March 1894, SRNSW NRS 985, mfm 2875.

85 Hutton to Cambridge, 22 April 1895, HP, A-2.
86 'Memoirs', HP, F-2.
87 Hutton to Peacocke, 19 May 1894, 7 April 1899, HP, A-5.
88 Hutton to Cambridge, 14 February 1894, HP, A-2.
89 Walker to Hutton, 17 March and 2 May 1894, SRNSW NRS 985, mfm 2875.
90 Hutton to Reid, 27 July 1895, HP, A-4.
91 'Notes of a conversation', between Reid and Hutton, 6 August 1894, HP, A-4.
92 Notes of interview between Brunker and Hutton, 16 August 1894, HP, A-4.
93 'Report by the Military Commandant for the year 1894', 133R, TNA CAB 9/1.
94 Hutton to Wolseley, 28 October 1895, HP, A-4; Hutton to Hampden, 5 August 1895, HP, A-3; Hutton to Cambridge, 29 August 1895, HP, A-2; Hutton to Nathan, 29 July 1895, HP, A-4; Hutton to Bridge, 29 October 1895, HP, C-2.
95 'Command of Artillery Forces and Permanent Artillery Regiment', 53M, 31 January 1896, TNA CAB 8/1.
96 Gipps to Hutton, 22 October 1895, HP, A-2.
97 Hutton to Wood, 3 November 1895, HP, A-5.
98 Preston, *Canada and 'Imperial Defence'*, p. 225.
99 Trainor, 'British imperial defence policy', p. 205.
100 'Lieutenant-Colonel Fox's Report on New Zealand Forces, 1893', 68R, 31 October 1893, TNA CAB 9/1.
101 Clarke, 'Marching to their own drum', p. 170.
102 Hutton to Cambridge, 20 January 1895, HP, A-2.
103 Strachan, *The Politics of the British Army*, p. 26.
104 Spiers, *The Late Victorian Army*, p. 155.
105 Huntington, *The Soldier and the State*, and Janowitz, *The Professional Soldier*, passim.
106 Hamer, *The British Army*, p. 14.
107 Morten, *Ministers and General*, pp. 199–200.
108 'Lieutenant-General Edward Hutton and "Greater Britain"', p. 122.
109 Clarke, 'Marching to their own drum', p. 161.
110 *Daily Telegraph* (Sydney), 19 December 1894, p. 4.
111 Clarke, 'Marching to their own drum', p. 125.
112 Hutton to Buller, 19 January 1896, HP, A-5.
113 Hutton to Cambridge, 22 August 1895, HP, A-2.
114 Spiers, *The Late Victorian Army*, p. 265.
115 Clarke, 'Marching to their own drum', p. 126.
116 Wood, *Chiefs of the Australian Army*, p. 17 (quoting from the *Sydney Morning Herald*, 6 August 1923).
117 Hutton, *Sydney Church of England Grammar School: Major-General Hutton's Speech*.

Chapter 4 Federal and imperial defence in Australia, 1893–96

1 'Memoirs', HP, F-2.
2 Trainor, 'British policy', pp. 334–6.

3 Hutton to Duke of Cambridge, 18 September 1893, HP, A-2.
4 'Memoirs', HP, F-2.
5 Hutton to Cambridge, 18 September 1893, HP, A-2.
6 'Lieutenant-General Edward Hutton and "Greater Britain"', p. 123.
7 'Memoirs', HP, F-2.
8 Hutton to Hampden, 4 July 1894, HP, A-3.
9 Hutton to Buller, November 1893, HP, A-5.
10 Buller to Hutton, 19 February 1894, HP, A-5; Hutton to Buller, 5 March 1894, HP, A-5.
11 Parkes to Hutton, 2 January 1894, HP, A-4.
12 Hutton to Parkes, 28 January 1894, HP, A-4.
13 Parkes to Hutton, 30 January 1894, and Hutton to Parkes, 31 January 1894, HP, A-4.
14 'Memoirs', HP, F-2.
15 *Mercury* (Hobart), 12 February 1894, p. 3.
16 Hutton to Duke of Cambridge, 14 February 1894, HP, A-2.
17 Trainor, 'British policy', p. 343.
18 Owen to Hutton, 14 February 1894, HP, C-2.
19 Hutton to Buller, 5 March and 28 May 1894, HP, A-5.
20 'Memoirs', HP, F-2.
21 Hutton to Cambridge, 29 August 1894, HP, A-2.
22 Walker to Hutton, 23 October 1894, SRNSW NRS 985, mfm 2875; Hutton to Buller, 29 October 1894, HP, A-5.
23 Trainor, 'British policy', pp. 345–6.
24 Hutton to Buller, 29 October 1894, HP, A-5.
25 Hutton to Cambridge, 5 November 1894, HP, A-2; 'Local Joint Naval and Military Committee Report of 1894', no. 159R', NAA CP601/2, vol. 1.
26 Hutton to Buller, 26 November 1894, HP, A-5.
27 Gipps to Hutton, 2 January 1894, HP, A-2.
28 Clarke, 'Marching to their own drum', p. 215.
29 'Memorandum', E.T.H. Hutton, HP, C-2.
30 Livingston, Jordan & Sweely, *Becoming Australians*, p. 123.
31 Hutton to Gipps, 26 November 1894, HP, A-2.
32 Clarke, 'Marching to their own drum', p. 213.
33 Hutton to Cambridge, 20 January 1895, HP, A-2.
34 Hutton to Cambridge, 24 March and 29 August 1895, HP, A-2.
35 Hutton to Hampden, 5 August 1895, HP, A-3.
36 Bridge to Hampden, 9 May 1895, HP, A-4.
37 'Memoirs', HP, F-2.
38 Darley to Reid, 11 May 1895, HP, A-4.
39 Hutton to Bridge, 4 May 1895, HP, C-2.
40 Hutton to Reid, 19 May 1895, HP, A-4.
41 'Memoirs', HP, F-2.
42 Hutton to Buller, 29 October 1894, HP, A-5.
43 'Memoirs', HP, F-2.
44 Hutton to Hampden, 5 August 1895, HP, A-3.
45 Hutton to Cambridge, 22 April and 22 August 1895, HP, A-2.

46 Clarke, 'Marching to their own drum', p. 220.
47 Hutton to Wood, 3 November 1895, HP, A-5.
48 Hutton to Peacocke, 20 May and 19 August 1895, HP, A-4.
49 Minute 'Australian defence', 29 September 1959, NAA A5954, 1211/3.
50 Clarke, 'Marching to their own drum', pp. 221–2.
51 Hutton to Nathan, 19 August 1895, HP, A-5.
52 'Report of Federal Military Conference', no. 119R, NAA CP601/2, vol. 1.
53 Walker to Hutton, 8 January 1896, SRNSW NRS 985, mfm 2875.
54 Hutton to Nathan, 5 January 1896, HP, A-5.
55 Hutton to Buller, 19 January 1896, HP, A-5.
56 Hutton to Grant, 17 February 1896, and Hutton to Nathan, 19 January 1896, HP, A-5.
57 Trainor, 'British policy', p. 360; Minute, 'Australian defence', 29 September 1959, NAA A5954, 1211/3.
58 Wilcox, *For Hearths and Homes*, p. 44.
59 'Memoirs', HP, F-2.
60 Wilcox, 'Relinquishing the past', p. 56.
61 Hutton to Barton, 14 July 1915, HP, A-4.
62 'Memoirs', HP, F-2; Hutton to Fisher, 28 May 1916, HP, A-4.
63 'Hutton, Lieutenant-Gen. Sir Edward, KCMG, CB', p. 552.
64 Barton to Hutton, 12 July 1915, HP, A-4.
65 Hutton to Cambridge, 22 August 1895, HP, A-2.
66 'Further Report of the Joint Naval and Military Committee, January 1896', no. 142R, 31 May 1896, 5/96, TNA CAB 9/1.
67 Legge to Hutton, 21 April 1896, HP, C-2.
68 Lassetter to Hutton, 20 June 1901, HP, C-3.
69 Johnson, *Volunteers at Heart*, p. 183; Mordike, *An Army for a Nation*, pp. 11, 43.
70 Mordike, *An Army for a Nation*, p. 43.
71 Trainor, 'British imperial defence policy', p. 217.
72 Trainor, 'British policy', pp. 281, 307.
73 Mordike, 'The origins of Australia's army', p. 12.
74 Trainor, 'British imperial defence policy', p. 208.
75 Trainor, *British Imperialism and Australian Nationalism*, pp. 103–4.
76 Coulthard-Clark, *Soldiers in Politics*, p. 191.
77 Trainor, 'British imperial defence policy', p. 212.
78 Mordike, 'The origins of the Australian Army', p. 1.
79 See Mordike, *An Army for a Nation*, pp. 23, 43; Trainor, 'British policy', pp. 336–7; Trainor, 'British imperial defence policy', p. 210.
80 'Lieutenant-General Edward Hutton and "Greater Britain"', p. 132.
81 *Bulletin*, 12 July 1893; *Daily Telegraph* (Sydney), 10 July 1893; *Truth*, 2 September 1894, and *Newcastle Morning Herald*, 21 August 1893 (all in Clarke, 'Marching to their own drum', pp. 236, 255).
82 *Sydney Morning Herald*, 24 August 1893 and 16 October 1893.
83 Clarke, 'Marching to their own drum', p. 122.
84 Ibid., p. 199.
85 Ibid.

86 Wilcox, 'Relinquishing the past', p. 56.
87 Nathan to Hutton, 27 November 1895, and Hutton to Nathan, 5 January 1896, HP, A-5.
88 Clarke, 'Marching to their own drum', p. 211.
89 Hutton to Darley, 20 January 1903, HP, A-3.
90 Hutton to Buller, 26 November 1894 and 22 April 1895; Hutton to Wood, 25 November 1894; Hutton to Nathan, 29 July 1895, all HP, A-5; Hutton to Wolseley, 17 January 1896, HP, A-4.
91 'Lieutenant-General Edward Hutton and "Greater Britain"', p. 118; Clarke, 'Marching to their own drum', p. 84.
92 Hutton to Buller, 28 May 1894, HP, A-5.
93 Hutton to Hampden, 4 July 1894, HP, A-3.
94 Hutton to Buller, 19 January 1896, HP, A-5.
95 Hutton to Cambridge, 29 August 1895, HP, A-2.
96 Author's italics. Clarke, 'Marching to their own drum', p. 202.
97 MacLean, 'The imperial federation movement in Canada, 1884–1902', p. ii.
98 Trainor, 'British policy', pp. 253–5.
99 Edwards to Hutton, 29 May 1894, HP, C-2.
100 Clark, *Kaiser Wilhelm II*, pp. 180–3.
101 Hutton, 'Our comrades of Greater Britain', NLA, Peth Pam 629, Defences Box 1, p. 15.
102 Wilcox, *Australia's Boer War*, p. 16.
103 Hutton, 'Our comrades of Greater Britain', p. 15.
104 Durrans, 'Imperial defence', p. 53.
105 May, *The Principles and Problems of Imperial Defence*, p. 294.
106 'Colonial defence', 1 April 1896, HP, A-5.
107 'John Gilbert, 4th Earl of Minto. Governor-General of Canada, 1898 – 1904; A Narrative, Chapter 1' (hereafter 'Minto Narrative'), December 1918, HP, A-1.
108 Strachan, *The Politics of the British Army*, p. 96.
109 'Minto Narrative'.
110 Ibid.
111 Gordon, 'The Colonial Defence Committee and Imperial Collaboration: 1885–1904', p. 534.
112 *Evening News*, 26 July 1893 (in Clarke, 'Marching to their own drum', p. 236).
113 Clarke, 'Marching to their own drum', pp. 65–6.
114 'Memoirs', HP, F-2.
115 'Minto Narrative'.
116 'Memoirs', HP, F-2.
117 Hutton to Gibbs, 1 July 1895, HP, A-2.

Chapter 5 Back in Britain, 1896–98

1 'Memoirs', HP, F-2.
2 Dennis et al., *The Oxford Companion to Australian Military History*, p. 159.
3 'General Principles of Colonial Defences', 57M, 19 May 1896, TNA CAB 18/17.

4 'Report of the Inter-colonial Military Committee, January 1896', 72M, 20 July 1896, TNA CAB 8/1.
5 'Memoirs', HP, F-2.
6 Hutton to AAG 5th Division, 11 September 1896, HP, F-1.
7 Ibid.
8 The two-power standard called for the Royal Navy to maintain a number of battleships at least equal to the combined strength of the next two largest navies in the world.
9 Hutton, 'Our comrades of Greater Britain', pp. 1–2, 8, 10.
10 Ibid., p. 2.
11 Ibid., pp. 8, 11.
12 Ibid., pp. 17–18; Souter, *Lion and Kangaroo*, p. 149.
13 Hutton, 'Our comrades of Greater Britain', p. 4.
14 Ibid., pp. 13, 14.
15 'Memoirs', HP, F-2.
16 'Narrative of a Visit to the German and French Manoeuvres in September 1897', HP, D-1.
17 Hutton, *Defence and Defensive Power of Australia*, p. 79.
18 Ibid.
19 E.T.H. Hutton, 'German and French Manoeuvres', *Aldershot Military Society Paper*, 7 December 1897, HP, A-4, pp. 21, 83.
20 MacLean, 'The imperial federation movement in Canada, 1884–1902', p. 176.
21 'Report of meeting at Guildhall, 3rd December, 1896', <https://archive.org>.
22 Trainor, 'British policy', pp. 253–4.
23 'Report of a conference between the Right Hon. Joseph Chamberlain, MP, and the premiers of the self-governing colonies of the Empire, June and July 1897', TNA CAB 18/9 and CO 885/6 (111).
24 Durrans, 'Imperial defence', p. 57.
25 Clarke, 'Marching to their own drum', pp. 49–50, 262.
26 Gordon, *The Dominion Partnership*, p. 137.
27 Knaplund, 'Intra-imperial aspects of Britain's defence question, 1870–1900', p. 138.
28 'Memoirs', HP, F-2.
29 Wolseley to Ardagh, 4 August 1898, TNA WO 32/6365.
30 'Mounted rifles for imperial service in war', 126M, TNA CAB 8/1.
31 Clarke, 'Marching to their own drum', pp. 265–7.
32 Melgund to Hutton, 20 January and 24 February 1896, HP, A-2.
33 'Minto Narrative'.
34 'Memoirs', HP, F-2.
35 *Globe* (Toronto), 8 July 1898, p. 6.
36 'Memoirs', HP, F-2.
37 Ibid.
38 Clarke, *Imperial Defence*, pp. 183, 142, 140, 203, 217, 218–19.
39 E.T.H. Hutton, 'A co-operative scheme for the defence of the Empire', p. 6 (reported in *The Times*, 14 May 1898).
40 'Minto Narrative'.
41 Hutton, 'A co-operative scheme for the defence of the Empire', pp. 1, 2.

42 Ibid.
43 Ibid. p. 3.
44 Ibid., p. 4.
45 *Canadian United Service Magazine*, vol. 4, no. 1, May 1898, p. 5.
46 'Memoirs', HP, F-2.
47 *Globe and Mail*, 3 August 1898, p. 1.
48 'Interview: Field Marshal Lord Wolseley and Colonel Hutton', 29 July 1898, HP, A-4.
49 Hutton, 'Our comrades of Greater Britain', p. 9.
50 'Interview between Lord Lansdowne and Colonel Hutton', 3 August 1898, HP, A-4.
51 'Interview between Right Hon. Joseph Chamberlain – Secretary of State for the Colonies and Colonel Hutton', 9 August 1898, HP, A-2.
52 Clarke, 'Marching to their own drum', p. 59.
53 'Minto Narrative'.
54 Seymour to Hutton, September 1898, HP, A-6.
55 Kitson to Hutton, 217 May 1898, HP, A-6.
56 'Memoirs', HP, F-2.
57 Ibid.
58 Ibid., p. 13.
59 'Minto Narrative'.
60 'Memoirs', HP, F-2.
61 Hutton to Minto, 9 August 1898, HP, A-2.

Chapter 6 Reforming the Canadian militia, 1898–99

1 Wood, *Militia Myths*, p. 3.
2 Miller, *Painting the Map Red*, p. 9.
3 Penlington, 'General Hutton and the problem of military imperialism in Canada', p. 156.
4 Durrans, 'Imperial defence', p. 117.
5 Penlington, 'General Hutton and the problem of military imperialism in Canada', p. 157.
6 Wood, *Militia Myths*, p. 3.
7 Miller, *Painting the Map Red*, p. 5.
8 *Canada. Parliament. House of Commons. Debates* (*CHCD*), 8th Parl., 3rd Sess., vol. 46, p. 4167.
9 *CHCD*, 3rd Sess., vol. 47, pp. 4930–46.
10 'Memoirs', HP, F-2.
11 Hutton to Minto, 31 January 1900, Libraries and Archives Canada (LAC), Minto Fonds (hereafter MF), MG27-IIBI, vol. 18, C-3114.
12 Penlington, 'General Hutton and the problem of military imperialism in Canada', p. 157.
13 'Memoirs', HP, F-2.
14 Miller, 'The public life of Sir Frederick Borden', pp. 53–4.
15 'Minto Narrative'.
16 Morton, *Ministers and Generals*, p. 135.
17 *Globe* (Toronto), 11 October 1898, p. 9.

18 *Ottawa Citizen*, 1 September 1898, p. 7.
19 *Canadian Military Gazette*, vol. 13, no. 17, 6 September 1898, p. 7.
20 Bell to Bell, 12 October 1898, HP, C-4.
21 'Lieutenant-General Edward Hutton and "Greater Britain"', pp. 132–3.
22 *Globe* (Toronto), 10 October 1898, p. 2.
23 *Canadian Military Gazette*, vol. 13, no. 20, 18 October 1898, p. 10.
24 Wood, *Militia Myths*, pp. 14, 24.
25 Brodrick to Palmer, 8 January 1898, TNA CO 537/476.
26 Wood, *Militia Myths*, pp. 27, 50, 69.
27 Buchan, *Lord Minto*, chapter 6.
28 Penlington, 'General Hutton and the problem of military imperialism in Canada', p. 156; Mowbray, 'Militiaman', pp. 24–5.
29 Durrans, 'Imperial defence', p. 33.
30 Ibid., p. 19.
31 Morton, 'Authority and policy in the Canadian militia, 1874–1904', p. 308.
32 Hutton to Ardagh, 21 November 1898, HP, C-2.
33 Hutton to Borden, 2 November 1898, HP, E-2.
34 Hutton to Borden, 8 October 1898, HP, A-3.
35 Hutton to Edwards, 12 February 1899, HP, C-3.
36 Hutton to Wood, 23 February 1899, HP, E-2.
37 Hutton to Chamberlain, 20 February 1899, HP, A-2.
38 Hutton to Borden, 30 May 1899, HP, A-3.
39 Winter, 'The evolution of the Canadian Army', p. 33.
40 Bell to Bell, 12 October 1898, HP, C-4.
41 Leech to Undersecretary of State for War, 30 November 1898, TNA WO 32/6290.
42 Assistant Adjutant General to Wolseley, 22 February 1899, TNA WO 32/6366.
43 Hutton to Minto, 30 March 1899, HP, A-2.
44 *Department of Militia and Defence for the Dominion of Canada, Report for the Year ended December 1898*, House of Commons Sessional Papers, no. 19, 1898 (hereafter *Report, 1898*), pp. 25–32, 39.
45 Ibid., p. 26.
46 Ibid.
47 Mowbray, 'Militiaman', p. 76.
48 'Memoirs', HP, F-2.
49 Ibid.
50 Ibid.
51 'The rural press on General Hutton', *Canadian Military Gazette*, 2 May 1899, p. 9.
52 Hutton to Edwards, 12 February 1899, HP, C-3; Hutton to Ardagh, 14 May 1899, TNA PRO 30/40/3.
53 Hutton to Seymour, 18 April 1899, HP, A-6.
54 'Report of the Department of Militia and Defence', 190R, 28 June 1898, TNA CA 9/1.
55 Mowbray, 'Militiaman', p. 55.

56 This approach had certainly worked for Lord Lansdowne, Secretary of State for War in Britain in the late 1890s. Morton, *Ministers and Generals*, p. 140; Spiers, *The Late Victorian Army*, p. 174.
57 Hutton to Ardagh, 21 November 1898, HP, C-2.
58 *Globe* (Toronto), 4 March 1899, p. 19.
59 *Ottawa Citizen*, 4 March 1899, p. 1.
60 Hutton to Minto, 20 November 1898, HP, A-2.
61 *Report, 1898*, p. 42.
62 Altham to Hutton, 28 May 1899, HP, C-3; Hutton to DGMS, 8 March 1899 and Hutton to QMG, 28 November 1898, LAC RG9-II-B-1, vol. 667, T-380.
63 Hutton to Harrison, 7 April 1899, HP, A-5.
64 AG to CSO, 23 February 1899, LAC RG 9-II-B-1, vol. 667, T-380; 'Mobilization for defence', E.T.H. Hutton, 15 May 1899, HP, A-3.
65 'Regulations for the Canadian Militia Army Medical Services, 20 May 1899', HP, A-2; 'Memoirs', HP, F-2.
66 *Canadian Military Gazette*, 14 July 1899, p. 115.
67 'Report of the Department of Militia and Defence for the year ended December 31st, 1898 – Remarks by the Colonial Defence Committee', 7 April 1899, HP, A-5; *Report, 1898*, p. 39.
68 Morton, *Ministers and Generals*, p. 141.
69 *Mail and Empire* (Toronto), pp. 8, 10, 12 June 1899, Canadian War Museum (CWM), Otter Diaries, 19910162–169.
70 Hutton to Minto, 28 May and 18 June 1899, HP, A-2.
71 Hutton to Sooble, 18 February 1899, HP, E-2.
72 *Canadian Military Gazette*, 15 November 1898, p. 1.
73 Hutton to Buller, 18 June 1899, HP, A-5.
74 Wolseley to Minto, 1 December 1899, LAC, MF, vol. 12.
75 Lee to Hutton, 8 March and 6 April 1899, HP, C-3.
76 Cited in 'Militia Order no. 50 (1) of 4th April, 1899', HP, C-3.
77 Roosevelt to Hutton, 31 October 1901, HP, A-2.

Chapter 7 Political difficulties and imperial imperatives, 1898–99

1 Durrans, 'Imperial defence', p. 36.
2 'Lieutenant-General Edward Hutton and "Greater Britain"', p. 164.
3 Mowbray, 'Militiaman', p. 43.
4 'Lieutenant-General Edward Hutton and "Greater Britain"', pp. 132–3.
5 Hutton to Wood, 23 February 1899, HP, E-2.
6 Strachan, *The Politics of the British Army*, p. 102; Aubrey, 'Major-General E.T.H. Hutton', p. 20.
7 'Major-General Hutton, CB', *Canadian Military Gazette*, 6 September 1898, p. 1.
8 *Montreal Gazette*, 3 September 1898, p. 6.
9 Hutton to Laurier, (prepared) 3–4 February 1900, HP, A-1.
10 *Canadian Military Gazette*, 18 October 1898, p. 9.
11 See, for example, Hutton to Minto, 20 November 1898, LAC, MF, vol. 15.
12 Minute (draft): Hutton to Laurier, (prepared) 3–4 February 1900, HP, A-1.
13 Hutton to Chamberlain, 20 February 1899, HP, A-2.

14 Ibid.
15 Aylmer to Domville, 11 January 1899, HP, C-3; Hutton to Borden, 16 January 1899, HP, E-2.
16 Foster to unknown, 7 March 1899, LAC RG9– II-B-1, vol. 667, T-380.
17 Hutton to Domville, 12 and 16 May 1899, HP, C-3.
18 *Gazette* (New Brunswick), 2 May 1899, HP, C-3.
19 Borden to Hutton, 29 May 1899, and Hutton to Borden, 31 May 1899, HP, A-3.
20 Hutton to Minto, 1 June 1899, HP, A-2.
21 Drummond to Hutton, 9 June 1899, HP, A-2.
22 Hutton to Minto, 18 June 1899, HP, A-2.
23 Hutton to Borden, 15 March 1899, HP, E-2.
24 Wolseley to Hutton, 17 March 1899, HP, A-4.
25 Mowbray, 'Militiaman', p. 47.
26 Miller, 'The public life of Sir Frederick Borden', p. 55.
27 Borden to Sifton, 9 May 1899, Provincial Archives of Nova Scotia (PANS), Borden Papers, MG2 149, F3, p. 5289.
28 Borden to Hutton, 30 January 1899, HP, A-3.
29 Laurier to Borden, 29 November 1899, PANS, Borden Papers, MG2 151, F1, p. 6081.
30 Hutton to Lady Minto, 17 June 1899, LAC, MF, vol. 18.
31 Hutton to Buller, 18 June 1899, HP, A-5.
32 Hutton to Minto, 30 June 1899, HP, A-2.
33 MacLean, 'The imperial federation movement in Canada, 1884–1902', p. 193.
34 Wood, *Militia Myths*, p. 55.
35 Parker to Hutton, 9 February 1899, HP, C-3.
36 Hutton to Ardagh, 21 November 1898, HP, C-2.
37 'Mobilization for Defence', 15 May 1899, HP, A-3.
38 Hutton to Minto, 31 January 1900, LAC MG27-IIBI, MF, vol. 18.
39 'Minto Narrative'.
40 Buchan, *Lord Minto*, chapter 6.
41 Hutton to Ardagh, 21 November 1898, HP, C-2.
42 *Report, 1898*, p. 41.
43 Morton, *Ministers and Generals*, p. 145.
44 'An Act Respecting the Militia and Defence of Canada', 1887, TNA WO 32/6367.
45 Penlington, 'General Hutton and the Problem of Military Imperialism in Canada', p. 160.
46 Lansdowne to Minto, 29 July 1900, LAC, MF, vol. 12.
47 Lansdowne to Minto, 4 November 1899, LAC, MF, vol. 12.
48 Spiers, *The Late Victorian Army*, p. 52.
49 Dundonald to Hutton, 29 June 1904, HP, C-4.
50 Aubrey, 'Major-General E.T.H. Hutton', p. 33.
51 'Memoirs', HP, F-2.
52 'Interview between Right Hon. Joseph Chamberlain – Secretary of State for the Colonies and Colonel Hutton', 9 August 1898, HP, A-2.
53 *Globe* (Toronto), 29 August 1898, p. 4.

54 *Canadian Military Gazette*, 6 September 1898, p. 7.
55 *Mail and Empire* (Toronto), 10 October 1898, CWM, Otter Diaries, vol. 1, 19910162–169.
56 'Lieutenant-General Edward Hutton and "Greater Britain"', p. 163.
57 Gillon, 'The triumph of pragmatic imperialism', p. 174.
58 *Report, 1898*, p. 40.
59 'Memoirs', HP, F-2.
60 Hutton to Edwards, 12 February 1899, HP, C-3.
61 Hutton to Wood, 23 February 1899, HP, E-2.
62 'Lieutenant-General Edward Hutton and "Greater Britain"', p. 157.
63 'Remarks by the Colonial Defence Committee', 7 April 1899, HP, A-5.
64 Hutton to Ardagh, 21 November 1898, HP, C-2.
65 *Globe* (Toronto), 4 March 1899, p. 19.
66 Hutton to Clauson, 24 April 1899, HP, E-2.
67 Hutton to Seymour, 18 April 1899, HP, A-6.
68 Hutton to Borden, 2 November 1898, HP, E-2.
69 Hutton to Borden, 30 May 1899, HP, A-3.
70 Hutton to Buller, 14 May 1899, HP, A-5.
71 Hutton to Wolseley, 31 December 1899, HP, A-4.
72 Miller, *The Canadian Career of the Fourth Earl of Minto*, p. 65.
73 Morton, *Ministers and Generals*, p. 197.
74 Morton, 'Authority and Policy in the Canadian Militia, 1874–1904', p. 359; Morton, *Ministers and Generals*, p. 133.
75 Preston, *Canada and 'Imperial Defence'*, p. 255.
76 Durrans, 'Imperial defence', p. 80.
77 Winter, 'The evolution of the Canadian Army'.
78 *Globe* (Toronto), 7 April 1899, pp. 1–2.
79 *Canadian Military Gazette*, 14 July 1899, p. 13.
80 Minto to Laurier, 25 March 1899, and Minto to Chamberlain 6 April 1899, TNA WO 32/6367.
81 'Interview between Lord Lansdowne and Colonel Hutton', 3 August 1898, HP, A-4.
82 Gordon, *The Dominion Partnership*, p. 154.

Chapter 8 Canada and an imperial war, 1899–1900

1 Wilcox, *Australia's Boer War*, p. 19.
2 Chamberlain to Minto, 3 July 1899, HP, A-2.
3 Van der Waag, 'South Africa and the Boer Military System', in Dennis & Grey, *The Boer War*, p. 41.
4 Clarke, 'Manufacturing spontaneity?', pp. 129–30.
5 Chamberlain to Minto, 3 July 1899, LAC, MF, vol. 14.
6 Clarke, 'Manufacturing spontaneity?', pp. 131–2.
7 Ibid.
8 Wilcox, *Australia's Boer War*, p. 20.
9 McGibbon, *The Path to Gallipoli*, pp. 107–8.
10 Canadian Military Gazette, 14 July 1899, p. 14.
11 Hutton to Wood, 8 June 1899, HP, A-5.

12 Laurier to Minto, 20 July 1899, LAC, MF, vol. 7.
13 Ibid.
14 Hutton to Chamberlain, 20 July 1899, HP, A-2.
15 'Memoirs', HP, F-2.
16 Minto to Hutton, 5 September 1899, HP, A-2.
17 Hutton to Minto (cipher), 5 September 1899, LAC, MF, vol. 15.
18 For the range of Hutton–Hughes correspondence throughout this period see: LAC RG14 E-I, vol. 1990.
19 Hutton to Minto, 11 August 1899, LAC, MF, vol. 15.
20 Penlington, 'General Hutton and the problem of military imperialism in Canada', pp. 164–5.
21 Hughes to Hutton, 10 October 1899, HP, A-3; Hutton to Minto, 20 October 1900, HP, A-1.
22 Foster to Headquarters, 9 October 1899, LAC RG9-II-B1, vol. 667, T-380.
23 Miller, *Painting the Map Red*, pp. 34–5.
24 'Lieutenant-General Edward Hutton and "Greater Britain"', p. 173.
25 Hutton to Minto, 30 January 1900, HP, A-1.
26 Morton, *Ministers and Generals*, p. 153.
27 Clarke, 'Manufacturing spontaneity?', p. 137.
28 Hutton to Chamberlain, 4 September 1899, HP, A-2.
29 'Lieutenant-General Edward Hutton and "Greater Britain"', p. 171.
30 Miller, 'The public life of Sir Frederick Borden', p. 66.
31 Chamberlain to Minto, 3 October 1899, LAC, MF, vol. 14.
32 Durrans, 'Imperial defence', p. 92.
33 Sanford Evans, *The Canadian Contingents and Canadian Imperialism*, p. 44.
34 Miller, 'The public life of Sir Frederick Borden', p. 53.
35 Durrans, 'Imperial defence', pp. 104–5.
36 'Memoirs', HP, F-2.
37 *Ottawa Citizen*, 5 October 1899, p. 4.
38 Chamberlain to Minto, 7 October 1899, LAC, MF, vol. 14.
39 Strathcona to Laurier, 11 October 1899, HP, A-2.
40 Hutton to Borden, 11 October 1899, HP, A-3.
41 Laurier to Minto, 12 October 1899, LAC, MF, vol. 7.
42 Chamberlain to Minto, 26 October 1899, LAC, MF, vol. 14.
43 Foster to Hutton, 7 October and 12 October 1899, HP, A-6.
44 'Memoirs', HP, F-2.
45 Hutton to Minto, 31 January 1900, LAC, MF, vol. 18.
46 'Memoirs', HP, F-2.
47 Foster to Borden, 25 October 1899, and Hutton to Borden, 26 October 1899, LAC RG9-II-B1, vol. 667, T-380.
48 Ibid., p. 44.
49 Hutton to Buller, October 1899, HP, E-2.
50 Hughes to Hutton, 27 October 1899, HP, C-3.
51 *Globe* (Toronto), 30 October 1899, p. 2.
52 Morton, 'Authority and policy in the Canadian militia, 1874–1904', p. 412.
53 Hutton to Minto, 31 January 1900, LAC, MF, vol. 18.
54 Laurier to Minto, 7 November 1899, LAC, MF, vol. 7.

55 'Memoirs', HP, F-2.
56 Borden to Smith, 12 December 1899, PANS, Borden Papers, MG2 152, 6198, F1.
57 Wilcox, *Australia's Boer War*, p. 26.
58 Chamberlain to Minto, 16 December 1899, LAC, Laurier Fonds, MG26-G, C-1171.
59 Strathcona to Laurier, 18 December 1899, LAC, Laurier Fonds, MG26-G, C-1171.
60 Hutton to Minto, 10 January 1901, HP, A-1.
61 'Memoirs', HP, F-2.
62 Hutton to Otter, 28 December 1899, HP, E-3.
63 Foster to Hutton, 22 December 1899, HP, A-6.
64 Hutton to Minto, 31 January 1900, LAC, MF, vol. 18.
65 Hutton to Laurier, (prepared) 3–4 February 1900, HP, A-1.
66 Hutton to Wolseley, 1 February 1900, HP, A-4.
67 'Lieutenant-General Edward Hutton and "Greater Britain"', pp. 188, 268–71.
68 Laurier to Strathcona, 15 January 1900, LAC, Laurier Fonds, MG26-G, C-1171.
69 Minto to Laurier, 18 January 1900, LAC, MF, vol. 18.
70 Penlington, 'General Hutton and the problem of military imperialism in Canada', p. 168.
71 Hutton to Minto, 20 January 1900, LAC, MF, vol. 15.
72 Hutton to Wood, 20 January 1900, HP, A-5.
73 'Memo of conversation between Laurier and Minto', 27 January 1900, LAC, MF, vol. 18.
74 'Privy Council Office, extract', LAC, MF, vol. 18.
75 Minto to Laurier, 30 January 1900, LAC, MF, vol. 18.
76 Hutton to Wickam, 16 January 1899, HP, C-3.
77 Borden to Laurier, 3 February 1900, LAC, MF, vol. 18.
78 Foster to White, 1 February and 29 January 1900, LAC, MF, vol. 18.
79 Borden to Laurier, and Pinault to Hutton, 3 February 1900, LAC, MF, vol. 18.
80 Mowbray, 'Militiaman', p. 81.
81 'Memorandum by the Canadian Cabinet', LAC, MF, vol. 18.
82 Graham to Privy Council, 3 February 1900, LAC, MF, vol. 18.
83 Hutton to Minto, 3 February 1900, LAC, MF, vol. 18.
84 Penlington, 'General Hutton and the problem of military imperialism in Canada', p. 170.
85 Hutton to Laurier, (prepared) 3–4 February 1900.
86 'Memorandum by the Canadian Cabinet', LAC, MF, vol. 18.
87 Hutton to Chamberlain, 5 February 1900, HP, A-2.
88 Minto to Chamberlain, 8 February 1900, LAC, MF, vol. 18.
89 Hutton to Minto, 8 February 1899, LAC, MF, vol. 15.
90 War Office to Hutton, and Hutton to War Office, 9 February 1900, HP, A-5; Hutton to Borden, 10 February 1900, HP, A-3.
91 Miller, 'The public life of Sir Frederick Borden', p. 102.
92 Gillon, 'The triumph of pragmatic imperialism', p. 172.

93 *Canadian Military Gazette*, 20 February 1900, p. 9.
94 *Ottawa Citizen*, 16 February 1900, p. 3.
95 Hutton to Minto, 18 August 1900, HP, A-1.
96 Hutton to Minto, 27 March 1901, LAC, MF, vol. 17.
97 *CHCD*, 8th Parl., 5th Sess., vol. 51, pp. 594–6.
98 Morton, Ministers and Generals, p. 162.
99 Durrans, 'Imperial defence', pp. 59–60.
100 Chamberlain to Minto, 3 July 1899, HP, A-2.
101 Buchan, *Lord Minto*, chapter 6.
102 Morton, 'Authority and policy in the Canadian militia, 1874–1904', p. 404.
103 Hutton to Wolseley, 1 August 1899, HP, E-2.
104 Hutton to Minto, 2 March 1900, HP, A-1.
105 Hutton to Minto, 10 January 1901, HP, A-1.
106 McGibbon, *The Path to Gallipoli*, p. 111.
107 Hutton to Minto, 10 January 1901, HP, A-1.
108 'Memoirs', HP, F-2.
109 Hutton to Wood, 20 January 1900, HP, A-5.

Chapter 9 Hutton's war in South Africa and raising an Australian army, 1900–03

1 Chamberlain to Hutton, 20 February 1900, HP, A-2; 'Interviews between Major General Hutton and high officials upon his return from Canada', 8 March 1900, HP, A-2.
2 Ibid.
3 Hutton to Minto, 2 March 1900, HP, A-1.
4 Wolseley to Minto, 2 March 1899, LAC, MF, vol. 12.
5 'Interviews between Major General Hutton and high officials upon his return from Canada', 8 March 1900, HP, A-2.
6 Lansdowne to Minto, 4 March 1900, LAC, MF, vol. 12.
7 Hutton to Eleanor Hutton, 24 March 1900, NLA MS1215.
8 Hutton to Minto, 14 April 1900, HP, A-1.
9 Hutton to Eleanor Hutton, 2 April 1900, HP, B-2.
10 Hutton to Eleanor Hutton, 7 April 1900, NLA MS1215.
11 'Lieutenant-General Edward Hutton and "Greater Britain"', p. 205.
12 Hutton to Laurier, 25 April 1900, LAC, MF, vol. 16.
13 Minto to Chamberlain, 12 May 1900, LAC, MF, vol. 14.
14 Hutton to Eleanor, 22 April 1900, HP, B-2.
15 Hutton to Eleanor Hutton, 14 September 1900, NLA MS1215.
16 Hutton to Minto, 23 September 1900, HP, A-1.
17 Hutton to Eleanor Hutton, 5 October 1900, HP, B-2.
18 *Sydney Morning Herald*, 11 August 1923, p. 14.
19 Hutton to Eleanor Hutton, 27 May 1900, NLA MS1215.
20 'An autobiography: General Chauvel', AWM MSS1406.
21 Hutton to Alderson, 3 June 1902, HP, A-6.
22 'Lieutenant-General Edward Hutton and "Greater Britain"', p. 218.
23 Hutton to Eleanor Hutton, 23 August 1900, HP, B-2.
24 Harries-Jenkins, *The Army in Victorian Society*, pp. 198–9.

25 Hutton to Eleanor Hutton, 13 May 1900, NLA MS1215.
26 Hutton to Eleanor Hutton, 22 June 1900, NLA MS1215.
27 Hutton to Minto, 14 May 1900, HP, A-1.
28 Hutton to Alderson, 3 June 1902, HP, A-6.
29 Hutton to Eleanor Hutton, 6 June 1900, NLA MS1215.
30 Hutton to Alderson, 3 June 1902, HP, A-6.
31 Hutton to Eleanor Hutton, 7 April 1900, NLA MS1215.
32 Hutton to Minto, 7 December 1900, HP, A-1.
33 Wilde, 'Joseph Chamberlain's proposal of an Imperial Council in March 1900', pp. 241ff.
34 Hutton to Minto, 14 April 1900, HP, A-1.
35 Hutton to Minto, 19 July 1900, HP, A-1.
36 Hutton to Eleanor Hutton, 4 August 1900, HP, A-1.
37 Hutton to Lansdowne, 5 October 1900, HP, A-3.
38 Satre, 'St John Brodrick and army reform, 1901–1903', pp. 117–39.
39 Hutton to Minto, 16 January 1901, HP, A-1.
40 Hutton to Minto, 8 February 1901, HP, A-1.
41 Hutton to Brodrick, 30 January 1901, HP, A-4.
42 Hutton to Minto, 8 February 1901, HP, A-1.
43 'Defence forces and defence, no. 254M', NAA CP601/2, vol. 1.
44 Satre, 'St John Brodrick and army reform, 1901–1903', pp. 117–39.
45 Hutton to Minto, 27 March 1901, HP, A-1.
46 'Defence forces and defence, no. 254M', NAA CP601/2, vol. 1.
47 Ibid.
48 Ibid.
49 Hutton to Minto, 16 January 1901, HP, A-1.
50 Forrest to Barton, 18 April 1901, NAA A2657, vol. 1.
51 Hopetoun to Barton, 2 June and 24 June 1901, NAA A2657, vol. 1.
52 Hopetoun to Barton, 3 August and 7 October 1901, NAA A2657.
53 *Daily Telegraph* (Sydney), 20 September 1901, p. 3.
54 War Office to Hutton, 22 November 1901, HP, A-4.
55 Hutton to Barton, 2 December 1901, and Barton and Forrest to Hutton, 3 December 1901, HP, A-4.
56 Hutton to Dibbs, 3 December 1901, HP, A-4.
57 Clarke, 'Marching to their own drum', p. 60.
58 'Notes of an interview between Rt Hon. Joseph Chamberlain – Secretary of State for the colonies and Major-General Sir Edward Hutton', 19 December 1901, HP, A-2.
59 Ibid.
60 Mordike, *An Army for a Nation*, p. 90.
61 'Lieutenant-General Edward Hutton and "Greater Britain"', p. 225.
62 Aubrey, 'Major-General E.T.H. Hutton', p. 50.
63 Norris, *The Emergent Commonwealth*, p. 122.
64 Crowley, *A New History of Australia*, p. 277; *Official Year Book of the Commonwealth of Australia*, 1908, no. 1, p. 894.
65 Souter, *Lion and Kangaroo*, pp. 59–60.

66 Perry, 'Lieutenant-General Sir Edward Hutton', p. 19.
67 'Commonwealth Defence Bill', 1901, NAA CP103/12 Bundle 3/A8.
68 'A study in British Commonwealth co-operation: Australian defence policy to 1938', NAA A5954, 784/2; *Sydney Morning Herald*, 24 July 1901, NAA A6, 1901/201.
69 'A study in British Commonwealth co-operation: Australian defence policy to 1938', NAA A5954, 784/2.
70 Hutton to Minto, 8 March 1902, HP, A-1.
71 Hutton to Ommanney, 24 February 1902, HP, A-2.
72 Hutton to Minto, 8 March 1902, HP, A-1.
73 'Lieutenant-General Edward Hutton and "Greater Britain"', p. 239.
74 *Official Yearbook*, no. 1, 1908, p. 1082; no. 12, 1919, pp. 1080–1; no. 13, 1920, pp. 999–1012.
75 'Report of the Federal Military Committee', AWM 3, [1].
76 'Memoirs', HP, F-2.
77 'Second Annual Report by Major-General Sir Edward Hutton, KCMG, CB, Commanding the Military Forces of the Commonwealth' (hereafter *Second Annual Report*), 1 May 1904, NAA A1195, 45.30/27793; 'Military Forces of the Commonwealth – Annual Report' (hereafter *First Annual Report*), E. T. H. Hutton, 1 May 1903, NAA A1195, 45.30/27793; Correspondence (various), Hutton, Forrest and Collins, February–May 1902, NAA B168, 1902/867 Part 1.
78 'Minute upon the defence of Australia' (hereafter Minute, 1902), E.T.H. Hutton, 7 April 1902, NAA A1195, 45.30/27793.
79 Ibid.
80 Hutton to Minto, 7 April 1902, HP, A-1.
81 Minute, 1902.
82 'Scheme of organisation of the military forces of the Commonwealth into a Field Force and into Garrison Troops', AWM 3, 677.
83 'Memoirs', HP, F-2.
84 Barton to Hutton, 6 April 1902, HP, A-4.
85 *Sydney Morning Herald*, 24 April 1902, p. 6.
86 *Register* (Adelaide), p. 4.
87 *West Australian*, 28 April 1902, p. 4.
88 Collins to Hutton, July 1902, NAA B168, 1902/2688.
89 Ibid.
90 Minute, 1902.
91 Hutton to Bigge, 29 April 1902, HP, A-2.
92 Bigge to Hutton, 17 July 1902, HP, A-2.
93 Hutton to Prince Arthur, 29 April 1902, HP, A-2.
94 'Memoirs', HP, F-2.
95 Collins to Hutton, 28 November 1902, NAA B168, 1902/2688.
96 Hutton to Ommanney, 19 August 1903, HP, A-2.
97 *Second Annual Report*.
98 'The military forces of the Commonwealth tables', AWM 3, [22].
99 Hutton to Bigge, 21 October 1902, HP, A-2.

Chapter 10 Difficulties and disappointments, 1903–04

1 Hutton to Northcote, 15 December 1903, HP, A-3.
2 Mowbray, 'Militiaman', pp. 100, 148–50.
3 'Lieutenant-General Edward Hutton and "Greater Britain"', pp. 227–8.
4 Tennyson to Forrest, 1 July 1903, Forrest Papers, NLA, MFM G 660.
5 'A study in British Commonwealth co-operation: Australian defence policy to 1938', NAA A5954, 784/2.
6 Forrest, *CPD*, vol. 7, 16 July 1903, pp. 2265, 2277.
7 'Extract from a speech by the Minister for Defence (Sir John Forrest), 16 July 1903', in Greenwood & Grimshaw, *Documents in Australian International Affairs 1901–1918*, p. 229.
8 Ibid., p. 230; McCay, *CPD*, vol. 7, 23 July 1903, p. 2277; 'Lieutenant-General Edward Hutton and "Greater Britain"', p. 249.
9 *Second Annual Report*; 'Draft of Commonwealth Military Regulations', NAA A2657, vol. 1.
10 Hutton to Ommanney, 19 April 1904, HP, A-2.
11 Hutton to Balfour, 27 June 1904, HP, A-2.
12 Lassetter to Hutton, 2 December 1901, HP, C-3.
13 Appendix A to *Organisation of the Military Forces of the Commonwealth, Commonwealth Parliamentary Papers (CPP)*, vol. 2, 1903, p. 60.
14 *Sydney Morning Herald*, 27 June 1904, p. 9.
15 *Monaro and Southern District Advertiser*, 12 March 1903, and *Cooma Express*, 26 May 1903, NAA B168, 02/1823 & 02/2688.
16 Wilkinson to Department of Defence, NAA B168, 02/2441[8].
17 McLean, *CPD*, 1st Parl., 2nd Sess., p. 3120.
18 Series of reports beginning 22 September, 1902, NAA B168, I 02/2688.
19 Roberts to Hutton, 5 June 1903, HP, A-4; Mordike, *An Army for a Nation*, p. 156.
20 Rushall to McCulloch, AWM3, 02/429.
21 Rushall to AAG, NAA B168, 02/1631.
22 Bou, 'Modern cavalry', in Dennis & Grey, *The Boer War*, p. 112.
23 Wilcox, *For Hearths and Homes*, pp. 50–1.
24 Hutton to Forrest, 16 November 1903, NAA B168, 1902/2688.
25 *Advertiser* (Adelaide), 15 June 1902, (clipping), HP, A-3.
26 See for example Price to Bridges, NAA B168, 02/2688.
27 Such newspapers for example included the *Argus* and the *Advertiser* (Adelaide).
28 Storrer to Watson, *CPD*, 2nd Parl., 1st Sess., p. 3393.
29 *Bulletin*, 17 March 1904, p. 21.
30 Northcote to Hutton, 11 February 1904, HP, A-3.
31 Bigge to Hutton, 19 April 1904, HP, A-2; 'Lieutenant-General Edward Hutton and "Greater Britain"', p. 256.
32 Hutton to Forrest, 25 March 1903, HP, A-4.
33 Ibid.
34 Hutton to Collins, 12 March 1902, AWM3, 02/359; Wilcox 'Relinquishing the Past', p. 57.
35 Mordike, 'Control by committee', p. 9.

36 'Select Committee: Case of Senator Lt. Col. Neild. Minutes of Evidence', NAA A1194, 45.30/27794.
37 'Select Committee Report, 1 September 1902', NAA A1194, 45.30/27794.
38 Collins to Forrest, 22 June 1903, NLA, MS 2553.
39 Forrest to Collins, 8 and 15 July 1903, NLA, MS 2553.
40 *Official Yearbook*, no. 1, 1907, p. 1051.
41 Kelly, *CPD*, 2nd Parl., 3rd Sess., p. 609.
42 Hutton to Ward, 7 June 1904, HP, C-4.
43 Hutton to Chapman, 13 November 1903, NAA B168, 1902/2688.
44 Wolseley to Hutton, 5 June 1902, HP, A-4.
45 Hutton to Ommanney, 23 December 1902, HP, A-2; 'Memoirs', HP, F-2.
46 Forrest to Collins, 6 November 1902, NAA B168, 1902/2688.
47 'Estimates of the Defence Department for the Financial Year, 1903–04', NAA A1194, 05.13/2472.
48 Vamplew, *Australians*, pp. 133, 412.
49 Hutton to Forrest, 4 May 1903, HP, A-4.
50 Hutton to Tennyson, 4 May 1903, HP, A-3.
51 *First Annual Report.*
52 Hutton to Chapman, 16 March 1904, NAA B168, 1902/867.
53 *Second Annual Report.*
54 Hutton to Minto, 16 May 1904, HP, A-1; *Second Annual Report.*
55 *Second Annual Report.*
56 Norris, The *Emergent Commonwealth*, p. 128.
57 *Second Annual Report.*
58 *First Annual Report.*
59 'Narrative of a staff ride by the Commonwealth military forces of New South Wales', NAA A1194, 12.42/4779.
60 'Narrative of instructional operations by a cavalry division', 4 May 1904, NAA B168, 1903/618.
61 *First Annual Report*; 'Comparative statement for militia and volunteers', NAA MP84/1, 1937/1/68.
62 Hutton to Brodrick, 18 August 1903, and Hutton to Ommanney, 19 August 1903, HP, A-2.
63 Collins to Hutton, 1 August 1903, NLA, MS 2553.
64 Hutton to Chapman, 1 March 1904, and Chapman to Hutton, 4 March 1904, NAA A2657, vol. 1.
65 Tennyson to Chapman, 8 January 1904, NLA, MS 479/3.
66 Hutton to Bigge, 12 May 1903, HP, A-2.
67 McMullin, *So Monstrous a Travesty*, pp. 103–4.
68 Hutton to Minto, 16 May 1904, HP, A-1.
69 Dawson to Hutton, May 1904, NAA B168, 1902/867.
70 Mordike, 'Control by committee', pp. 10–11.
71 Hutton to Northcote, 31 May and 4 June 1904, and 23 February 1903, HP, A-3.
72 Miller, *The Canadian Career of the Fourth Earl of Minto*, p. 61.
73 Hutton to Dawson, 21 June 1904, NAA B168, 1904/4592.
74 Dawson to Hutton, 28 June 1904, NAA B168, 1904/4592.

75 Ibid.
76 Wood, *Chiefs of the Australian Army*, p. 45.
77 Collins to Garran, 29 March 1904, NAA B168, 1904/184 Part 3; Garran to Collins, April 1904, NAA B168, 1904/184 Part 3.
78 'Memorandum by a committee in regard to the command and administration of the military and naval forces', NAA B168, 1904/184 Part 3.
79 Strachan, *The Politics of the British Army*, pp. 68, 121–2; Wood, *Chiefs of the Australian Army*, pp. xviii–iv.
80 'Extracts: Clarke Forrest', 26 June 1904, AWM3, 04/62.
81 Hamer, *The British Army*, pp. 179, 182–3, 194–5; Strachan, *The Politics of the British Army*, pp. 104–5.
82 'Lieutenant-General Edward Hutton and "Greater Britain"', p. 226.
83 Hutton to McCay, 7 September 1904, HP, A-4.
84 Ibid.
85 'An Act to amend the Defence Act 1903', NAA B168, 1904/184 Part 3.
86 Hutton to Lee, 13 October 1903, HP, C-3.
87 Hutton to Kelly Kenny, 10 November 1903, HP, C-3.
88 'Memoirs', HP, F-2.
89 Hutton to Collins, 20 August 1904, HP, A-6.
90 McCay to Deal, 7 September 1904, HP, A-6.
91 *Major-General Sir Edward T. H. Hutton, KCMG, CB*, pp. 14–15.
92 'Memoirs', HP, F-2.
93 Legge to Hutton, 12 January 1908, HP, C-4.
94 Williams to Hutton, 1 July 1908, HP, C-4.
95 Deakin to Clarke, 3 October 1905, Deakin Papers, NLA, 15/3522–3.
96 Wilcox, *For Hearths and Homes*, p. 54.
97 'Memoirs', HP, F-2.
98 Hutton, 'The bond of military unity', pp. 239–40.
99 Wood, *Chiefs of the Australian Army*, p. 46 (quoting from the *Argus*, 10 November 1904).
100 Bean, *The Story of ANZAC*, vol. 1, p. 178.
101 Smith-Dorrien to Hutton, 27 July 1903, HP, C-3.

Chapter 11 The new Australian army and imperial defence, 1902–04

1 Thompson, 'The language of imperialism', p. 152.
2 Tennyson to Chamberlain, 17 April 1900, NLA, MS 479.
3 Wilde, 'Joseph Chamberlain's proposal', p. 227.
4 Durrans, 'Imperial defence', pp. 113, 114.
5 'Lieutenant-General Edward Hutton and "Greater Britain"', p. 191.
6 'Memoirs', HP, F-2.
7 Gordon, *The Dominion Partnership*, p. 145; Wilde, 'The Boxer Affair and Australian responsibility for imperial defence', p. 56.
8 Wilde, 'Joseph Chamberlain's proposal', pp. 241–2, 243.
9 Hutton to Kelly Kenny, 4 August 1902, HP, A-1.
10 Hutton to Minto, 10 January 1901, HP, A-1; 'Lieutenant-General Edward Hutton and "Greater Britain"', p. 192.

11 Gordon, 'The Colonial Defence Committee and imperial collaboration: 1885–1904', p. 535.
12 Thompson, 'The language of imperialism', p. 155.
13 Parkin to Hutton, 4 October 1900, HP, A-3.
14 Lascelles, 'The colonies and imperial defence', pp. 858–9.
15 Gordon, 'The Colonial Defence Committee and imperial collaboration: 1885–1904', p. 536.
16 'Lieutenant-General Edward Hutton and "Greater Britain"', p. 230.
17 Lascelles, 'The colonies and imperial defence', p. 859.
18 Mordike, *An Army for a Nation*, p. 118.
19 Ibid., p. 104.
20 Hutton to Collins, 11 August 1902, NAA B168, 1902/2688.
21 'Lieutenant-General Edward Hutton and "Greater Britain"', p. 23.
22 'Notes of an interview between Rt Hon. Joseph Chamberlain – Secretary of State for the Colonies and Major General Sir Edward Hutton', 19 December 1901, HP, A-2.
23 Hutton to Roberts, 22 July 1902, HP, A-4.
24 Hutton to Brodrick, 24 February and 7 April 1902, HP, A-4.
25 Hutton to Ommanney, 23 December 1902, HP, A-2.
26 Hutton to Tennyson, 23 February 1903, HP, A-3.
27 Hutton to Ommanney, 19 August 1903, HP, A-2.
28 'Major-General French's defence scheme', TNA WO 32/6365.
29 'Defences of the Colony', 20 July 1900, HP, A-4.
30 McGibbon, *The Path to Gallipoli*, p. 131.
31 'Colonial co-operation in imperial defence', 271M, 2 August 1901, TNA CAB 8/1.
32 Nathan, 'Colonial co-operation in imperial defence', 16 August 1900, NAA CP103/12 Bundle 3/A8.
33 Altham to Ardagh, 20 October 1900, TNA WO 32/6365.
34 Ibid.
35 Chamberlain to Ranfurly, 6 September 1901, NAA A6661, 972.
36 'The organization of colonial troops for imperial service', TNA CO 537/300.
37 Wilson to Onslow, 19 February 1902, TNA CO 537/300.
38 'Colonial troops for imperial service in war', 293M, 13 June 1902, TNA CA 8/1.
39 'A study in British Commonwealth co-operation', NAA A5954, 784/2.
40 Durrans, 'Imperial defence', p. 92.
41 Gordon, *The Dominion Partnership*, p. 155.
42 Durrans, 'Imperial defence', p. 143.
43 'Extract from a speech by the Secretary of State for the Colonies (Mr J. Chamberlain)', in Greenwood & Grimshaw, *Documents on Australian International Affairs*, pp. 222–3.
44 Ibid.
45 'A study in British Commonwealth co-operation: Australian defence policy to 1938', NAA A5954, 784/2.
46 Ibid.

47 Deakin to Barton, 6 July 1902, NLA, Tennyson Papers, MS479/6/2.
48 Durrans, 'Imperial defence', p. 149.
49 Roberts to Hutton, 3 October 1902, HP, A-4.
50 Lascelles, 'The colonies and imperial defence', p. 884.
51 Knaplund, 'Intra-imperial aspects of Britain's defence question, 1870–1900', p. 141; Otte, 'The Foreign Office and defence of empire, 1856–1914', in Kennedy & Neilson, *Imperial Defence*, p. 9.
52 Nicholson to Hutton, 22 November 1901, HP, A-4.
53 Hutton to Nicholson, 10 March 1903, HP, A-5.
54 Hutton to Minto, 29 August 1902, HP, A-1.
55 Hutton to Kelly Kenny, 4 August 1902, HP, A-3.
56 Hutton to Prince Arthur, 4 August 1902, HP, A-2.
57 Hutton to Tennyson, 23 February 1903, and Hutton to Darley, 20 January 1903, HP, A-3.
58 Hutton to Brodrick, November 1902, HP, A-4.
59 Ommanney to Hutton, 20 November 1902, HP, A-2.
60 'Minute upon defence by General Officer Commanding the Military Forces: Remarks by the Colonial Defence Committee', 22 October 1902, HP, A-3.
61 Tennyson to Chamberlain, 11 March 1903, NLA, Tennyson Papers, MS479/2/279.
62 Hutton to Tennyson, 9 March 1903, HP, A-3.
63 Hutton to Forrest, 9 May 1903, NAA B168, 1902/2688.
64 Hutton to Nicholson, 10 March and 17 March 1903, HP, A-5.
65 Hutton to Brodrick, 18 August 1903, HP, A-4.
66 Brodrick to Hutton, 3 November 1903, HP, A-4.
67 Roberts to Hutton, 5 June 1903, HP, A-4.
68 Hamilton to Hutton, 23 December 1903, 7 April 1899, HP, A-5; Hamilton to Otter, 23 December 1903, CWM, 58 A1, 102.32.
69 Clauson to Hutton, 4 June 1903, 6 August 1903, HP, A-5.
70 Hutton to Clarke, 7 October 1906, HP, A-3.
71 'Correspondence in regard to the policy of Australian defence', HP, A-5.
72 Souter, *Lion and Kangaroo*, p. 115.
73 Meaney, 'British and Australian identity', p. 79.
74 Souter, *Lion and Kangaroo*, p. 109.
75 Cole, 'The problem of "nationalism" and "imperialism" in British settlement colonies', p. 177.
76 Souter, *Lion and Kangaroo*, pp. 21, 22.
77 *Courier* (Brisbane), 28 July 1902, p. 4.
78 'Lieutenant-General Edward Hutton and "Greater Britain"', p. 244.
79 'Australian and Canadian opinion on military defence', in Greenwood & Grimshaw, *Documents on Australian International Affairs*, p. 225.
80 Wilde, 'The Boxer Affair and Australian responsibility for imperial defence', pp. 64–5.
81 'Minister for Defence for the Prime Minister, 15 March 1902', in Greenwood & Grimshaw, *Documents on Australian International Affairs*, p. 115.

82 Forrest to Barton, 15 March 1902, HP, A-4.
83 'Minister for Defence for the Prime Minister, 15 March 1902', in Greenwood & Grimshaw, *Documents on Australian International Affairs*, p. 115.
84 'Speech by Mr Andrew Fisher (Labor), 5 August 1903', in Greenwood & Grimshaw, *Documents on Australian International Affairs*, p. 232.
85 *Sydney Morning Herald*, 28 July 1902, p. 6.
86 Hutton to Tennyson, 9 March 1903, HP, A-3.
87 Hutton to Darley, 20 January 1903, NLA, Tennyson Papers, MS479/6/2.
88 Robinson, Gallagher & Denny, *Africa and the Victorians*, p. 9.
89 Hutton to Arnold Foster, 12 October 1903, HP, A-4.
90 May to Hutton, 19 September 1904, HP, C-4.

Chapter 12 The twilight years, 1905–23

1 Hutton to HQ Aldershot, 7 June 1906, HP, C-4.
2 Hutton to Methuen, 17 May 1906, HP, C-4.
3 Douglas to Haldane, 18 February 1907, TNA WO 138/31. Lieutenant-General Sir Charles Whittingham Horsley Douglas, Adjutant-General to the Forces, was in charge of personnel and therefore the natural person to deal with such a serious complaint.
4 Hutton to French, 14 November 1906, TNA WO 138/31.
5 'An address upon the military power and organization or our colonies', E.T.H. Hutton, 17 March 1905, HP, F-1.
6 'Prime Minister's proposals for the re-organization of the regular army and militia', 24 February 1905, TNA 30/60/50.
7 Wilcox, 'Relinquishing the past', pp. 58–9.
8 'Papers laid before the Conference: Naval and military defence', NAA CP103/2, Bundle 3A2.
9 Durrans, 'Imperial defence', p. 165.
10 Hutton to Deakin, 24 January 1906, NLA, Deakin Papers, 15/3553–4.
11 Hutton to Barton, 14 July 1915, HP, A-4.
12 'Memoirs', HP, F-2.
13 'Correspondence in regard to the policy of Australian defence', September 1915, HP, A-5.
14 'Memoirs', HP, F-2.
15 Hutton to Haldane, 28 May 1916, HP, A-4.
16 'Memoirs', HP, F-2.
17 Strachan, *The Politics of the British Army*, p. 236.
18 Haldane to Hutton, 24 May 1913, and Hutton to Haldane, 28 May 1913, HP, A-4.
19 Birdwood to Hutton, 30 September 1916, HP, A-6.
20 Hutton to French, 2 January 1915, HP, A-4.
21 Kitchener to Hutton, 26 March 1915, TNA WO 138/31.
22 White to Hutton, 4 July 1915, HP, A-6.
23 Chauvel to Hutton, 9 September and 23 November 1916, HP, A-6.
24 Chauvel to Hutton, 4 February 1917, HP, A-6.
25 Godley to Hutton, 1 December 1915, HP, C-4.

26 Birdwood to Hutton, 30 September and 1 December 1916, HP, A-6.
27 Hutton to Barton, 14 July 1915, HP, A-4.
28 Earle, 'The Officers' Training Corps', p. 33.
29 Bruche, 'The land and air defence forces of Australia', pp. 758, 771.
30 'Lieutenant-General Edward Hutton and "Greater Britain"', p. 263.

Bibliography

UNPUBLISHED OFFICIAL AND PERSONAL RECORDS

Australia

	Australian War Memorial (AWM)
AWM1	Pre-Federation and Commonwealth records
AWM3	Department of Defence central registry file, 1902–05
AWM130	New South Wales Mounted Rifles, South Africa, 1899–1900
AWM 3DRL/2507	Papers of H.L. Harnett
AWM 3DRL/3310	Papers of P.R. Ricardo
AWM 3DRL/3607	Papers of J.M. Antill
AWM 3DRL/7545	Papers of T. Kelly
AWM PR00318	Papers of A.W. McKenzie
AWM PR00535	Papers of H.G. Chauvel
AWM PR82/149	Papers of R.D. Fraser
AWM PR85/084	Papers of B. Spurway
AWM PR86/126	Papers of F.W. Bretag
AWM PR86/261	Diary of J.C. Hoad in South Africa, 1900
AWM PR87/207	Papers of J.A.K. Mackey
AWM PR90/107	Papers of F. Livingstone-Learmonth
MSS1063	G. Verney, 'Building an Australian Army, 1870–1904', paper presented to the Canberra Chapter of the History of Australian Defence and Foreign Policy Association, 26 May 1982
MSS1406	Chauvel Memoirs

National Archives of Australia (NAA) (Canberra)	
A2	Correspondence file
A6	Correspondence file
A8	Correspondence file
A1194	Library material
A2657	Volumes of papers of historical interest, 1901–10
A5954	Shedden Collection
A6006	Folders of copies of Cabinet papers
A6443	General Correspondence files relating to the Australian contingents in the South African (Boer) War
A6661	Correspondence and printed matter
A6662	Miscellaneous correspondence relating mainly to local (non-imperial) matters
CP103/2	Minutes of proceedings and papers laid before the Imperial Conference
CP103/12	Records of Imperial Conferences

National Archives of Australia (NAA) (Melbourne)	
B168	Correspondence files
B3756	Correspondence files
B3778	Historical collection of correspondence files of the Victorian Department of Defence
B6121	Naval historical files
MP84/1	Correspondence files
MP153/16	Australian state defence papers
MP372/10	Correspondence and files of the Office of DQMG
MP372/14	Copies of memoranda and letters concerning reorganisation of the defence forces
MP372/15	Inward correspondence and files of the office of DGMS
MP372/19	Outward correspondence and files of the office of DGMS
MP372/23	Correspondence and files of the office of DQMG
MP372/24	Outward correspondence and files of the office of DQMG
MP372/26	Inward correspondence and files of the office of DAG
MP481/2	Minutes of meetings
MP598/30	Typescript of Jensen's defence production in Australia and supporting evidence
MP729/1	Victorian series, defence

MP744/3	General correspondence of the Headquarters Brigade Office, Queensland Defence Force
MP744/6	Letter book of Robert Collins, Secretary of the Department of Defence

National Archives of Australia (NAA) (Brisbane)

M4214	Personal papers of Colonel Howel Gunter

National Archives of Australia (NAA) (Hobart)

P2456	Reports by Colonel J.G. Hoad, Australian attaché to the Japanese army during Russo-Japanese War

National Library of Australia (NLA)

NLA, MFM G 660–61	Forrest Papers
NLA, MFM G 10271–82	Wolseley Papers
NLA, MFM G 24422	L. Trainor, 'British Policy to New South Wales, Queensland and Victoria during the Secretaryship of State for the Colonies of the Marquess of Ripon, 1892–1895'
NLA, MFM M 936–37	Hopetoun Papers
NLA, MS 51	Edmund Barton Papers
NLA, MS 479	Hallam Tennyson Papers
NLA, MS 1215	Letters and press cuttings 1900–04 (collected by E.T.H. Hutton)
NLA, MS 1540	Papers of Alfred Deakin, 1804–1973 (bulk 1880–1919) [manuscript]
NLA, MS 2553	Records, 1903–21 (Department of Defence)
NLA, MS 8655	Warren Perry Papers
NLA, Nf 355.209944 H984	E.T.H. Hutton, *Defence of NSW: Mobilization – Port Jackson District*, 1894
NLA, Npf 355.4509944 H984	E.T.H. Hutton, *Defence of NSW*
NLA, Peth Pam 629, Defences Box 1	E.T.H. Hutton, *Our Comrades of Greater Britain*, Edward Stanford, London, 1896

State Library of New South Wales (SLNSW)

A 871 – A 1052	Henry Parkes Correspondence
B 1680	Barham Diary
MLMSS 2105	Steel Diary
MLMSS 6114	Perry, W., 'Military Reforms in the Colony of New South Wales, 1893–96: The work of the Commandant, Major-General E.T.H. Hutton', 1996

State Record of New South Wales (SRNSW)

NRS 905	Main series of letters received [Colonial Secretary]
NRS 906	Special bundles [Colonial Secretary]
NRS 910	Registers of Minutes and Memoranda [Colonial Secretary]
NRS 985	Copies of letters to naval and military officers
NRS 1251	Boer War: Regimental orders for the New South Wales Mounted Rifles
NRS 1252	Boer War: Regimental orders for the 6th Regiment, Imperial Bushmen, New South Wales and the 3rd Mounted Brigade.
NRS 1253	Boer War: Regimental orders

Library of the University of New South Wales (CANBERRA)

Microfilm 1173 pts A-2 – G-1 (20 reels)	Papers of Edward Thomas Henry Hutton (1848–1923)

Canada

Canadian War Museum (CWM)

19910162–169	Otter Diaries, vol. 1, 1896–98

Libraries and Archives Canada (LAC)

MG26-G	Sir Wilfrid Laurier fonds
MG27-IIB1	Gilbert John Elliot-Murray-Kynynmound, 4th Earl of Minto fonds
MG29-E29	George Denison fonds
RG9-II-B1	Department of Militia and Defence fonds, headquarters records

Provincial Archives of Nova Scotia (PANS)	
MG 2	Frederick Borden Papers

United Kingdom

National Archives of the United Kingdom (TNA)	
CAB 5	Committee of Imperial Defence: colonial defence memoranda, 1902–39
CAB 9	Colonial Defence Committee and Committee of Imperial Defence
CAB 11	Colonial Defence Committee and Committee of Imperial Defence
CAB 18	Committee of Imperial Defence: miscellaneous reports and papers
CAB 21	Cabinet Office and predecessors: registered files
CAB 37	Cabinet Office: photographic copies of Cabinet papers
CAB 41	Photographic Copies of Cabinet letters in the Royal Archives
CO 44	Colonial Office and predecessors: Canada, formerly British North America, Acts
CO 46	War and Colonial Department and Colonial Office: Canada, formerly British North America, Government Gazettes
CO 418	Colonial Office: Australia original correspondence
CO 537	Colonial Office and predecessors: confidential general and confidential original correspondence
CO 885	War and Colonial Department and Colonial Office: subjects affecting colonies generally
DO 119	High Commissioner for South Africa correspondence
PRO 30/40	Ardagh Papers
PRO 30/60	Balfour Papers
WO 32	War Office and successors: registered files (General Series)
WO 105	Roberts Papers
WO 106	Directorate of Military Operations and Military Intelligence, correspondence and papers
WO 138	War Office: personal files

British Library (BL)	
Call numbers 50078–50114	Edward Hutton Papers

PARLIAMENTARY PUBLICATIONS

Australia

Annual Report upon the Military Forces of the Commonwealth for the Period January 1902 – 30th April, 1903, by Major-General Sir Edward Hutton, KCMG, CB, Commanding, 1903 Session, vol. 2.

Commonwealth of Australia Gazette, 1901/02–1909.

Commonwealth of Australia, Parliamentary Papers (CPP)

Commonwealth Military Forces Table 1903, 1903 Session, vol. 2.

Commonwealth Parliamentary Debates (CPD), 1901–04.

Defence: Correspondence regarding a Conference between representatives of His Majesty's Government and the Governments of the Self-Governing Dominions on the subject of Naval and Military defence, 28 May 1909, 1909 Session, vol. 2.

Journal of the Senate, 1901–04.

Memorandum on Australian Military Defence and its Progression since Federation, 1909 Session, vol. 2.

Military Forces of the Commonwealth (Reduction in Estimates – Report by Major General Hutton, 9 October 1902), 1903 Session, vol. 2.

Minute upon the Defence of Australia by General Hutton, 1901–02 Session, vol. 2.

Official Year Book of the Commonwealth of Australia, Nos 1–13.

Organisation of the Military Forces of the Commonwealth, 1903 Session, vol. 2.

Report of the Military Board, 1906, 1907 Session, vol. 2.

Second Annual Report by Major-General Sir Edward Hutton, KCMG, CB, Commanding the Military Forces of the Commonwealth, 1905 Session, vol. 2.

New South Wales

New South Wales Parliamentary Debates, 1893–95.

New South Wales Legislative Council Journal, 1893–95.

Canada

Canada. Parliament. *House of Commons. Debates*, 8th–9th Parliaments, Vols 46–54, 1898–1900.

Department of Militia and Defence for the Dominion of Canada, *Report for the Year Ended December 1898*, House of Commons Sessional Papers, no. 19, 1898.

Department of Militia and Defence for the Dominion of Canada, *Report for the Year Ended December 1899*, House of Commons Sessional Papers, no. 19, 1899.

ARTICLES AND UNPUBLISHED THESES

Adams, R., 'The military view of the Empire, 1870–1899: As seen through the journal of the Royal United Services Institution', *Royal United Services Institution Journal*, vol. 143, no. 3, 1998, pp. 58–64.

Anderson, O., 'The growth of Christian militarism in mid-Victorian Britain', English Historical Review, vol. 86, no. 338, 1971, pp. 46–72.

Atkinson, L., 'Australian defence policy: A study of empire and nation (1897–1910)', PhD thesis, Australian National University, 1964.

Aubrey, R., 'Major-General E.T.H. Hutton: A study of his relations with the Canadian Government', BA thesis, Carleton University, Ottawa, 1957.

Baden-Powell, R., 'Training for territorials', *Royal United Service Institution Journal*, vol. 52, no. 369, 1908, pp. 1469–1501.

Badsey, S., 'Fire and sword: The British Army and the Arme Blanche controversy 1871–1921', PhD thesis, University of Cambridge, 1981.

Bailies, H., 'Technology and imperialism: A case study of the Victorian army in Africa', *Victorian Studies*, vol. 24, no. 1, 1980, pp. 83–104.

Beckett, I.F.W., 'The South African War and the late Victorian Army', in Grey & Dennis, *The Boer War*.

Bethune, E.C., 'The uses of cavalry and mounted infantry in modern warfare', *Royal United Service Institution Journal*, vol. 50, no. 339, 1906, pp. 619–36.

Bou, J., 'Ambition and adversity: Developing an Australian military force, 1901–1914', *Australian Army Journal*, vol. 9, no. 1, 2012, pp. 71–88.

——'Cavalry, firepower and swords: The Australian light horse and the tactical lessons of cavalry operations in Palestine, 1916–1918', *Journal of Military History*, vol. 71, 2007, pp. 99–125.

——'Modern cavalry', in Grey & Dennis, *The Boer War*.

Bruche J. H., 'The land and air defence forces of Australia', *Royal United Services Institution Journal*, vol. 76, no. 504, pp. 756–72.

Buckner, P., 'Whatever happened to the British Empire', *Journal of the Canadian Historical Association*, vol. 4, no. 1, 1993, pp. 3–32.

Burroughs, P., 'Imperial defence and the Victorian army', *Journal of Imperial and Commonwealth History*, vol. 15, no. 1, 1986, pp. 55–72.

——'John Robert Seeley and British imperial history', *Journal of Imperial and Commonwealth History*, vol. 1, no. 2, 1973, pp. 191–211.

——'The mid-Victorian navy and imperial defence', *Journal of Imperial and Commonwealth History*, vol. 30, no. 2, 2002, pp. 102–14.

Clarke, G., 'Manufacturing spontaneity? The roles of the commandants in the colonial offers of troops in the South African War', in Dennis & Grey, *The Boer War*.

Clarke, S.J., 'Marching to their own drum: British Army officers as military commandants in the Australian colonies and New Zealand 1870–1901', PhD thesis, University of New South Wales, 1999.

Cohen, A., 'Joseph Chamberlain, Lord Lansdowne and British foreign policy 1901–1903: From collaboration to confrontation', *Australian Journal of Politics and History*, vol. 43, no. 2, 1997, pp. 122–34.

Cole, D., 'The problem of "nationalism" and "imperialism" in British settlement colonies', *Journal of British Studies*, vol. 10, no. 2, 1971, pp. 160–82.

Colvin, J., 'Sir Wilfrid Laurier and the imperial problem, 1896–1906', PhD thesis, University of London, 1954.

Coulthard-Clark, C., 'Australia's Monroe doctrine: An attempt to keep the islands English', *Pacific Islands Monthly*, vol. 57, no. 12, 1986, pp. 40–2.

Darwin, J., 'Imperialism and the Victorians: The dynamics of territorial expansion', *English Historical Review*, 1997, vol. 112, no. 447, 1997, pp. 614–42.
Durrans, P., 'Imperial defence: The Canadian response during Joseph Chamberlain's tenure of office as Colonial Secretary 1895–1903', MA thesis, Carleton University, 1964.
Earle, H., 'The Officers' Training Corps', *Royal United Services Institution Journal*, vol. 67, no. 465, 1922, pp. 26–38.
Elias, R., 'The land forces of Australia', *Royal United Services Institution Journal*, vol. 34, no. 152, pp. 205–28.
Gillon, B.T., 'The triumph of pragmatic imperialism: Lord Minto and the defence of the Empire, 1898–1910', MPhil thesis, University of Glasgow, 2009.
Gordon, D., 'The Colonial Defence Committee and imperial collaboration: 1885–1904', *Political Science Quarterly*, vol. 77, no. 4, 1962, pp. 526–45.
Haycock, R., 'The proving ground: Sam Hughes and the Boer War', *Journal of Canadian Studies*, vol. 16, no. 3, 1981, pp. 14–25.
Hitsman, J.M. & Morton, D., 'Canada's first military attaché: Capt. H.C. Thacker in the Russo-Japanese War', *Military Affairs*, vol. 34, 1970, pp. 82–4.
Howe, S., 'The slow death and strange rebirths of imperial history', *Journal of Imperial and Commonwealth History*, vol. 29, no. 2, 2001, pp. 131–41.
Hutton, E.T.H., 'A co-operative system for defence of the Empire', *Selected Papers*, no. 1/05, Royal Canadian Military Institute, Toronto, 2005, pp. 1–6.
——'Mounted infantry', *Royal United Service Institution Journal*, vol. 30, no. 135, 1886, pp. 695–738.
——'Some recollections of the Zulu War, 1879: Extracted from the unpublished reminiscences of the late Lieut-General Sir Edward Hutton', *Army Quarterly*, vol. 16, 1928, pp. 65–80.
——'The art of marching', *Royal United Service Institution Journal*, vol. 37, no. 184, 1893, pp. 621–54.
——'The Territorial Army and its field artillery', *Royal United Services Institution Journal*, vol. 52, no. 369, 1908, pp. 1585–88.
'Hutton, Lieutenant-Gen. Sir Edward, KCMG, CB', *Royal Society of Arts Journal*, vol. 59, 1911, p. 552.
Johnson, B., 'Australia, New Zealand and imperial defence (military) 1902–1914', MA thesis, Monash University, 1983.
Johnson, R.A., 'Fourth prize essay', *Royal United Service Institution Journal*, vol. 50, no. 338, 1906, pp. 492–527.
Keyser, F.G., 'The different systems of signalling in the field', *Royal United Service Institution Journal*, vol. 37, no. 181, 1893, pp. 245–67.
Knaplund, P., 'Intra-imperial aspects of Britain's defence question, 1870–1900', *Canadian Historical Review*, 1922, pp. 120–42.
Lascelles, E.F.W., 'The colonies and imperial defence: The question of the provision of an imperial service army reserve', *Royal United Services Institution Journal*, vol. 50, no. 341, 1906, pp. 855–89.
Leece, D., 'Who was Edward Thomas Henry Hutton?', *Journal of the Royal United Institute of New South Wales*, vol. 63, no. 2, 2012, p. 30.

Lehane, R.J.R., 'Lieutenant-General Edward Hutton and "Greater Britain"': Late Victorian imperialism, imperial defence and the self-governing colonies', PhD thesis, University of Sydney, 2005.

Liik, G., 'External threats as a factor in Australian politics, 1870–1900: The background to Australian Defence', PhD thesis, University of Sydney, 1974.

Luvaas, J., 'G.F.R. Henderson and the American Civil War', *Military Affairs*, vol. 20, 1956, pp. 139–53.

MacLean, G., 'The Imperial Federation Movement in Canada, 1884–1902', PhD thesis, Duke University, 1958.

Meaney, N., 'British and Australian identity: The problem of nationalism in Australian history and historiography', *Australian Historical Studies*, vol. 32, no. 116, 2001, pp. 76–136.

——'Britishness and Australia: Some reflections', *Journal of Imperial and Commonwealth History*, vol. 31, no. 2, 2003, pp. 121–35.

Melhuish, K., 'Australia and British Imperial Policy: Colonial autonomy and the imperial idea, 1865–1902', PhD thesis, University of Sydney, 1965.

Miller, C., 'Hutton, Sir Edward Thomas Henry', Dictionary of Canadian Biography Online, <http://www.biographi.ca>.

——'Sir Frederick William Borden and military reform, 1896–1911', *Canadian Historical Review*, vol. 50, no. 3, 1969, pp. 265–84.

——'The public life of Sir Frederick Borden', MA thesis, Dalhousie University, 1964.

Miller, S., 'The British way of war: Cultural assumptions and practices in the South African War, 1899–1902', *Journal of Military History*, vol. 77, no. 4, pp. 1329–48.

Mordike, J., '*Control by committee: The first Military Board, 1905', paper presented to Australian War Memorial History Conference*, 6–10 July 1987, pp. 1–12.

——'The origins of Australia's army', *Australian Defence Force Journal*, no. 87, 1991, pp. 7–19.

Morton, D., 'Authority and policy in the Canadian Militia, 1874–1904', PhD thesis, University of London, 1968.

Mowbray, J.A., 'Militiaman: A comparative study of the evolution of organisation in the Canadian and British voluntary citizen military forces 1896–1939', PhD thesis, Duke University, 1975.

'National horse supply and our military requirements, The', *Royal United Service Institution Journal*, vol. 52, no. 362, 1908, pp. 510–31.

Page, R., 'Canada and the Empire during Joseph Chamberlain's tenure as Colonial Secretary, 1895–1903', DPhil thesis, St John's College, Oxford, 1971.

——'Canada and the imperial idea in the Boer War years', *Journal of Canadian Studies*, vol. 5, 1970, pp. 33–49.

Penlington, N., 'General Hutton and the problem of military imperialism in Canada, 1898–1900', *Canadian Historical Review*, vol. 24, no. 2, 1943, pp. 156–71.

Perry, W., 'General Sir Edward Hutton', *Stand-to*, vol. 4, no. 4, 1954, pp. 21–3.

——'Lieutenant-General James Gordon Legge: Australia's first Chief of the General Staff', *Victorian Historical Journal*, vol. 48, no. 3, 1977, pp. 179–226.

——'Lieutenant-General Sir Edward Hutton: The creator of the post-Federation army', *Australian Army Journal*, no. 291, 1973, pp. 19–27.

——'Military reforms of General Sir Edward Hutton in New South Wales: 1893–96', *Australian Quarterly*, vol. 28, no. 4, 1956, pp. 65–75.

——'Military reforms of General Sir Edward Hutton in the Commonwealth of Australia, 1902–04, *Victorian Historical Magazine*, vol. 29, no. 1, 1959, pp. 34–57.

——'The military life of Major-General Sir John Charles Hoad', *Victorian Historical Journal*, vol. 29, no. 3, 1959, pp. 169–204.

'Rural press on General Hutton, The', *Canadian Military Gazette*, 2 May 1899.

Satre, L.J., 'St John Brodrick and army reform, 1901–1903', *Journal of British Studies*, vol. 15, no. 2, 1976, pp. 117–39.

Schuyler, R.L., 'The Recall of the legions: A phase of the decentralization of the British Empire', *American Historical Review*, vol. 26, no. 1, 1920, pp. 18–36.

Shields, R., 'Australian opinion and defence of the Empire', *Australian Journal of Politics and History*, vol. 10, 1964, pp. 41–63.

Strachan, H., 'The early Victorian army and the nineteenth-century revolution in government', *English Historical Review*, vol. 95, no. 377, 1980, pp. 782–809.

Streets, H., '"The right stamp of men": Military imperatives and popular imperialism in late Victorian Britain', PhD thesis, Duke University, 1998.

Thompson, A., 'The language of imperialism and the meanings of empire: Imperial discourse in British politics, 1895–1914', *Journal of British Studies*, vol. 36, no. 2, 1997, pp. 147–77.

——'Thinking imperially? Imperial pressure groups and the idea of empire in late Victorian and Edwardian Britain', DPhil thesis, Corpus Christi College, Oxford, 1994.

Trainor, L., 'British imperial defence policy and the Australian colonies, 1892–96', *Historical Studies*, vol. 14, no. 54, 1970, pp. 204–18.

——'Convenient conflict? From federal defence to Federation', in Dennis & Grey, *The Boer War*.

Tucker, A., 'Army and society in England 1870–1900: A reassessment of the Cardwell reforms', *Journal of British Studies*, vol. 2, no. 2, 1963, pp. 110–41.

Tyquin, M., 'The SS "Drayton Grange": The tragedy of the last Australian troopship from the Boer War', *Health and History*, vol. 3, 2001, pp. 94–103.

Van der Waag, I., 'South Africa and the Boer military system', in Dennis & Grey, *The Boer War*.

Wilcox, C., 'Relinquishing the past: John Mordike's *An Army For a Nation*', *Australian Journal of Politics and History*, vol. 40, no. 1, 1994, pp. 52–65.

Wilde, R., 'Chamberlain's proposal of an Imperial Council in March, 1900', *Canadian Historical Review*, vol. 37, no. 3, 1956, pp. 225–46.

——'The Boxer Affair and Australian responsibility for imperial defence', *Pacific Historical Review*, vol. 26, no. 1, 1957, pp. 51–65.

Winter, C.F., 'The evolution of the Canadian Army', transactions of the semi-annual meeting of the Officers' Association of the Militia of Canada, Ottawa, 5 April 1899, <http://archive.org>.

Wood, W.A., 'The Sudan contingent of 1885 and the anti-war movement', *Labour History*, no. 3, 1962, p. 53.

Wormell, D., 'John Robert Seeley (1834–95): Educational reformer, historian and political scientist', PhD thesis, University College London, 1977.

BOOKS AND MONOGRAPHS

Adams, R.J.Q., *Balfour: The Last Grandee*, John Murray, London, 2007.
Alomes, S., *A Nation at Last? The Changing Character of Australian Nationalism 1880–1988*, Angus & Robertson, Sydney, 1988.
Anderson, B., *Imagined Communities: Reflections on the Origins of Nationalism*, Verso, London, 2006.
Andrews, E., *The Anzac Illusion: Anglo-Australian Relations During World War I*, Cambridge University Press, Melbourne, 1993.
——*The Department of Defence*, vol. 5, Australian Centenary History of Defence, Oxford University Press, Melbourne, 2001.
Annan, N. (ed.), *Ideas and Beliefs of the Victorians: An Historic Revaluation of the Victorian Age*, Sylvan Press, London, 1949.
Arnold-Forster, M., *The Right Honourable Hugh Oakeley Arnold-Forster: A Memoir*, Arnold, London, 1910.
Badsey, S., *Doctrine and Reform in the British Cavalry 1880–1918*, Ashgate, Aldershot, 2008.
Bartlett, T. & Jeffery, K. (eds), *A Military History of Ireland*, Cambridge University Press, Cambridge, 1996.
Bean, C.E.W., *The Story of ANZAC*, vol. 1, Angus & Robertson, Sydney, 1921.
Beaumont, J. & Vere Hole, W., *Letters from Louisa*, Allen & Unwin, St Leonards, 1996.
Beckett, I.F.W., *Britain's Part-time Soldiers: The Amateur Military Tradition 1558–1945*, Pen and Sword, London, 2011.
——(ed.), *Victorians at War*, Society for Army Historical Research, London, 2007.
Beckett, I.F.W. & Gooch, J. (eds), *Politicians and Defence: Studies in the Formulation of British Defence Policy, 1845–1970*, Manchester University Press, Manchester, 1981.
Belich, J., *Replenishing the Earth. The Settler Revolution and the Rise of the Anglo-World, 1783–1939*, Oxford University Press, Oxford, 2009.
Bell, D., *The Idea of Greater Britain: Empire and the Future of World Order, 1860–1900*, Princeton University Press, Princeton, 2007.
——*Victorian Visions of Global Order: Empire and International Relations in Nineteenth-century Political Thought*, Cambridge University Press, Cambridge, 2007.
Beloff, M., *Britain's Liberal Empire, 1897–1921* (2nd edn), Macmillan, Basingstoke, 1987.
Berger, C., *Imperial Relations in the Age of Laurier*, University of Toronto Press, Toronto, 1969.
——*The Sense of Power: Studies in the Ideas of Canadian Imperialism, 1867–1914*, University of Toronto Press, Toronto, 1970.
Bond, B., *The Victorian Army and the Staff College 1854–1914*, Eyre Methuen, London, 1972.

Bowman, T. & Connelly, M., *The Edwardian Army: Recruiting, Training and Developing the British Army, 1902–1914*, Oxford University Press, Oxford, 2012.
Brendon, P., *The Decline and Fall of the British Empire, 1781–1997*, Jonathan Cape, London, 2007.
Bridge, C. & Fedorowitch, K. (eds), *The British World: Diaspora, Culture and Identity*, Frank Cass, London, 2003.
Brief History of the King's Royal Rifle Corps 1755–1948, A (3rd edn), Wellington Press, Aldershot, 1948.
Brown, J.M. & Louis, W.R., *The Oxford History of the British Empire*, vol. 4, Oxford University Press, Oxford, 1999.
Browne, H., *Joseph Chamberlain, Radical and Imperialist*, Longman, Essex, 1974.
Buchan, J., *Lord Minto, A Memoir*, T. Nelson & Sons, London, 1924.
Buckner, A. (ed.), *Canada and the British Empire*, Oxford University Press, Oxford, 2008.
Buckner, P. & Francis, R. (eds), *Rediscovering the British World*, University of Calgary Press, Calgary, 2005.
Cain, P. & Hopkins, A.G., *British Imperialism: Innovation and Expansion, 1688–1914*, Longman, London, 1993.
——*British Imperialism 1688–2000*, Longman, New York, 2002.
Cannadine, D., *Ornamentalism: How the British Saw Their Empire*, Oxford University Press, Oxford, 2001.
Chandos, J., *Boys Together: English Public Schools, 1800–1864*, Yale University Press, New Haven, 1984.
Clark, C., *Kaiser Wilhelm II: A Life in Power*, Penguin, London, 2009.
Clarke, G., *Imperial Defence*, Imperial Press, London, 1897.
——*My Working Life*, J. Murray, London, 1927.
——(ed.), *The Defence of the Empire: A Selection from the Letters and Speeches of Henry Howard Molyneux, Fourth Earl of Carnarvon*, Murray, London, 1897.
Colomb, J.R.C., *The Defence of Great and Greater Britain*, Stanford, London, 1880.
Cook, T., *The Madman and the Butcher*, Allen Lane, Toronto, 2010.
Coulthard-Clark, C.D., *A Heritage of Spirit: A Biography of Major-General Sir William Throsby Bridges*, Melbourne University Press, Melbourne, 1979.
——*Duntroon: The Royal Military College of Australia*, Allen & Unwin, Sydney, 1986.
——*No Australian Need Apply: The Troubled Career of Lieutenant-General Gordon Legge*, Allen & Unwin, Sydney, 1988.
——*Soldiers in Politics*, Allen & Unwin, Sydney, 1996.
Crotty, M., *Making the Australian Male: Middle-class Masculinity 1870–1920*, Melbourne University Press, Carlton South, 2001.
Crowley, F., (ed.), *A New History of Australia*, William Heineman, Melbourne, 1974.
——*Big John Forrest*, UWA Press, Nedlands, WA, 2000.
Cunningham, H., *The Volunteer Forces: A Social and Political History 1859–1908*, Croom Helm, London, 1975.
Darwin, J., *The Empire Project: The Rise and Fall of the British World-System, 1830–1970*, Cambridge University Press, Leiden, 2009.

——*Unfinished Empire: The Global Expansion of Britain*, Allen Lane, London, 2012.
Dawson, G., *Soldier Heroes: British Adventure, Empire and the Imagining of Masculinities*, Routledge, London, 1994.
Dennis, P. et al. (eds), *Oxford Companion to Australian Military History*, Oxford University Press, Melbourne, 1995.
Dennis, P. & Grey, J. (eds), *The Boer War: Army, Nation and Empire*, Army History Unit, Canberra, 2000.
Dilke, C., *Problems of Greater Britain*, Macmillan, London, 1890.
——*The British Empire*, Chatto & Windus, London, 1899.
Dilke, C. & Wilkinson, S., *Imperial Defence*, Macmillan, London, 1892.
D'Ombrain, N., *War Machinery and High Policy: Defence Administration in Peacetime Britain, 1902–1914*, Oxford University Press, Oxford, 1973.
Dunlop, J.K., *The Development of the British Army, 1899–1914*, Methuen, London, 1938.
Eddy, J. & Schreuder, D. (eds), *The Rise of Colonial Nationalism: Australia, New Zealand, Canada and South Africa First Assert Their Nationalities, 1880–1914*, Allen & Unwin, Sydney, 1988.
Eldridge, C.C., (ed.), *British Imperialism in the Nineteenth Century*, Macmillan, London, 1984.
——*British Imperialism in the Nineteenth Century*, St Martin's Press, New York, 1984.
——*Victorian Imperialism*, Hodder & Stoughton, London, 1978.
Fedorowich, K. & Thompson, A.S. (eds), *Empire, Migration and Identity in the British World*, Manchester University Press, Manchester, 2013.
Fergusson, N., *Civilization: The West and the Rest*, Allen Lane, London 2011.
——*Empire: How Britain Made the Modern World*, Allen Lane, London, 2003.
Feuchtwanger, E.J., *Democracy and Empire: Britain, 1865–1914*, Edward Arnold, London, 1985.
Field, L., *The Forgotten War: Australian Involvement in the South African Conflict of 1899–1902*, Melbourne University Press, Melbourne, 1979.
Fielding, J. & O'Neill, R., *A Selected Bibliography of Australian Military History 1891–1939*, Australian National University, Canberra, 1978.
Francis, R. & Smith, D. (eds), *Readings in Canadian History Post-Confederation*, Holt, Rinehart & Winston, Canada, 1982.
French, D. & Reid, B.H. (eds), *The British General Staff: Reform and Innovation c. 1890–1939*, Taylor & Francis, Hoboken, 2002.
Froude, J.A., *Oceana: or, England and Her Colonies*, Longmans, London, 1898.
Gallagher, J., *The Decline, Revival and Fall of the British Empire: The Ford Lectures and Other Essays*, ed. A. Seal, Cambridge University Press, 1982.
Godley, A., *The Life of an Irish Soldier*, E.P. Dutton & Company, London, 1939.
Goldman, C.S. (ed.), *The Empire and the Century*, John Murray, London, 1905.
Gooch, J., *The Plans or War: The General Staff and British Military Strategy, c. 1900–1916*, Routledge & Kegan Paul, London, 1974.
Gordon, D., *The Dominion Partnership in Imperial Defense, 1870–1914*, Johns Hopkins Press, Maryland, 1965.

Graham, G., *The Politics of Naval Supremacy: Studies in British Maritime Ascendancy*, Cambridge University Press, Cambridge, 1965.

Grebert, R., *The Australian Army Slouch Hat and Rising Sun Badge*, New South Wales Military Historical Society, Sydney, 2002.

Greenwood, G. (ed.), *Australia: A Social and Political History*, Angus & Robertson, Sydney, 1955.

Greenwood, G. & Grimshaw, C. (eds), *Documents in Australian International Affairs 1901–1918*, Thomas Nelson, Melbourne, 1977.

Grey, J., *A Military History of Australia* (rev. edn), Cambridge University Press, Melbourne, 1990.

Guha, R., *Selected Subaltern Studies*, Oxford University Press, New York, 1988.

Hamer, W., *The British Army: Civil–Military Relations 1885–1905*, Clarendon Press, Oxford, 1970.

Harries-Jenkins, G., *The Army in Victorian Society*, Routledge & Kegan Paul, London, 1977.

Harris, S., *Canadian Brass: The Making of a Professional Army, 1860–1939*, University of Toronto Press, Toronto, 1988.

Harrison, J.F.C., *Late Victorian Britain, 1870–1901*, Fontana Press, London, 1990.

Headrick, D.R., *The Tools of Empire: Technology and European Imperialism in the Nineteenth Century*, Oxford University Press, New York, 1981.

Hill, A., *Chauvel of the Light Horse: A Biography of General Sir Harry Chauvel*, Melbourne University Press, Melbourne, 1978.

Hobsbawn, E., *The Age of Empire: 1875–1914*, Weidenfeld & Nicolson, London, 1987.

Holmes, R., *The Little Field Marshal: A Life of Sir John French*, Weidenfeld & Nicolson, London, 2004.

Honey, J. R., *Tom Brown's Universe: The Development of the Victorian Public School*, Quadrangle/New York Times Book Co., New York, 1977.

Horne, C.F., *Source Records of the Great War, vol. 1*, National Alumni, New York, 1923.

Horner, D. (ed.), *The Commanders: Australian Military Leadership in the Twentieth Century*, Allen & Unwin, Sydney, 1984.

Howard, M., *The Continental Commitment: The Dilemma of British Defence Policy in the Era of the Two World Wars*, Temple Smith, London, 1972.

Huntington, S., *The Soldier and the State: The Theory and Politics of Civil–Military Relations*, Harvard University Press, Cambridge, Mass., 1957.

Hutton, E.T.H., *Address by Major-General Hutton, CB, ADC to HM the Queen, Commanding Canadian troops* [1898], Canadian Institute for Historical Microreproductions, Ottawa, 1986.

——*A Narrative of the Tour of Inspection through the Western Division of New South Wales*, September 30th to October 19th, 1895, Geo. Murray & Co., Sydney, 1895.

——*Defence of New South Wales, Charles Potter*, Govt. Printer, Sydney, 1894.

——*Defence of New South Wales: Mobilization Port Jackson District: Orders and Memoranda*, Govt. Printer, Sydney, 1894.

——*Horse-breeding for Military Remounts: Extract from Lecture*, Agricultural Gazette of NSW, Sydney, 1894.

——*Lecture on Mounted Infantry – Its Present and Its Future*, Gale & Polden, Aldershot, 1889.
——*Military Forces of the Commonwealth: Minute upon the Defence of Australia*, Robt S. Brain, Government Printer for the State of Victoria, Melbourne, 1902.
——*Narrative of a Staff Ride by the Commonwealth Military Forces of New South Wales in the Locality of Penrith-Camden-Liverpool, 8th, 9th and 10th September, 1904 and Remarks Thereon by Major-General Sir E.T.H. Hutton, KCMG, CB, Commanding the Military Forces of the Commonwealth*, Govt. Printer, Sydney, 1905.
——*Report and Schedules of the Intercolonial Military Committee: Assembled at Sydney, New South Wales, 29th January, 1896*, Charles Potter, Govt. Printer, Sydney, 1896.
——*Sydney Church of England Grammar School: Major-General Hutton's Speech, December 21st, 1894*, Printed at the Times Office, North Sydney, 1894.
——'The bond of military unity', *The Empire and the Century*, John Murray, London, 1905.
——*The Defence and Defensive Power of Australia*, Angus & Robertson, Melbourne, 1902.
Hutton, E.T.H., Rouse, R. & Dangar, H.C., *The Australian Horse Trade and Its Development for Military and Domestic Purposes*, Charles Potter, Govt. Printer, 1896.
Hutton, E.T.H. & Thompson, J.L., *Horse-breeding for Military Remounts: and Horses for Indian and European Markets*, Charles Potter, Govt. Printer, Sydney, 1894.
Hyam, R., *Britain's Imperial Century 1815–1914*, Palgrave, Basingstoke, 2002.
Hyam, R. & Martin, G., *Reappraisals in British Imperial History*, Macmillan, London, 1975.
Industrial Progress of New South Wales, The, Government Printer, London, 1872.
Inglis, K.S., *The Australian Colonists*, Melbourne University Press, Carlton, 1974.
Janowitz, M., *The Professional Soldier: A Social and Political Portrait*, Free Press, Glencoe, 1960.
Jay, R., *Joseph Chamberlain: A Political Study*, Oxford University Press, Oxford, 1981.
Jenks, E., *A History of the Australasian Colonies*, Cambridge University Press, London, 1912.
Johnson, D., *Volunteers at Heart: The Queensland Defence Forces, 1860–1901*, University of Queensland Press, St Lucia, 1975.
Johnson, F.A., *Defence by Committee: The British Committee of Imperial Defence, 1885–1959*, Oxford University Press, London, 1960.
Jones, S., *From Boer War to World War: Tactical Reform of the British Army, 1902–1914*, University of Oklahoma Press, Norman, 2012.
Jose, A.W., *History of Australasia*, Angus & Robertson, Sydney, 1909.
Keith, A. (ed.), *Selected Speeches and Documents on British Colonial Policy 1763–1917*, vol. 2, Oxford University Press, Oxford, 1918.

Kendle, J.E., *The Colonial and Imperial Conferences, 1887–1911: A Study in Imperial Organization*, Longman, London, 1967.

Kennedy, G. & Neilson, K. (eds), *Imperial Defence: The Old World Order 1856–1956*, Routledge, London, 2008.

——*The British Way in Warfare: Power and the International System, 1856–1956: Essays in Honour of David French*, Ashgate, Burlington, 2010.

Kitson Clark, G., *An Expanding Society: Britain 1830–1900,* Melbourne University Press, Melbourne, 1967.

——*The Making of Victorian England*, Methuen & Co, London, 1962.

Kochanski, H., *Sir Garnet Wolseley: Victorian Hero*, Hambledon Press, London, 1999.

Kohn, H., *The Idea of Nationalism: A Study in Its Origins and Background*, Macmillan, New York, 1967.

Kubicek, R.V., *The Administration of Imperialism: Joseph Chamberlain at the Colonial Office*, Duke University Press, Durham, NC, 1969.

Langer, W., *The Diplomacy of Imperialism, 1890–1902,* Alfred A. Knopf, New York, 1972.

Livingston, K.T., Jordan, R. & Sweely, G., *Becoming Australians: The Movement towards Federation in Ballarat and the Nation*, Wakefield Press, Kent Town, 2001.

Luvaas, J., *The Education of an Army: British Military Thought, 1815–1940, Cassell*, London, 1965.

McGibbon, I.C., *The Path to Gallipoli: Defending New Zealand, 1840–1915*, GP Books, Wellington, 1991.

Macintyre, S., *A Concise History of Australia (3rd edn)*, Cambridge University Press, Melbourne, 2009.

——*The Oxford History of Australia, vol. 4, 1901–42, The Succeeding Age*, Oxford University Press, Melbourne, 1993.

McKernan, M. & Browne, M. (eds), *Australia: Two Centuries of War and Peace*, Australian War Memorial, Canberra, 1988.

McMullin, R., *So Monstrous a Travesty*, Scribe Publications, Melbourne, 2004.

Major-General Sir Edward T.H. Hutton, KCMG, CB, Biographical Press Agency, London, 1905.

Marsh, P.T., *Joseph Chamberlain: Entrepreneur in Politics*, Yale University Press, New Haven, 1994.

Matthew, H.G.C., *The Liberal Imperialists: The Ideas and Politics of a Post-Gladstonian Elite*, Oxford University Press, London, 1973.

Maurice, J.F., *History of the War in South Africa, 1899–1902*, vols 1–4, Hurst & Blackett, London, 1906–10.

Maxwell, L., *The Ashanti Ring: Sir Garnet Wolseley's Campaigns 1870–1882*, Leo Cooper, London, 1985.

May, E.S., *The Principles and Problems of Imperial Defence*, Swan Sonnenschein & Co., London, 1903.

Meaney, N., *A History of Australian Defence and Foreign Policy 1901–23, vol. 1, The Search for Security in the Pacific, 1901–14*, Sydney University Press, Sydney, 1976.

Military Forces, The (reply to Mr Cameron's question on 7th November, 1895, respecting report by Major-General Hutton on), Govt. Printer, Sydney, 1895.

Miller, C., *A Knight in Politics: A Biography of Sir Frederick Borden*, McGill-Queen's University Press, Montreal, 2010.

——*Painting the Map Red: Canada and the South African War, 1899–1902*, Canadian War Museum and McGill-Queen's University Press, Montreal, 1993.

——*The Canadian Career of the Fourth Earl of Minto: The Education of a Viceroy*, Wilfrid Laurier University Press, Waterloo, 1980.

Monger, G.W., *The End of Isolation: British Foreign Policy 1900–1907*, Nelson, London, 1963.

Mordike, J., *An Army for a Nation: A History of Australian Military Developments 1880–1914*, Allen & Unwin, Sydney, 1992.

Morton, D., *A Military History of Canada*, Hurtig Publishers, Edmonton, 1990.

——*Canada and War: A Military and Political History*, Butterworth, Toronto, 1981.

——*Ministers and Generals: Politics and the Canadian Militia, 1868–1904*, University of Toronto Press, Toronto, 1970.

——*The Canadian General: Sir William Otter*, Hakkert, Toronto, 1974.

Moyles, R. & Owram, D., *Imperial Dreams and Colonial Realities. British Views of Canada, 1880–1914*, University of Toronto Press, Toronto, 1988.

Nasson, B., *The South African War, 1899–1902*, Arnold, London, 1999.

Nicholls, B., *The Colonial Volunteers: The Defence Forces of the Australian Colonies*, Allen & Unwin, Sydney, 1988.

Norris, R., *The Emergent Commonwealth; Australian Federation: Expectations and Fulfilment 1889–1910*, Melbourne University Press, Melbourne, 1975.

Omissi, D.E. & Thompson, A.S. (eds), *The Impact of the South African War*, Palgrave, Basingstoke, 2002.

Operations of General Hutton's Force, South African Campaign, 1900: Itinerary Maps and Plans of Engagements, War Office, London, 1900.

Orde, A., *The Eclipse of Great Britain: The United States and British Imperial Decline, 1895–1956*, Macmillan Press, Basingstoke, 1996.

O'Sullivan, E.W., *The Power of Mounted Riflemen*, Age Office, Queanbeyan, 1894.

Owen, R. & Sutcliffe, R. (eds), *Studies in the Theory of Imperialism*, Longman, London, 1972.

Page, R., *The Boer War and Canadian Imperialism*, Canadian Historical Association, Historical Booklet, no. 44, Ottawa, 1987.

Pakenham, T., *The Boer War*, Weidenfeld & Nicolson, London, 1979.

Penlington, N., *Canada and Imperialism, 1896–1899*, University of Toronto Press, Toronto, 1965.

Porter, A. (ed.), *The Oxford History of the British Empire*, vol. 3, Oxford University Press, Oxford, 2001.

Porter, B. (ed.), *Bibliography of Imperial, Colonial and Commonwealth History Since 1600*, Oxford University Press, Oxford, 2002.

——*Critics of Empire: British Radicals and the Imperial Challenge*, Palgrave Macmillan, New York, 2008.

——*Empire and Superempire: Britain, America and the World*, Yale University Press, New Haven, 2006.
——*The Absent-minded Imperialists: Empire, Society and Culture in Britain*, Oxford University Press, Oxford, 2004.
——*The Lion's Share: A Short History of British Imperialism, 1850–1995* (3rd edn), Longman, London, 1996.
Preston, R., *Canada and 'Imperial Defense': A Study of the Origins of the British Commonwealth Defense Organization, 1867–1919*, Duke University Press, Durham, 1967.
Prickett, S., *Romanticism and Religion: The Tradition of Coleridge and Wordsworth in the Victorian Church*, Cambridge University Press, Cambridge, 1976.
Reader, W., *Professional Men: The Rise of the Professional Classes in Nineteenth-Century England*, Weidenfeld & Nicolson, London, 1966.
Roach, J., *Secondary Education in England 1870–1902: Public Activity and Private Enterprise*, Routledge, New York, 1991.
Roberts, A., *Salisbury: Victorian Titan*, Weidenfeld & Nicolson, London, 1999.
Robinson, R. & Gallagher J., *Africa and the Victorians: The Official Mind of Imperialism*, Macmillan, London, 1981.
Robinson, R., Gallagher, J. & Denny, A., *Africa and the Victorians: The Climax of Imperialism in the Dark Continent*, St Martin's Press, New York, 1961.
Robson, R. (ed.), *Ideas and Institutions of Victorian Britain*, G. Bell & Sons, London, 1967.
Ross, A.T., *Armed and Ready: The Industrial Development and Defence of Australia 1900–1945*, Turton & Armstrong, Sydney, 1995.
Rothblatt, S. (ed.), *Ideas and Beliefs of the Victorians*, MIT Press, Cambridge, Mass., 1999.
Said, E., *Orientalism: Western Conceptions of the Orient*, Penguin, Harmondsworth, 1985.
Sanford Evans, W., *The Canadian Contingents and Canadian Imperialism: A Story and a Study*, T. Fisher Unwin, London, 1901.
Sawer, G., *Australian Federal Politics and the Law 1901–1929*, Melbourne University Press, Carlton, 1956.
Schreuder, D. & Ward, S. (eds), *Australia's Empire*, Oxford University Press, Oxford, 2008.
Schurman, D.M., *Imperial Defence, 1868–1887*, ed. J. Beeler, Frank Cass, London, 2000.
Seeley, J., *The Expansion of England*, Cambridge University Press, New York, 2010.
Shand, A., *The Life of General Sir Edward Bruce Hamley*, vol. 2, William Blackwood & Sons, London, 1896.
Shannon, R.T., *The Age of Salisbury, 1881–1902: Unionism and Empire*, Longman, London, 1996.
——*The Crisis of Imperialism, 1865–1915*, Hart-Davis, MacGibbon, London, 1974.
Sinclair, K., *A Soldier's View of Empire*, Bodley Head, London, 1982.
Skelley, A., *The Victorian Army at Home: The Recruitment and Terms and Conditions of the British Regular, 1859–1899*, Croom Helm, London, 1977.

Souter, G., *Lion and Kangaroo: The Initiation of Australia*, Sun Australia, Sydney, 1992.
Spiers, E., *Haldane: An Army Reformer*, Edinburgh University Press, Edinburgh, 1980.
——*The Army and Society 1815–1914*, Longman, London, 1980.
——*The Late Victorian Army*, Manchester University Press, Manchester, 1992.
Stanley, G., *Canada's Soldiers: The Military History of an Unmilitary People*, Macmillan, Toronto, 1960.
Stevens, P. & Saywell, J. (eds), *Lord Minto's Canadian Papers: A Selection of the Public and Private Papers of the Fourth Earl of Minto, 1898–1904*, vol. I, Champlain Society, Toronto, 1981.
Stirling, J.F., *Colonials in South Africa, 1889–1902*, Blackwood, Edinburgh, 1907.
Stockings, C., *The Making and Breaking of the Post-Federation Australian Army, 1901–09*, Land Warfare Studies Study Paper no. 311, Canberra, 2007.
——*The Torch and the Sword: A History of the Army Cadet Movement in Australia*, UNSW Press, Sydney, 2007.
Stockings, C. & Connor, J. (eds), *Before the Anzac Dawn: A Military History of Australia to 1915*, UNSW Press, Sydney, 2013.
Stockwell, S. (ed.), *The British Empire: Themes and Perspectives*, Blackwell, Oxford, 2008.
Stone, J. & Schmidl, E.A., *The Boer War and Military Reforms*, University Press of America, Lanham, 1988.
Strachan, H. (ed.), *Big Wars and Small Wars: The British Army and the Lessons of War in the Twentieth Century*, Routledge, London, 2006.
——*The Politics of the British Army*, Clarendon Press, Oxford, 1997.
——*Wellington's Legacy: The Reform of the British Army 1830–1854*, Manchester University Press, Manchester, 1984.
Thompson, A.P., *Imperial Britain: The Empire in British Politics c. 1880–1932*, Pearson Education, Essex, 2000.
——*The Empire Strikes Back? The Impact of Imperialism on Britain from the Mid-nineteenth Century*, Longman, Harlow, 2005.
——*The Imperial Idea and Its Enemies: A Study in British Power* (2nd edn), Macmillan, London, 1985.
Trainor, L., *British Imperialism and Australian Nationalism: Manipulation, Conflict and Compromise in the Late Nineteenth Century*, Cambridge University Press, Cambridge, 1994.
Vamplew, W. (ed.), *Australians: Historical Statistics*, Fairfax, Syme & Weldon Associates, Sydney, 1987.
Vandervort, B., *Wars of Imperial Conquest in Africa, 1830–1914*, Taylor & Francis, Hoboken, 2012.
Vazenry, G., *Reorganisation of the Australian Military Forces*, Australian War Memorial, Canberra, 1965.
Von Der Goltz, C., *The Nation in Arms: A Treatise on Modern Military Systems and the Conduct of War* (5th edn), trans. P. Ashworth, Hugh Rees, London, 1906.

Ward, R., *Concise History of Australia*, University of Queensland Press, St Lucia, 1992.
Warren, A., *Wait for the Wagon: The Story of the Royal Canadian Army Service Corps*, McClelland & Stewart, Canada, 1961.
Webster, A., *The Debate on the Rise of British Imperialism*, Manchester University Press, Manchester, 2006.
Welsh, M., *Science in a Pickelhaube: British Military Lesson Learning at the RUSI (1870–1900)*, Royal United Services Institute for Defence Studies, Whitehall, 1999.
Wilcox, C., *Australia's Boer War: The War in South Africa 1899–1902*, Oxford University Press, Melbourne, 2002.
——*For Hearths and Homes: Citizen Soldiering in Australia, 1854–1945*, Allen & Unwin, St Leonards, 1998.
——*Red Coat Dreaming: How Colonial Australia Embraced the British Army*, Cambridge University Press, Melbourne, 2009.
Williams, R., *Defending the Empire: The Conservative Party and British Defence Policy, 1899–1915*, Yale University Press, London, 1991.
Wolseley, G., *The Story of a Soldier's Life*, vol. 2, Archibald Constable & Co., Westminster, 1903.
Wood, E., *From Midshipman to Field Marshal*, Methuen, London, 1907.
Wood, J., *Chiefs of the Australian Army*, Australian Military History Publications, Loftus, 2006.
Wood, James A., *Militia Myths: Ideas of the Canadian Citizen Soldier, 1896–1921*, UBC Press, Vancouver, 2010.
Young, R., *White Mythologies: Writing History and the West*, Routledge, London, 1990.

NEWSPAPERS AND PERIODICALS

Age (Melbourne), 1899–1904.
Australian Star, 1899–1901.
Bulletin (Sydney), 1893–1905.
Canadian Military Gazette, 1898–1900.
Canadian United Services Magazine, 1898.
Daily Telegraph (Sydney), 1894–1900.
Globe (Toronto), 1898–1900.
Illustrated Sydney News, 1893–96.
La Presse (Montreal), 1899.
Mail and Empire (Montreal), 1899–1900.
Montreal Gazette, 1899–1900.
Ottawa Citizen, 1899–1900.
Punch (Melbourne), 1900–04.
South Australian Advertiser, 1900–03.
Sydney Morning Herald, 1892–1904.
Toronto Globe, 1898–1900.

Index

Milton Keynes UK
Ingram Content Group UK Ltd.
UKHW020652070923
428198UK00007B/47